SHOT DOWN OVER ITALY

SHOT DOWN
OVER ITALY

*A true story of courage and survival
in Nazi-occupied Italy during World War II*

John W. Lanza

Bright
Spot
BOOKS

Caldwell, NJ 07006

Visit website at www.ShotDownOverItaly.com

Library of Congress Control Number: 2010906479

ISBN: 978-0-9827529-0-6

Printed in the United States of America

First Edition, June 2010

This book is dedicated to Goffredo Sarri and Riccardo Becattini and their families for helping two American airmen to escape from and evade the enemy for two months during World War II after they were shot down over Nazi-occupied Italy on May 26, 1944.

It is also dedicated to the crew of the B-25 bomber that was shot down: pilot Major William Clark Hunter; co-pilot Second Lieutenant Walter H. Brickner; navigator Second Lieutenant John H. Kinney; bombardier Second Lieutenant Laverne E. Reynolds; engineer/gunner Sergeant John W. Denny, Jr.; radio operator/waist gunner Technical Sergeant Alfred J. Todd; and my uncle, tail gunner Sergeant William A. Lanza, without whose amazing memory this book could not have been written.

Contents

List of Photographs, Maps and Illustrations

Preface

On June 6, 1984, the fortieth anniversary of D-Day, President Reagan reminded the nation of the sacrifices of a generation of veterans, and renewed the nation's pride in those who gave so much so that we would continue to be a free nation.[1] Tom Brokaw characterized these veterans as the "greatest generation," and went so far as to say: "This is the greatest generation any society has produced."[2] Since then, many stories have been told about ordinary people having extraordinary experiences during World War II, and we have grown to appreciate the "greatest generation" that has been aging around us.

Sergeant William A. ("Bill") Lanza of Revere, Massachusetts, my uncle (always "Uncle Willie" to me), was one of those ordinary people who had extraordinary experiences during the war, only none of us knew it because he never talked about them. He was an aerial gunner on a B-25 bomber that was shot down over Italy, and with the help of the Italian Resistance, evaded the enemy for two months, living in a cave with another member of his crew, Technical Sergeant Alfred J. Todd of Oriskany Falls, New York. Todd was a radio operator/waist gunner.

Bill and Todd were known as Guglielmo and Alfredo by their Italian friends. They were crew members of the 321st Bomb Group, whose motto was "perseverance, vision and duty."[3] They had to draw on all these attributes and more to evade capture for a couple of months. "I felt it was my duty not to be captured," said Bill. Luck is the best attribute to have during war, and they had plenty of it, thanks to the Tuscan families of Goffredo Sarri and Riccardo Becattini, who helped them evade the enemy during the summer of 1944.

My uncle and his family lived upstairs from our family when I was growing up in Revere. While I knew that he and three of his brothers had been in the war, and that his mother, my grandmother, died while they were overseas, I never knew his story, probably because he signed a document certifying that he wouldn't talk about it. It was common practice for returning evaders to sign such a document to protect those who helped them and not compromise future clandestine operations. These documents were declassified and made part of the public domain in 1995, but most evaders were unaware of this and remained silent.[4]

In the spring of 2006, I had retired in the nick of time because my ninety-two-year-old father, a fiercely independent man, needed my help. His friends were telling my two brothers and me that he was running out of gas. As a result, I spent a lot of time traveling from my home in Caldwell, New Jersey to his home, "Fairweather by the Sea," as he liked to call it, an apartment complex for senior citizens in Beverly, Massachusetts.

My father was a trumpet player whose senior years were filled with music, which no doubt soothed his soul because he was a professional musician until the age of eighty-eight. Now, he was struggling. My father was always my "go to" guy, and I now found myself in the unfamiliar role of being his "go to" guy.

While I was adjusting to this reversal of roles, I spent some time with my uncle, my father's younger brother, who lived nearby and in 2006 was ninety years old. I had the time, so I asked him about his wartime experiences. He was surprised that I was interested. He mentioned that a nephew and his two grandsons had some interest, noting that his wife and three daughters had little interest. He told me that one of his nephew's friends had even interviewed him about his wartime experiences about twenty years ago for a term paper at Boston College, for which he received an "A."[5] He was glad to share his experiences with me as well.

Having done a fair amount of reading about World War II and having just returned from a visit to the beaches of Normandy, I was all ears. Every Memorial Day and Veterans Day, I call my uncle; my brother Ron, a Marine who was wounded in Vietnam; and my college roommate, Rocky Stone, a retired Army Lieutenant Colonel who also served in Vietnam. I thank them for their service.

As my uncle spoke of his wartime experiences, I was surprised to find such a story in my own backyard. I wished that I had asked him about the war sooner. However, I was too busy raising five kids, commuting to New York City and trying to survive five bank mergers. I was a typical third-generation offspring of an immigrant family, focused on getting a good formal education, which invariably takes you to places you've never been before and never imagined you would go.

Preface

The trend continues with the fourth generation as my kids are even more spread out geographically. I guess this is the American way. When I visited Italy to meet the families that helped the two Americans, I was surprised to find that this isn't the Italian way. The people I sought out in Italy and their families have remained close to home.

As I listened to my uncle, I thought it might be a good idea to write down his story to pass on to my children. As I got into it and began doing research to gain historical perspective, I found that many others were conducting similar research on relatives who served in the Army Air Forces during World War II. Some were even developing websites in memory of relatives who served their country well. Among all those I came across, one individual stood out, John T. Fitzgerald. When I first ran across him, he was in the early stages of consolidating the history of the 321st Bomb Group in a website in memory of his father, a decorated flyer. Through him and others, as I dug up more information, my uncle remembered more. It was a good experience for both of us.

In the meantime, my father's health had declined and he ran out of gas in January 2007. I still miss my "go to" guy. My uncle remained as the last of eight brothers and sisters, all of whom were nice to me growing up. At my father's funeral, my uncle told me that he felt guilty being the last one standing. I told him that, like my father, he was built to last. My mother wasn't built to last. Her focus was in doing what it took to ensure that my two brothers and I received a college education despite the odds. If it weren't for her persistence, I wouldn't be writing this story now.

My uncle wasn't the only silent member of his generation. Alfred Todd was even more silent. After months of searching, I tracked down his widow, Blanche Todd, a lovely lady with whom I have had many pleasant conversations over the past few years. She would have tears in her eyes talking about her beloved "Toddy." I was surprised to hear that he never discussed his wartime experiences with her or their four children. I was also saddened to learn that they lost their son, Robert, at the age of nineteen in an automobile accident. She had a difficult time remaining composed while talking about him. The family still honors his memory every year with a wrestling scholarship in his name to a deserving student-athlete at Vernon-Verona-Sherrill Senior High School in Verona, New York.

3

SHOT DOWN OVER ITALY

To help explain why her husband never discussed his wartime experiences, I sent Mrs. Todd a copy of the document he signed certifying that he wouldn't talk about them, even with a spouse. It's a shame that those who evaded the enemy during the war, often with the most interesting stories, weren't allowed to talk about them. When my uncle returned home from the war, he was contacted by the *Boston Globe*, but had to explain to the reporter that he was bound to secrecy. The reporter understood and left him alone. It was a different time.

In time, I tracked down the family of Major William Clark Hunter, the pilot of the B-25, who went down with the ship after ensuring that the six members of his crew had bailed out. His family was glad to hear from me, especially since I had dug up a lot of information about him which I shared with them. They are very proud of the good major and they should be. He is a genuine war hero.

I also tracked down Second Lieutenant Laverne E. Reynolds, the bombardier, who spent the rest of the war in prison camps in Germany. He is another charter member of the silent generation who seldom spoke of his wartime experiences. Nevertheless, he shared with me some of his memories, which his daughter said were painful for him to recall.

Eventually, I was able to track down the families of two other crew members and a friend of the third. Sadly, all three have passed. Steve Denny, the son of Sergeant John W. Denny, Jr., the engineer and top-turret gunner and also a prisoner of war, told me that his father didn't speak to him about his prison experiences until he was an adult and able to handle it. I knew from my research that his father had sent away for his POW Medal in 1988, and Steve told me that the day he received it was the proudest of his life.

Judy Ellen Kinney, the daughter of John H. Kinney, the navigator, told me that every time she asked her father about the war, he chose to remain silent. She believed the war visions were too troubling for him to repeat. Like Bill and Todd, Kinney escaped from and evaded the enemy thanks to the help of partisans. He too had to certify in writing that he wouldn't talk about his wartime experiences.

It took me the longest time to find Walter H. Brickner, the co-pilot, who also evaded the enemy with the help of partisans. My uncle had heard that Brickner was a good athlete, and he was indeed. I learned from his golfing buddy, Jim Wood, a southpaw like Brickner,

Preface

that he had been a professional baseball player. Wood told me that even though they were members of the same country club and golfed together often, Brickner never spoke of his wartime experiences. Like Bill, Todd and Kinney, he was another silent evader who certified in writing that he wouldn't disclose his wartime experiences, and never did. It's amazing to hear something like this in today's tell-all society.

I didn't know much about the war in Italy when I began this journey, so it took a while to get up to speed. In reading about the battles taking place in southern Italy during the first half of 1944, I found many different viewpoints of the same battles. The political and military leaders of the different nations forming the Allied forces often saw things differently, as did authors from those countries. War requires leaders to make difficult decisions with dire consequences that are analyzed for years, sometimes decades or longer. So much has been written on World War II that I found myself reading the same things over and over, but from different points of view. As expected, powerful political and military leaders sought to take credit for what went right and to absolve themselves of blame for what went wrong. As a retired banker in New York City, I was familiar with this type of politics.

In Italy, the Allies were fighting an aggressive campaign in a country of treacherous mountains and muddy valleys. The Germans were dug in on the mountains while the Allies were in exposed positions in the valleys. The winter of 1943-1944 was one of the worst winters in years. C. L. Sulzberger, a well-known *New York Times* war correspondent, called it a "winter of deep discontent."[6] Operating under unimaginable conditions of misery, nobody had anything good to say about anything. Understanding this, I simply digested what I read and did my best to describe the events fairly to give historical perspective to this story. The following winter was even colder, and Denny and Reynolds experienced it in the miserable confines of their respective prison camps.

The Italian Campaign was complex. There were several wars going at the same time in Italy. There was a ground war between the Allies and Germany with land battles raging under intolerable conditions. My uncle felt sorry for the soldiers fighting under such adverse circumstances. There was the air war in which he was engaged that carried its own dangers, such as shrapnel from enemy flak ripping through planes, as was the case on his last mission. In addition, the partisans, who formed the Italian Resistance, were fighting a guerilla war against Mussolini's Fascists, in essence a civil war, and were emerging as a force against the Germans occupying central and northern Italy. After they were shot down, the four Americans who evaded capture received clandestine aid from the partisans.

While it took some time, I located and visited the families in Italy who helped Todd and my uncle evade the enemy. I was touched by the warmth of the receptions I received from both families. There was no doubt that each had fond memories of the two Americans who dropped in on them during the war, and stayed for a couple of months. I found that while the Americans seldom talked about the war, the Italian partisans talked about it all the time. I also found that different people had different recollections about the same events, so here again I simply digested what I heard and described the events in this story to the best of my ability.

When I gave my uncle a draft of an early chapter, he was quick to point out that this war wasn't about him, noting that he was one of the lucky ones. He said the true heroes were men like Major Hunter. I agreed that he was indeed one of the lucky ones and that Hunter was a true hero. Still, I pointed out that his memory is the thread that was used to weave the story.

In sum, this is another compelling story of ordinary men like my uncle having extraordinary wartime experiences. While war is horrible and full of inhumanity, this story shows the human side of war at its best, such things as his pilot sacrificing his life to save the lives of his crew, and two Italian families helping two Americans at the risk of their own lives.

Chapter 1

BEFORE THE STORM

World War I, which began in 1914 and ended in 1918, was supposed to be the war to end all wars.[1] It had destroyed more lives than all previous wars. Over 65 million men and women were mobilized on both sides to serve in that war, of which over 37 million were casualties. Over 8 million people lost their lives, 21 million were wounded, and almost 8 million had been imprisoned or were missing.[2] The numbers were staggering.

William A. Lanza ("Bill") was born in February 1917, a couple of months before the United States entered that war in April 1917. Despite the firm intention on the part of many nations to avoid another world war, Bill and three of his brothers would serve in World War II in which the numbers would be even more staggering. Over 100 million men and women would be mobilized on both sides to fight in that war, and more than 50 million people would die.[3]

Bill's Family Background

Bill was born in East Boston, a diverse city of immigrants that came to America in waves since the middle of the 19th century. The Canadians came in the 1840s, the Irish in the 1850s, the Russian and Eastern European Jews in the 1890s, and the Italians at the turn of the century. During the first years of the 20th century, East Boston probably had the largest Jewish community in New England. By the time Bill was born, the major ethnic group was the Italians.[4] Years later, when Bill was shot down over Italy, the land of his ancestors, his saving grace was his Italian heritage.

Bill was the fourth of eight children born to William and Mary Lanza, two Italian immigrants who came to America to find a better life. He had five brothers, two older (Jimmy and Tony, later to also be called Jimmy by musicians) and three younger (Dan, Rudy and Tavio), as well as an older (Anna) and younger sister (Rita). He grew up in a working-class family.

Of his parents, he said: "My father was tough on us. He expected us to work all the time. On the other hand, my mother was the nicest person in the world. She was 'Aces,' but he was tough on her too. We all loved her so much, but my father dominated her and us, and we did what he told us."

Bill's family lived on the first floor in one of the three-story tenement houses that lined Morris Street in East Boston, not far from Logan Airport. Of the other tenants, he said: "A young woman with two sons lived on the top floor. I can't recall her name, but she was a fine woman who had a husband who used to come around and give her a hard time. My father didn't think very much of him, none of us did. Once he was fresh with my father in the hallway, and my father beat the hell out of him. My father had a short fuse and we all knew it."

The Kid Upstairs

"The Graziano family lived on the second floor. They were a family of five with two sons and a daughter. The oldest son, Jerry, was very talented and became a big-time musician. His younger brother Tony followed him into the music business and so did his younger sister, Agnes. I believe she was on the business end as a copywriter.

"Mr. Graziano loved music and got along great with my father, who played the guitar and piccolo. He looked like Tom Mix, the 'King of the Cowboys,' and everyone used to kid him about it. In fact, Jerry used to love Tom Mix and even carried news clippings of him in his pocket. Mr. Graziano was a music teacher and played the accordion, and both his sons could play it too.

"Jerry was the best friend of my older brother Jimmy, the musician, who was older than him. They went to music lessons together as kids, played together in Jerry's jazz band as teenagers, and played together in Jimmie McHale's band on radio as young men. My father was responsible for my brother becoming a good trumpet player. After buying him a trumpet and paying for a few lessons, Jimmy wanted to drop the trumpet. My father said that if he did he'd wrap it around his neck. My brother knew he would, so he stuck with it and played professionally until he was eighty-eight years old.

"Jerry was something else. His main instrument was the violin, but he could play anything. Our grammar school bought a xylophone and he learned to play that too, even once played it in front of the whole school. He was a likeable kid and got along well with everyone. A couple of times when I was about ten [and Jerry twelve], I went with him to Egleston Square in Roxbury where he practiced for Sam Cohen's Sunday Amateur Nights. I helped him strap on his accordion, and was impressed by how well he played it."

Cohen used to have his amateur nights at the Columbia Theater on Washington Street in Boston. For two decades from 1917 to 1937, Cohen's amateur nights alternated with vaudeville and second-run films at Loew's Columbia Theater on Washington Street in Boston, then gave way to burlesque.[5] Washington Street eventually became the "Combat Zone" in Boston, known for its adult entertainment. This was a far cry from Cohen's amateur nights.

"My brother always thought Jerry was a musical genius because music came so easy to him. He loved playing with him and was influenced by him. When Jerry changed his name from Generoso Graziano to Jerry Gray, he encouraged my brother to change his name from Tony Lanza to Jimmy Lane, and he did for a while. When my father got wind of this, he dropped the Lane but kept the Jimmy.

Tony became Jimmy to musicians, and eventually to most of his immediate family as well. However, Jimmy the musician married an Irish lass, Dorothy Gladys Haley, whose sister Irene married another Jimmy Lanza, who was a sweater manufacturer in East Boston and the cousin of Jimmy the musician. That side of the family always called Jimmy by his birth name, Tony.

Bill notes: "A lot of people I grew up with changed their last name to sound less ethnic. My brother is one of the few who changed only his first name after my father let him have it for changing his last name. My oldest brother Jimmy never had a problem with this, but he had other problems. He had infantile paralysis, which most people call polio today. He had trouble getting around, and wore an iron brace on one leg. He went to work in my brother-in-law's store, and died in a fire in that store when a kerosene stove blew up. It was a real tragedy for our family."

By coincidence, after Bill was shot down over Italy, he would run across a youngster limping through the woods with an iron brace just like his brother's. A lot of people had infantile paralysis then, including President Franklin Delano Roosevelt, who led the effort to conquer the disease. He championed the cause by celebrating his birthday with charity balls and by helping to establish the National Foundation for Infantile Paralysis. Comedian Eddie Cantor appealed to radio listeners to send dimes to the White House to fight the disease, which led to the March of Dimes that helped to fund the vaccine developed by Dr. Jonas Salk to prevent the disease.[6]

Before the vaccine, an estimated 50,000 people were afflicted by polio each year. After the vaccine, it was a different story. Virtually all babies today receive the Salk vaccine and, according to the March of Dimes, there has been no new case of the disease in the Western Hemisphere since 1991.[7] As a related point of interest, when the nation decided to honor Roosevelt with a coin, there was never any doubt that the coin would be the dime that has borne his image since 1946.[8]

Bill looked up to his brother the musician, who was blowing the horn in the clubs in Boston and on radio. It was the era of the big bands. "My brother was around some good musicians, like Jerry and Al Avola, who was also from East Boston. Once, he was with a carload of musicians going to Boston, and stopped by the store to get some change. Gene Krupa was with him and I was pretty impressed." Krupa became one of the most influential drummers of the twentieth century. Jerry would make his mark as well, as would Avola, a talented jazz guitarist.

"When Jimmy and Jerry were young men, they went to New York a couple of times to see some great musicians like Tommy Dorsey. Jerry was pulled to the brighter lights and drew the interest of Artie Shaw. I remember when Jimmy went with him for an interview with Shaw at Ben Marden's Riviera, just over the George Washington Bridge in New Jersey. This was in the mid-thirties. Jerry got the job and became Shaw's arranger and his music career took off."

Jerry Gray was indeed a musical genius. At the age of seven, he was an accomplished violinist and at the age of twelve he was a concertmaster with the Boston Junior Orchestra. At the age of thirteen, he was a violin soloist in that Orchestra.[9] When he was a young man playing in nightclubs and living at home with his parents in Medford, just a few miles north of Boston, he composed *String of Pearls* on the piano one evening while his parents were at the movies.[10] The song would become one of the top tunes of all time.

When Gray teamed up with Shaw in 1936, he arranged some of his top hits, most notably his top hit, *Begin the Beguine.*[11] His buddy from East Boston, Al Avola, played guitar on the record. Shaw, who had also changed his name from Arshawsky to sound less ethnic, was a handsome man and a self-proclaimed perfectionist both professionally and personally. Professionally, some considered him the best jazz clarinetist of his time, but he was seldom satisfied with his work. Personally, he was married eight times, including to some of the most beautiful women of his time such as Lana Turner and Ava Gardner, but he wasn't satisfied with any of them either. He lived a life of constant change and was often miserable. Gray's life, on the other hand, was just about the music.[12]

While Gray was forming an alliance with Shaw that would bring good music to ears of their nation in the midst of the Great Depression, across the ocean two dictatorial leaders, Hitler and Mussolini, were forming an alliance that would bring anything but good music to their respective nations or any other nation for that matter. When Shaw walked out on his band in 1939, Glenn Miller offered Gray a job the next day.[13] Jerry knew Miller liked Shaw's band because he had stacks of his records in the room he kept at the Hotel Pennsylvania in New York City.[14]

When Gray joined Miller, another alliance was formed that would bring good music to help boost the morale of a nation during wartime. Across the ocean, a storm was brewing as the alliance between Hitler and Mussolini was tightened with the Pact of Steel on May 22, 1939 in which the two dictators agreed to support each other in time of war. The storm gained momentum the following year with the Tripartite Pact of September 27, 1940. This brought Japan into the fold to form the Axis powers that would wreak havoc on the world and, in the end, on their respective nations.[15]

Though Miller hired Gray as an arranger, when he heard Gray's composition of *String of Pearls,* he tweaked it here and there and it became a big success.[16] After that, he encouraged Gray to compose as well as arrange, and Gray composed other hits for Miller, such as *Pennsylvania 6-5000, Caribbean Clipper, Sun Valley Jump, Here We Go Again, The Spirit is Willing,* and *The Man in the Moon.* Gray's list of arrangements included such hits as *Elmer's Tune, Moonlight Cocktails, Adios, American Patrol, Anvil Chorus, Chattanooga Choo Choo, I've Got a Gal in Kalamazoo* and the final version of the band's hit *St. Louis Blues March.*[17]

Glenn Miller recognized talent and surrounded himself with talented people. He was more than a good band leader; he was a good leader. The result was success. From 1939, the start of World War II, to late 1941, when Pearl Harbor was bombed and the United States entered the war, the Glenn Miller Orchestra was the most popular band in America.[18]

Miller was also a true patriot. When the United States went to war, he was thirty-eight years old, yet he volunteered to serve his country. In 1942, he was commissioned as a captain. In 1943, he wanted to replace the stiff martial music with dance-band music and wrote to Gray, his civilian band's arranger, about his plans: "We have authorization for a 14-man arranging staff to provide music for the Army Air Forces Technical Training Command, and it is my plan to place you in charge of this when you get one of uncle's zoot suits."[19] Soon afterward, Jerry signed up and donned one of Uncle Sam's "zoot suits."

Miller also brought with him several members of his civilian band and formed the Army Air Forces Overseas Orchestra.[20] Over the next two years, his band pursued a rigorous schedule entertaining the troops through radio broadcasts and visits to military bases. One month, his band played at thirty-five different bases and did forty broadcasts.[21]

In July 1944, when the war was in full force, Miller was promoted to major. At that time, Bill and Todd were missing in action and living in a cave in enemy territory. They wouldn't be hearing Miller tunes that summer. Miller's music was popular with the troops and Miller wanted to be as close to the fighting men as possible. The liberation of Paris on August 25, 1944 was a significant event of the war, and Miller was planning to have a Christmas broadcast from Paris.

On December 12, Miller and David Niven, the British actor, heard that Gray was cooking an Italian dinner using ingredients his mother sent him from the States, so they invited themselves to dinner. They dropped by the attic room Gray shared with bassist Trigger Alpert for a hearty meal. Before he left, Miller asked Jerry if he'd like to fly over to Paris with him the next day, but Jerry had a cold and didn't feel well. He told him he'd follow later with the rest of the band. That was the last time Jerry saw Miller.[22]

Due to inclement weather, Miller wasn't able to take off until a couple of days later, in weather that was still miserable. On December 15, Miller boarded a small plane for Paris to make arrangements for the Christmas broadcast. Tragedy then struck the popular band leader. His plane disappeared over the English Channel. Neither he nor his plane was ever found.

The cause of Miller's death remained a mystery until 1985 when the British Ministry of Defense explained that his plane was accidentally struck by one of a number of bombs dropped in the waters by Royal Air Force pilots who were returning from a mission and released their bombs over the ocean instead of landing with live bombs. Since no evidence of the crash was ever found, Miller's tombstone in Arlington National Cemetery still shows him as missing in action.[23]

According to Kathryn Shenkle, the historian of Arlington National Cemetery, "The band performed the scheduled Christmas broadcast from Paris under the direction of Jerry Gray. Glenn Miller's Army Air Force Band continued successfully. Its last concert was on November 13, 1945, at the National Press Club dinner for President Harry Truman in Washington, D.C., where Generals Dwight Eisenhower and Hap Arnold thanked the band for a job well done."[24] For his efforts in keeping Miller's band going until the war's end, Sergeant Gray was awarded a Bronze Star.[25] The kid upstairs served his country well.

Today, Miller's swing music is still associated with World War II. There is an exhibit honoring him at the National Museum of the United States Air Force at Wright-Patterson Air Force Base in Ohio. The following quote by Jimmy Doolittle, one of the war's biggest heroes, appears in the exhibit: "Next to letters from home, the Major Glenn Miller Army Air Force Band was the greatest morale builder we ever had in the Europe Theater of Operations." The exhibit includes a photo of Jerry Gray standing between Glenn Miller and Bing Crosby.

Even today, Europeans associate Miller's music with World War II. For example, at a 2007 dinner gathering of the World War Cultural Association in Reggio Emilia, Italy, the attendees dressed in World War II uniforms and danced to the music of Glenn Miller. The

Association's members, including Michele "Mick" Becchi, a friend to many Americans researching relatives who served in Italy during the war, share a passion for helping future generations to avoid the tragic errors that led to World Wars I and II.[26]

Early Influences

Unlike the kid upstairs, Bill had no musical talent. So while Bill's father had a soft spot for music, he had no soft spot for education. It was work that counted, so a formal education was never an option for Bill. Like so many other immigrants, Bill's father was enterprising, always looking for ways to support his family. He was principally a storekeeper and over the years had a cheese shop, a grocery store and a variety store. According to Bill, he was also an excellent carpenter.

Bill remembers: "I loved sports when I was a kid. I was a pitcher in the sixth grade, and it was a big deal for me when I was elected captain of the baseball team. I also played guard in street football. In those days, we ran track in grammar school, and I was on the track team. Once, we had a meet at Tech Field [at MIT—Massachusetts Institute of Technology] and broke a school record in the relay. Our coach treated us to apple pie and ice cream. Funny, I still remember that day so clearly, maybe because after that I had to work all the time." Four years earlier in 1925, Jimmy Doolittle also had a good experience at MIT, receiving one of its first doctorates in aeronautical engineering.[27]

Bill continues: "When I was twelve, in the sixth grade, my father made a push cart for me to use in delivering sulfur candles to drug stores in the North End, the Italian section of Boston. We bought barrels of sulfur powder from Everett Chemical, and my brothers melted the sulfur and poured it into candle molds. Then, we'd pack the candles in boxes of fifty with William Lanza & Sons stamped on the boxes. My father sold them and I delivered them. The stores sold them to Italian immigrants who made wine. They used the candles, which you could smell a mile away, to fumigate the wine barrels. I used to take the ferry from East Boston to the North End. The ferry cost me a penny in those days."

The sulfur served as a purifying agent to keep the barrels clean and free from fungi or bacteria which could spoil the taste and smell of the wine. Much later, during the war, Bill would fumigate the grapes on the farm in Tuscany with a sulfur spray, to help the farmers who were helping him to evade the enemy.

At an early age, Bill was drawn to airplanes. "We lived near Logan Airport [at that time East Boston Airport or simply Boston Airport] and I used to like to walk there to watch the planes take off and land. Like most kids, I was fascinated by them and the pilots that flew them, guys like Charles Lindbergh and Jimmy Doolittle. I still remember when Lindbergh came to Boston after his historic flight. I was ten years old and he was the biggest hero in the world. I walked to the airport by myself to see him land."

Lindbergh received a hero's welcome that would impress any youngster. Thousands of people came to Boston Airport to see Lindy. As Bill excitedly watched, Lindbergh flew into view at about two o'clock in the afternoon. Cannons exploded, boat whistles tooted loudly, sirens filled the air, bells rang, and thousands of people cheered wildly as he touched down. The *Spirit of St. Louis* was greeted by the spirit of Boston.[28]

The mayor of Boston and the governors of all the New England states were at the Airport to greet him. In addition to this civil welcome, Lindbergh was extended a military welcome from the 26th Division of the National Guard.[29] Little did Bill know that fourteen years later he would become part of the 26th Division when it was called into Federal service as a result of World War II. Interestingly, in 1927, the commander of the 26th Division was Major General Edward L. Logan, for whom Boston Airport would be renamed Logan Airport in 1943.[30]

State and city officials joined Lindbergh in a nine-mile motorcade to a reception in the Boston Commons. Bill recalls: "I followed the motorcade for a while as it moved slowly down Maverick Street in East Boston. I got a good glimpse of Lindbergh. The motorcade continued down Meridian Street, where President Kennedy's father lived as a kid. After that, I believe it went over the bridge to Chelsea and later the bridge to Boston. It was one of the most memorable days of my life. At the time, I never thought for a minute that I might someday be flying in a plane, let alone flying on combat missions during a war."

At the Boston Commons, the crowd was said to be the largest since 1919 when the 26th Division returned from World War I and marched in review before hundreds of thousands of people.[31] One reason for the turnout was that many offices and stores gave their employees half a day off to see Lindbergh. That evening and the next day, up until the time he took off for another city, was filled with speeches and activities as Boston rolled out the red carpet for the popular aviator. Lindbergh kept up this pace in a hectic three-month nationwide tour in which he visited all forty-eight states and ninety-two cities. The tour was sponsored by Daniel Guggeheim, a multimillionaire and aviation enthusiast.[32]

From age twelve to twenty-two, Bill worked with his father in his stores. He worked part-time while he was in school and full-time after two years of high school. "My two older brothers didn't even go to high school, so at least I went for two years. Even though I didn't get a formal education, I got another kind of education. When you work in a store you learn to deal with all kinds of personalities, and you need to get along with them if you want them to come back."

Ralph "Jake" Turner, a gifted educator and headmaster of the former Emerson School for Boys in Exeter, New Hampshire, used to tell his students that education was "learning to live with and for others while learning to think for oneself." By that definition, Bill received a pretty good education. He also picked up a few street smarts along the way. "My father never paid me, but I took what I needed, and even slipped my mother money from time to time."

In his two years of high school, he also received a bit of an education on military discipline. "Believe it or not, I received military training in my two years of high school. All the boys in the Boston public schools had to become cadets. We had to buy our own uniforms and they gave us mock rifles. We went through drills as if we were in the military. The drilling was done during school just like any other course. I seem to remember that our instructor was a captain in the National Guard."

From the time of the Civil War up to the time of the Vietnam War, military training was a required course for male students in Boston's public schools. The Boston School Boy Cadet course was taught by reserve officers and the training included marching, maneuvers, posture and inspection. All cadets started as privates and were promoted based on their leadership abilities. Every year, they would march in the Boston School Boy Cadets parade, which would draw thousands of flag-waving spectators. Like Bill, many of them later became real soldiers.

Their high school training gave them a distinct advantage over those who never had military training throughout high school.[33]

On June 2, 1932, when Bill was fifteen years old, he marched in the annual Boston school cadets' parade. He was among 17,000 school boys from thirteen high schools and eighteen intermediate schools. The cadets were reviewed at four different spots by, respectively, a representative of the mayor, the governor himself and his staff, the superintendent of schools, and a member of the school committee. Cadets were judged on "carriage, alignment, appearance and discipline."[34] It was a big deal to be selected the outstanding regiment and the best band.

Twelve years later on June 4, 1944, about 500,000 people turned out for the cadet parade to watch 14,000 cadets in what was described as one of the best displays put on by schoolboys in the eighty-one years of the program. On that day, far away in Italy, Bill was hiding in a cave behind enemy lines.

The last school boy cadets' parade was held on May 24, 1960. During the 1950s, educators, administrators and parents began questioning the benefits of military training. Some figured now that we have the atomic bomb, why do we need soldiers? The crowds dwindled as did the appropriations for the program. Ray Barron, who survived three years of combat in World War II fighting against Fascism and Nazism, donated his own money that year to keep the parade alive, and was called by some a "fascist for supporting military drill in the schools."[35]

Since Bill was unable to play team sports, he brought an individual sport to the store: "I liked to box and kept a pair of boxing gloves and a bag in the basement of the store. I would take out my frustrations on that bag. Sometimes when my friends came around, we would box in the basement. One of my friends, Muzzy Mazzarino, became pretty good, and decided to become an amateur boxer.

"I remember once when he was starting out and was pretty green. He was sparring with another boxer and the guy opened up on him. Afterwards in the locker room, he was getting more and more upset with this guy for taking advantage of him. I kept telling him to forget about it, but the more he thought about it, the madder he got. Finally, he went after the guy. They broke it up before anyone got hurt. After that, he wasn't green anymore.

"Boxing was big in those days. I used to go with Muzzy to his fights in and around Boston. He fought in Boston at Mechanics Hall and the Boston Arena, and outside Boston in Medford, Lowell and Brockton, Rocky Marciano's home town. Muzzy had a good jab and a great inside right punch. With it, he could hit like a mule and would drop a guy like a sack of potatoes. He had quite a few knockouts." So did Marciano, who became the only undefeated heavyweight champion in boxing history. Notably, Jimmy Doolittle also had quite a few knockouts as an accomplished boxer.[36]

"Every Monday night was amateur night at the Boston Arena. You had to win three three-round bouts to be the champ. One night, Ted Williams was in the crowd. Williams was a loud guy and he was sitting near the ring. Muzzy was fighting an Irish guy from Charlestown for the championship, and he overheard Williams betting on him to beat the Irish guy. He got all excited and won the fight. He never stopped talking about it because we all loved Williams.

"I was always a sports fan. I followed the Red Sox and I liked to watch hockey and football. I used to take money from the store to go to Bruins games at the Boston Garden, and I really enjoyed going to semi-pro football games. But boxing was my favorite sport, and it helped me later in the service. When I was in the infantry, I was an instructor in hand-to-hand combat.

"In 1941, just before I was drafted for a year of service, Muzzy was thinking of going pro and wanted me to manage him. When I got drafted, he said he'd wait for me to get back. I didn't make it back for almost five years, and he never turned pro. Muzzy wasn't drafted because he worked in the shipyard. After that, he went into the florist business. His father was a florist and Muzzy carried on in the family tradition that is still going strong. Muzzy's Day Square Florist is still a family-owned business in East Boston. His son Joe runs the business now, but Muzzy's wife is there every day helping him with flower arrangements." A photo of Muzzy with his fists up adorns a wall, a reminder of days past.

Like Muzzy, Bill spent a lot of time with his father. "My brothers all worked in the store at one time or another, but I was a steady worker all those years. I probably spent more time with my father than any of my brothers and sisters. Since he always spoke to me in broken English, I could understand and speak Italian, but I never considered myself fluent. Years later, this experience would come in handy when I was shot down over Italy."

During Prohibition (1920 to 1933), Bill's father sold wine in his store. "Most people didn't feel that drinking booze was a crime. It helped them to relax. Years later in the Air Corps, after every bombing mission, we all got a shot of whiskey to help us relax. My father helped the people in the neighborhood to relax. A glass of wine had always been a part of our meals."

Bill's father had been making and drinking wine for most of his life. During Prohibition, wine was treated differently than other types of alcohol as a result of the Volstead Act that exempted wine used for sacramental purposes, so the door was open to skirt around the law.[37] A lot of people became holier.

The thirties brought the Great Depression and Bill's family struggled like most other families, but he always had a job in his father's store. "Adversity builds character" certainly applied to the generation that weathered that decade. They were used to hard times, so when the war came they were willing to make the sacrifices necessary to win the war.

In 1939, Bill's parents sold the store and bought a three-story house in Revere, just north of Boston. There was a large barn in the backyard and his enterprising father dug out a cellar and put his carpentry skills to good use by making the barn into a two-story residence that he connected to the three-story residence. His father loved the house because it had a backyard where he could grow flowers, vegetables and of course grapes for his wine. Another family lived on the third floor, Jimmy on the second floor with his new wife, and everyone else on the ground floor and in the rear residence. Though smaller in scale, this living arrangement was similar to the housing arrangement Bill would find on the farm that harbored him and Todd when they were shot down over Italy.

When his father sold the store, Bill got a job working for the Waldorf Commissary in Boston, which supplied food to the popular Waldorf restaurants known for their quick service. Two years later, he was drafted into the Army for a year of service that Pearl Harbor expanded to almost five years of service. When he left home, he had no idea how important the time he spent listening to his father's broken English would be three years later when he was shot down over Italy. Also, he had no way of knowing how heavy the burden of having four sons in the war would weigh on his mother.

Like the Graziano family on the second floor at Morris Street, the Lanza family on the first floor would, like so many other families, do their part during the war. Bill was with the Army Air Forces in the Mediterranean Theater, while his three younger brothers all served in the Navy in the Pacific Theater. Dan was in the Seabees in New Guinea, Rudy was on the USS *Canberra* and later was land-based in Okinawa. Tavio was also in Okinawa, assigned to an LST (Landing Ship, Tank), a naval vessel to support amphibious operations.

Oldest brother Jimmy was ineligible for the draft because he had infantile paralysis, and Jimmy the musician missed the draft because he was married with a child on the way and had a wartime job. He was a welder of destroyer escorts in the Hingham Ship Yard. Destroyers were desperately needed to escort convoys and protect them from the German U-boats (submarines) that were sinking Allied ships at an alarming rate.[38] Jimmy worked days welding destroyer escorts and nights blowing the horn in nightclubs. Weekends sometimes found him entertaining the men and women at military bases, including the one on Cape Cod that Bill was stationed at when he first went into the service.

Chapter 2

PREPARING FOR THE STORM

Bill Lanza was inducted into the United States Army on March 6, 1941 at the age of twenty-four to serve for a year in the 101st Infantry Regiment of the 26th Infantry Division, called the Yankee Division. He and others from Revere boarded a bus on that day for a ride into Boston to be processed for military duty. Among those on the bus was Frank Alvino, who became one of Bill's closest friends in the Infantry.

The Yankee Division, consisting of soldiers from all six New England states, had a proud history, having served on the front lines throughout World War I.[1] Not only that, but it earned more combat decorations than any other activated National Guard division during World War I.[2] After the December 7, 1941 surprise attack on Pearl Harbor, things changed dramatically for Bill and many other inductees, and he ended up serving until the end of the war. Frank wasn't so lucky.

Infantry Training

As a member of the 26th Infantry Division, Bill was originally stationed at Camp Edwards on Cape Cod where he received three months of basic training. "Camp Edwards was close to home and one weekend my brother Jimmy was in a band that entertained us with swing music, including some of the songs that his friend Jerry arranged for Glenn Miller. That music was to follow us to Europe and for the rest of our lives. Miller's music meant a lot to the old veterans like me. We grew up listening and dancing to this music, and when I heard it, I always thought of Jerry."

After basic training at Camp Edwards in eastern Massachusetts during the spring of 1941, Bill participated in maneuvers, or infantry training exercises, at Fort Devens in western Massachusetts during the summer of 1941.[3] Following that, he participated in the First Army "Carolina Maneuvers" during the fall of 1941, where more than a half-million troops engaged in mock warfare in the rolling terrain and numerous streams of North and South Carolina. The goal was to add some realism to training. There were two armies—the Red Army and the Blue Army—and umpires determined the casualties and decided on the prisoners of war.[4]

Bill recalls that he was in the Red Army, in which he and his buddy, Frank Alvino, had quite an adventure. "Frank and I were in a scout patrol of four men and a driver, who was assigned to our company to drive our Weapons Carrier [a 4 x 4 general purpose truck used to carry weapons[5]]. Our job was to find the enemy. Our patrol leader ordered us on a foot patrol in the woods, while he and the soldier drove off in a different direction. As we made our way through the woods, we came upon enemy troops. Frank wanted to engage them, but I didn't. I figured we would be captured and be out of the war. I convinced him, and we reported their position back to our patrol leader.

"Soon afterward, we set up a blockade and captured a command car [a vehicle for a senior officer and staff]. It was a big deal to capture a senior staff officer. Our patrol leader ordered the other soldier to drive the command car back to our base with our prisoners of war. As soon as he got in the vehicle, the car sped off, and his helmet came flying out of the car. He was now their prisoner of war. Our patrol leader was ticked, and told us to stay put while he went to complain to the umpires. We figured that the officers were too embarrassed to play fair. Our rifles had blanks, so there wasn't too much we could do to stop the vehicle.

"While we waited, we came across an abandoned farmhouse. When we looked in the window, we saw a mattress and thought we found gold. We got little sleep on maneuvers, so we decided to take a nap. We ended up sleeping there that night. The next day, we couldn't find anyone but a farmer, who invited us to dinner with his family. We had the best meal in a long time, and gave his kids some money in appreciation. That night, we slept in the abandoned farmhouse again, and had another good night's sleep.

"The next day, the farmer drove us to the highway, and we hitchhiked back to the base, about forty or fifty miles away. It wasn't a problem getting a ride in those days. People had great respect for the uniform. We figured we would be in for it back at the base, but instead our sergeant apologized for deserting us. I still can't believe we came out of that okay."

People did indeed have great respect for soldiers, as Bill would again experience on his trip back to Massachusetts. "After the Carolina Maneuvers, the Yankee Division returned to Camp Edwards in a large convoy. As we drove through towns along the way, soldiers would be asked to direct traffic. When our convoy went through York, Pennsylvania, I was the traffic guard. People from the town were coming up to me, saying nice things and giving me packages of goodies like beer, food and cigarettes. Later, I loaded all my presents on a truck. Everyone was behind us 100 percent. It's a good thing too, because the day after we arrived at Camp Edwards, Pearl Harbor was attacked."

When the war broke out, the need to protect our shores from enemy infiltration grew in importance. To address this national security concern, the Yankee Division was called upon to patrol the North Atlantic coast to prevent the landing of spies or saboteurs.[6] Bill became part of this initiative. He was assigned coastal patrol duty that included patrolling the Maine coast for spies and saboteurs, and later the Long Island coast after saboteurs landed there.

The importance of coastal patrol duty was escalated after four German saboteurs landed on a Long Island beach on June 13, 1942 and four days later another four landed on a Florida beach. Their purpose was to strike a blow against America's ability to manufacture vital equipment for the war. Fortunately, the nation's guard was up and all eight saboteurs were arrested by June 27, 1942 before any of them had a chance to accomplish a single act of destruction.[7]

After coastal patrol duty, Bill was deployed for additional infantry training at Fort Meade in Maryland, Fort Jackson in South Carolina, and Camp Gordon in Georgia. "We went on numerous maneuvers. There was a lot of sweating in the infantry but you all suffered together and built a strong camaraderie among each other. You learned to work as a team under adverse circumstances." He also learned to get used to sleeping on the ground, which stood him in good stead when he was shot down over Italy.

As an infantryman, Bill had extensive training on weapons. Originally trained as a rifleman in a rifle company, he became a corporal in a weapons platoon where he was in charge of a squadron of two machine gunners and three mortar launchers. In time, he would be on the receiving end of mortar barrages. His boxing came in handy as well when he became an instructor in hand-to-hand combat. "This training taught me how to fall and tumble. For example, my lieutenant used another soldier and me to demonstrate how to jump off a moving truck. I think this experience was invaluable in helping me to later avoid injury when I landed after bailing out of a plane in trouble."

Because of his training on unarmed defense and the fact that he knew how to use a gun, he once drew an interesting assignment. "When I was at Fort Meade, a friend and I were ordered to pick up two men who had gone AWOL and bring them back to the base. He had to go to Massachusetts to get his prisoner, and I had to go to North Carolina to get mine. I picked up the kid in a guard house and got him back okay, but his prisoner escaped out a window when he went to the head. My prisoner was a farmer from the Midwest and, while we got along, he knew that I would do what it took to get him back."

While Bill was focusing on his prisoner during the spring of 1943, a large group of Allied prisoners of war across the ocean were digging a tunnel for a daring escape from Stalag Luft III, a high-security prison camp in what is now Zagan, Poland, about 125 miles (about one-hundred air miles) southeast of Berlin.[8] Stalag Luft is short for _Stammlager Luft_ which means "permanent camp for airmen." As the war escalated, the Germans were busy establishing prison camps such as these and the prisoners were busy trying to escape from them. For some time, the prisoners at this camp had been preparing for what has become known as the "Great Escape."[9]

After dark on March 24, 1944, the first prisoner started through a narrow two-foot tunnel, secretly and painstakingly dug over a two-year period about thirty feet below ground, to an opening by a nearby forest. The tunnel was supposed to reach the woods, but it came up just short. The plan was for about 250 prisoners to escape. All night long, prisoners made their way through the tunnel. As the seventy-seventh prisoner emerged from the tunnel, he was seen by a guard and the chase was on. Of the seventy-six prisoners who escaped, only three got away. The other seventy-three were recaptured and returned to prison. Then, in violation of the Geneva Convention, fifty of them were executed.[10]

Bill didn't know it at the time, but he would soon become an airman. Ten months later, he too would be bailing out of a B-25 in enemy territory, but he would be lucky enough to evade capture. Two members of his crew wouldn't be so lucky. One would end up in Stalag Luft III, the "Great Escape" prison, and the other in Stalag VII-A, where many violations of the Geneva Convention would occur.

Joining the Army Air Forces

With the war escalating abroad, Bill's friends at home were asking him when he was going overseas. It was the middle of 1943 and he had been in the service for over two years. While the Yankee Division served on the front lines during World War I, it didn't see action in World War II until after almost four years of training.[11] Before that happened, Bill saw a notice at Camp Gordon, Georgia, looking for volunteers with experience in handling weapons for combat duty overseas with the Army Air Corps, and he signed up. Even though the name of the Army Air Corps was changed to the Army Air Forces on June 20, 1941, Bill and many other former airmen still call it the Army Air Corps.[12]

For a guy who used to walk to the airport as a kid to watch the planes take off and land, joining the Air Corps was a no-brainer. "I was anxious to go overseas. I had also decided that I wanted to die clean, not in the mud, and figured my weapons training would be put to good use as an aerial gunner. Thirteen of us signed up. We were all non-commissioned officers. Our company commander called me in to ask me why I signed up. I told him I was anxious to go overseas and that the Air Corps looked attractive to me. I also told him I always liked the idea of flying."

When Bill signed up for the Army Air Forces in July 1943, there was a dire need for aerial gunners. The training program had just been expanded to produce 140,000 gunners a year as soon as possible. General Henry "Hap" Arnold, the Commanding General of the Army Air Forces, declared that gunnery training was to be given "a priority on personnel, base facilities, and equipment, including combat-type airplanes, ahead of all other training activities in the United States."[13] Like Bill, Arnold served in the infantry before taking to the air. After graduating from West Point, he was an infantry officer until he became the first qualified Army pilot in 1911.[14]

Bill trained with the 310th Bomb Group at Columbia Army Air Base in South Carolina. In July 1943, Columbia was not only a relatively new airfield but one that already had a rich history. The air base was the result of a crash defense program in 1940 to develop a nationwide grid of strategically-located landing fields. Columbia was selected as one of 250 landing fields and construction work began on June 6, 1941 on 600 acres of land. The airport was almost completed when Pearl Harbor was bombed on December 7, 1941. The day after, the Army Air Corps moved in and by early February it was decided that the base's primary mission would be to train medium bomber crews. Later that month, the most famous B-25 crews of all time were assembled at Columbia for one of the most dangerous and important missions of the war.[15]

The B-25 was a relatively new aircraft in World War II. It was the result of a March 1939 proposal by the Army Air Corps for the design of a medium bomber that could carry a bomb load of 3,000 pounds over a range of 2,000 miles at a top speed of over 300 mph. Lee Atwood, the chief engineer of North American Aviation, took charge of the project and produced the B-25, suggesting that it be named in honor of General "Billy" Mitchell, one of the top American airmen of World War I. Mitchell foresaw the importance of air power in war and promoted its development more than anyone else. The Air Corps agreed with Atwood's suggestion, and it was named the North American B-25 Mitchell, the only military aircraft named after a specific person. It was accepted by the Army in February 1941, a month before Bill was drafted.[16]

The B-25 was a versatile and durable aircraft that has always had a special place in the hearts of many Americans because sixteen of them were used by Doolittle's Raiders in the April 18, 1942 bombing of Japanese cities in retaliation for the bombing of Pearl Harbor. Bill was training as an infantryman at the time, and shared the pride of the nation for these courageous men and their incredible mission. Many books have been written about the mission. Among them are the World War II classic, *Thirty Seconds Over Tokyo* by Ted Lawson, and several books by the Raiders' official historian, Colonel Carroll V. Glines, including *The Doolittle Raid: America's Daring First Strike Against Japan*.

The Doolittle Raid came at a low point in the morale of the United States, following the sudden attack on Pearl Harbor and its being unprepared to strike back in force. It was a mission that required great courage on the part of the pilots and crews, all volunteers, because there was a great risk that they would not survive the mission. Their task was formidable. Unbeknownst to them at the time, they were going to be trained to take off from an aircraft carrier near the coast of Japan to bomb selected targets on the Japanese mainland.

Columbia Army Air Base in Columbia, South Carolina, was the place at which the crews volunteered for this critical mission. However, when they volunteered for the mission, it wasn't yet called the Columbia Army Air Base. It was called the Lexington County Army Air Base. It wouldn't be renamed until April 2, 1942.[17] In February 1942, the Army Air Forces had decided that the field's primary use would be as a bombardment training station, and issued orders to the 17th Bomb Group at Pendleton Field in Oregon to move to the Lexington County Army Air Base.

Shortly after the 17th Bomb Group arrived at their new base, they were met by Lieutenant Colonel James H. "Jimmy" Doolittle, who was selected by Arnold to assemble and train the crews for the mission. Later, he talked Arnold into letting him lead the mission as well.[18] Doolittle knew that these crews had been flying the B-25s longer than anyone else and he needed experienced crews for the mission. He explained that he was looking for volunteers to take part in a secret "dangerous, repeat, dangerous" mission that required experienced B-25 crews. Twenty-four crews volunteered for the mission.[19]

When Doolittle ordered the Army engineers at the air base to mark off one of the runways to resemble the flight deck of an aircraft carrier and happened to have the plans for one, Russell B. Maxey, one of the Army engineers, knew something strange was going on. When Doolittle would tie ropes to a B-25 tail, rev up the engines, then release the aircraft in a burst to try to take off before the lines they had painted on the runway, he would be wondering what was going on. According to Maxey, "They practiced until they got pretty doggone good at it. Then one day they were gone."[20]

Dolittle and the twenty-four B-25 crews were off to Eglin Field, an isolated field in the wooded swamps near Pensacola, Florida to train for weeks in utmost secrecy for their dangerous mission. At the start of training, only Doolittle knew the mission objective. It was to be withheld from the crews during their training to prevent it from leaking to the enemy.[21]

First, the crews had to learn how to take off in the short distance of an aircraft carrier with a bomber that wasn't designed for this purpose. They strained the capabilities of the B-25s because it was unheard of at the time for planes of that size and weight (with full bomb loads) to take off in such a short distance.[22] B-25s normally required runways of at least 1,200 to 1,500 feet, but they had to learn to lift off by 450 feet or less.[23]

The pilots also had to learn to fly their B-25s at extremely low levels since the plan was for them to fly from an aircraft carrier to and over the Japanese mainland at an altitude of only 500 feet to evade enemy fighters and anti-aircraft guns.[24] B-25s normally flew at heights above 10,000 feet and typically descended to no lower than 8,000 on bomb runs. Flying lower than this was something done by smaller, more maneuverable fighter bombers, not medium-bombers like Mitchell B-25s.

After intense training, they departed for San Francisco Bay in early April to board the USS *Hornet* with plans to take off 400 to 450 miles from the Japanese coast to bomb selected targets in Japan. After hitting their targets, they were supposed to find and land on secluded airfields in China, a country with no love for the Japanese.

On their way to the Japanese coast in a convoy consisting of carriers, cruisers and destroyers traveling in radio silence, the Raiders were briefed on the targets and given maps to help them locate them.[25] This intelligence had been collected by Captain Davey Jones, the pilot of Plane #5, and Lieutenant Tom Griffin, the navigator of Plane #9.

According to Griffin, "When our training first started in February, 1942, Lieutenant Colonel Jimmy Doolittle sent Davey Jones and me to Washington, D.C. to work with Air Force Intelligence in gathering together information we would need to supply each crew about the exact location of potential targets in the Japanese Islands. We got this information and also maps of Japan and China, enough to supply twenty crews even though only sixteen went on the mission. This information was given out during our eighteen-day trip across the Pacific with each crew receiving specific targets to hit."[26]

As they were approaching the Japanese coast, the USS *Hornet* ran into trouble. The aircraft carrier was spotted by a Japanese picket boat, formerly a fishing boat recruited into the naval service to be part of the picket line of boats patrolling off the Japanese coast as an early warning system for enemy ships or aircraft.[27] While the picket boat notified the Japanese Combined Fleet Headquarters before it was destroyed by the Americans, the Japanese figured that an air attack could not be forthcoming before August 19. They assumed that the aircraft carriers were carrying short-range, carrier-type aircraft that couldn't be launched that far from shore. They never suspected one was carrying longer-range, medium bombers.

In any case, the fact that the convoy was spotted forced the Raiders to lift off immediately on April 18 when they were about 650 miles from Japan. Their early departure increased the possibility of running out of gas before reaching the Chinese airfields.[28] This dangerous mission became even more dangerous.

The planes flew low across the ocean and reached Japan without being detected by the Japanese Army and Navy interceptors, which were far overhead.[29] In dramatic fashion, the Raiders bombed military installations, factories, oil stores, gas and electric companies and other targets. Japanese leaders had led the population to believe that the war could never penetrate their shores, so the attack was a total shock to the Japanese general public. It was a total shock to Japanese leaders as well. They had yet to put up full defensive precautions against an air attack because they figured the spotted carriers could not have launched planes until the next day when they were closer to mainland Japan.[30]

It was an incredibly well-conceived plan, and the Raiders implemented it in impressive fashion. Unfortunately, however, none of them made it to their landing destinations. All but one plane ran out of gas and crashed in China. Eleven of those crews bailed out in China before their planes crashed, three landed in the waters off the China coast and ditched their planes, and one plane had a crash landing in China. The only plane to land did so in the Soviet Union.[31]

Of the eighty airmen on the mission, three were killed during the raid, eight were captured by the Japanese, and five were imprisoned when they landed in Russia.[32] Of the eight Japanese prisoners of war, only four survived—three were executed by a firing squad and one died in prison. After he lost all the aircraft, Doolittle felt as though he failed on the mission, but everyone else felt otherwise. Despite great odds, Doolittle's Raiders succeeded in their dangerous mission, greatly boosting the morale of the American public when it was needed most.[33]

Three of Doolittle's Raiders—Davey Jones, Tom Griffin and Griff Williams—returned to duty and each ran into trouble again and had to bail out of a disabled aircraft.[34] You might call all three "double heroes." In fact, Jones was one of the prisoners who helped to dig the tunnel for the "Great Escape." However, before that fateful night, he and other Americans were moved to another part of the camp. This time, he caught a break because the move probably saved his life. Luck is a valuable asset during wartime, and this move was his rabbit's foot.[35]

It was fitting that the B-25 Mitchell delivered the first blow in retaliation for the bombing of Pearl Harbor because its namesake, Billy Mitchell, predicted Pearl Harbor years before it happened. After an inspection tour of the Pacific and Far East, Mitchell submitted a report in 1924 that predicted war with Japan, including the attack on Pearl Harbor. He predicted that the Japanese would some day attack Pearl Harbor at 7:30 a.m. and Clark Field in the Philippines at 10:40 a.m. On December 7, 1941, Japan attacked Pearl Harbor at 7:55 a.m. and Clark Field in the Philippines a couple of hours later.[36]

Mitchell's report was largely ignored and he died in 1936, five years before his prophecy came true. However, his steadfast promotion of air power eventually started paying dividends during World War II.[37] Today, the B-25 and other war planes that flew in combat during World War II are affectionately known as "warbirds," and the B-25 is considered by many to be a venerable old "bird."

Mitchell's promotion of air power was also appreciated after the war when in 1946 he was posthumously awarded by Congress a special Congressional Gold Medal for his "outstanding pioneer service and foresight" in the field of American military aviation.[38] It is also noteworthy that Mitchell's protégé, Hap Arnold, led the Army Air Forces during World War II.[39]

Columbia Army Air Base in July 1943 was an impressive place to be for a young man like Bill. It was the air base at which Doolittle recruited the volunteers for his famous mission and where some of the Raiders were now instructors. Not only that, but top movie stars were on the base making a war movie.

Bill remembers it well: "It was exciting to be around some of the heroes of Doolittle's Raid. It was also exciting to be at a base where a movie was being filmed. They were using our B-25s to film scenes for *A Man Named Joe*, starring Spencer Tracy and Van Johnson. It was about a deceased B-25 pilot, played by Tracy, who returned as the guardian angel for a young pilot, played by Johnson, who was in love with Tracy's girlfriend."

Fred Smith, a B-25 pilot in training at Columbia at the time, had an opportunity to fly to Chicago on a weekend leave with one of Doolittle's Raiders who was an instructor at the base. Bill Pound was the navigator of Plane #12 which, despite encountering enemy fighters, successfully bombed the Ogura refinery, two factories and a large warehouse along the docks of Yokohama.[40] Pound was planning to attend a Cubs game and Smith was planning to see his folks. After they took off for Chicago, Smith turned to Pound: "Bill, you're the navigator. What course should we take?" The Raider replied: "Turn on WGN in Chicago [the Cubs station] on your radio compass and follow the needle!" He did just that, and they arrived safely in Chicago.

When Bill Lanza reported to Columbia, he was assigned to a crew that included pilot Second Lieutenant Alfred E. Vancil, co-pilot Second Lieutenant Connally O. Briles, navigator/bombardier Second Lieutenant Thomas B. Dunn, engineer Sergeant Ronald J. Kane, and radio operator/waist gunner Staff Sergeant Robert F. Mygrant. Bill was the top-turret gunner. The objective of their training was to create a closely-knit, well-organized team of highly-trained specialists.[41]

"We trained together as a crew at Columbia and we also trained individually in our specialty. We became familiar with the B-25 and our responsibilities on combat missions. We had instructors in the classroom and in the air so that we could learn to function as a team as well as to become proficient in our specialties. Classroom training included identifying aircraft and understanding ballistics. The class to identify aircraft was something else."

As the importance of aircraft grew in World War II, the need to quickly identify a plane as being friendly or hostile became critical. This was no small matter because there were so many planes in the skies during the war. While the Army Air Corps had only a few hundred airplanes before the war, it had produced almost 80,000 airplanes by the end of the war, and this included more than a hundred different types.[42]

The different types of American aircraft were identified by function, using a letter for each function. For example, A meant Attack, such as the Douglas A-20 Havoc that operated primarily at low levels to support ground troops. B was for Bombardment, such as the North American B-25 Mitchell that operated at 8,000 to 10,000 feet to bomb targets behind enemy lines. C meant Cargo, such as the Douglas C-47 Skytrain used to transport troops and supplies. L meant

Liaison, such as the Stinson L-5 Sentinel, or "Flying Jeep," used for reconnaissance and rescuing Allied personnel in remote areas. P meant Pursuit, such as the Republic P-47 Thunderbolt used to pursue enemy aircraft in the skies as well as enemy trains, tanks and other vehicles on the ground. T meant Training, such as the North American T-6 Texan used to train fighter pilots during the war.[43]

In addition to many types of American planes, there were many types of planes from other nations, both friendly and hostile. Since an enemy aircraft could dart out of the clouds or approach from the position of the sun, it was necessary to recognize the outline of a hostile aircraft immediately before it was too late. It was indeed a daunting task to train American airmen to instantly determine if another plane were hostile or not. An exhibit at the Smithsonian National Air and Space Museum in Washington, D.C. displays 202 of the 220 models of planes American airmen were taught to instantly identify during World War II. The exhibit includes planes from Russia (6), Italy (13), Germany (30), Japan (37), Great Britain (37) and the United States (79).

To address this critical need to quickly identify aircraft, Army Air Force psychologists developed a training apparatus called a tachistoscope. The device flashed images of friendly and enemy aircraft, starting with large images flashed at slow speeds and gradually decreasing the size of the images and time of exposure. Eventually, pilots and gunners were able to identify the spec of a plane in the distance in 1/100th of a second. This was a form of subliminal training that is effective because the human brain is able to take in all the information it needs to build a response to an image flashed in 1/100th of a second.[44] Bill was impressed: "It was quite a course."

"I was being trained as an aerial gunner to fire 'twin fifties,' two fifty-caliber machine guns, from the top turret of a B-25 bomber. In the infantry, I had been trained to fire a machine gun but not two at once and not from a fast-moving bomber shooting at a faster-moving fighter. I had to take classroom training in ballistics, and then I had to practice what I learned to develop the skill I needed to do my job on combat missions."

One of the concepts being taught was "lead," and they had skeet ranges with targets that closely resembled the flight paths of enemy planes. The position of the clay pigeon determined how you would lead it. They would be released from different positions and the gunners would learn to quickly pick it up, track it, and give it the lead necessary for the bullet and the target to come together at the same point.[45]

"I loved skeet shooting. My friend Bob Mygrant and I liked to spend time at the range. We'd even go on our own when we had a chance. We'd take turns loading the clay pigeons for each other. I loved it so much that after the war I thought of opening a skeet-shooting range north of Boston on Route 1. I even wrote to *Popular Mechanics* for plans for a skeet-shooting range, but nothing ever came of it. By coincidence, years later I worked with a young lady in the Post Office who was the skeet-shooting champion of Massachusetts."

While skeet shooting helped gunners get used to firing ahead of a target to hit it, there was a lot more involved in hitting a fast-moving fighter from a bomber flying at a good clip. To be prepared to destroy an attacking fighter, gunners went through extensive classroom training to understand ballistics, the science of the motion of projectiles in flight.[46]

While Bill had to learn his specialty, gunnery, he also had to learn how to function as a member of the team. As a gunner, he needed to constantly search the sky for enemy fighters, especially coming out of the sun or the clouds. Failure to spot a sneak attack could be fatal. When spotting a fighter or fighters, a gunner needed to alert the crew by sounding off in terms familiar to the entire crew.

A clock system and a level system alerted them to the location of the attack. In the clock system, the nose of the bomber pointed toward 12 o'clock, the tail 6 o'clock, the left wing 9 o'clock and the right wing 3 o'clock. In the level system, "high" meant above the bomber, "level" meant on the same level, and "low" meant below the bomber. Thus, "two fighters at 4 o'clock high" alerted the crew to two fighters just behind, above and to the right of them.

Bill got to practice his gunnery skills at Myrtle Beach on the Atlantic coast, about 125 air miles southeast of Columbia. The War Department took over the Myrtle Beach Municipal Airport in South Carolina, and it became the Myrtle Beach General Bombing and Gunnery Range in March 1942.[47] Its five bombing ranges were used for practicing different types of bombing, such as demolition, pattern, skip and night bombing.

Precision bombing ranges required considerably less land area than gunnery ranges. In June 1943, the Army Air Forces determined that for safety reasons precision bombing ranges required 2 x 2 miles or 4 square miles. On the other hand, air-to-ground gunnery ranges required 4 x 6 miles or 24 square miles, and air-to-air gunnery ranges required 20 x 40 miles or 800 square miles. Also, an air-to-air gunnery range had to be located over water areas. Large-size air-to-air gunnery ranges were required because, for example, .50-caliber projectiles fired from 20,000 feet, as aerial gunners do in heavy bombers, could carry twenty-one miles.[48]

"When we practiced air-to-air gunnery, a tubular cloth target called a sleeve was trailed behind another aircraft on a cable, and we tried to hit it. We would use color-coded ammunition so our instructors could later tell who hit the target and how many times. When we practiced air-to-ground gunnery, we would have to hit targets on the ground as we flew by at low levels, maybe 400 or 500 feet. After I qualified as an aerial gunner, I received my wings.

"Early in our training at Myrtle Beach, I had a funny experience. Dunn, our navigator/bombardier, was a friend of mine and invited me to go with him on a practice bombing run. The weather was very poor and I was in the nose of the plane with him while he was toggling off bombs. He was complaining that he couldn't see his bombs hit the target. He could sight the target through the cross-hairs of his bombsight, but he just couldn't see the bombs hit it. He asked me to sight the target and release a few, and I was glad to oblige, but I had no luck either.

"Later, the training instructor asked him how he did and he said he did okay. When we landed, the instructor saw that the bombs were still in the bomb bay. I always kidded him about that. I could kid him because the truth was that he was damn good at his job. I trained with him in the States, flew with him on our long trip to Europe, and on three of my last four missions in which we had great success. Luckily for him, he wasn't on my last mission.

"I had another funny experience when we had high-altitude training in a low-pressure chamber on the ground. I remember all of us—Vancil, Briles, Dunn, Kane, Mygrant and me—going into the chamber with an instructor for the first time. We went up to the equivalent of pressure at eight or nine thousand feet and then escalated to about fourteen thousand feet. We all had our oxygen masks on and the instructor asked me to take my mask off and do something for him. He gave me a pencil and a piece of paper and asked me to subtract five from one hundred and keep subtracting. I subtracted five and wrote down ninety-five. When I got to ninety, I

Sergeant William A. Lanza
Courtesy of the Lanza Family

couldn't think of what came next. I started to smile and then laughed a little. The rest of the crew started to laugh too. Pretty soon I was laughing my brains out and so was everyone else. It drove across the point of how the lack of oxygen at high altitudes affects your brain."

The purpose of the program was to be sure the airmen could handle the stresses of low pressure and to teach them how to survive at a high altitude, most notably how to prevent illness or death from lack of oxygen. From March 1942 to September 1944, about 623,000 airmen participated in the high-altitude training program.[49]

After Columbia and Myrtle Beach, Bill and his crew underwent advanced flight training at Greenville Army Air Base, also in South Carolina. "We did a lot of formation flying at this base. We had done our share of formation flying at Columbia, but our pilots were learning and sometimes the planes were all over the sky. At Greenville, they were much improved and getting better." Greenville, built in 1942 to support the war effort, was used as a training base for the crews of B-24 heavy bombers as well as B-25 medium bombers.[50]

Heavy bombers flew higher and further and carried more destructive power than medium bombers. They were capable of flying deep into enemy territory on strategic missions to impede the enemy's economic ability to wage war by bombing the factories that built the weapons and the refineries that fueled them. Medium bombers typically flew tactical missions to cut enemy supply lines and support the troops at the front. The faster and more maneuverable light bombers, such as the A-20 Havoc, and fighter bombers, such as the P-47 Thunderbolt, flew closer to the ground on tactical missions to attack more precise targets such as troop concentrations, trains and vehicles. Considerable training was necessary to prepare airmen for combat in these sophisticated flying machines.

South Carolina did more than its share during World War II as hundreds of thousands of soldiers and aviators were trained at bases in that State. South Carolina is where the official and personal correspondence of General Mark Clark is archived today. Clark, the commander of the Fifth Army during the Italian Campaign, served as the president of The Citadel in Charleston from 1953 to 1965.[51] As we will see later, he was a controversial leader during the Italian Campaign.

After Bill's training in South Carolina, his crew was sent to Hunter Field in Savannah, Georgia where they picked up a new plane and were outfitted for combat overseas. According to Bill, "We picked up a new D-model B-25 and I got a little stick action. Vancil, our pilot, gave each of us a shot at flying the new plane. I'll never forget it. I sat in the pilot's seat and he sat next to me in the co-pilot's seat. He let me fly for a while. It was a great experience. When I was a kid, I was fascinated by planes and I'm still impressed with the way the pilots handled their planes during the war. I never dreamed I would one day be flying one, even if it was for a short time."

Roundabout Route to Europe

After becoming familiar with their new aircraft, the crew departed for Morrison Field in West Palm Beach before heading overseas. "We were scheduled to take off from Morrison Field in West Palm Beach, Florida, and wouldn't know our destination until after we took off."

They took off for Europe on February 4, 1944 via a roundabout route called the South Atlantic Air Route. At the time, it was common for airmen to cross the Atlantic by way of South America during the winter because a North Atlantic Air Route—making stops in countries such as Canada, Greenland, and Iceland—was too cold.[52] The typical South Atlantic Route of about 10,000 miles was considerably longer than the typical North Atlantic Route of about 2,700 miles, but it was much safer during the winter months.[53]

Soon after leaving Morrison Field, the crew learned that they were headed to Casablanca in Morocco, North Africa, for further orders. The plane headed south, making its first stop at Borinquen Field in San Juan, Puerto Rico. "Mygrant was always full of ideas and he had a good one in Puerto Rico to chip in and buy a case of whisky. The whiskey turned out later to be a valuable commodity. We could have sold it for a hundred dollars a bottle."

The next stop was at Atkinson Field in the middle of a jungle near Georgetown, British Guiana (on the northern coast of South America, now called Guyana). During the war, the United Kingdom leased it to the United States.[54] This was part of the barter deal in which the Americans provided the British with destroyers in exchange for the right to lease some of their air and naval bases. Today, Guyana is the only South American country whose official language is English. From this jungle, they departed on a long trip in two stops over a much larger

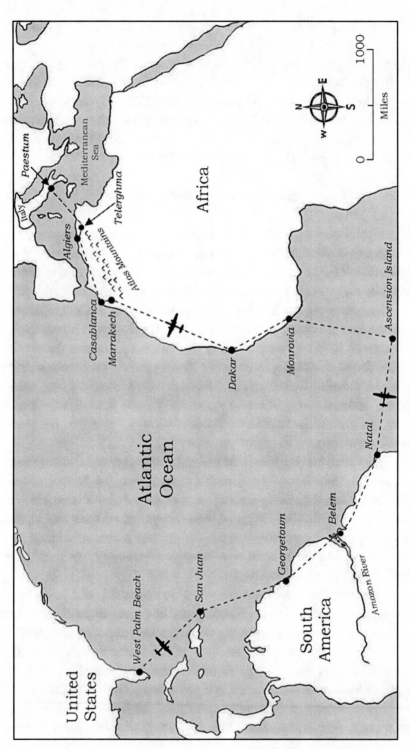

South Atlantic Route to Europe

jungle, the Amazon Jungle. This was not a place where you wanted to get lost. It would be very difficult to locate and reach a fallen plane in that vast wilderness of stifling heat, as we will soon see.[55]

Their first destination in Brazil was Val-de-Caes Field near Belem, a great port of the Amazon River about ninety miles from the country's north coast. To get there, they flew across the Equator, whereupon Bill and his crew partook of a tradition among airmen to get their "short snorters." A short snorter was a dollar bill on which they wrote the date they crossed the Equator and obtained signatures of crew members as witnesses to this event. This tradition followed them to the drinking establishments of Europe.[56]

The word "snort" is slang for a stiff drink, and a "short" is less than a full measure. When airmen were drinking, one might challenge the others to see who bought the drinks. The airman with no short snorter or the least impressive short snorter would spring for the drinks. Some airmen were lucky enough to obtain the names of famous people, and others expanded the tradition by obtaining signatures on foreign currency as they traveled from one country to another, sometimes from Allied crews of foreign aircraft. The bills were swapped, sold, strung together, and viewed by some as status symbols of their travels.[57]

The tradition carried over to the astronauts who carried one-dollar bills signed by their fellow crew members and, true to tradition, anyone unable to produce their short snorters during a mission would be buying drinks for the crew back on earth. It was a tradition that helped airmen to get acquainted. It also helped them get the autographs of famous people in history, such as Neil Armstrong.[58] An interesting thing about the tradition is that, similar to selling liquor during Prohibition, it was against the law to deface the nation's currency.

One of the most impressive short-snorter strings was assembled by Hank Myers, the pilot of the predecessors of *Air Force One*—President Roosevelt's personal plane, the *Sacred Cow*, and President Truman's personal plane, the *Independence*. In addition to the signatures of Roosevelt and Truman, he had the signatures of Churchill, Stalin and Eisenhower, as well as many other distinguished figures who crossed the equator or flew to another country in a plane piloted by him. His short snorter was thirty-five feet long. Needless to say, he never had to spring for drinks.[59] Today, short snorters are valuable collectors' items. In fact, there is an impressive display of them at the National Museum of the United States Air Force. Muses Bill: "I had my short snorter for years, but have no idea where it is now."

The flight from British Guiana to Belem was almost a thousand miles of jungle and cattle ranches. Brazil had one of the largest commercial herds of cattle in the world, and Bill saw them up close.[60] "Vancil liked to fly close to the ground, sometimes too close for comfort. He got a kick out of chasing the cattle. I remember the scene as being very beautiful as we buzzed along, but it was anything but relaxing to fly that close to the ground in a B-25 Mitchell." Today, the Amazon's seventy-three million cows outnumber the human population about three to one.[61]

"Vancil also liked to fly close to the treetops of the jungle, a hair-raising experience. He had a close call once when he had to dip his wing and almost clipped the treetops. We said someone ought to talk to him. I guess he was told to fly low, but we worried because he took chances." The Amazon Jungle has three-hundred species of wild animals, and the Amazon River has its fearful anaconda and piranha. "When we flew over the Amazon River, he buzzed some sailboats. I think Vancil would have made a good pursuit pilot."

A couple of months later, on April 11, 1944, a B-24H Liberator on its way to Europe crashed in the Amazon Jungle. The plane and its ten-man crew were about an hour from Belem when the pilot reportedly requested weather information. A ground station in Brazil provided the information but nothing was ever heard from the aircraft after that. The crew remained missing for the next fifty-one years.

On July 4, 1995, a fifteen-man team from the U.S. Army Identification Laboratory in Hawaii went to Brazil to begin the arduous process of locating the remains of that crew in the dense Amazon Jungle. After three weeks, they found their remains and dog tags about fifty miles northeast of the Amazon River city of Macapa, which is about 250 miles northwest of the plane's destination of Belem. After a memorial service in Macapa, they brought the boys back home. After two and a half years of attempting to locate surviving relatives of the crew members, the remains of the entire crew were buried with full military honors in Arlington National Cemetery on February 20, 1997.[62]

Unlike this unfortunate crew, Bill's crew made it safely to Belem, and after a layover, took off for Natal, another long trip of over fourteen-hundred miles, arriving there safely as well. "Natal is just about the closest point to Africa from the Americas, but we still broke up the Atlantic crossing with a stop on Ascension Island, which is about the halfway point." During the war, the U.S. Army built an airfield called Wideawake Airfield on the southwestern corner of this small, desolate island of only thirty-four square miles.[63]

Wideawake was an apt name for the airfield, because you needed to be wide awake to find it. The name, however, came from local birds called sooty terns which made loud, distinctive calls that woke people early in the morning.[64] Nevertheless, crews needed to be on their toes to find this tiny island and its airfield, and many were because over 25,000 U.S. planes touched down on Wideawake on their way to and from the Mediterranean and European theaters of war.[65]

Bill could appreciate the difficulty of locating this spec in the vast Atlantic: "We were having trouble locating the island. Dunn was our navigator and he and Vancil were looking at the radio compass and having a heated debate. I was behind them in the crawlway over the bomb bay, listening and crossing my fingers. Fortunately, they brought us in safely."

It wasn't unusual for even experienced crews to have trouble finding the island. Jack Valenti, former head of the Motion Pictures Association of America, was a B-25 pilot who flew 51 combat missions during the war. On his way home, as he was honing in on the island, using his radio compass to guide him, the needle on the compass went crazy and he overshot the island. He brought the plane down lower and with the help of his navigator located the island, but his landing was bumpy because he didn't know the runway ran uphill.[66] Nevertheless, his aircraft proved once again to be durable under adverse circumstances. After he reached the States, he never piloted a plane again; but he remembered the B-25 Mitchell as a "faithful, steady companion."[67]

Bill notes: "One interesting thing about the trip that most people are unaware of is that we traveled across the Atlantic with two homing pigeons in a cage, which we would release to identify our location in the event that we went down in the ocean. When we were having problems locating the island, I was hoping it wasn't time to release the pigeons."

During the war, long-distance communications wasn't what it is today, and pigeons were a supplemental and emergency means of communications. The earliest documented use of pigeons during wartime was by the Romans more than 2,000 years ago. Soon after Pearl Harbor, the Signal Corps, which focused on communications, recruited experienced pigeon handlers from pigeon fancier organizations. A pigeon fancier was the name given to those who bred pigeons. They also went looking for trained pigeons. By October 1943 they had enough pigeons to sustain their own breeding program for what was called the pigeon service. At its peak, the pigeon service of the Signal Corps had 150 officers, 3,000 enlisted men, and 54,000 pigeons.[68]

It took about eight weeks to train a reliable messenger from the time the bird broke free from its egg. Pigeons were tough birds. They could handle being released from an aircraft going 375 miles per hour at 35,000 feet through weather as cold as forty-five degrees below zero and carry a message a long distance. The pigeon service sent an estimated 30,000 messages via pigeon overseas and an outstanding 96 percent reached their destinations. The subsequent improvements in communications technology made the pigeon service obsolete and it was disbanded in 1957.[69]

Not only did Bill's hometown supply manpower to the war effort, but it supplied pigeon power as well. Bill knew someone who was a pigeon fancier: "Joe Martoni, who lived next door to my wife's family on Chelsea Street in East Boston, trained homing pigeons for racing. He trained them on the roof of his three-decker apartment house. His pigeons were quicker than most, and the Army used them during the war."

From Ascension Island, Bill and the crew flew to Roberts Field near Monrovia, Liberia, on the west coast of North Africa, arriving there in late February. In North Africa, they made several stops. The first was in Dakar, Senegal, which was then called French West Africa. Dakar was the westernmost point in Africa, and had a steel mesh runway on a rocky plateau overlooking the Atlantic Ocean. It was a place where malaria was a serious concern.[70]

The next flight was over the Atlas Mountains to Marrakech, Morocco, then on to his destination, Casablanca, also in Morocco. They arrived in Casablanca on February 22, 1944, eighteen days after leaving the States. Casablanca was familiar to many Americans then and now because of the film by the same name that won the Academy Award for Best Picture in 1943.

Bill recalls: "Casablanca is a city that brings back fond memories, such as spending time with my friend Mygrant, who later won the

Distinguished Flying Cross. Once, when we were in a gift shop in Casablanca, he recognized Ella Logan, a Hollywood star. She was with her agent and he asked for her autograph. Not only did she gladly oblige, but she even posed for a photo with him. It was always exciting to see a movie star, and many of them were overseas entertaining the troops." This star had a unique experience. She claimed to have snubbed Adolf Hitler in a nightclub in Cologne, Germany when she toured Europe in the 1930s.[71]

In Casablanca, the planes were serviced as airmen prepared for different assignments in the European or Mediterranean Theaters. Bill's crew was assigned to the 446th Bomb Squadron of the 321st Bomb Group in Italy.

"In Casablanca, we learned to depend less on ballistics and more on feel in firing at a target. In the States, we had to do some figuring with our ballistics training, but now we learned with the help of experienced British instructors to simply react quickly to the position of the target. The computing was done beforehand for each position we may see the target in. All we needed to add was the speed of our plane. It was a matter of feel, sort of like skeet shooting; only in a moving aircraft you had to factor in the speed of the plane because a bullet from a moving plane keeps the forward speed of the aircraft as well as its own velocity. It was easy to learn and apply."

At that time, the British were more experienced with turret gunnery under wartime conditions. In fact, the idea for putting power-operated gun turrets in American bombers came in the summer of 1940 from the success the British Royal Air Force was having with them in their bombers. It wasn't until December 5, 1941 that the Army Air Corps made plans to procure and install them in its bombers.[72]

After a week's stay in Casablanca, Bill flew to Algiers, Algeria for a stopover, then on to Telerghma, Algeria, an airfield on a high flat plateau in the Atlas Mountains. "It was windy and freezing, one of the coldest places I'd ever been to." While in Algeria, he spent a day in nearby Constantine, the historic city named for Constantine the Great. One of the largest cities in Algeria, it stands on a rocky plateau overlooking a deep gorge through which flows the Ruhmel River, about eight hundred feet below.[73]

Bill recalls: "It was such a unique city. It looked as though an earthquake split the city in half." One could see how a visitor could have this impression because at one point, the cliffs of the gorge are only fifteen feet apart.[74] During the war, Constantine was one of the historic sites that were put to military use, becoming an important staging area for the Allies.[75]

Bill's next stop was at an airfield near Mount Vesuvius in Pompeii, Italy, where they arrived on March 1, 1944 and stayed for a few days. From there, he flew next to Paestum, where he and his crew became the newest members of the 321st Bomb Group. About three weeks later, the volcano would erupt and destroy the planes of the 340th Bomb Group located near the base of Mount Vesuvius, and crews of the 340th would relocate to the home base of the 321st in Paestum.

At Paestum, Bill was not only experiencing the history being made during the war, but he was also viewing another important site of ancient history. Paestum was the archaeological site of three ancient Greek temples that date back to the eighth century BC. The site was near the airfield which had been the home of the 321st since the middle of February. Before Bill arrived in Italy, the 321st had moved a number of times from French Morocco to Algeria to Tunisia and to Italy. Paestum was its third base in Italy. The 321st essentially followed the path of the war in the Mediterranean Theater. It would soon move again to Corsica as the Allied troops pushed the Germans up the peninsula of Italy.

When the Allies invaded Italy in September 1943, one of Paestum's three famous temples, the Temple of Neptune, was used by American troops as its headquarters.[76] It was unlikely that the ruins would be bombed. It wasn't just headquarters. According to Bill, who was there in the spring of the following year: "We hid our bombs in the ruins because we felt nobody would bomb them. Nobody did."

Ready for Action

As a member of the 321st Bomb Group, Bill was part of a larger organization—the 57th Bomb Wing—that was under the command of Brigadier General Robert D. Knapp, who until his promotion had been the commander of the 321st Bomb Group. The 57th Bomb Wing consisted of (1) medium bomb groups of B-25 Mitchells, (2) light bomb groups of A-20 Havocs, and (3) fighter groups such as the P-40 Warhawks that escorted bombers on their missions in addition to attacking smaller targets that required flying closer to the ground and firing at smaller targets.[77]

The 321st Bomb Group was one of the three medium bomb groups under the command of General Knapp. The two others were the 310th Bomb Group, with which Bill trained in the States; and the 340th Bomb Group, which would soon lose all its planes to the eruption of Mount Vesuvius.[78] Each of the three bomb groups had four bomb squadrons. In Bill's bomb group, the four squadrons were the 445th, 446th, 447th and 448th, and he was in the 446th. Each squadron had approximately fifteen assigned aircraft and each B-25 at that time had five crew members.[79] The commander of the 321st, Lieutenant Colonel Charles T. Olhmstead, would soon be replaced by Colonel Richard H. Smith.[80] In less than the two years since the 321st was formed in July 1942, there had been five command changes, a reflection of the many changes taking place in the rapid buildup of air power.

Two days after Bill arrived in Italy, the 57th Bomb Wing became a combat organization in which all B-25s in the Mediterranean Theater of Operations were placed under the same command for the first time. These changes were made to carry out an aggressive bombing campaign to choke German communications north of Rome by bombing ships, harbors, railroads and their marshalling yards, bridges, airfields, supply dumps and other targets to cut the flow of men, equipment, and supplies to the German front lines and eventually push the enemy northward toward Germany.[81] This was aptly named Operation Strangle.

Bill was now part of a precision bombing team that underwent considerable training in the States to prepare for overseas combat, and continued to hone their skills overseas. He was well aware of how dangerous his job was and how important it was for each crew member to carry out his assigned duties as expected. He knew what could happen when a team is out of sync. He had heard that, during a training exercise at Columbia before he got there, six bombers flying in a close formation were lost when one plane got too close to another. With regard to the responsibilities of crew members, Jack Valenti once said: "It's all about duty...it is because they will not betray their buddies, their comrades-in-arms. They will not let them down, because each of us knows that our buddies will not let us down."[82]

Bill would soon see action. From his training, he knew the routine. On bombing missions, the lead ship typically had a specially-trained bombardier to operate the Norden bombsight that was used to sight the target for all the planes in the formation. The Norden bombsight was state-of-the-art at the time, a closely-guarded top-secret weapon. In fact, because the Doolittle Raid was likely to be a one-way trip, they didn't want to risk its getting into the hands of the enemy, so it was replaced with a simpler, manual sight.[83]

The Norden was critical for high-altitude precision daylight bombing, but the Doolittle mission would involve low-altitude precision daylight bombing. Because the Raiders would be flying so low, they didn't need the sophisticated Norden bombsight. One of the Raiders, Captain Ross Greening, designed a simple replacement bombsight that was built by the machine shops at Elgin Field where they trained. The bombsight was connected to the cockpit through a pilot direction indicator to give the pilot turn directions without relying on voice communications.[84]

The Norden bombsight was very important during the war because it enabled a bombardier to drop its bombs within fifty-five feet of a target from three miles up by simply sighting the target and keying into the Norden's analog computer the key elements necessary for a successful hit—the speed and altitude of the aircraft and the wind conditions. The Norden would then take control of the aircraft and release the bombs at the right moment.[85]

The designer of the bombsight, Carl Norden, was a Dutchman born in the Dutch colony of Semerang, Java (now Indonesia). At age five, his family moved to Holland and at age thirteen to Germany. He received his technical education in Switzerland. After receiving a degree in mechanical engineering, he immigrated to the United States in 1904 and went to work developing defense control systems for the military.

In 1917, Norden started his own company and in 1921 began work on his bombsight. He produced the first generation of his bombsight in 1929 and kept improving the design throughout the 1930s. When the war broke out, he was so proud of having produced a precision instrument that minimized collateral damage to civilian populations near military targets that he sold his rights to his bombsight to the United States government for one dollar.[86]

The Norden was used to obtain the utmost in "saturation bombing." The entire formation dropped their bomb loads on the cue from the lead ship, thereby ensuring a heavy concentration or "saturation" of bombs on the target.[87] This was also called "blanket bombing" because by staying in a tight formation and dropping their bombs at the same time they would create a blanket of bombs that were all close together and enhance their chance of destroying the target. It was critical for all crews to remain focused and stay in formation because a problem with one plane, especially the lead ship, could adversely affect the entire group.[88] In light of the importance of the lead ship, enemy anti-aircraft cannons were aimed at it to disrupt the bomb run. This is what happened on Bill's last mission.

A bombing mission for a B-25 Mitchell bomb group involved some or all of the four squadrons arranged in box formations. A box formation consisted of six aircraft in two "V" formations. Each "V" was called an element and consisted of a lead ship with two wing ships flying off its wings and behind it. The rear element in the box formation would fly above or below the lead element to stay away from its trailing air turbulence.[89] Bill would experience this turbulence months later over Italy when he bailed out of his aircraft.

Two box formations constituted a flight and had a flight leader who was responsible for the leadership of twelve aircraft in the flight. The lead ship carried the Norden bombsight with the bombardier responsible for aiming the bombs of the flight.[90] Of the twenty-eight missions that Bill would fly, twenty-six consisted of two flights with approximately twenty-four aircraft and the other two consisted of three flights of approximately thirty-six aircraft. The reason for the approximation is that spare aircraft flew on each mission for contingency purposes. For example, the most planes to complete any of his missions would be thirty-eight and the fewest twenty-one.[91] When a plane completed a mission, it was said to have flown a sortie.

The leader of the mission was called the flight commander and was typically one of the flight leaders. The flight commander would determine the type of formation to be flown for the mission and the signals to change the formation. The other planes would adjust their positions based on the signals going down the chain of command so that the changes were made in a precise, efficient manner.

Each flight flew not more than fifty feet apart and sometimes closer in tighter formations. The lead flight was typically lower than the other one or two flights behind it. Whether the flight to the left or right of the leader was higher or lower depended upon the

47

direction the formation would turn after dropping their bombs. If they made a right turn, the flight on the left would be placed higher, and vice versa.[92]

Bill would develop an appreciation for formation flying: "It was pretty amazing to see so many planes flying so close to one another. The lead pilot of every element knew who to follow and if everyone did their job down the chain of command, it was an impressive sight. This required a lot of skill and discipline, and our leaders did a great job in ensuring that we had both.

"Fighters would also escort us to protect against enemy fighters." The fighters would also have a flight commander to lead their formation. Twelve Spitfires would fly as escorts on twenty-two of Bill's missions, and six and eight Spitfires, respectively, on two others. P-47s and P-40s would escort him on the other four missions.[93] The British Spitfire looked more like a racer than a warplane; the American P-47 Thunderbolt clearly looked like the rugged aircraft that it was; and the American P-40 Warhawk had a look somewhere between the two. However, they were all lethal weapons. The B-25 also had formidable weaponry that enemy fighters were hesitant to engage. The P-47 has a special place in Bill's heart because, as we shall see much later, one probably saved him from being captured or worse.

Flying in precise formations was considered to be the most effective defense against enemy fighters.[94] In addition to concentrating the power of the defense, sticking together in precise formations concentrated the power of the attack as well. Good leadership in giving orders and strict discipline in following orders were necessary for tight formations. According to the *Pilot Training Manual for the B-25*, "leading a formation requires accurate, precise flying and excellent judgment."[95] There was no room for debate in the sky while flying in a tight formation. Any objections down the line were to be held until after the mission. The man in charge was the boss with a great responsibility resting on his shoulders.

Future Escape and Evasion Partner

Three months after his arrival in the Mediterranean Theater of Operations, Bill would spend a couple of months hiding from the enemy with another airman, Technical Sergeant Alfred J. Todd. Todd

Technical Sergeant Alfred J. Todd
Courtesy of the Todd Family

was born in 1919 in rural Holland, Ohio to Ray and Corinne Todd. Soon after his birth, the family moved to another rural community in Oriskany Falls, New York, about eighteen miles southwest of Utica and about fifty miles southeast of Syracuse. Alfred, called "Toddy" by his family, grew up on a farm. His family raised dairy cows, grew many different kinds of vegetables, and had acres of strawberries. Many years later, it would be in these same strawberry fields that his mother would sense disaster on the day that his plane was shot down.

Todd attended nearby Vernon High School (now Vernon-Verona-Sherrill Senior High School). At that time, he had to walk a couple of miles to school each day because there were no buses. After high school, he studied agriculture at and graduated from nearby Morrisville College. His dream was to be a veterinarian, but he lacked the funds to follow his dream. Instead, he followed the route taken by many young Americans at that time. On September 24, 1940, he signed up to serve his country. Interestingly, the pilot of the plane that Todd was shot down in during the war also grew up on a farm, and his son, a tot at the time of the incident, grew up to become a veterinarian.

Todd joined the Army Air Corps and was trained as a radio operator and waist gunner for combat duty overseas on a B-25 Mitchell. He received training as a radio operator at Fort Monmouth, New Jersey. Later, he received training as a combat crew member at Drew Field in Tampa, Florida, the site of today's Tampa International Airport. In 1940, the U.S. Government leased Drew Field from Tampa for twenty-five years or until the end of the war. It was estimated that as many as 120,000 combat crew members were trained at Drew Field, which was given back to Tampa in 1945. After Drew, Todd received additional training at Barksdale Field in Shreveport, Louisiana prior to heading overseas for combat duty. Shreveport was always a special place for the bombardier on Todd's last mission (Second Lieutenant Laverne E. Reynolds) because this is where he met and married the love of his life.

Todd, like Bill, would fly on many missions over Italy as a member of the 446th Bomb Squadron, 321st Bomb Group, 57th Bomb Wing, 12th Air Force. On his last mission, this farm boy would jump out of a distressed aircraft seconds behind Bill, a city boy. Together, they would evade the enemy for a couple of months in the confines of a cave on a wooded hill in Tuscany, next to a farm with families whose humanity and courage they would appreciate for the rest of their lives. However, like many World War II veterans who escaped from and evaded the enemy, Todd never discussed his wartime experiences with his wife or his four children. Consequently, little information was passed down to his family until the conception of this book.

Chapter 3

ITALY IN CHAOS

When Sergeant Bill Lanza arrived in Italy on March 3, 1944, the country that his parents emigrated from was in chaos. To understand the chaos, it is necessary to review how Italy was governed for two decades before Bill arrived, and how this form of government led to the current state of the nation. It shows what can happen to a country when its leader becomes too powerful and risks the future of his country to seek more power.

Mussolini Leads Italy to War

Since 1922, when Bill was only five years old, Italy had been a Fascist state under Benito Mussolini. Fascism is "a political philosophy that puts the nation above the individual and has a centralized autocratic government headed by a dictatorial leader. It involves dictated economic and social regimentation and forcible suppression of opposition."[1] It is the antithesis of a democracy in which individuals are free to express their opinions. In a Fascist state, the dictator rules and becomes a powerful figure.

Mussolini rose to power using force and a strong conviction that Italy needed a powerful dictator to restore Italy's power and prestige in the world. He wanted to create a new Roman Empire that would dominate the Mediterranean Sea, as well as a colonial empire in parts of Africa to enhance his prestige on the world stage.[2] He became a dominating force in Italy during Fascism and sought to expand his power beyond Italy's borders with force. He was known as *Il Duce*, which means the leader, and he led Italy into war.

Mussolini did some things which endeared him to the people. He had strong beliefs and one of them was cultivating the land to enable the Italian people to be self-sufficient. Italy had been dependent on foreign wheat imports for years, and he was determined to improve this situation. In 1926, his government embarked on a massive government-investment project to reclaim some 6,600,000 acres of swampland (called the Pontine Marshes) southeast of Rome.[3] The land had once been fertile soil for the Ancient Romans, who built and maintained ditches to drain the stagnant water into the Tyrrhenian Sea. When Rome was sacked by barbarians, the area became a swampland for centuries, and it bred mosquitos that caused malaria.[4]

In 1926, the work of reclaiming the Pontine Marshes was begun with the building of canals and pumps to drain the land for rural and urban development. During the thirties, the Fascist government placed families of war veterans on the land, each with a farmhouse and several parcels of land, along with tools and livestock necessary to cultivate the land. Moreover, they were given fifteen years to pay for and become owners of their property. This rural development project, along with other cultivation initiatives, yielded results in 1938 when Italy managed to produce more wheat than it consumed for the first time in modern history.[5]

In addition to rural development, the Pontine Marshes project resulted in the creation of five new towns during the thirties—Littoria (renamed Latina in 1945), Sabaudia, Pontinia, Aprilia and Pomezia, each with a town hall, parish church, school, police headquarters, Fascist headquarters, cinema, sports fields and playgrounds, along with surrounding villages.[6] It was an urban development project that is impressive even by today's standards. Unfortunately, during the war, the Germans flooded the area to slow down the Allied troops in pursuit. This resulted in the return of the malaria problem, which wasn't conquered again until the 1950s.[7]

Mussolini did other things which did not endear him to the people. He favored war over peace. In 1932, he wrote that "Fascism repudiates the doctrine of Pacifism," and added: "War alone brings up to its highest tension all human energy and puts the stamp of nobility upon the peoples who have the courage to meet it."[8] His growing obsession with making war led to an alliance with another powerful leader with an even greater obsession for making war, Adolf Hitler.

Italy in Chaos

Mussolini aligned with Germany and Japan during the mid-1930s and built an African empire by forceful means. In so doing, he alienated former allies Great Britain and France.

When Germany invaded Poland in 1939, Great Britain and France declared war on Germany, the beginning of World War II. In 1940, Italy entered the war on Germany's side to form the Axis powers against the Allied powers in Europe. The day after Japan's December 7, 1941 attack on Pearl Harbor, the U.S. declared war on Japan, the third Axis power. Three days later, Germany and Italy declared war on the United States. This prompted the United States to join the Allies in fighting against Germany and Italy in North Africa during 1942. By January 1943, Mussolini had lost his African empire and it was becoming apparent that the battlefront was moving toward Italy. Consequently, his strong hold on power in Italy was beginning to weaken. Italy was losing faith in Fascism and its powerful dictator who led the country to war.

With victory assured in North Africa, the Allies were planning to invade Sicily, but were debating whether or not to pursue the enemy on to the Italian mainland. Rather than deploy troops to Italy, the Americans favored using them in a buildup for an invasion of France from across the English Channel. Winston Churchill, on the other hand, felt that the Allies should invade Italy. To elicit American support, he traveled to Washington, D.C. in May 1943.[9]

Churchill asserted that Germany was unlikely to put up a strong fight for the Italian mainland and that only nine Allied divisions would be needed to succeed in Italy.[10] The U.S. Joint Chiefs of Staff, led by General George C. Marshall, worried that a war in Italy would become a war of attrition and drain manpower and supplies from the main objective of invading Europe through France.[11] For the United States, the invasion of France was always the priority. Even though Churchill would prove to be wrong on both of his assertions, he was successful in gaining American support for an invasion of Italy. The war of attrition that the Americans worried about would follow.

On July 9-10, 1943, the Allies invaded Sicily. The U.S. Twelfth Air Force led by General Carl "Tooey" Spaatz, the U.S. Seventh Army led by General George Patton and the British Eighth Army led by General Bernard Montgomery were powerful Allied forces. As they moved closer to the Italian mainland, the Italian government was torn between those who continued to support Mussolini and those who wanted to depose the dictator and end the war. Those who were sitting on the fence most likely fell into the anti-Fascist camp on July 19 when the Allies bombed Rome. In the largest single bombing raid in history up to that time, 1,000 tons of bombs rained down on the capital city where the nation's leaders were debating the future of their country. This bombardment upset the King, the Pope, the Fascist General Counsel, and the general public. This was the crowning blow that tipped the scales in favor of ousting Mussolini from power.[12]

The day after the bombing, King Victor Emmanuel III tried to talk Mussolini into stepping down, but his words fell on deaf ears. This convinced the King that he would have to use another tactic to depose him. Count Dino Grandi, once an avid supporter of Mussolini, had become a strong adversary when Mussolini aligned with Germany in the war instead of with Great Britain and France. He had urged the King to remove Mussolini from power. Now that the King was in agreement with him, he was ready to do his part.

When an elected official is voted out of office, he or she simply re-enters society in a different role. When a dictator is thrown out of office, the transition isn't so smooth. When Napoleon was deposed, he was exiled, and a similar fate awaited Mussolini. The fall from such absolute power can be devastating, especially when you are on the world stage.

On July 24-25, Mussolini met with the Fascist Grand Council to plead his case for staying the course. Grandi followed him with a strong case for his removal. In addition, he introduced a three-page resolution to remove Mussolini from power and to restore constitutional authority to the King. The resolution was put to a vote and the Council voted 19 to 7 in favor of the monarchy resuming all powers. Later that day, the King met with Mussolini and informed him that he was being replaced by General Pietro Badoglio, a tough pill for Mussolini to swallow. But that wasn't all. As soon as he left the King, he was arrested and sent to prison.

A new government was formed under Badoglio who, on July 28, announced the end of Mussolini and his Fascist party. Badoglio had never been a supporter of Mussolini. In 1922, when Mussolini was forcing his way into power, he had pleaded with King Victor Emmanuel III to allow him to put an end to Mussolini's aggressive behavior. The King, wishing to avoid further conflict, had allowed Mussolini to get his foot in the door. Once his foot was in the door, he ruled for twenty years.

Mussolini was a student of history and thought he understood its lessons. His ambitions led him to believe that, as a dictator with great power, he could create a new Roman Empire. However, not only did he lack the industrial resources to accomplish this, he never understood that the majority of the Italian people never embraced Fascism, viewing it as a passing phase that they hoped would end.[13]

The news of the end of Mussolini and Fascism touched off a celebration by Italians who thought this would end the conflict and suffering for their country. It also touched off demonstrations, in some cases violent reprisals, against Fascists. This prompted Badoglio to order the police to disperse all public meetings and processions, and to put the country under martial law to maintain order. When the Allies started bombing again on August 1, many Italians were in a state of confusion.[14] The confusion would turn to fear a month later when the disastrous alliance between Hitler and Mussolini would rear its ugly head again and be felt for some time to come.

On August 3, the new Italian government put out peace feelers (tentative proposals for a peace settlement) to the Allies through diplomatic channels. By the middle of August, the Allies had captured Sicily and were preparing to invade Italy. Meanwhile, large numbers of German reinforcements had been entering the country from the north because Hitler was worried about his Italian allies without Mussolini at the helm. It was estimated that between July 25 and August 6, six German divisions entered Italy through the Brenner Pass, the mountain pass through the Alps between Italy and Austria. Some would argue later that if Badoglio had acted to close the Brenner Pass when he replaced Mussolini, the Allies wouldn't have had to deal with so many German troops during the battles that lay ahead.[15]

As the Allies prepared to invade Italy, major changes occurred in the leadership of the ground forces. In the invasion of Sicily, Commanding General Sir Harold G. Alexander had two legendary commanders under him—Patton and Montgomery—who stormed through Sicily in just thirty-nine days.[16] Alexander would lose both of them for the major battles of Italy.

In Sicily, Patton was involved in a pair of regrettable events in which his temper got the best of him. He slapped a couple of soldiers, and he lost his command.[17] While he would later be given command of the Third Army in France under Eisenhower, he was lost to Alexander for the invasion of Italy. Instead, Alexander would have to rely on less-experienced General Mark W. Clark, who was given the command of the Fifth Army. After Montgomery would lead the Eighth Army on to the toe of Italy and up to Salerno, linking up with Clark, he too would be assigned to help Eisenhower with the invasion of France. Moreover, he would take his more experienced units with him. Consequently, Alexander would also have to rely on less-experienced General Sir Oliver W. H. Leese.[18]

Clark was a West Point graduate with a few weeks of combat experience in World War I. He was a charming, aggressive leader who wanted the responsibility of command and action. Eisenhower had made him his Deputy Commander in Chief for the invasion of North Africa in what was known as Operation Torch. He was young and rising fast, and Eisenhower gave him command of the Fifth Army for the invasion of Italy at Salerno. He was a young leader in command of an army of sixteen nationalities, a tough assignment for even a seasoned leader.[19] By comparison, the enemy commanded for the most part only one nationality in Italy because it was difficult to count on the Italian Fascists when the Fascist state was crumbling.

Invasion of Italy

While considering the peace feelers of the Italian government, the Allies invaded Italy in early September, 1943. The British Eighth Army under Montgomery landed at the toe of Italy on September 3 and the U.S. Fifth Army under Clark made an amphibious landing at Salerno on September 9. Both Armies had troops from a number of Allied nations, and the plan was to link up, secure most of southern Italy, and open the road to Rome.[20] This was easier said than done.

Hitler had other plans. Intent on keeping the war as far from Germany as possible, he had been sending troops to Italy and shoring up for the battles ahead. Field Marshall Albert Kesselring, the German commander in southern Italy, felt that the main landing would be at Salerno and was prepared for it. As a result, the Fifth Army met with strong resistance. Clark was unable to establish a secure beachhead

Italy
Key Locations

and the Germans, occupying the hills surrounding the Gulf of Salerno, nearly cut his Army in two.[21]

The Badoglio government had been on the brink of surrender, and the invasion of Italy prompted it to capitulate. The Armistice was signed in Sicily on September 3, and Badoglio broadcast the news to the nation by radio on September 8. He said:

> *"The Italian Government, recognizing the impossibility of continuing the unequal struggle against the overwhelming power of the enemy, with the object of avoiding further and more grievous harm to the nation, has requested an armistice from General Eisenhower, Commander in Chief of the Anglo-American Allied Forces. This request has been granted. The Italian forces will therefore cease all acts of hostility against the Anglo-American forces wherever they may be met. They will, however, oppose attack from any other quarter."* [22]

Franco DiGangi, who in 2007 celebrated his fiftieth year as owner of a barber shop in Caldwell, New Jersey, remembers that broadcast. He was a fourteen-year old boy living in Cerisano, a small hilltop village in the province of Cosenza in the region of Calabria on the foot of Italy. His village looked down on Cosenza, the main city in the province, which was about four or five miles away to the northeast. Since Cosenza was a junction on the Italian rail network, it was a target of Allied bombing. He remembers one bombing mission that occurred just before the Armistice.

"My friends and I were playing on the side of the hill that overlooks Cosenza when we heard the familiar hum of the Allied bombers in the distance. As they flew over our heads, heading toward Cosenza, they were attacked by Italian fighters. Machine-gun shells were falling like rain all around us. We were holding our heads and running under trees to protect from being hit by the shells. Fortunately, none of us were hurt."

The same could not be said for the people of Cosenza. According to DiGrangi, "After the bombing, many of its wounded citizens were brought to the convent in our village. Hundreds of them were lined up on the floor of the convent, some screaming in pain. The people in our village did their best to help them. It was very sad."

Franco cannot recall the exact date of this incident. It could have been on September 3 when Allied fighters and light bombers attacked road junctions and bridges in Cosenza, or on September 4 when Allied fighter bombers and light bombers attacked roads and a railroad junction in Cosenza.[23]

Several days later when Badoglio broadcast that Italy had surrendered to the Allies, there were celebrations throughout Italy that were short-lived. Franco remembers the celebration in his village. "Everyone thought the war was over. There was a great celebration, and people were dancing in the streets around bonfires. The celebration stopped when we saw a large German convoy heading our way. My father was the *maresciallo* of the *carabinieri* in the village, similar to chief of police in the United States. The headquarters were in the first building as the Germans entered the village so my father met with the German commander when he entered the village. The commander asked him what the fires were for, and he told them that we were celebrating a saint.

"The Germans didn't know that the road up the hill to the village didn't go down the other side towards Cosenza, so they had to go back down the hill. Before they left, they went to the bakery and took everything. There wasn't too much my father could do to stop them. Their trucks turned around in the large square near the convent, and left the village."

News of the surrender had other repercussions. Prisoners of war held in prison camps in Italy were released but would soon run into trouble. As soon as Italy surrendered, Hitler wasted no time in ordering his troops to disarm the Italian soldiers and seize control of central and northern Italy. As a result, released prisoners of war behind enemy lines were forced to go into hiding to evade capture. Bill and Todd would meet some of them down the road, and the co-pilot of their plane that was shot down over Italy (Second Lieutenant Walter H. Brickner) would be brought by partisans to others hiding deep in the woods east of where Bill and Todd were hiding in a cave.

Prisoners of war at a camp in Laterina, about thirty miles southeast of Florence, were among those released and went into hiding throughout the Tuscan countryside to evade German capture. Many found their way to the thick forests around Monte Scalari in northeastern Figline Valdarno. Those forests also became the preferred shelter for many young men from Florence who had opted to join the partisans. The residents of the area, mostly farmers, supported the partisans, helping to hide, feed and shelter them at the risk of their own lives.

A partisan is defined as "a member of a group that has taken up armed resistance against enemy occupying forces."[24] The Italian partisans formed the Resistance that was opposed to the Fascism of Mussolini and the Nazism of Hitler. When Mussolini was ousted and Italy surrendered to the Allied powers in September 1943, the Italian armed forces were effectively disbanded, and the Italian Resistance began to grow as many of the soldiers joined its ranks to more effectively resist the Germans occupying Italy and the Fascists supporting them.[25]

The partisan cause would continue to gain momentum and become a force for the Germans to deal with the following summer when they would be retreating through the area where Bill and Todd would be hiding. The Germans' response to partisan resistance would be severe, and among other things a tragic incident would befall eighteen partisans not far from where Bill and Todd were hiding.[26]

With the invasion of Italy, the Allies were now in Europe south of Germany in what Churchill called the "soft underbelly of Europe."[27] It didn't turn out to be soft because Hitler was determined to shore it up to keep the Allies as far from Germany as possible. He had been establishing strategic positions on the high ground throughout Italy and the battle for the Salerno beachhead was the first of many uphill battles that Clark's Army would face during the Italian Campaign. Four months later, Clark would be mindful of the danger of not properly establishing a beachhead when his Army staged another amphibious landing at Anzio.

When Mussolini was ousted from power and imprisoned, Hitler was determined to rescue his ally, and the result was a dramatic rescue that would result in more chaos in Italy. On July 26, Hitler summoned six officers to Wolf's Lair to pick one for a special mission to rescue Mussolini. Wolf's Lair was his military headquarters in the forests of East Prussia, so-named because Wolf had been one of Hitler's boyhood nicknames. From the six, he chose Otto Skorzeny for the mission.

Skorzeny was an imposing six-foot-four-inch captain of the elite

Waffen SS fighting forces. He, like Hitler, was a proud Austrian who still resented losing land to the Italians in World War I. This made him an obvious choice for the mission. Hitler wanted Mussolini back in power as soon as possible because he feared that without him Italy might switch sides in the war.[28] Skorzeny had the formidable task of locating and rescuing Mussolini, and delivering him to Hitler.

Well aware of this threat to free Mussolini, the new Italian government had moved Mussolini from place to place to frustrate would-be rescuers. It was a cat and mouse game of high intrigue. He was moved from Rome to Gaeta, about 75 miles south of Rome on the coast, where he was met by Admiral Franco Maugeri, the chief of Italian Naval Intelligence. A couple of days later in late July, he was shipped to the island of Ponza. In early August, he was shipped to the island of Maddalena, off the northeastern coast of Sardinia.

While Mussolini was on Maddalena, he complained to Maugeri that Italians were "too individualistic" and "too cynical," and didn't submit to Fascism the way the Germans submitted to Nazism. He stated: "That's why Hitler has had an easier time than I. Germans are born Nazis; Italians had to be made into Fascists."[29]

The Jews in Germany would disagree with that assessment, as would many other Germans who didn't subscribe to Nazism. Like the Italians, the Germans were led to war by a dictator that risked the future of his country in his quest for world power. After World War I, the German government deliberately let its currency, the mark, plunge in value in order to pay off its war reparations in devalued currency, and the worthless mark wiped out the life savings of the middle and working classes. Hitler got his foot in the door to power by contending that you couldn't trust Germany's leaders and needed someone like him to stop the printing of worthless money. Once he was in power, German citizens who opposed Nazism, like Italian citizens who opposed Fascism, were unable to voice a counter viewpoint without being suppressed by force.

The strategy to move Mussolini around to prevent his rescue worked very well for a while, as evidenced by the fact that at different times Skorzeny suspected Mussolini of being on two islands that he was never on—Ventotene and San Stefano. In late August, Mussolini was moved to an inn near a small village at the foot of Gran Sasso, the tallest mountain in the Apennines at 9,500 feet. In early September, he was taken to that village, where he rode in a cable car up to a ski resort perched on a small plateau on Gran Sasso, about 7,000 feet up the mountain. There he was held prisoner in the resort's Hotel Campo Imperatore.[30]

Skorzeny learned that Mussolini was being held at this hotel and planned a daring rescue. The plan called for him and his men to board a dozen gliders to be towed to the mountain, and then released to land on the rocky plateau. On September 12, he led the surprise commando operation and, incredibly, his lead glider skidded to halt about fifty feet from the hotel, and the others skidded in behind him. With little resistance from the Italian *carabinieri*, the Italian military police, Skorzeny rescued Mussolini.[31]

In another daring feat, he and Mussolini were flown off the cliff in a small German-built Fiesler-Storch spotter plane, the same plane which in 1938 had inspired the development of the U.S.-built L-5 Stinson spotter plane that was used in Italy during the war for reconnaissance and delivering supplies to the partisans.[32] The pilot initially refused to make the flight because he thought the three-person load was too heavy for the aircraft, but he relented under Skorzeny's pressure. After takeoff, the plane went into a dive but the pilot skillfully leveled it out to avert disaster.[33] Two days later, Mussolini was delivered to Hitler at his headquarters in Wolf's Lair.[34]

While Mussolini was being rescued, the situation in Salerno was desperate. Yet, Clark's troops fought gallantly, aided by strong air and naval support, and held the beachhead.[35] By September 15, with the Eighth Army approaching from the south, the Germans decided to withdraw northward and the Allies occupied Salerno and surrounding areas. Valuable airfields would be built in nearby Paestum, one of which (Guado Airfield) would become Bill's home base six months later when he arrived in Italy.

On September 20, the Eighth Army linked up with the Fifth Army and pushed northward.[36] On September 28, the Allies captured valuable airfields in Foggia on the east coast, from which they could now fly strategic bombing missions in Austria, the Balkans and Germany.[37] By October 1, they also took Naples on the west coast as a valuable shipping port. At this time, Bill was far away in the States training to be a gunner in the Army Air Corps. A year later, he would be sailing out of Naples back to the States. In between, he would have wartime experiences he would never forget. However, like many veterans who evaded capture with clandestine aid, he would remain silent on them for most of his life.

Now in control of central and northern Italy, the German Army formed a neo-Fascist government under Mussolini. Hitler and the Nazis pulled the strings, and Mussolini was the leader of this puppet government in name only. It was called the Italian Social Republic, but came to be known as the Salò Republic because it was headquartered in Salò, a small town on Lake Garda, halfway between Verona and Milan in northern Italy.[38] The return of Fascism effectively began a civil war in Italy, as most citizens were fed up with it, and this sentiment led to the growth of the Italian Resistance movement.

Mussolini was now virtually a prisoner in his own country, an old man who was hated by most Italians for having made Italy a battleground of destruction. His wife would later write that, after July 1943, he thought his star had completely faded and that he was a defunct leader. She would write that he greatly feared the German intentions for his country. Hitler's intentions were to defeat the Allies and their supporters, and he was now disappointed in Mussolini. Joseph Goebbels, one of Hitler's close associates, went so far as to say that Mussolini had become weak like his Italian heritage.[39]

Mussolini was not disposed to mount a campaign of suppression against the nineteen members of the Fascist Grand Council that voted against him, particularly his son-in-law, Galeazzo Ciano. Hitler, on the other hand, was disposed to suppress them, and Mussolini became his puppet. Four months later, in January 1944, Hitler pressured him to convene a kangaroo court in Verona. The result was that Mussolini's son-in-law and four others in captivity were shot to death, while another was given a long prison sentence. The other thirteen were sentenced to die while in captivity.[40] When her father did not prevent the death of her husband, Mussolini's daughter Edda became another victim of the chaos that her father brought to Italy.

On September 26, Florence was bombed for the first time. Although the bombing was intended to hit only military targets, non-military targets were hit as well, prompting citizens in Florence and other cities on major roads or railway lines to start thinking about finding shelter outside the city. In Figline Valdarno, a town on the Arno River about fifteen miles southeast of Florence, Goffredo Sarri

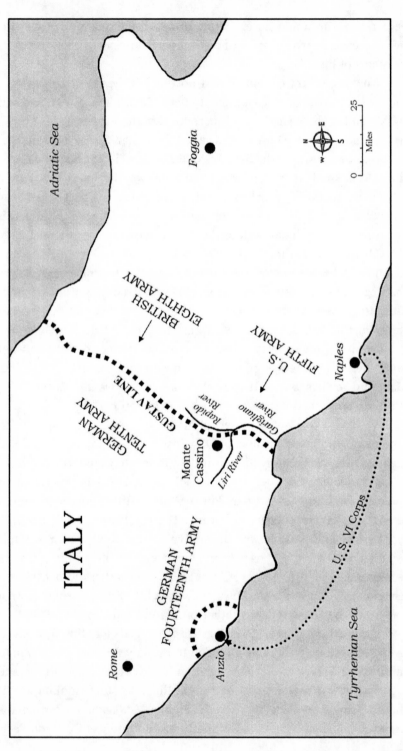

Stalemate at the Gustav Line and Anzio Beachhead – January to May 1944

was among those citizens thinking about finding shelter for his family outside the city.

Those who were already in the Italian Resistance fighting against Mussolini's Fascism were joined by former Italian soldiers willing to take up arms against the Germans occupying their country. The Fascists who continued to support the Germans became enemies of the people, most of whom wanted to be liberated from Fascism and the Nazis who occupied their country. As a result, the partisans had many supporters, particularly the farmers.[41] As we will see later, the partisans and farmers were of great help to Allied airmen like Bill and Todd who were shot down over Italy.

By the end of September, central and northern Italy were effectively ruled by German martial law, and the Germans made it known that partisan attacks on German soldiers would be met with severe reprisals in which citizens would be rounded up and killed, with multiple citizens sacrificed for each German killed. They also threatened to arrest one member of each family of any soldier in hiding, and to hold that person hostage until the soldier gave himself up. In this reign of terror, the Resistance was growing.

Gustav Line

The Germans anticipated the Allies' entering Naples on October 1, 1943. Consequently, before retreating to the Gustav Line about sixty miles to the north, they destroyed the city to prevent the Allies from using it effectively.[42] They were to continue this path of destruction up the peninsula of Italy. The following day, Churchill sent a telegram to General Alexander stating: "I hope...by the end of the month or thereabouts...that we shall meet in Rome."[43] As we will see, Churchill's optimism soon met with the harsh reality of the Gustav Line. What Churchill thought would take a month to accomplish took nine months of unimaginable human suffering and sacrifice.

After Naples, the Allies were faced with muddy valleys and rocky mountains, in addition to serious German firepower on the mountains. At the Gustav Line, the Allies faced the German Tenth Army with its formidable wall of interlocking defenses that ran across the narrowest part of Italy from Gaeta on the west coast to Ortona on the east coast. As described in the book, *Monte Cassino: The Hardest Fought Battle of World War II,* the Gustav Line "was an awesome piece of military engineering, the most formidable defensive system encountered by the British or Americans during the war."[44]

Anchoring the line was Monte Cassino, a mountain from which the Germans could see for miles. This defensive stronghold would prove difficult to capture because of the rocky terrain and terrible winter weather that lay ahead. To make matters worse for the Allies, the only road to Rome from Naples was through the valley of the Liri River, and Monte Cassino hovered over the entrance to the valley.[45]

The towering Monte Cassino and the rapidly-flowing Rapido River in front of the mountain were impediments of nature that the Germans utilized to fortify the Gustav Line.[46] The Germans supplemented these natural obstacles with significant man-made impediments by flooding the Rapido and other rivers to create conditions that made it difficult for the Allies to utilize their tanks and heavy artillery. In short, the deck was stacked against the Allied ground forces.

On top of Monte Cassino was a historic abbey of great religious and architectural importance that was founded in the sixth century by St. Benedict. Known as the Monte Cassino Benedictine Abbey, it was a national treasure. It was also one of Christianity's most sacred sites, and its buildings were beautified by some of Italy's finest artists. In addition, its library was one of the most important in the world, containing over forty thousand manuscripts, including masterpieces of Latin literature by distinguished writers such as Tacitus, Cicero, Horace, Virgil and Ovid.[47]

With the Germans dug in around the abbey and the Allies approaching, Catholics on both sides of the war were concerned about the abbey and its treasures. This wasn't a religious war—Catholics were on both sides. In October 1943, an Austrian engineer convinced the abbot of the monastery of dangers that lay ahead, and from October to early December some seventy thousand volumes were boxed up and transported to Rome to prevent their destruction.[48]

The abbey was a complex of buildings and courtyards with walls twenty feet thick at its base that made it look like a fortress. The Germans were dug in on the high ground around the abbey, and some of the Allied leaders thought they had actually occupied the abbey itself. Their mountaintop positions were fortified by mortar, gun and machine-gun emplacements blasted out of solid rock and protected by mines and barbed wire.[49] Consequently, the only way to inflict real damage was through the air.

By early November 1943, with winter creeping in, the Allies experienced the jarring existence of the Gustav Line. Hitler was determined to hold this line and the Allies were determined to penetrate it, even though the odds were against them. The Germans had the strong strategic advantage of having established the high ground at Monte Cassino, which towered 1,700 feet above the town of Cassino.[50]

While the Allies were stalemated at the Gustav Line south of Rome, many people in Rome and north of Rome, both now under German occupation, were in hiding. Those with the most cause for fear were Jews and officers of Badoglio's government. Underground meetings were taking place in churches, cellars and caves as the Resistance movement was growing. Of the seven thousand Jews in Rome, about a thousand had already been taken away by the Germans. The rest were terrified and in hiding.[51]

Many were hiding in Catholic convents and monasteries, even in the domes of churches. When the Germans occupied Rome in 1943, Pope Pius XII instructed Catholic nuns and monks to reach out and shelter political fugitives and Jews. It was later estimated that 4,200 Jews in Rome were saved by these nuns and monks.[52]

People in Hiding

In September 1943, the Resistance began to come together for the common purpose of making life difficult for the Nazis occupying their country and the Fascists who supported them. The political parties that were outlawed during Fascism—Communist Party, Socialist Party, Christian Democratic Party, Partito d'Azione (a republican liberal party), and other minor parties—began to come together below the Gustav Line in Naples under the Committee of National Liberation.[53]

Gradually, similar committees began to appear throughout central and northern Italy. With the help of the Allies, the Resistance carried out clandestine activities during the rest of the war. According to the book *At War In Italy 1943-1945: True Adventures in Enemy Territory*, the Resistance had "four basic missions: (1) gather and transmit intelligence; (2) rescue Allied airmen; (3) conduct psychological efforts to expand anti-Nazi opposition within the populace; and (4) engage in sabotage and harassment of the enemy."[54]

Thousands of young men in Italy joined the partisans to end the Fascist regime once and for all. They had the spirit of rebels fighting for their freedom and made life difficult for the Fascists and the Nazis. They conducted secret meetings and carried out clandestine operations, employing standard tricks of the trade such as sabotage and surprise attacks. The Germans responded with their own clandestine operations against the partisans and by terrorizing civilians suspected of supporting them.

Italy became a battleground with both overt and covert operations. The overt operations involved ground forces battling along the front lines, air forces dropping bombs behind enemy lines, and naval forces unleashing firepower along the coast. The covert operations involved clandestine activities taking place behind enemy lines where Resistance fighters were being aided by Allied intelligence operatives.

In Florence, numerous arrests were taking place on charges of helping released British prisoners of war or other vague unspecified charges. Citizens were being interrogated in the search for Jews. The families of young men drafted by Mussolini's Fascist Army who didn't report for duty were being terrorized. In one case, when a young man failed to show up, the Germans went to his house looking for his father. When his mother told them he was away, they decided to take their young boy instead. At that point, the father came out and gave himself up, and was shot.[55]

Behind the lines, many people were in hiding, including Jews trying to avoid concentration camps, escaped prisoners of war, refugees whose homes were either bombed or in danger of being bombed, anti-Fascists who didn't report after being drafted into Mussolini's Salò Republic Army and their families, former Italian soldiers with anti-Fascist sentiments, airmen who were shot down, and the partisans.

Few behind enemy lines in central and northern Italy felt safe. The Italians were prisoners in their own country, and hoping to be liberated by the Allies. It was a situation they would have to live with for months because liberation would be slow. The Allies would be bottlenecked for almost half the year at the Gustav Line. Even after breaking through that line, they would still be strapped by losing troops to the invasion of France at Normandy.

Italy in Chaos

Eight months later, when Bill and Sergeant Todd would be shot down just east of Figline Valdarno, they would be among many people hiding in the area. They too would experience the humanity and unselfishness of farmers who helped to hide, shelter and feed them for a couple of months.

Changes in Leadership

The Italian Campaign would have been a challenge even for battle-tested leaders such as Patton and Montgomery. Losing them to the preparations for the invasion of France made a difficult situation even more difficult for Alexander, the Allied commander in Italy. The first several months of the Italian Campaign under Eisenhower, the Supreme Commander of the Mediterranean Theater of Operations, were described by his successor, General Sir Henry Maitland Wilson, as a "slow, painful advance through difficult terrain against a determined and resourceful enemy, skilled in the exploitation of natural obstacles by mines and demolition."[56] The next five months under Wilson would be characterized by stalemate at the Gustav Line and controversy stemming from a number of things. The terrain, weather, and personnel situation all favored the enemy. The Germans held the high ground, which was difficult to scale in winter conditions, and their Army was essentially one nationality versus multiple nationalities for the Allies.

In December 1943, the last month of Eisenhower's tour of duty as Supreme Commander of the Mediterranean Theater, three notable events occurred. First, Kesselring ordered his men not to occupy the monastery itself in establishing German defensive positions on Monte Cassino, and informed the Allies of this, but some Allied commanders didn't believe him.[57] Second, the Allies suffered heavy losses while trying to capture Monte Cassino and were frustrated in the face of the formidable Gustav Line.[58] And third, Churchill proposed to break the stalemate with a bold, surprise amphibious landing behind enemy lines to cut off supply routes to the Gustav Line.

While the major fighting occurred south of Rome, the major bombing occurred north of Rome, where the Germans occupied central and northern Italy. Many families in towns near strategic targets and therefore in danger of Allied bombing became displaced families looking for a safe haven. In the town of Figline Valdarno, Goffredo Sarri, who had been worried about his family's safety, moved the family to a nearby farm in the village of Vaggio. His concerns were well-founded because Allied bombs had destroyed his business and would later destroy his home. Farms were safer than towns because the Allies knew that the farmers were their friends and were always careful not to drop bombs on farms. Six months later, Bill and Todd would learn just how helpful farmers could be, and Goffredo Sarri would become their savior.

In early January 1944, Eisenhower left to become the Supreme Allied Commander in Europe where he would lead Operation Overlord, the code name for the invasion of France at Normandy. Wilson replaced him. At the next level, the command remained the same for the ground forces under Alexander, but changed for the air and naval forces. Admiral Andrew Browne Cunningham was replaced by Admiral Sir John H.D. Cunningham to lead the naval forces, and Air Marshall Arthur Tedder was replaced by General Ira C. Eaker to lead the air forces. Under Eaker, the Allies would dominate the air war in Italy.

Eaker sought to establish daytime bombing and to establish airfields closer to the enemy so that fighters had the range to provide protection for the bombers. He was successful on both counts. He already had a good track record in the eyes of Hap Arnold, the Commanding General of the Army Air Forces. He would finish his military career as one of the most important figures in air warfare, and receive a special Congressional Gold Medal for his contribution to aviation and the security of his country. This put him in the company of other legendary airmen who had received the honor before him— the Wright Brothers, Charles Lindbergh and Billy Mitchell.[59]

During the summer of 1942, Arnold sent Eaker to England to head the Eighth Air Force and to complement the British efforts of nighttime bombing runs with American daylight runs. He found, as had the British before him, that without fighter support a bomber crew could only expect to survive between fourteen and fifteen missions, significantly below the twenty-five missions expected at that time.[60] Fighters didn't have the range to cover the bombers on some of their raids, and he wanted to change this situation in Italy by establishing airfields closer to the bombing targets.

Progress was made toward this goal when the invasion of Italy led to the establishment of airfields in Paestum near Salerno on the east coast, and in Foggia on the west coast. This enabled Eaker to ensure that bombers were escorted by fighters on their daylight missions. Later, as fighting moved from southern to central Italy, airfields would be established in Corsica to again be nearer the targets in central and northern Italy and ensure fighter escorts. Bill would be among those airmen who moved from Paestum to Corsica.

Battles of Monte Cassino

The Allied plan was to push the Germans northward, liberating Rome in the process. The Allies, especially Churchill, felt that the capture of Rome would give them a major psychological boost because it would be the first major Axis capital to fall and would enable the Allies to establish still more airfields closer to Germany. The German leaders understood this and countered with a formidable defensive line across the country about seventy miles south of Rome. Under Kesselring, the Germans had retreated from southern Italy to this front line, which Kesselring designated as the Gustav Line.

In January 1944, Churchill's proposal for an amphibious landing was given the code name Operation Shingle, and was put into action. Rather than becoming a decisive battle, it was to become only the first of four major battles over five months of trying to capture Monte Cassino.[61] On January 22, about fifty thousand men in the U.S. VI Corps of the Fifth Army made an early-morning amphibious landing behind enemy lines at Anzio, Italy.[62] Anzio was selected for the landing site because it was within striking distance of Rome, but still within range of Allied aircraft operating from Naples.

To help pave the way for the landing at Anzio, medium bombers, including B-25 Mitchells from the 321st Bomb Group, which Bill would join in a couple of months, bombed all lines of communications leading to the area for a few days before the landings. This bombing blocked three vital highways, and helped to make the amphibious landing a success as the landing forces met no opposition.[63]

James Arness, later to become Marshall Matt Dillon of the long-running TV show Gunsmoke, was among those who landed at Anzio. He wanted to be an aviator, but his six-foot-seven-inch height disqualified him, so he joined the Third Infantry Division and participated in the Anzio landing. As the tallest man on his landing craft, he was chosen to be the first man off to test the depth of the water. It was only up to his waist. Arness was among the casualties at Anzio, sustaining a severe wound from a machine-gun bullet in his right leg that resulted in his lifelong slight limp.[64] Most viewers probably never noticed this because on the TV show his deputy Chester had a pronounced limp, and his wasn't even real.

The landing was a complete surprise, but its leader, Major General John Lucas, secured the beachhead for an inevitable German counterattack instead of striking inland to cut the supply route from Rome to the Gustav Line.[65] Like Clark, Lucas remembered that the failure to secure a beachhead at Salerno was almost fatal, so he dug in to wait for his tanks and heavy artillery. Clark agreed with Lucas's decision.[66]

Lucas's hestitation gave Kesselring time to regroup. He brought in his Fourteenth Army, a contingent of 70,000 men that grew to over 135,000 by mid-March.[67] As a result, they pinned Lucas's men down on the beachhead.[68] They remained pinned down during the long, harsh winter, forcing the Allies to continue to wage battles through the winter rather than wait for better weather in the spring. The combination of the German high ground, concentrated defenses, rugged terrain, and miserable weather put the troops at Anzio at a significant disadvantage.[69] Churchill was incensed by this lost opportunity and Lucas lost his command as a result.

Communications is always a problem, and with different nationalities fighting together with different commands, the problems escalate. Eisenhower himself had expressed such a concern with the invasion of Italy. Lucas believed he was the victim of mixed signals. His immediate superior, Clark, advised him not to stick his neck out because he did at Salerno and got in trouble. Lucas took this advice and secured the beachhead against a counterattack rather than opt to continue inward to disrupt enemy supply lines. On the other hand, Churchill envisioned and expected that Lucas would move inward and cut off enemy supply lines. Whether this pursuit would have led to the desired results has been much debated, but the bottom line is that the decision cost Lucas his command.[70]

It is noteworthy that on January 24 a special order from Hitler to all German troops was intercepted by the Allies. The order stated:

"The Gustav Line must be held at all costs for the sake of political consequences which would follow a completely successful defense. The Fuehrer expects the bitterest struggle for every yard."[71] This left no doubt that Hitler was prepared to defend the Gustav Line at all costs. On the Allied side, Clark was likewise determined to break through the Gustav Line, ordering his men to make repeated frontal attacks against it.[72] The result was that some of the bitterest fighting under some of the worst conditions of the war took place at the Gustav Line.

The failed plan to cut the German supply lines to the Gustav Line prompted the Allied commanders to debate the issue of whether or not to bomb the abbey. On February 3, Alexander established a new corps in Clark's Fifth Army called the New Zealand Corps and put General Sir Bernard Freyberg, a national hero in New Zealand, in charge of it. His objective was to capture Monte Cassino.

After assessing the situation, Freyberg concluded that the abbey was a fortress that must be bombed. The Americans were not in favor of the bombing. The other Allies reluctantly supported Freyberg.[73] Among those in favor was Clark's superior, Alexander. Eaker, the head of the Mediterranean Allied Air Forces, flew over the abbey on February 13 and thought he saw military personnel in the building.[74] After much debate, Clark conceded despite his reservations and agreed to give the order as long as it was approved at the highest level. It was, by Wilson, the Supreme Allied Commander of the Mediterranean Theater.[75]

National treasures are held in high regard in Italy, and the abbey, the most venerable abbey of Christendom, was considered such a treasure.[76] Nevertheless, on February 15, 1944, heavy and medium bombers dropped 453.5 tons of bombs on the complex, followed the next day by concentrated artillery barrages and additional bombs by fighter bombers.[77] The abbey was utterly destroyed, yet the Germans still held their high ground because they weren't in the abbey, and thus were able to hold off the Allied troops. The senior U.S. diplomat to the Vatican, Harold Tittmann, was told by a spokesman for the Vatican that the bombing was "a colossal blunder—a piece of gross stupidity."[78]

The decision to bomb the abbey was one of the most controversial decisions of World War II. Not only did the bombing destroy a national treasure, but the irony of the bombing was that it worked to the tactical advantage of the Germans. After the bombing, they

Monte Cassino Abbey
Courtesy of Museo Historeale di Cassino

Before
Bombing

After
Bombing

Today

felt free to occupy the ruins, and the rubble provided much better defensive cover than the abbey before its destruction.[79]

The destruction of the Benedictine Abbey of Monte Cassino is a symbol of the cruelty of war. After the war, it was completely rebuilt and restored to its former beauty, and many of its treasures that were removed before the bombings were returned intact. It also stands today as a symbol of the ability of people to recover from the abyss of war.

Since Italy was a battleground in World War II, its citizens have experienced the cruelty of war first hand, and have a strong incentive to prevent the country from becoming a battleground again. Mussolini's lost bid for world power brought terrible suffering to its citizens and incredible destruction to many of its towns. What's more, the suffering was inflicted upon many civilians who never supported him to begin with. In a dictatorship, there is great risk associated with expressing views against the dictator, and most citizens are not prepared to take that risk.

Today, in the hope that future generations will learn from the errors of past generations, the *Museo Historeale di Cassino* stands at the foot of Monte Cassino in the town of Cassino, a town which, like the abbey atop Monte Cassino, was utterly destroyed during the war. The *Museo Historeale* shows this destruction in a way that stirs the emotions, as does a compelling movie. Its designer, Carlo Rambaldi, is a master of special effects who won three Academy Awards for his work in the movies *E.T.*, *Alien* and *King Kong*. Working with the Ministry of Cultural Heritage and Activities, he designed a museum that shows how the abbey was sacrificed to the absurdity of war, using images of destruction, lights, special technologies, carefully chosen rhetoric, and powerful music.[80]

Chapter 4

BOMBS AWAY

In early March, 1944, the Germans were still holding a strong position atop Monte Cassino, leaving the Allied commanders little choice but to attack the high ground again by air. While the Allied leaders were not in agreement to bomb Monte Cassino in mid-February, they were very much in agreement to bomb it in mid-March, as well as the town of Cassino, whose citizens had been evacuated when the Germans took over the town in late 1943.[1]

The Gustav Line was now heavily defended by fifteen German divisions.[2] By May, the German Army at Monte Cassino alone would grow to twenty-three German divisions.[3] To counter, the Allies would need considerably more than the nine divisions Churchill estimated the Allies would require for the war in Italy.[4]

On March 15, in the greatest air effort to date in the Mediterranean Theater, hundreds of heavy and medium bombers, supported by hundreds of fighters and fighter bombers, dropped tons of high explosives on Monte Cassino and the town of Cassino.[5] According to the historical records of the 321st Bomb Group for that day, Cassino became the most bombed area in the world with 2,500 tons of bombs dropped on it by 12th and 15th Air Forces."[6]

It was a miracle that St. Benedict's tomb, in the centre of the abbey, was never destroyed during the two devastating bombings of Monte Cassino. Months later, after the capture and liberation of Rome in June, General Alexander informed the Pope of its survival. The Pope was deeply moved and assured Alexander that he understood the military necessity for the bombing and the inevitable destruction of the monastery.[7]

After the second bombing of Monte Cassino on March 15, the Germans were still dug in after the battle to take the hill was unsuccessful. Both sides were worn out from bitter fighting, cold weather, and heavy casualties. It was time for a new strategy to pull back the ground initiative and step up the air initiative. It was time for air power on a massive scale.[8] Billy Mitchell was probably smiling in his grave.

New Bombing Strategy

Bill Lanza didn't realize it at the time, but he would become part of one of the outstanding air campaigns of World War II. Despite growing to twenty-one divisions, the Allied ground forces would be faced with formidable obstacles and have to rely on an air interdiction campaign to stifle the German supply lines and pave the way for a victory in Italy.[9]

On March 19, the day of Bill's first mission, the Allied leaders disclosed a new plan, called Operation Strangle, which was designed to strangle enemy troops by cutting off all their lines of supply.[10] Medium bombers and fighter bombers were to carry out the plan. The primary job of the medium bombers was to block highways and railroads by knocking out bridges, viaducts, marshalling yards and other communications lines. The primary job of the fighter bombers was to strafe and bomb all enemy transport on the highways and railroads.[11]

Concentrated attacks against bridges were something new for the 321st Bomb Group at that time. Previously, it flew few missions against this type of pinpoint target. The targets were broader, such as airfields or railroad marshalling yards. According to the March 26, 1944 issue of its internal newspaper, *321 In The News*, "In comparative size the average rail and road bridge is about the smallest target ever given bombers and perfection is required to bomb such an objective successfully. Experience has shown that unless numerous direct hits are scored on a bridge it will remain standing even though the pattern of bombs falls across it."[12]

Because bombing bridges called for a high level of precision bombing, the bombers had to make longer bomb runs, closer to the targets, increasing the possibility of being hit by flak. As we will see later, Bill would get shot down trying to bomb a bridge. Not long after that, he and Todd would witness fighter bombers destroy a train that traveled over that very bridge.

Flak was the nemesis of aviators. The term is an abbreviation of the German words *flugabwehr-kanone* that translates to "air-defense cannon."[13] A large 88-mm shell over three feet in length and weighing about thirty-two pounds when fired from an 88-mm flak cannon would jettison a metal projectile weighing about twenty pounds and filled with an explosive toward the target aircraft. The metal projectile was timed to detonate at the estimated altitude of the aircraft in a burst of black smoke that set off splinters of metal, called shrapnel, into any aircraft in its vicinity. Typically, anti-aircraft cannons were placed around potential bombing targets with the intent of aiming the shells to explode near the lead ship on a bomb run to disrupt the run, which is exactly what happened later when Bill's plane was shot down. The 88-mm flak burst had a spherical kill zone of about thirty feet, so explosions near an aircraft could be deadly.[14]

For protection, bomber crews wore flak suits—also called flak jackets or flak vests—because aircraft on a bomb run were often "holed" by flak and, worse still, crew members were hit by the fragments. Data collected in 1942 on U.S. bomber crews showed that 70 percent of the casualties were caused by flak fragments, or by flying pieces of plexiglass or metal ripped from the aircraft by flak concussions. Wearing flak suits and steel helmets were said to reduce fatalities by 50 percent and injuries by 70 percent. Consequently, airmen didn't want to fly combat missions without them.[15]

On March 13, the flak was deadly. A plane in Bill's bomb group ran into intense and accurate flak that killed one crew member and badly wounded another. On the same mission, two members of another crew received severe flak wounds. As we will see later, a direct hit by an 88-mm projectile can cause severe damage to an aircraft.

With Operation Strangle in effect, the missions were directed against the German lines of communication north of Rome. More specifically, as indicated in the records of the 321st for that month: "Railroad bridges and marshalling yards along the main Rome-Florence road received our particular attention and it got so that toward the end of the month our crews could almost fly blind to these particular localities and drop their bombs on dead reckoning."[16]

The hard-luck bomb group of the 57th Bomb Wing had to be the

340th Bomb Group. The group was located near the base of Mount Vesuvius, which had been acting up for several days. On March 22, it erupted in all its destructive glory, roaring and rumbling and spewing forth stones and ashes, destroying the living quarters of the 340th as well as their eighty-eight B-25 Mitchells, and forcing the evacuation of the entire camp. It was a devastating loss. Yet, recovery was swift. Crew members were housed in a tobacco warehouse at Paestum, which was used by Bill's bomb group for briefings. Meanwhile, the Allied industrial machine flexed its muscle in supplying replacement B-25s. Within a week, the 340th was flying missions again, and by April 15, less than a month after the eruption, it was a fully-recovered fighting unit.[17] Said Bill: "It was amazing how quickly we were able to replace planes."

On March 30, his fourth mission, Bill was flying in a formation of twenty-four B-25 Mitchells, escorted by P-40 Warhawk and P-47 Thunderbolt fighters, to bomb a railroad bridge in Orvieto. His pilot was Lieutenant Leon R. Hawkes and two of his tent mates were flying with him. Sergeant Malcolm B. Leonard was the engineer in the front of the D-model Mitchell bomber, and Sergeant Hoyt V. Harrison was the radio operator/gunner in the waist of the plane. Bill was just behind and above Harrison as the top-turret gunner. They were attacked twice by enemy fighters.[18]

According to the mission report, the first attack occurred near Viterbo on their way to the target. An estimated eight Messerschmitt 109s (ME 109s) and three to six Foche Wulf 190s (FW 190s) attacked them, but weren't aggressive and were driven off by the P-40s and P-47s. It was a cloudy day, visibility was poor, and they were unable to bomb the bridge in Orvieto. Consequently, they headed for their alternate target, a railroad bridge northwest of Orte and about twenty-five miles south of Orvieto. Visibility continued to be poor and only twelve of the planes ended up dropping their bombs. Reportedly, none hit the target bridge.[19]

After dropping their bombs, they were attacked again. The first flight element of twelve B-25s was not attacked, but the second one was, by six to nine ME 109s and three to six FW 190s.[20] Bill, who was in the second element, remembers: "I saw one of the fighters come out of the clouds at 12 o'clock and fire at us, so we all opened up. Harrison was tugging at my leg and I was kicking back trying to free my leg so I could concentrate on the fighters. He was trying to alert me to the fighters coming from 6 o'clock, but I was focusing on the plane attacking from 12 o'clock. Later, he told me that one of the enemy fighters was so close that he could see the pilot's white scarf when he flew by his window."

According to the mission report, the enemy fighters "worked in teams of two or three usually from 6 o'clock with one coming in from above and doing a split S and diving, others climbing and breaking to the right or left."[21] Despite plenty of air activity, the formation had no casualties, and only two B-25s were holed on the mission. Two tail gunners claimed a hit on an FW 190, as did one of the escort fighter pilots. At the end of the month, it was reported that one FW 190 was destroyed and another was probable.[22] Bill notes, "In the frenzy of an attack, it's tough to tell who hit what. I thought I hit one, but they gave credit to two guys on the end. We had a lot of firepower and this was one of the few missions I was on that enemy aircraft attacked us. The Germans respected our firepower. We would see enemy fighters in the distance, but the only time they attacked was when there were clouds. On most of my missions, flak was the main threat, but you had to be ready for anything."

Most of the missions Bill flew during the latter half of March and during April had bridges as the targets. The mission reports show five bridges were targets during the latter half of March, and nineteen during April.[23] However, other targets drew their attention as well. In fact, it was on a mission to bomb an airport that Bill's plane ran into trouble.

On April 14th, Bill flew on a mission to bomb the Viterbo Aerodrome, one of the principle German fighter bases in central Italy. Thirty-eight planes flew on this mission, the most of any mission he flew on. The formation consisted of three flights of twelve planes each in two six-plane boxes. Captain Paul T. Cooper, later to become the leader of the 321st Bomb Group, led the mission. He was also the leader of the first flight, with Lieutenant E.E. Stocking to his left leading one flight and Captain R.H. Neuman to his right leading the other flight. In addition to the thirty-six aircraft in the three flights, two additional aircraft were flying in the rear element, and Lieutenant Fenton M. Dalley was the pilot in one of them.[24] The flak was intense and accurate as nineteen planes, half of them, were hit by flak. Despite this barrage, the formation's bombs hit through the center of the field and landing strip, and hits on or near three hangars were reported, as well as hits in the barracks southeast of the aerodrome.[25]

On the breakaway after dropping their bombs, the formation was making a gradual right turn when Lieutenant Norman J. Lundmark, the bombardier in the first element of the second flight, witnessed flak breaking around the rear element, then saw Dalley's ship begin to nose down and go into a vertical dive. He said the aircraft was going at tremendous speed when it leveled out flying upside down at an altitude of between 3,000 and 5,000 feet, then disappeared from his vision heading in a direction northeast of the target.[26]

Sergeant William W. Britton, Jr., the tail gunner on the lead ship of the fourth element in the second flight, heard that a plane was in trouble, picked up the ship, and saw it plummeting toward the ground where it hit a road and exploded. Neither witness saw any parachutes because nobody had a chance to bail out.

Soon the families of the crew would be notified. Dalley's father in Utah and the mothers of the other five crew members—co-pilot Lieutenant James E. Kelley of Nebraska, bombardier Lieutenant Allen E. Wingrove of Pennsylvania, engineer/gunner Corporal Francis R. Ellis of Indiana, radio operator/gunner Sergeant Jack L. Phelps of Tennessee, and turret-gunner Sergeant Daniel R. Smith of Mississippi—would receive the dreaded notifications that their sons were missing in action. While praying for their safe return, they would later be notified that their sons had been killed in action.[27] The pain of war extends far beyond the battlefield, and is acutely felt by the families of fallen heroes.

Bill was in Lieutenant Hawkes's plane, one of the nineteen planes hit by flak. When the shrapnel from flak rips through the skin of an aircraft, anyone in its path is scarred if they're lucky and killed if they're not. Hawkes' crew was lucky. For his role in the mission, Bill was awarded the Air Medal. According to Bill, "I was just doing my job." His citation stated:

> *For meritorious achievement while participating in aerial flight as turret gunner of the B-25 type aircraft, upon the commencement of the bomb run over Viterbo, Italy on 14 April 1944, Sergeant Lanza's plane was damaged by intense*

anti-aircraft fire. As his pilot determinedly held the crippled plane on course and enabled the bombardier to release his bombs upon the target with devastating effect, Sergeant Lanza displayed outstanding skill and courage in the performance of his assignments. On many combat missions, his proficiency and devotion to duty have reflected great credit upon himself and the military service of the United States. [28]

John Kinney, who would later be shot down with Bill, flew with the mission leader, Captain Cooper, and also received the Air Medal for this mission. His citation read:

For meritorious achievement while participating in aerial flight as navigator of B-25 type aircraft. On 14 April 1944, Lt. Kinney flew as lead navigator of a large formation attacking Viterbo Airdrome, Italy. Despite intense anti-aircraft fire which destroyed one bomber and damaged nineteen others, Lt. Kinney skillfully directed his pilot on a perfect course to the target enabling the formation to cover the objective with a devastating bomb pattern. His proficiency in combat reflects great credit upon himself and the United States Army Air Corps. [29]

Three days later, Bill was on another mission with Lieutenant Hawkes, this time to bomb a railroad bridge about eight miles west of Viterbo. "I was in the top turret and we were nearing the target when the tail of another ship went whizzing by me." The lead aircraft of the formation, always the prime target of anti-aircraft cannons, had taken two direct hits which severed the tail assembly, killing three members of the crew.

According to one of the two survivors, the navigator Lieutenant William S. Hough, "the plane climbed out of control and fell off on its back. Captain [Weymouth] Crowell succeeded in getting the ship off its back and out of a spin." Crowell ordered Hough and his co-pilot, Lieutenant Floyd A. Elliott, to bail out. Elliott, who became a prisoner of war, said much later of Crowell, who went down with the plane: "I believe he was unable to leave his seat because of the centrifugal force caused by the plane spinning to the right. My seat was near enough the center of the spin that I was able to overcome this force."[30]

Sergeant Zdenaek Hajny, in another plane in the formation, also saw the tail assembly fly past the side of his plane, followed by the plane on its back, after which he said it "turned right side up and went into a slow flat wide spiral down." He saw the two chutes [Hough's and Elliott's] and reported that "the ship crashed into the north end of the town NNE [between north and northeast] of the target, bursting into flames immediately upon impact."

Thanks to the efforts of Captain Crowell, Hough and Elliot were able to bail out and survived the war. Elliott, who was from Columbia, Missouri, became a prisoner in the same prison camp where the Great Escape had taken place, while Hough, who was from Kokomo, Indiana, evaded the enemy for a couple of months. By no means did they have an easy time, but they were among the fortunate survivors to return home, having lost five of their comrades whose sacrifices, especially that of Captain Crowell, they would never forget and always appreciate.[31]

Their lost comrades were, in addition to Captain Crowell of Willamina, Oregon; bombardier, Lieutenant Alfred W. Kreutz of Newberg, Oregon; engineer Joseph M. Johnson of Kopperl, Texas; radio operator/waist gunner Sergeant Charles W. Doss, Jr. of Groesbeck, Texas; and aerial gunner Sergeant Herbert J. Graham of Porterville, California. The families of these war heroes would have a rough time for a long time.[32] This was another sad day for the 321st, and more sad days lay ahead.

In late April, Bill's bomb group moved to Solenzara, Corsica to be closer to their targets in central and northern Italy.[33] Corsica, a French island, was known to the Ancient Greeks as Kallisto, or "the most beautiful."[34] It had dense forests, high mountains with scenic streams, and sandy beaches. Today, most of its population is concentrated in its two main towns—Ajaccio, where Napolean was born, and Bastia, its capital, where Bill's personal effects were sent after he was shot down.[35]

War is nerve-racking and it helps to have good friends to support each other. Bill's tent mates fit that bill. They included two friends he trained with in the States—Sergeants Mygrant and Kane from California and Massachusetts, respectively—and two friends he made in Paestum—Sergeants Hoyt V. Harrison and Malcolm B. Leonard from California and New York, respectively. Their tent also included Sergeant Francis P. Bufkin, Jr. from Tennessee, a new friend who Bill said had a great sense of humor. According to Kane, "We all got along great. We were good buddies."[36]

They shared the day's experiences together, played poker together, and let off steam together. Notes Bill: "We used to get a shot of whiskey after every mission to help us relax. We were always tense after a mission, and were so glad to make it back in one piece. Mygrant suggested we save our shots and have a party every now and then. We all thought that was a good idea."

During the war, Corsica's east coast was dotted with Allied airfields where more than fifty thousand military personnel passed through the island between 1943 and 1945, leaving the Corsicans with all kinds of memories. Many of them were captured in a book entitled *U.S.S. Corsica*, written (in French) by Dominique Taddei, a native who was a child during the war. The memories range from pleasant ones, such as the Americans helping the Corsicans build a destroyed bridge, to sad memories, such as the gathering of the personal effects of airmen who didn't make it back from missions.[37]

One of Bill's memories involves a leisure activity with an element of danger. "Mygrant was full of ideas. Once, he suggested we go hunting for wild boar with our pistols, so we all went along. Harrison always had his holster on, ready for target practice. Some of the guys even took their guns into town. We found no boar but got separated and some of us found an abandoned stone house in the woods and started shooting at it for target practice. We were really pumping away. We didn't know that Leonard was inside the building until he looked out the window. We were lucky we didn't kill each other."

While danger was sometimes lurking off duty, it was always lurking on duty. Operation Strangle was in full force, and the 12th Air Force medium bombers, including those of the 321st, were busy bombing railroad bridges, tracks, tunnels and marshalling yards; viaducts; and fuel dumps north of Rome.[38]

The month of April took its toll as the Allied air forces flew mission after mission to cut off enemy supplies while the Allied ground forces prepared for Operation Diadem, the fourth Battle of Monte Cassino. The Allies were awaiting better weather and reinforcing for a major offensive to break through the Gustav Line and take Rome. Operation Strangle was a critical element in the Allied strategy to break through the formidable Gustav Line and capture Rome.

In supplying the front lines with ammunition, motor fuel and troop reinforcements, the Germans depended on waterways, roadways and railways. At that time, Mediterranean Army Air Force Intelligence estimated that 700 tons of daily supplies arrived by water, 800 tons by road, and 80,000 tons by rail. It didn't take a rocket scientist to see the merits of disrupting the Italian rail network in order to "strangle" the German supply network. Consequently, Operation Strangle focused mainly on bombing marshalling yards and bridges of the rail system of northern and central Italy.[39]

As the Allied air forces were busy bombing enemy supply lines in northern and central Italy, the Allied and Axis ground forces at the Gustav Line remained at a relative standstill, wet, freezing, and exhausted. When the weather improved, the Allied troops mounted a spring offensive, the fourth and decisive major battle at Monte Cassino.

On May 11, they attacked the town of Cassino, including the high ground of Monte Cassino. For days, they kept shelling the German positions in and around the monastery.[40] The Allied forces kept up the pressure and the exhausted Germans, many of them wounded, capitulated to the Polish II Corps on May 18.[41] Today, many of those valiant Polish soldiers lie in the Polish cemetery located on the mountain close to the abbey. On the grave of their commander, General Wladyslaw Anders, you will still find red poppies signifying the Polish blood shed for freedom.

The assault on Cassino finally broke down the Gustav Line. It took four battles in five months with over 50,000 casualties suffered by the Allies and the Germans to take Cassino.[42] Once Cassino was in Allied hands, the German defenses at the Gustav Line began to disintegrate, and the Germans retreated to a new line, referred to as the Hitler Line, about ten to twelve miles north of the Gustav Line. The Allied troops punctured this line rather quickly and General Clark headed for Rome and liberated the city on June 4.[43]

The U.S. VI Corps of the U.S. Fifth Army suffered greatly during the four months it took to break through the Gustav line. They were pinned down on the Anzio beachhead from their amphibious landing on January 22 until the entire U.S. 36th Infantry Division made an amphibious landing on the beach on May 22. During March, April and the first part of May, recalled one veteran, the Anzio beachhead resembled the Western Front during World War I, and the VI Corps sustained many casualties, the vast majority from air and artillery attacks. During these four months, they suffered over 29,200 combat casualties and 37,000 non-combat casualties. Of the combat casualties, the Americans were hardest hit with 16,200, or more than half of them. By comparison, German combat losses were estimated at 27,500, reflecting their significant strategic advantage.[44]

Bill remembers how poor the situation was for the troops at the Anzio beachhead: "Our troops were pinned down in wet and freezing weather, exposing them to both the elements and enemy firepower. We used to fly along the coast near Anzio but were careful to stay out of range of the German heavy artillery. Still, we could see the shells dropping in the middle of our troops. It was terrible. They couldn't move. Fragmentation bombs were dropped on them too. Oh, I felt so bad for them." Like flak aimed at aircraft formations, fragmentation bombs are aimed at troop concentrations. Both distribute metal splinters which can be deadly. Fragmentation bombs were used by both the Allies and Axis powers, another harsh reality of war.

Private Runo Palmquist of the U.S. Fifth Army's 3rd Infantry Division, 15th Infantry Regiment was one of the sitting ducks on the beaches of Anzio. He wasn't at Anzio during the battles in January and February. When Monte Cassino was bombed in mid-February, he was sixty miles away in Naples and yet could see the bombing in the distance.

"When we shipped out to Anzio, we were all jammed into the hull of the ship that was being attacked by Stuka dive bombers," said Palmquist. Stuka was short for _sturzkampfflugzueg_, the German word for dive-bomber. It was the air element of Germany's _Blitzkrieg_, or lighting war. The tactical precision bomber was feared by its adversaries. The actual name of the plane was the Junkers Ju.87.[45]

Palmquist continued: "The explosions of the bombs were powerful and shaking the ship. We all knew we were in big trouble if one hit us, but we were lucky and made it to Anzio in one piece." Palmquist was among the many soldiers sent to reinforce the beachhead. The original 36,000 men that landed at Anzio with Lucas on January 22 were increased to 60,000 by early February, and would increase to 90,000 by May.[46]

Before Palmquist arrived, the Germans were trying to drive Lucas's men into the sea, but with air and naval support they held their ground. By late February, their attack lost momentum and the Germans began to withdraw. When Palmquist landed at Anzio, a stalemate had set in with flurries of mortar or sniper fire.[47] However, they were subjected to steady artillery shelling for a couple of months. The Germans overlooked the Allied troops from their positions in the surrounding hills. Months later, when Palmquist would stand on one of those hills, he would see for himself the great advantage the Germans held at Anzio.

To help prevent the men pinned down on the beach from being easy targets, the Allies employed smoke pots to generate smoke every day from dusk to dawn from the middle of March until the Anzio breakout in mid-May.[48] While the smoke improved the odds of not being hit, survival was still a matter of luck.

Palmquist noted: "It was awful. We had our smoke pots going to cloud the air, but this didn't stop the artillery shells. Without the smoke as a defensive safeguard, the Germans would have been able to direct accurate artillery fire on our positions. Even though we could hear the shells whistling as they approached, enabling us to hit the dirt, if it was heading for your foxhole, you didn't stand a chance.

"One day, a buddy of mine in the next foxhole went to relieve himself. While he was gone, an artillery shell landed in his foxhole. When he returned and saw the damage, he had a complete breakdown and had to be taken to the hospital. The following day, we all decided to visit him in the hospital. He was still in shock and didn't recognize any of us."

Palmquist went on to see considerably more action. The 3rd Infantry Division sustained more casualties than any other American division in World War II. Nicknamed the "Blue and White Devils," it was in combat for 531 days, won thirty-six Medals of Honor, and had in its ranks Audie Murphy, the most highly decorated soldier of World War II. After the Allied troops broke out of the Anzio beachhead in May, Palmquist was among the first soldiers to enter Rome. After fighting in Italy, he was part of Operation Dragoon, the invasion of southern France in the middle of August, and fought up through France and into Germany during the winter. "On Christmas eve, we each got a bottle of beer. I put mine aside and it was so cold that it froze. The bottle, like everything else around me, exploded."

Runo and his wife, Norma, live in South Windsor, Connecticut.

Among other things, Runo has a strong faith. According to his friend Ron Lanza (the author's brother, a wounded Vietnam veteran): "Runo exemplifies what his generation of soldiers was all about. He talks little about his wartime experiences, yet clearly this humble man has strength, compassion and a purpose that manifests itself in his longtime leadership within the church family I am privileged to share with him."

Poor weather hampered medium bomber missions in early May, but activity became hectic as the month wore on. During the month, the 12th Air Force supported the major spring offensive of the Allied ground forces to break through the Gustav Line, while continuing to "strangle" the enemy by attacking its lines of communications north and northwest of Rome. The 321st Bomb Group had the busiest and most successful month in its history in terms of sorties flown, targets blasted, and percentage of bombs hitting their targets.[49] But again, there was a price to pay because the 321st Bomb Group lost fourteen aircraft, the most lost in any single month, although most crews bailed out before their planes crashed.[50] The 446th Bomb Squadron alone had 19 crew members lost in action, including the seven on Bill's plane.[51]

On May 12, the 321st had its busiest day since it began combat operations in late March, 1943.[52] The Group flew five missions involving 114 aircraft, a new record.[53] Two of the missions were directed at a command post in Pico, Italy. The first attack cost the Group one plane with twenty-three "holed" by flak. Bill flew on the second attack late in the afternoon mission that "resulted in a good concentration of bombs covering the target area despite another heavy barrage of anti-aircraft fire."[54]

Several planes were hit, including Bill's plane. "We caught flak in our right engine. Oh, what a concussion! It knocked the nacelle [engine cover] off. Our plane was damaged so badly that we couldn't make it back to our home base in Corsica, so our pilot, Lieutenant [Vernon] Lewis, landed at an airfield [Capodochina Airfield] near Naples.

"After we landed, Captain Cooper's plane came in with a wounded crew member, Sergeant [Joseph M.] Foley—one of my friends and a former infantryman like me. I watched as they took him off the plane. He was hit by flak and was rushed to the hospital. He pulled through and years later, I worked with him at the Post Office in Boston."

"Lieutenant [John] Fitzgerald also landed with us and he and Captain Cooper returned to our home base that day, but we remained overnight while our engine was being repaired. At dinner, an M.P. [Military Policeman] made conversation with our engineer [Sergeant John Bober, Jr.] and me. He was commending us for the good job we were doing and the risks we were taking, and offered to take us to town. He had a jeep and we went to Naples that night with friends of his, and had a helluva good time."

The next morning, while Bill was asleep near Naples, his bomb group in Solenzara, Corsica was awakened in the wee hours by an air raid alert. Just north of them in Alesan, the hard-luck 340th was the victim of another disaster.[55] It wasn't a mountain that erupted this time, it was much worse. After dropping flares to light up the area, an estimated twenty to thirty German fighter planes attacked them around four o'clock in the morning, bombing and strafing everything in sight for about an hour and fifteen minutes. Many men were killed in their beds, others in their trenches as fragmentation and other anti-personnel bombs exploded all around them. Their planes with full bomb loads were exploding and fires were raging.[56] There was a tremendous loss of life and aircraft. It was war at its worst, a devastating blow to the 340th Bomb Group.

Before the Germans raided the airbase of the 340th, they had attacked Poretta Airfield, about fifteen miles north of Alesan Field, at about ten o'clock at night, killing a number of men and destroying twenty-five Spitfires.[57] The two attacks were red flags that prompted men at other airbases to protect themselves better from surprise attacks.

"When we returned to our base, everyone was digging foxholes, worrying about another attack." Axis Sally, who made propaganda radio broadcasts for the Germans from Radio Berlin, had announced that the 310th Bomb Group would be next and after that the 321st Bomb Group. This warning sent the men rushing to deepen their fox holes.[58]

Bill's tent mate, Kane, recalls the broadcast that prompted them to deepen their foxholes. Her broadcasts had an impact. Edward F. Logan, Jr., a B-17 pilot during the war who wrote a memoir entitled *Jump, Damn It, Jump!* noted that Axis Sally would sometimes correctly name the target for the day's mission, which would cause them to cancel the mission. He wondered how the Germans obtained this information.[59]

Axis Sally, also called the "Berlin Bitch," was Mildred Gillars. She was born in the United States and led a complicated life that couldn't possibly be summarized in a paragraph. She was greatly influenced by a professor—Otto Max Koischwitz—with whom she had an affair in New York City and who later renounced his U.S. citizenship to become an officer for the Nazi radio service in charge of propaganda broadcasts. During the war, she continued her affair with him while also working for him doing propaganda radio broadcasts for Radio Berlin. After the war, she was convicted of treason for the Nazi broadcast of a play entitled *Vision for Invasion*, which Koischwitz, deceased by now, had written. She served twelve years in a Federal prison after which she was paroled and thereafter lived a quiet and reclusive life, succumbing in 1988 at the age of 87.[60]

Bill recalls: "Danger was all around us. I remember a very sad day [May 15] when Lieutenant Walsh and his crew were killed when his plane crash-landed on the runway, and blew up. I knew Lieutenant Walsh. He lived in the Boston area like me. I had also heard that one member of his crew, Sergeant Orechia, had been relieved but insisted on flying one more mission." According to the mission summary, the plane exploded because it was saturated with gasoline from leaking fuel lines.[61] Bill continues: "Everyone was upset. Colonel Smith, our group commander, raised hell after that plane blew up. We flew the next day, and he told us that if anyone ever smells fumes, we have the right to bail out."

On the same day, one of Bill's friends narrowly escaped disaster. "Mygrant was on a mission to bomb a harbor, Portoferraio, on the island of Elba, off the west coast of Tuscany, and his plane was hit badly by flak, forcing the entire crew to bail out into the Tyrrhenian Sea. They were later rescued by British Air-Sea Rescue. Bob was a good man and, fortunately, a good swimmer as well. He was back in our tent that night, and later received the Distinguished Flying Cross for that mission. It was good to have him back in our tent." According to the mission report of the squadron for that day, Mygrant's plane blew up just after the last man bailed out.[62]

Mygrant's plane was Lieutenant John Fitzgerald's wing ship, and he witnessed the rescue. In a news article, he said: "The crew had bailed out and were floating in their Mae Wests about three miles from the island. When I found them, there were two Spitfires keeping

93

the Germans away until the rescue boat's arrival." He praised the men of the Air-Sea Rescue team: "They had plenty of guts and a lot of Americans owe them their lives."[63] Mae Wests are what servicemen called their inflatable life jackets because they were puffed up in front, reminding them of the popular, buxom movie star.[64]

Another plane on that mission, Lieutenant Rolland Othick's ship, also got hit over Portoferraio. According to Lieutenant George Gibbons, the co-pilot of the lead plane of the three-plane element directly behind Othick's three-plane element, "His right engine was smoking badly and oil was coming out of his nacelle. He slid out of the formation with a diving turn to the left and then turned right and headed toward Pianosa Island." While he lost sight of the aircraft, his gunner, Sergeant Isom Burrow, watched the trail of black smoke and reported that he saw the plane land on a runway strip on German-controlled Pianosa Island, which is situated about eight miles southwest of Elba. He said it looked like a successful belly landing "because the airplane did not explode upon hitting the runway but created a big cloud of red dust."[65]

The dust settled to reveal tragedy. The bombardier, Lieutenant Patrick Griffin, lay dead and both the radio operator, Sergeant Woodrow Youngblood, and gunner, Sergeant Edward Miller, had been wounded. Griffin was buried on Pianosa Island. Youngblood and Miller were both hospitalized.[66] Pilot Othick and co-pilot Lieutenant Estel Mayfield were sent to Stalag Luft III, the "Great Escape" prison camp. When Miller got better, he joined them. Engineer Alvie Cobb was sent to Stalag XVII-B and, when Youngblood recovered, he was sent to Stalag Luft IV.[67]

According to Bill, "After Pianosa Island fell into Allied hands [on June 17], Mygrant went there on leave to check on the men who crash-landed on the island. He learned from one of the natives, most likely a prison guard or family member of a prison guard, that Griffin was given a ceremonial burial. The native also gave him a picture of the ceremony. When I made it back to Allied lines and visited my old base for a few days, he gave me the picture."

Pianosa is a small, flat island of about four square miles, located between Corsica, where Napoleon was born in 1769, and Elba, where he was exiled in 1814 following his fifteen-year rule of Europe.[68] His fate was similar to Mussolini's in that both were exiled and both recovered, but without the power they once had and were used to for many years. Both of them, like Hitler, were powerful men who thought they could do no wrong. When a dictator falls from power, the landing is rarely soft. Interestingly enough, in the middle of the 1800s, Pianosa became a place of exile for criminals as a penal colony that remained a prison until the end of the twentieth century.[69]

The capture of Elba on June 17 was worrisome to Kesselring. The possibility of another amphibious landing in Italy behind German lines was always a source of anxiety for him. The Normandy invasion assuaged his fears somewhat, but he couldn't see any other reason for the Allies capturing the remote island.[70] As far back as August 1943, the Germans were worried about an amphibious landing in Tuscany, at Grosseto, Piombino or Livorno.[71]

Pianosa Island is mostly known for its fictional portrayal in Joseph Heller's popular anti-war novel, *Catch-22*. Heller took literary license in giving this island what it never had, a U.S. Army Air Corps airfield.[72] It may have had a runway during the war because, as previously noted, Sergeant Burrow said he saw Lieutenant Othick crash-land on one.

Heller was an Army Air Corps bombardier stationed in Italy who flew sixty combat missions and wrote this satire of the military bureaucracy and the insanity of war.[73] The impact of the book is still felt because people still refer to a no-win situation as a "Catch-22." The fact of the matter was, however, that the Allies did win and it was through the sacrifice and courage of men who were willing to do more in the line of duty.

Bill didn't view *Catch-22* positively: "We didn't appreciate the novel because it poked fun at what we went through over there. A war is difficult to manage, especially a war as big as that one." Many veterans still feel this way. Nevertheless, the United States Air Force Academy still recommends the book to help students recognize the dehumanizing aspects of a military bureaucracy.[74]

Heller's main character, a bombardier named Yossarian, had a different mindset than most airmen who didn't try to get out of missions. For example, Bill was proud that he never went on sick call, "I flew every mission I was assigned to. I even volunteered for one mission when the gunner had the shakes." The "shakes" is a term used to describe the anxiety or fear of flying after a harrowing experience.

In this man's case, on his previous mission, his plane went into a spin, which is usually curtains, but the pilot leveled off the plane and they made it back.

Harry George was a pilot in the 340th Bomb Group who also didn't think much of Heller's book. He said the stuff in it was absurd. Like Bill and Todd, George was shot down over Italy and also evaded the enemy by living in mountain caves with the help of three Italian farmers. Among other things, he took issue with the remark that the number of missions men had to fly was raised to mess with their minds, noting that you couldn't roll crews off the production lines the way you could roll aircraft. He said it takes over a year to train a pilot and six to nine months to train a bombardier-navigator.[75] The Luftwaffe ran into a manpower shortage of trained pilots in 1944, and the result was a rapid increase in the loss rate of their planes and crews.[76]

By increasing the missions flown by experienced crews and by continuing to roll aircraft off the assembly lines, the Allies took over domination of the skies from the Luftwaffe. The people who worked in aircraft factories were very proud of their contributions to the war effort. Harry Desko and his wife Alice helped to build B-25s during the war. They worked at the North American Aviation plant in Kansas City, Missouri, which built 6,608 B-25s (2,290 B-25Ds and 4,318 B-25Js).[77] "One day, we built thirteen from scratch," noted Harry with pride. Over the years, he and his wife did their best to preserve the history of that plant, giving presentations with their impressive display of photographs along with a model of a B-25 with a six-foot wingspan.[78]

The way Bill saw it, nobody liked going on bombing missions, but this was war and in times of war you do what you have to. He says: "The crews were unbelievable. They had nerves of steel. Every time we went up, it got a little harder, but everyone pushed themselves. Most of us were tense on the bomb run. After the bombs were released, it was getaway time." He thought Captain Cooper said it best: "Let's get the hell out of here!"

In his book, *This Time, This Place*, Jack Valenti, who flew fifty-one missions, explains what it was like to go on a bombing mission. There was the excitement when briefed by intelligence, the anticipation in taxiing toward the runway, the anxiety of taking off with a full bomb load, the gratitude for doing it successfully, and the linking up with the formation for the trip to the target. On the bomb run, however, heading into a field of flak, "it was all head-down concentration, because the plane had to be flown steady, steady, steady, so the lead planes could sight on the target. Then came the fear, sweaty, throat-grabbing, belly-twisting fear. It never varied."[79]

If the crews were lucky, they avoided the flak, dropped their bombs, and high-tailed it out of there safely. Very often, they were hit by the shrapnel from the exploding flak. Said Valenti: "When your plane was hit by shrapnel, you could feel the crunch and crack, and you could only pray that it hadn't hit anything vital."[80] It was routine for aircraft to be "holed" by shrapnel and it was routine for the ground crews to patch the holes with sheet metal. It was not routine for something vital to be hit, whether it be part of the aircraft or part of the body of someone in the aircraft. Unfortunately, Bill would soon find himself in an aircraft in which something vital was hit.

Chapter 5

SHOT DOWN

The Italian Campaign was in full force during May 1944. The Allied troops south of Rome mounted a spring offensive to break through the Gustav Line while bombing activity north of Rome picked up. The ground fighting was intense and the bombs were dropping at an accelerated pace. Because the same targets were bombed time and time again, the enemy got better at aiming their cannons at the attacking aircraft. Since the German engineers were able to repair bridges quickly, the Allied bombers were called upon to destroy them again.

As the Germans retreated, they too would destroy the bridges behind them in order to delay the troops in pursuit. Thanks to a British civil servant, Donald Bailey, who built model bridges as a kid and put his hobby to good use later by inventing the Bailey Bridge, the Allies were also able to replace bridges quickly. During the war, Allied engineers built Bailey Bridges totaling over 420 miles. Eisenhower considered the Bailey Bridge to be one of the three pieces of equipment, along with radar and the heavy bomber, that most contributed to the Allied victory in Europe.[1]

With German heavy artillery dug in around bridges that were likely to be bombed again, air crews had to muster all their courage to fly into the range of the feared German 88-mm anti-aircraft flak cannons because a direct hit could cut a plane in half. Bill Lanza saw this happen on a previous mission when the tail section of the lead ship went flying by his plane. Hitler was a strong advocate of the 88-mm cannons for their versatility and performance. He believed they were a more effective weapon against enemy bombers than fighter planes. As a result, the 88's were consistently given a high production priority in his arsenals of weapons.[2]

Bad weather hampered medium bomber missions in early May. However, when the weather improved later in the month, bombing activity was hectic. For example, the 321st Bomb Group flew fifty missions in May, almost double the twenty-eight missions flown in April.[3] This increased activity would take its toll.

In late May, Bill was assigned to fly with Major William Clark Hunter, whom he greatly respected. "Major Hunter was 'all balls.' Boy, was he a tough guy! He looked the part too. Most of us carried only our standard Army issue .45-caliber pistols in a shoulder holster, but he also carried a .38-caliber pistol on his hip. He was so determined to hit the target that he would take us on long bomb runs, increasing our chances of hitting the target but also increasing the chances of getting hit by German anti-aircraft fire. We lived dangerously with him at the helm, but boy were we effective!"

Bill thought Major Hunter was a tough Texan, but in fact he was a tough Indiana guy. His parents were married on the Clark family farm and he was raised on the Hunter farm in Williamsport, Indiana, the oldest of three boys. He was always called by his middle name, Clark, also the maiden name of his mother. His family had been grain farmers in the area for a long time, and his two younger brothers and their sons continued the tradition. Clark chose a different career path, and obtained a mechanical engineering degree from Purdue University on July 12, 1938. He was always grateful to his parents for providing financial support for his education despite their desire for him to carry on in the family tradition.

Purdue had a rich history in aviation and this most likely had an influence on Clark. During the 1930s, Purdue built its own airport, the first university-owned airport in the United States. With its own airport, it also became the first university in the United States to offer college credits for flight training.[4] Clark was in the Reserve Officers' Training Corps (ROTC) at Purdue, and five days after he graduated went on active duty.[5]

Clark wanted to fly. He enlisted in the Army Air Corps on May 12, 1940. He trained at Kelly Field in San Antonio, Texas. The airfield had been training "flying cadets" since it opened in 1917. In 1941, they were renamed "aviation cadets" and Clark was one of them. Between

Major William Clark Hunter
Courtesy of the Glaze, Hunter and McDonald Families

January 1939 and March 1943, over 6,800 men graduated from Kelly's Advanced Flying School.[6] The most famous pilot to receive aviation training at Kelly was Charles Lindbergh. Two years after graduating first in his class at Kelly Field in 1925, Lindbergh became a national hero when he became the first man to fly solo across the Atlantic.[7]

While in cadet training at Kelly Field, Clark met his future wife, Jean Collins, at a weekly cadet tea dance at the Gunter Hotel in San Antonio. Spanish customs prevailed at those dances. Young ladies would ride to the dances with their mothers. According to John Loeblein, who wrote about the social life at Kelly during the war, "they had to be chaperoned or else no nice girl would come."[8] He wrote that "those moonlight dances were out of this world." Clark no doubt felt the same way as he danced the night away with a very nice, very pretty young lady who would become his wife.[9]

Clark graduated from Kelly's Advanced Flying School and married Jean on July 31, 1941 in Oklahoma City. He was twenty-six and she was nineteen. At that time, he was in training at Will Rogers Field, named for the cultural and political icon from Oklahoma. The maid of honor, Jean's sister, Betty Blackburn, remembers Clark as a handsome, reserved, quiet man of whom she was in awe.

On August 15, 1942, while he was training at Key Field in Meridian, Mississippi, Clark and Jean had a child, William Clark Hunter, Jr., always called Bill. When Clark left for overseas duty, Jean and little Bill moved back to San Antonio to be near her family. Although Bill did not grow up with his birth father, he looked like him and always felt close to him.

The first three missions Bill Lanza flew with Major Hunter went very well. His friend Dunn was the navigator. He knew none of the other crew members. The targets were hit and they experienced little flak and no enemy fighters. The missions were flown north of Rome on May 17, 19 and 25, about the time the Allies were breaking through the Gustav Line. The way Bill saw it, "The only way to lick the Germans was to cut their supply lines."

Bill was part of a mighty offensive to do just that, and the Allied bombing north of Rome to disrupt supply routes to the German front line was finally paying dividends. The fourth battle of Monte Cassino was being won by the Allies and there was finally light at the end of the tunnel for the troops pinned down on the Anzio beaches. The stage was set for the liberation of Rome.

The May 17 target was the Viterbo airfield, located forty-seven miles northeast of Rome. Bill was familiar with this target. The last time he had seen it, on April 14, his plane was riddled by flak, which knocked the cover off one of the engines. It was the mission for which he was awarded the Air Medal. Captain Bounds led the May 17 mission comprising thirty-seven B-25s in three flights, and Hunter led one of the flights. The mission report stated: "Target very well covered with bombs starting east of road and crossing to southwest and west of landing ground."[10]

The May 19 target was a viaduct in Borge San Lorenzo, 207 miles northwest of Rome and sixteen miles northeast of Florence. Captain Wilson led the mission with twenty-five B-25s in two flights, and Hunter again led one of the flights. According to the mission report, "Excellent coverage of the target was reported with many strings [of bombs] right on center and two reports of seeing the bridge disintegrate."[11]

The May 25 target was a railroad bridge in Todi, 158 miles northeast of Rome. Hunter led the May 25 mission with twenty-five B-25s in two flights. Bill said he was an effective leader, and he peaked on this day. The mission report stated that all bombs landed in the target area with direct hits on both approaches to the bridge as well as on the center of the bridge. The mission operated at peak efficiency with a 100 percent bombing accuracy.[12] This meant that all bombs landed within an area six-hundred feet in radius from the center of the objective.[13]

On this day, the 12th Air Force had its most active day against enemy forces in Italy. Most medium bombers, including those in Hunter's formation, pounded bridges in central and northern Italy while light bombers and fighter bombers were supporting the ground troops engaged in the fourth battle of Monte Cassino.[14]

The excellence of the mission Hunter led prompted General Robert Knapp, the Commanding General of the 57th Bomb Wing, to cite it as the best he had ever seen in the following telegram that was received by the 321st Bomb Group on May 27, the day after Hunter was killed in action.

CONGRATULATIONS ON THE EXCELLENT BOMBING THE 321 BOMB GROUP HAS BEEN DOING DURING THE PAST FEW WEEKS. THE SUPERB BOMBING OF THE TODI ROAD BRIDGE ON MAY 25 WHERE YOUR STRIKE PHOTOGRAPHS SHOW 100% ACCURACY WAS THE BEST I HAVE EVER SEEN. IT IS MY

INTENTION AND PLEASURE TO REQUEST THAT THE 321 BOMB GROUP BE GIVEN A CITATION FOR THE MAY MISSIONS.[15]

Reynolds, Hunter's bombardier who sighted the Todi Road Bridge target, wouldn't be there either to read this citation, nor would be Brickner, Todd and Lanza, who also flew with Hunter on the May 25 mission. They would all be flying their last combat mission the next day.

Last Mission

On May 26, 1944, Bill flew for the fourth time with Hunter, who was again leading the mission. It was his last mission—a day he would never forget. It was just eleven days before the Allied forces in Italy liberated Rome on June 4, and thirteen days before the Allied forces in England crossed the English Channel for the Normandy Invasion on D-Day, June 6.

When the day began, Bill was thinking about the next day: "I was scheduled for some rest and relaxation in Egypt after this mission and was looking forward to the break. As luck would have it, I ended up having practically no rest or relaxation for the next couple of months." Still, his fate would be far better than that of some of the other crew members.

This was Bill's twenty-eighth mission. Unbeknownst to him, studies in England during World War II showed that odds of a crew member surviving twenty-five missions were not high. Less than 25 percent of bomber crew members made it to twenty-five missions because half the crew was either sick, wounded, transferred or mentally disabled. The odds improved to 50 percent of completing twenty-five missions once a member made it to twenty missions. Bill had already beaten these odds, but his luck was about to change.[16]

Bill was also flying his fourth mission with Todd, whose mother that day sensed he might be in trouble. His mother, Corinne, was picking strawberries on the family farm back in rural New York State, and a bird kept buzzing her. This wasn't normal, and she viewed it as an omen that something was wrong. She told her husband about it and was worried about her son Toddy. She would talk about this omen the rest of her life because her son was about to be shot down in enemy territory about four thousand miles away.

On this day, Bill was flying with a crew comprised of individuals from different parts of the United States. He was from Massachusetts, Hunter from Indiana and Todd from rural New York State. The others were co-pilot Second Lieutenant Walter H. Brickner from Pennsylvania, bombardier Second Lieutenant Laverne E. Reynolds from South Dakota, navigator Second Lieutenant John H. Kinney from California, and the engineer Sergeant John W. Denny, Jr. from Tennessee. Hunter was the oldest at 29, Bill was next at 27, Todd was 25, Bricker, Kinney and Reynolds were 24, and Denny was the youngest at 21. While Bill was flying his fourth mission with Hunter and Todd, this was only his second with Brickner and Reynolds, and his first with Denny and Kinney.

While many airmen trained with the same crew in the States, the crews were typically broken up overseas as the crew members replaced other crew members when positions opened up with other crews. According to Reynolds, when he got to Italy, he never flew with any of the crew members he trained with in the States. Bill, on the other hand, occasionally flew with some of those he trained with in the States.

Each day's flying assignments were posted for all to see. Said Bill: "Every day you looked at the bulletin board to see if you were flying. If you weren't flying, your time was yours unless someone was practicing landings or something like that and wanted you to go along. If you were flying, the names were sometimes familiar, sometimes not. Whatever the case, you just went up and did your job."

Orders for the missions on May 26 were sent by General Robert D. Knapp of the 57th Bomb Wing to Colonel Richard H. Smith, commander of the 310th, 321st and 340th Bomb Groups. It was his responsibility to implement those orders. The orders called for four missions by the 321st Bomb Group to bomb three bridges and a viaduct, each with a complement of planes from its four squadrons.[17]

On May 26, revised orders were received with different targets for two of those missions, one of which Bill was on. Instead of bombing a bridge and a viaduct in Poggibonsi, they were ordered to bomb a bridge and viaduct in Incisa in Val d'Arno, which is about twenty miles northeast of Poggibonsi. The first mission was to bomb the viaduct at 4:05 p.m., and the second mission, led by Hunter, was to bomb a bridge at 4:35 p.m. Since the viaduct and the bridge were near each other, if the flak was heavy on the first mission, it was likely to be heavy and more accurate on the second mission.[18]

As the crew members on Hunter's mission assembled for their briefing at 2:20 p.m., they were wearing their Mae West vests. Over them were their parachute harnesses to which they would attach their parachutes in the event of a bailout. The purpose of the briefing was to provide useful information to help them find the target, and to let them know what to expect from the enemy in the target area.[19] Intelligence officers briefed them using information collected from post-combat interviews with crew members who had flown missions in the target area. According to Brickner, they were told to expect heavy flak on the mission.[20] This was not a mission for the weak of heart.

After a twenty-minute briefing, the officers broke first and headed for the planes in trucks, and the enlisted men followed in their trucks. Bill recalls: "The mission was a nightmare all around. The truck I was riding in to my plane was delayed because we had to cross a runway that was in use by another flight [the one to bomb the viaduct].[21] When I got to my plane, the engines had already been started and the hatch was up. Todd saw me and lowered the hatch so I could board. I still don't know if the other gunners in that truck made their planes. In the rush, I never received a flak jacket or an escape kit, and I didn't even know if I had a parachute because I didn't see one when I boarded the ship. The escape kit would have come in handy later on the ground. It's probably a good thing that I forgot my .45-caliber pistol because I probably would have used it later on the ground and got in trouble. Not only did I forget my gun for the first time, but I also forgot my dog tags and a religious medal that I had worn on every mission but this one. Everything was going wrong."

A flak jacket was in essence a bullet-proof vest for airmen. It consisted of steel plates sewn in canvas that clipped together at the shoulders and hung in the front and back of the airman. It protected his vital parts from pieces of shrapnel from flak bursts that ripped through the thin metal or plexiglass that stood between him and the shrapnel.[22]

The escape kit was also called an escape and evasion kit because it was intended to help a downed airman escape from and evade the enemy. It was a small tightly-packed plastic box about the size of a paperback book that could be kept in the pant-leg pocket of an airman's flight suit. The contents could vary, but typically it contained a map of the area, called a silk map even though some were made of rayon;

a small compass in a case that could be swallowed in an emergency and utilized later; currency appropriate for use in the country they were flying over; a plastic bag and water purification pills; medications such as Benzedrine tablets to stay awake; morphine with a syringe to alleviate pain if necessary, along with bandages and adhesive tape; matches in a waterproof container; and photos of the airman in a suit that could be used in making a phony ID card such as a passport.[23]

Dog tags identified military personnel and were required to be worn at all times when on duty. They were small rectangular-shaped aluminum tags like those worn by dogs, hence the name. They had a small hole for a chain so they could be worn around the neck. There were two of them, both the same, so in the event an airman was killed in action, one could be collected while the other could remain with the body. If an airman went to a prisoner of war camp, the enemy collected one of them. If an airman were buried in a foreign cemetery, one would be buried with the body and the other placed on the grave marker. The information on the dog tag evolved from 1940 to 1946 and differed depending on the period in which it was issued and whether or not you were an officer. All of them had the airman's name, serial number, inoculations and blood type. Some also had the name and address of next of kin.[24]

Todd never received an escape kit either. Two months later, they were told during an intelligence briefing that the kits were in the front of the plane. They also learned later that they never received flak suits because, due to a shortage of flak suits, the crew of another ship on an earlier mission borrowed and didn't return them in time for their mission.[25]

The two morning missions were to create road blocks in towns not far from Rome. Reynolds, the bombardier on the afternoon mission with Bill, was also on one of the morning missions in which his aircraft encountered a problem. When they reached the target area, the bomb bay doors wouldn't open. Consequently, the aircraft returned to the base without having dropped its bombs. In other respects, both morning missions went well. Neither mission group ran into flak, but then again the heavy artillery was not likely to be positioned near road bridges. It was more likely to be positioned near railroad bridges because the Germans utilized the railways to transport the majority of their manpower and equipment to the front lines.[26]

The first afternoon mission group, which was taking off when Bill was trying to get to his plane, consisted of twenty-four B-25s escorted by twelve Spitfires. They ran into "heavy, intense and accurate" flak in the target area, and seventeen of the planes were "holed" by flak fragments. The right rudder and a section of the right stabilizer were shot off one aircraft, yet the pilot miraculously flew his aircraft back to Corsica where he and his crew bailed out before it crashed. His crew was fine, but he broke his leg when he landed. Several others in the formation were wounded by flak, but none seriously.[27] The fact that seventeen planes were hit by flak did not bode well for Hunter, who would soon lead a formation into the same general target area.

Hunter taxied to the runway and was preparing for takeoff at 3:21 p.m. Ever since side-by-side seating was designed for an aircraft, the pilot has been positioned on the left of the co-pilot in the pilot's compartment, also known as the flight deck. To Hunter's right was his co-pilot, Brickner. Even though Brickner was flying only his second combat mission, he had to be ready to assume Hunter's duties at any time during the flight if necessary.[28]

Walt Brickner was a professional baseball player before going off to war. His dream was to be a major leaguer. Before the war, he was heading in the right direction. Fresh out of high school in 1939, he signed with the Dover Orioles of Dover, Delaware in the Eastern Shore League.[29] Timing is important in sports, and luck just wasn't with him in his timing. He started his professional career in 1939, the same year that Hitler started World War II. While a storm was brewing overseas, he was progressing very well in his baseball career, but things changed when the storm hit.

After a short season with the Orioles in 1939, he played two full seasons with the Moultrie Packers of the Georgia-Florida League. He was always a slick-fielding, lefty first baseman with the versatility to play the outfield, and before the war he was hitting well to boot. In 1940, he had to be happy because the Moultrie Packers were an affiliate of his hometown Philadelphia Phillies, and he was performing well. He played 117 games and had a batting average of .318 with a slugging average of .400. In 1941, again playing for the Packers, now a Pittsburgh Pirates' affiliate, he played 132 games and had a batting average of .337 with a slugging average of .457.[30]

After a record of 47 wins and 91 losses in 1940, the Packers turned it around in 1941, winning 79 games and losing 61 to finish in second

Second Lieutenant Walter H. Brickner
Courtesy of the Museum of Idaho

place.[31] While the Packers were knocked out of the playoffs in the second round, Brickner had to feel pretty good about his contribution to the team. Little did he know at the time that he wouldn't be playing baseball again until late summer 1945.

When the storm hit in late 1941, Brickner chose to weather it. On January 28, 1942, less than two months after Pearl Harbor, Brickner decided to put his baseball career on hold, and he enlisted in the Army Air Corps.[32] After his pilot training, he was shipped overseas, and on May 15, 1944, was assigned as a co-pilot in the 446th Bomb Squadron of the 321st Bomb Group. Nine days later, he was ready to go on his second and last mission.[33]

In front of and below Hunter in the nose of the aircraft was the bombardier, Reynolds, who had already been on one mission that day. Laverne Reynolds grew up on a farm one mile north of Stickney, South Dakota. Stickney was a small town where he attended two different one-room country schools until high school. His grandparents lived near the high school in Plankinton, about ten miles away, so he stayed with them throughout high school. He was a lineman on the football team and in his senior year he must have been a tired lineman because he worked nights. He was the night telephone operator from 10:00 p.m. to 7:00 a.m. As to the pay, Reynolds notes: "I made only $20 a month of which twenty cents was taken out for Social Security." Despite this rigorous routine, he did well in school.[34]

In 1938, Reynolds enrolled as a student at South Dakota State College (now University) with the thought of teaching and coaching football in high school after graduation. Don Smith, the student who headed his floor one year, later turned out to be one of the best-known heroes of the war. After graduation, Smith became one of Doolittle's Raiders. He was the pilot of plane #15 who survived a plane crash at sea after successfully bombing a large aircraft factory in Japan, only to be in another plane crash seven months later in the British Isles that took his life in November 1942.[35]

In October 1939, Reynolds began his own journey that led to the war. He joined the South Dakota National Guard in the 109th Engineer Regiment. In February 1941, after he had completed two years and three months of college, his regiment was activated for a year of federal service. He and his friends were sent to Camp Claiborne in Louisiana for basic training as part of the 34th Infantry Division.

Shot Down

When Pearl Harbor was attacked in December 1941, Reynolds was thrust into the war for its duration. In early January 1942, his regiment was sent to Fort Dix in New Jersey where his company was broken up into two new companies. One of his friends, Harvey Schroeder, was in the one that shipped overseas, and he was in the one that remained at Fort Dix.

According to Reynolds, "During the summer of 1941, several of my friends and I tried to transfer to the Air Corps, but we were told that they didn't have any positions available at that time. However, when the war broke out they needed people so my friends decided to switch to the Air Corps. My folks didn't want me to fly, but I flipped a coin and it came up heads for me, so I joined my friends in the Air Corps and went home to await my orders."

His orders took him to two airfields in Alabama (Maxwell Field and Pryor Field), one in California (Santa Ana Army Air Base), and one in New Mexico (Kirkland Army Air Field) before he received his bombardier wings in April 1943. He then went to another airfield in New Mexico (Carlsbad Army Airfield) for navigation training, after which he went to Barksdale Field in Shreveport, Louisiana for crew assignment and training with a crew on a B-26. Although he trained with B-26 Marauders, he would end up flying in combat with B-25 Mitchells.

When he arrived in Shreveport, there were a number of bombardiers waiting for crew assignment, so he had some time on his hands. One day, he met two young ladies on a bus who were looking for the hospital on the base. Being the good soldier, he guided them to the hospital. One of the young ladies was Aline Gates, who, like him, was from a small town, but in a much warmer climate near Dodson, Louisiana. He asked her out on a date, and they hit it off. The relationship grew and led to marriage in Shreveport on October 9, 1943.

Three months later, the honeymoon ended. Reynolds received orders for overseas combat duty. The crew went to Savannah, Georgia to pick up a B-26. Some of the crew flew the aircraft overseas and others traveled by ship. Reynolds went by ship and the crew reunited in Casablanca, then flew together to Italy. Reynolds liked his crew, especially his pilot, Second Lieutenant Fred G. Ritger. Consequently, he was disappointed at the news that greeted him in Italy: "The crew I trained with was split up. We became replacements and were assigned to various B-25 squadrons. I never flew a mission again with my original crew."

Second Lieutenant Laverne E. Reynolds
Courtesy of the Reynolds Family

Reynolds was assigned to the 446th Bomb Squadron of the 321st Bomb Group to fly in B-25s. In March 1944, his bomb group was transferred to Solenzara, Corsica. On May 25, he was the lead bombardier for Hunter and operated at peak efficiency with a 100 percent bombing efficiency. The following day, he was about to fly on his thirty-ninth and last mission.

A crawlway led from the bombardier's compartment in the nose of the aircraft to a compartment behind the flight deck, sometimes referred to as the navigator's compartment. Typically, the bombardier on most B-25s was also the navigator and was positioned in the nose of the aircraft. In a lead aircraft, however, a bombardier with expertise in the Norden bombsight was positioned in the nose and concentrated on bombing. The lead navigator, on the other hand, was positioned behind the flight deck and concentrated on navigating. The lead navigator was Kinney.[36]

John Kinney was from the West Coast. He was born in Los Angeles and grew up in Sacramento. He loved the West Coast dearly, and would return to his native California after the war. But that's not all he loved dearly when he left the States for combat duty overseas.[37]

In 1940, Gwen Ellen Haines moved to Sacramento from Chicago with her family. Their new home overlooked a lawn and palm tree center divide at E Street and 21st Street, not far from the California State Capitol. Kinney and his friends would play football on the lawn of the center divide, and she would watch them play. How many passes he caught in those games is not known, but he caught something much more important, the eye of Gwen. He was twenty and working as an aeronautical draftsman. She was still in high school, but it was love at first sight.

On March 3, 1942, about three months after Pearl Harbor, Kinney enlisted in the Army Air Corps. He completed his preflight training in Santa Ana, California in June and his primary flight training in King City, California in August. Then, he and Gwen married in Sacramento on August 23. She took a job in the California State Capitol and he continued to receive navigation, bombardier and gunnery training at various locations such as Las Vegas, Nevada; Victorville, California; Carlsbad, New Mexico; and Columbia, South Carolina. Upon completion of his training, he headed for combat duty in Italy.

Kinney had studied aero engineering and put it to good use by training to be proficient in the skills of a navigator, namely pilotage (identifying present position and direction of flight through features on the ground), dead reckoning (plotting and flying a course based solely on mathematical calculations), radio navigation (obtaining position information from ground radio stations), and celestial navigation (determining position by reference to two or more celestial bodies.)[38] He learned his lessons well, and was the lead navigator on this mission.

On the aircraft leading the mission, Reynolds as lead bombardier and Kinney as lead navigator needed to be in sync with Hunter. Kinney was responsible for knowing the exact position of the aircraft at all times and for getting the formation to the target area. Once in the target area, Reynolds would take over on the bomb run, using the Norden bombsight to zero in on the target and put the formation on the bomb run to hit the target. Hunter, as commander of the ship, needed to orchestrate the process for it to be successful.

According to the *Pilot Training Manual for the B-25*, under a given set of conditions, such as the speed and altitude of the aircraft and the speed and direction of the wind, "there is only one point in space where a bomb may be released to hit a predetermined object on the ground."[39] It was up to Reynolds to find that point in space through the use of the Norden bombsight. Since the bombardiers on the other ships would release their bombs when Hunter's ship released its bombs, Reynolds' job was critical to the success of the mission. Consequently, if something bad happened to the lead ship and threw it off course, it would adversely affect the entire formation. German anti-aircraft batteries were keenly aware of this and, as one might logically conclude, aimed for the lead ship with their powerful cannons.

Because Hitler himself put such a strong emphasis on the importance of ground anti-aircraft defense, Germany had by 1944 more manpower devoted to anti-aircraft defense than was employed in the entire aircraft industry.[40] This emphasis strengthened its anti-aircraft proficiency, but it weakened its air power. So while there were fewer German fighters in the air to attack Allied bombers, the Germans had become better at shooting Allied aircraft out of the sky.

Just behind and above Kinney in the upper turret compartment was the engineer and top-turret gunner, Sergeant John W. Denny, Jr. The pilot depended on the engineer to know the aircraft's engines and armament equipment like the back of his hand.

Second Lieutenant John H. Kinney
Courtesy of the Kinney Family

SHOT DOWN OVER ITALY

Denny grew up on a farm in Neptune, Tennessee, a small rural community about thirty-five miles northeast of Nashville. His father was a dirt farmer, which is to say that he farmed his land without hired hands, but nevertheless used a mule to pull the plows. Someone once wrote that a poor dirt farmer had little cash but survived through his crop, his home garden, and an occasional slaughtered pig. Denny's father didn't have a pig, but the black family down the road raised hogs, so the two families traded with each other as farming families in rural America often do.[41]

Denny helped on the family farm until he went off to war. After graduating from high school in 1942, he enlisted in the Army Air Corps. Like many young men who grew up on farms, he was mechanically inclined, and attended the Airplane and Engine Mechanics School in Biloxi, Mississippi. Next, he trained as an engineer on a Mitchell B-25 bomber in Greenville, North Carolina. Following that, he was shipped overseas for combat duty in April 1944. He could never have envisioned the hellhole he would end up in after he was shot down.[42]

The bomb bay was behind and below Denny and a tight crawlway over it led into the radio operator's compartment occupied by Technical Sergeant Alfred Todd, the radio operator and waist gunner. The Mitchell bomber was loaded with radio equipment that the crew depended upon for communicating with one another and with other aircraft. Todd was responsible for knowing all there was to know about this equipment. Another tight crawlway behind Sergeant Todd led to the tail gunner's compartment, where Bill was positioned to defend the ship in the event of a surprise attack by enemy fighters. This was Todd's twenty-seventh combat mission and Bill's twenty-eighth.

Todd and Bill came from different backgrounds. Todd grew up in a small town in a rural area. Bill grew up in a large city in an urban area. Todd had one brother. Bill had five brothers and two sisters. Todd had completed high school and college. Bill had to leave high school after two years, but had been behind the counter of his father's stores for twelve hours a day by the time he entered the service. They may not have selected each other as tent mates, yet they would soon end up as cave mates.

As gunners, Denny, Todd and Bill were expected to be experts in aircraft identification, able to quickly distinguish between enemy and friendly aircraft and in the event of an enemy attack to quickly alert all crew

Sergeant John W. Denny, Jr.
Courtesy of the Denny Family

members to the position of an attacking aircraft using the clock system. They were also expected to be thoroughly familiar with their machine guns, and with each other's machine guns in case of an emergency.

Bill and Denny each manned flexible twin (double-barreled) fifty-caliber machine guns in their respective turrets. Todd in the waist compartment manned two flexible single-barreled fifty-caliber machine guns, one on each side of the aircraft. Reynolds, in the nose of the aircraft, also manned a flexible single-barreled fifty-caliber machine gun.[43] The turret gunners had to have good coordination. In case of a surprise attack, the safety of the ship depended on their having accurate eyes and steady hands, along with a delicate touch and a good sense of timing.[44]

The Mitchell B-25s had considerable firepower that enemy fighters were not eager to engage. Consequently, in his twenty-eight missions, Bill encountered few instances in which German fighters attacked a tight formation of B-25s. When they did, they would have a barrage of B-25 machine guns firing at them from all angles. And that's not all. They would be pursued by Allied escort fighters, just as swift and maneuverable as they were, aiming to blow them out of the sky. The shortage of German fighters for attacking Allied bombers was a good indication that the once mighty Luftwaffe wasn't so mighty anymore.

In all but his last four missions—those flown with Major Hunter in a B-25J aircraft—Bill was a top-turret gunner in a B-25C or a B-25D aircraft. He flew twenty-one missions in a C model and three in a D model. In the C and D models, the top turret was in the back of the aircraft, but in the J model it was moved forward right behind the flight deck. In a B-25J, the top turret was manned by the engineer. As a result, on this mission Bill manned the tail turret, a different experience. "When I was in the top turret, I always knew what was going on. In the tail turret, I didn't know. So when we got in trouble, I was guessing."

Major Hunter's shiny new unpainted aluminum B-25J aircraft was to lead a formation consisting of twenty-six B-25s flying in four boxes of six aircraft each, and trailing two spare aircraft for contingencies. The formation was to be escorted by twelve Spitfires that were ready to engage any fighters that tried to attack the bombers. The Spitfire was a British single-seat fighter that played a major role in defending England against the Luftwaffe in the Battle of Britain, where it earned legendary status in British air history—another venerable old "warbird."[45]

Hunter's new B-25J, which came off the assembly line in Kansas City, Missouri less than two months earlier on April 1, had arrived in Italy via the South Atlantic Route in late April. The B-25Js were flying off the assembly line at that time, and rushed overseas unpainted. They were manufactured exclusively at the Kansas City plant, which produced 4,318 B-25Js during the war. It was a solid, dependable aircraft. Generals Eisenhower and Arnold both used converted B-25Js as their personal transport planes.[46]

Many of the B-25Js remained unpainted during the hectic month of May, and without a logo design on the fuselage. However, each had markings on the twin tail fins to identify its bomb group, its bomb squadron, and the individual aircraft. On Hunter's aircraft, a red tip on the twin tail fins identified the 321st Bomb Group, a Roman numeral II identified the 446th Bomb Squadron (I was for the 445th, III for the 447th and IV for the 448th), and a tail number identified each ship.

The tail number on Hunter's ship, 327650, was derived from its serial number, 43-27650. The first two digits of the serial number indicated the year in which the aircraft was ordered, 1943, not the year in which it was delivered, 1944. Since it was assumed that all Army aircraft would be produced in the forties, the first digit was removed, along with the hyphen, to obtain the tail number. In 1941, when it was determined that a readily-visible number was necessary for identifying Army aircraft, the Army decided to identify planes with numbers of no less than four digits painted on the tail fins that were large enough to be seen from at least 150 yards away.[47]

Hunter's unpainted aluminum warbird gleamed in the sun, and had to be covered with camouflage netting when on the ground.[48] It gleamed in the sky too. Bill felt like a sitting duck in the shiny bird, especially on this sunny day.

Major Hunter led the group into the sky at 3:21 p.m. He was the flight leader of the planes from his 446th squadron, and Lieutenant Donald Armstrong was the flight leader for the planes from his 448th squadron. Since Hunter was also the leader of the entire formation, Armstrong was under his command on this mission.[49]

As with every mission, the planes took off and assembled into their formation in a rapid and orderly manner. They all knew their places and assembled at precisely 3:42 p.m. The aircraft in the 446th flight led by Hunter formed into two boxes of six aircraft each, one behind the other. The aircraft in the 448th flight led by Armstrong flew to Hunter's right, also in two boxes of six aircraft each, one behind and below the other. Each box contained two three-plane elements that flew in a "V" formation with a lead ship and a wing ship off each of its wings. Each trailing element, however, flew at different levels to avoid the turbulence left in the wake of the element in front of them. The turbulence caused by an aircraft slicing through the sky with spinning propellers could be substantial, as Bill would soon find out.

As the formation assembled into place, Hunter's leading three-plane element had Lieutenant Charles Burandt just off his left wing and Lieutenant Vernon Lewis just off his right wing. Both would later be challenged in trying to avoid a collision with Hunter's plane after it was clobbered by flak and knocked off course.

Lieutenant Frank Lonsdorf, piloting the wing ship on the rear element of Armstrong's flight, would later give an eyewitness account of what happened to Hunter's plane after it was hit, as would Sergeant Seaton Coleman, the top-turret gunner of the lead ship in that element flown by Lieutenant L.T. Lyons. The squadron leader of the Spitfire escort, a British fighter pilot by the name of Walmesley (rank and first name unknown), would also provide an eyewitness account of what happened to the distressed aircraft.[50]

For various reasons, two of the planes in the formation never even made it off the ground, hence the need for spares. This left the formation with twenty-four aircraft and no spares in the sky. By 3:55 p.m., they rendezvoused with the twelve Spitfires that would escort them to the target and protect them from enemy fighters. The mission objective was to bomb a railroad bridge over the Arno River just north of Incisa in Val d'Arno, a small town about twelve air miles southeast of Florence. Because the bridge was expected to be well-guarded by flak cannons, they had an alternate target, a road bridge in Cecina.[51] Cecina was on the way back to the base from Incisa.

At precisely 4:00 p.m., Hunter's navigator, Kinney, charted a northeast course to the target area about 174 miles away. His course was true and within a half-hour they were approaching the target area.[52] Tension built as Hunter got ready to lead the formation on the bomb run. All crew members knew their responsibilities. For the mission to be successful, every crew member in every aircraft needed to concentrate on doing his job.

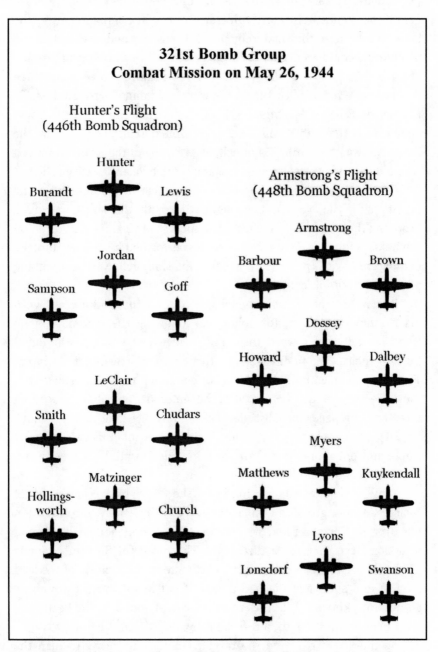

**321st Bomb Group
Combat Mission on May 26, 1944**

Hunter's Flight
(446th Bomb Squadron)

Hunter
Burandt
Lewis

Jordan
Sampson
Goff

Armstrong's Flight
(448th Bomb Squadron)

Armstrong
Barbour
Brown

Dossey
Howard
Dalbey

LeClair
Smith
Chudars

Matzinger
Hollings-worth
Church

Myers
Matthews
Kuykendall

Lyons
Lonsdorf
Swanson

Last Mission: Major Hunter led 24 Mitchell B-25s into combat on May 26, 1944, the day that his plane was shot down over Italy.

A bomb run begins at the Initial Point and it ends at the Release Point. The planes were most vulnerable during the few minutes of the bomb run because they had to fly precisely straight and level so that the bombardier could accurately sight the target. Harry D. George, a co-pilot of a B-25 that was also shot down over Italy, said: "Those two or three minutes were terror-filled times...We were goddamned sitting ducks..."[53] Lieutenant Edward V. Crinnion, a pilot who flew in the 446th Bomb Squadron of the 321st Bomb Group, had similar sentiments. To him the bomb run was "four minutes of hell, as everyone in the formation was a sitting duck, flying straight and level, unable to take any evasive action."[54]

Bombardier Reynolds had the critical task of zeroing in on the target using the Norden bombsight. Since all the ships would be dropping their bombs on his lead, the success of the mission rested on Reynolds' shoulders. The day before, he performed his job as Hunter's bombardier with perfection as the mission achieved a bombing accuracy of 100 percent.

Perched in the plexiglass-enclosed nose of the lead aircraft with his Norden bombsight, Reynolds was following the landmark Arno River as it flowed toward the target bridge just north of the small town of Incisa. The bombsight was turned on and ready for his input. The bombsight contained an analog computer that would calculate the trajectory of the bombs after he entered data about the wind direction, airspeed and altitude of the aircraft.[55] Like most systems, its output was only as good as its input, so Reynolds had to carefully gauge and enter precise information in order to attain a precise hit. The previous day, he had done just that.

While Reynolds was zeroing in on the target bridge just north of Incisa, German gunners east of the target bridge were zeroing in on his aircraft. German radar was tracking his aircraft for the range and direction necessary for a direct hit. The powerful 88-mm cannons fired potent twenty-pound shells to detonate in the vicinity of the lead aircraft and spew forth jagged pieces of hot metal to rip through its aluminum skin. As lethal as these pieces of metal could be to any crew member in its path, a direct hit by a shell could be far worse.[56]

As the aircraft neared the target, Hunter was ready to turn the control of the aircraft over to the autopilot that was connected to the bombsight so that, as Reynolds lined up the target in the cross hairs of the bombsight, the aircraft would respond to his fine-tuning.

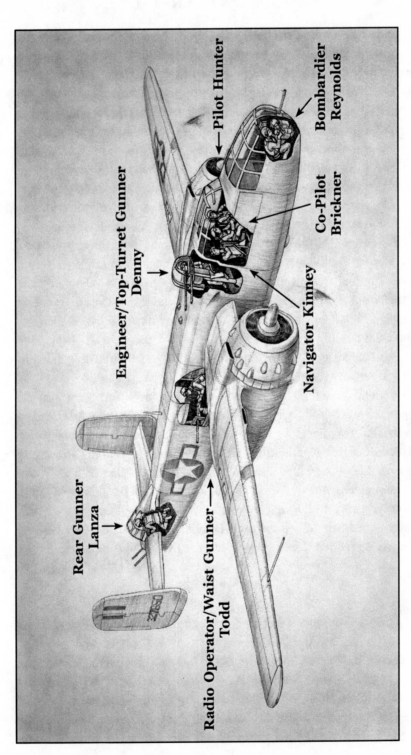

Pilot Hunter

Bombardier Reynolds

Co-Pilot Brickner

Engineer/Top-Turret Gunner Denny

Navigator Kinney

Rear Gunner Lanza

Radio Operator/Waist Gunner Todd

Crew Positions on Bomb Run

Reynolds did his fine-tuning by feel as he peered through the sight, carefully turning knobs to line up the aircraft until the target stopped moving in the crosshairs of his sight. At that point, the Norden analog computer took over the aircraft and the bomb run began with the bombs to be released by the computer at the precise point that it calculated the trajectory necessary for the bombs to hit the target.[57]

According to the mission report, the bomb run started at 4:31:30 p.m., its Initial Point. The expectation was that they would be over the target and release their bombs in three and a half minutes at 4:35 p.m., the anticipated Release Point. As they entered the bomb run, the flak was heavy. They would soon find out that it was also accurate.

Bill notes: "On the approach to a bomb run, I was always nervous, probably in the same way a football player gets butterflies before a game. The fear was always there, but you overcame it. When we were on the bomb run and the flak was flying, I was concentrating more on doing my job than anything else. I was scanning the sky for enemy fighters and could see all our planes behind us. I was a little more nervous than usual on this mission because I didn't have a flak suit on to protect my vital parts."

Reynolds had his earphones on and was concentrating only on the target. Meanwhile, black puffs of exploding shells were discharging deadly flak fragments in their direction. Far below, the Arno River was winding like a snake through the valley, and German cannons on the east side of the valley were spitting up heavy artillery.[58] The bomb-bay doors were wide open on all the aircraft, and the bombardiers in the other aircraft had their fingers on their bomb release buttons, all anxiously waiting to release their bombs as soon as Hunter's aircraft released its bombs. Then, they would get the hell out of there.

Disaster Strikes

Almost three minutes into the bomb run and thirty-five seconds before bombs away, disaster struck! Hunter's plane was pounded by enemy flak![59] Brickner said later that flak fragments struck the right engine, wings and fuselage.[60] Walmesley later reported that the aircraft received a direct hit in its right engine. Kinney thought the first burst of flak hit the nose, wounding Reynolds, and that the second burst knocked out the right engine, cut the hydraulic system, and penetrated the oil lines.[61] While everything on the mission up to this point was precise, this was a traumatic event in which precision was no longer the modus operandi.

Sixty-five years later, Reynolds, who was in the nose, said it wasn't hit and that he wasn't wounded. However, he said he heard someone yelling that either he was hit or the plane was hit. It was Kinney who was hit. He was hit in the knee by flak for which he later received a Purple Heart. Bill figured it must have been Denny who was hit because he was told later on the ground by partisans that Denny was in pain when he was picked up by the enemy. He was indeed in pain, excruciating pain, but it wasn't from a flak wound.

With a dead right engine no longer able to create the thrust necessary to keep pace with the left engine, the nose of the aircraft pulled sharply to the right (yawed right in pilot nomenclature), further complicating the situation by blocking the wind that helped to buoy up the right wing. Without pilot intervention, the aircraft was in danger of turning over and going into a spin. Once a plane goes into a spin, the centrifugal force of the spin and the force of the downward plunge could pin the crew against the fuselage and prevent them from bailing out.[62]

Hunter needed to act quickly to regain control of the aircraft, and Brickner needed to help him in this multitasking endeavor. To prevent an explosion, they shut down the fuel lines to the right engine. To reduce the drag of the right propeller, they tried to feather it, a procedure to turn the sharp sides of the propeller blades into the wind. B-25s are built to operate with one engine, but that's after feathering the dead propeller to give it the least resistance to the air. According to Brickner, the engine could not be feathered, adding to their problems.[63]

To understand what Hunter was up against in regaining control of his aircraft, it is helpful to understand how a pilot flies a B-25 Mitchell bomber under normal conditions, using directional controls to change the pitch, roll, and yaw of the aircraft, and throttle controls to change the thrust of the aircraft. Basically, the flight controls enable a pilot to alter the angles of the aircraft's control surfaces so that the relative wind hits them in ways that allow the pilot to control the flight of the aircraft.

The pilot controls an aircraft's pitch (nose up or down) with a column, called a stick; and the aircraft's roll (bank left or right) with a steering wheel attached to the column, called a yoke. For nose down, he pushes the stick forward, causing the elevators (hinged sections on the back wings) to go down to meet the resistance of the relative wind in such a way that it pushes the tail up, and thus the nose down. For nose up, he pulls the stick back, causing the elevators to go up so that the relative wind pushes the tail down, nose up.[64] To roll right, he turns the yoke to the right, which moves the ailerons (hinged sections on the outboard portions of the front wings) in opposite directions (right aileron up, left aileron down) so that the relative wind causes the plane to bank right. To roll left, he turns the yoke to the left, which has the opposite effect. Cables connect the stick and yoke to the elevators and ailerons.[65]

The pilot controls the yaw, or right- or left-movement of the aircraft with foot pedals connected by cables to the twin rudders (hinged sections on the tail fins). By stepping on the left rudder pedal, he can move the rudders to the left so that the relative wind pushes the tail right, causing the nose to yaw left. Likewise, by stepping on the right pedal, he can cause the nose to yaw right.[66]

Hydraulics assist the pilot in operating these directional controls in much the same way as power steering helps a driver to steer a car. Basically, hydraulics provide power from fluid under pressure.[67] Consequently, severed hydraulic lines are a pilot's nightmare, akin to losing power steering in a car.[68] Without these hydraulic assists, brute strength is necessary to bring a distressed aircraft under control, especially one the size of a Mitchell bomber.

The pilot controls the power of the aircraft with mixture controls (a rich, or higher fuel/air mixture, helps to prevent the engine cylinder heads from overheating at high speeds), propeller controls (an increase in the pitch, or angle, of the propeller blades results in more appropriate bites of the wind for any increase in a propeller's revolutions per minute), and throttle controls (an increase in the volume of fuel, like stepping on the gas, creates more power).[69]

Because Hunter's aircraft was large (over 67 feet wide and 53 feet long), heavy (about 33,000 pounds normally loaded), and fast (about 200 mph on the bomb run), its momentum was substantial when it lost its right engine.[70] To overcome the sudden loss of power in the right engine and the abrupt swing of the nose to the right, Hunter had to do a number of things, the most important of which was to stop the aircraft from yawing right by using every ounce of his strength to push down hard on the left rudder pedal.[71] Brickner no doubt was doing the same with his left rudder pedal.

Since the aircraft lost half its power when the right engine was destroyed, Hunter also had to quickly increase the power in the left engine. He went "full bore"—full speed ahead on the mixture controls, the propeller controls and the throttle controls. When he did so, the engine roared as would a car engine when flooring it, but considerably louder. The higher-powered engine and the faster-spinning propellers also caused the aircraft to shiver with intensity.

Bill, in the back of the plane, was shaken when the plane was hit: "When we got hit the first time, the concussion was so great that it pulled the triggers out of my hands. I figured it was time to get out of the tail turret because I didn't have a parachute on."

Kinney thought the first flak burst hit the nose, but it most likely hit the rear of the aircraft where Bill was positioned and felt its impact. It could be that the elevators were damaged by the concussion. If so, this would make it even more difficult for Hunter to lift the nose of the aircraft, a problem he would later encounter.

Bill continues: "As I started to back out of the rear turret, we got clobbered again, worse than before. Oh, what a concussion! That was probably the blast that knocked the right engine out. Before the blast, I could see all the planes behind me. After it, they all disappeared. I wasn't sure what the damage was, but I knew it was bad because someone yelled 'I'm hit!' or 'We're hit!'"

Reynolds, unlike Bill, said he was never nervous on a bomb run, which is probably why he had registered 100 percent accuracy on the previous day's mission. This is pretty amazing considering that he was nearly blinded a few weeks earlier on a combat mission. "I was hit in the face around my nose and between my eyes and my face was covered with blood. I had to keep my eyes shut all the way back to the base." He received the Purple Heart for that incident. Fortunately, he escaped serious injury and wasn't scarred for life.[72]

On this day, with his earphones glued to his head and his eyes glued to the target through his Norden bombsight, Reynolds remained focused and released his bombs despite the disruptions. He always thought they hit the target. Over six decades later, he learned that only six ships released their bombs, and that some reportedly hit just short of the bridge and others just over the bridge on the northwest bank of the river.

Hunter was focused too, on saving his crew and his ship. With the help of Brickner, he was strenuously trying to control the ship, which had left the formation, peeling ninety degrees to the right and down. His wing ships, piloted by Burandt and Lewis, had also left the formation to avoid a collision with Hunter's ship. They ended up returning to the base with an escort of two Spitfires.[73]

In the back of the plane, Bill was trying to brace himself: "When I stood up, the plane was in a dive. It was vibrating violently, the noise was deafening, and black smoke from the flak had entered the ship through the bomb bay doors. The smoke had the strong smell of gunpowder. I located my chute and put it on, then sat down, staring at Todd who was on the interphone. I was ready to go."

While Todd had Bill's attention, the disabled aircraft had the attention of the residents in the valley below. They were watching this drama unfold in the sky above them. One of the observers, teenager Amerigo Sarri, would later tell Bill that, after his plane was hit, the roar of the engine (when Hunter revved up the left engine) could be heard throughout the valley.

When Hunter's aircraft suddenly swung right and plunged down, he was fortunate to avoid hitting his two wing ships, which recovered and headed home. Armstrong led the remaining twenty-one aircraft to the alternate target, a road bridge in Cecina. That bomb run was successful, with direct hits reported. Cecina was about fifty-three miles southwest of Incisa.[74]

After dropping their bombs in Cecina, all but one of the Mitchells flew the remaining 113 miles back to their home base in Solenzara, Corsica. The one exception was Lieutenant Alan Sampson's plane that made an emergency landing at the 310th Bomb Group's field in Ghisonaccia, Corsica, because his bombardier, Lieutenant Warren Williams, was wounded by flak fragments and needed immediate medical attention. Ghisonaccia is about twelve miles north of Solenzara. One of Bill's friends from Massachusetts, Sergeant Edward Leary, was also hit by flak, in his right leg, and received medical attention at the home base. The only aircraft not to return from the mission was Major Hunter's.[75]

Abandon Ship

While Hunter had been successful in preventing the aircraft from rolling over, he was still struggling to regain control. His course had abruptly changed ninety degrees from northeast to southeast. He was losing altitude and was heading toward the mountains, lots of them. Realizing the extent of the problem, he gave the order for all crew members to abandon ship.[76]

The plane was leaving the Arno River Valley and flying toward the Pratomagno Mountains, the Catenaia Alps (Alpe di Catenaia) beyond them, and the Luna Alps (Alpe della Luna) beyond them still, all part of the Apennines, the chain of mountains that run up the spine of the Italian peninsula. The three mountain ranges reached heights of 5,078, 4,639 and 4,770 feet, respectively.[77] The aircraft's loss of altitude while heading toward these mountains put Major Hunter and his crew in a frightful situation.

Bill got the signal to bail from Todd. "Todd was on the interphone listening carefully for further instructions. When he looked at me and pointed to the escape hatch, it was time to go. The plane was diving and we had trouble opening the hatch. We were kicking it and, when the plane leveled off a bit [thanks to Hunter] the hatch gave way. You could see the patchwork on the ground below. I figure that we were at about 7,000 feet.

"I never had any experience in jumping before, and was trying to remember what we were told. I remembered something about a hinge. When I sat down with my back to the front of the plane and dropped my legs though the hatch, they were whipped back up, and I fell backwards. I could hear the flak—Boom Boom Ba Boom! It was deafening, but I had to go, so in one motion I just put my legs down again, braced my arms against the aft side of the hatch so I wouldn't hit my face, and slid out feet first.

"Wham! I slammed against the bottom of the fuselage, just as I felt a terrible concussion from a flak burst. I was gripping the rip cord tightly with my right hand and instinctively yanked it when I hit the plane. My chute opened almost immediately. As my chute opened, I could see the bottom of the ship above me. It looked so close. Then I felt a jolt. Oh what a jolt! It felt like the force of a hundred horses pulling on my shoulders."

In a B-25J, there is a front escape hatch and a back escape hatch, and the bail-out procedures are different. To bail through the front hatch, the correct procedure is to stand at the forward edge of the hatch facing the rear of the plane, crouch, place your hands on the aft side the hatch and drop feet first through the hatch, using your hands

Aircraft in Distress: Major Hunter pulls aircraft out of a dive, enabling Sergeants Lanza and Todd to bail out over enemy territory.

and arms to protect your face and head from injury. This is basically what Bill did, but through the rear hatch. To jump from the rear hatch, the correct procedure is to stand at the aft edge of the hatch, facing the front of the plane, crouch and grip the aft edge of the hatch by your feet, then roll out headfirst as if your hands and feet were a hinge.[78] Otherwise, as Bill experienced, you could be whipped against the bottom of the aircraft by the air turbulence.

Todd followed right behind Bill. He didn't pull his cord as quickly and, when his chute mushroomed, he was at about the same altitude as Bill. The formation had banked to the right after aborting the bombing. Lieutenant Lonsdorf was flying the wing ship in the rear element of the second box in Armstrong's flight and saw the two men bail out in rapid succession. He could see the wounded aircraft beneath his right wing and slightly off to the right heading in the same direction as the formation. About ten seconds later, he saw another man bail out, but his chute didn't open for about seven or eight seconds. That was Denny, the engineer and top-turret gunner. Lonsdorf then lost sight of Hunter's plane because he had to concentrate on flying his own plane.[79]

Bill recalls: "When I last saw our ship, it was banking dizzily and pouring black smoke from the right engine. The impression it left me with was that Major Hunter was desperately trying to bring it under control." Bill's gut feeling, however, was that it would never be brought under control. This is what he reported to military intelligence two months later.[80]

As did Bill and Todd with the back hatch, Kinney had trouble opening the front hatch. It looked to him as though constant treading on the door caused the hinges to bind, but in several moments of struggling he finally forced it open.[81]

It is difficult to know exactly who bailed first out of the front hatch. According to the intelligence briefing of Kinney, the next one out of the aircraft was Denny.[82] However, sixty-five years later, Reynolds said he was the first one to bail out of the front hatch. Since Denny landed near Todd, it seems as though he must have been the next man out because two witnesses in other aircraft saw the first three chutes blossom one after another.

Denny in the upper turret most likely saw Kinney below him struggling to open the front hatch. Having seen Lanza and Todd bail

131

out of the back hatch, Denny probably climbed over the bomb bay into the waist compartment and bailed out of the back hatch too.

When Hunter gave the signal to bail, Reynolds says he left his position in the nose of the aircraft and crawled through the narrow passageway under the flight deck into the navigator's compartment. When he got there, Kinney was kicking the hatch, bad knee and all, to get it open. Once the hatch was open, he says Kinney gave him the signal to bail and out he went. Reynolds figures he jumped at 6,000 feet and recalls: "After I jumped, I wished I had stayed on the plane. It looked like it was going back to the base."

Hunter must have brought the plane under control because just as Kinney was about to jump, Brickner called him back, saying that they might be able to make it. To Reynolds, who was descending in his chute, the plane looked under control, and Reynolds doesn't recall seeing any smoke. The oil probably drained out of the smoking engine and cut off the trailing black smoke. Bill always thought Hunter was trying to make it to the east coast to ditch the plane in the Adriatic Sea.

Kinney stated that Major Hunter was desperately trying to trim the aircraft, but was unable to do so.[83] An aircraft is trimmed when its wings and fuselage are level with the ground, such as when a plane floats in for a landing (an aircraft could be also trimmed at a slight descent). A trimmed aircraft would have relieved the flight control pressures felt by Hunter, relieving him from the physical exertion of trying to level the plane.[84] Unable to hold altitude with a mountain coming up fast, Hunter ordered Kinney to jump.[85]

Kinney said he bailed out at about 4,000 feet, but noted that the altitude of the country below was 3,000 feet.[86] Brickner stated later that he thought Kinney bailed at 3,000 feet.[87] Since they were traveling over terrain with peaks and valleys, estimating distances from the ground in panic mode is not an exact science.

Hunter also ordered Brickner to jump, and Brickner thought he went out the hatch at about 2,000 feet. As he left the ship, he said that Hunter was still struggling to level the aircraft, and that it was losing altitude at 1,500 to 2,000 feet per minute.[88] This left Hunter with insufficient time to save himself.

Kinney said he saw Brickner bail out before the plane disappeared over a mountain ridge.[89] The ridge was in the Centenaia Alps, on the other side of which was the Upper Tiber Valley, and beyond that the Luna Alps.

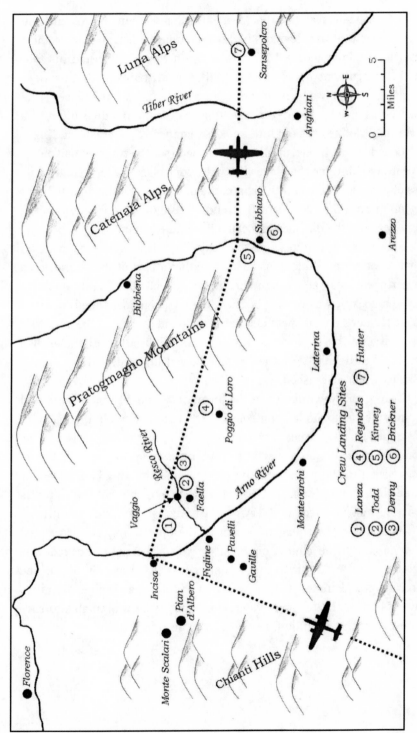

Flight Path of Aircraft and Landing Sites of Crew

It is conceivable that the reason Hunter was unable to trim the aircraft was that the elevators had been damaged. This would account for Brickner later telling Bill's friend Dunn that Hunter had his foot on the instrument panel when he left him to bail out. If this were the case, Hunter was caught between a rock and a hard place. If he released the stick, the aircraft would nose down into a dive and it was curtains. It looks as though he took his chances on a crash-landing.

Lonsdorf had picked up the ship in time to see the two men bail out. It appeared to him that the plane was under control except for a continuous loss of altitude. Then, he lost sight of it again. However, he reported that his tail gunner, Staff Sergeant Holtzendorf, using his binoculars, saw the plane crash in the distance and catch fire immediately.[90]

Subsequent accounts given to Kinney by reliable partisans made no mention of a fire. While it is conceivable that a part of the aircraft may have ripped loose and caught fire upon impact, it is highly doubtful that the cockpit was on fire because the partisans described in detail Major Hunter's personal effects that were found on him in the aircraft.[91] Not only that, but a report sent to the family three months later also described in detail the clothes he was buried in, namely those he was wearing when he crashed.

Two other eyewitnesses in the formation thought that Hunter had brought the ship under control. Staff Sergeant Seaton L. Coleman, the upper turret gunner in an aircraft flying in the same element as Lonsdorf, saw the ship starting down on a steep angle after it was hit, veering to the right with the right engine smoking badly. He saw three chutes open (Lanza, Todd and Denny) and thought the ship was brought under control at a very low altitude, but he didn't see it hit.[92]

Walmesley, the squadron leader of the Spitfire escort, also stated that he saw three chutes open, after which the plane headed east under control.[93] The truth of the matter was that the only reason the aircraft looked under control was that Hunter was giving his all to save his crew. He did save his crew but, sadly, he was unable to save himself. By any definition, he was a true hero of the war.

Chapter 6

PARTISAN HELP

Watching the action in the air from a farm in Vaggio, a small village in Tuscany, were, among others, Riccardo Becattini, a farm worker, and Amerigo Sarri, a teenage boy. Riccardo was also a partisan, and Amerigo's father, Goffredo, was a partisan leader. They saw the plane get hit and the three chutes open in their vicinity while the aircraft continued on a southeasterly course toward the mountains. Partisans helped Allied airmen who were shot down, and would soon spring into action to try to reach the airmen before the Fascists or the Germans.

High above, Bill Lanza was quietly descending into enemy-occupied territory. "When I jumped, the Germans were still shooting, but when my chute opened, the flak stopped. They had me like a clay pigeon, but I guess they wanted to capture me instead. I was thinking that it was decent of them not to blow me away. As I was descending, I could see Todd drifting away from me." Bill must have been facing north as he descended because the aircraft was headed in a southeasterly direction and he remembers seeing the aircraft and Todd to his right.

"At one point, my chute started to oscillate. I was swinging back and forth, and that's not all. About that time I noticed a fire far below on my left, and I was thinking I might be going from the frying pan into the fire. I was up pretty high, so I tried to steady the chute by pulling on the shroud lines, but this didn't seem to help so I stopped pulling. Fortunately I drifted away from the fire. It was very quiet and I felt very vulnerable. I was wondering how I was going to get out of this mess. As I got closer to the ground, I could see cliffs and was worried I might hit them, but fortunately I drifted over them. I could also hear vehicles, and then the ground seemed to come up mighty fast.

"Since I had never jumped before, I didn't know how to land. I remembered someone saying you should relax so I tried to relax but, boy, did I get a belt when I hit the ground! I landed on an incline on a farm and fell back on my buttocks and hit my head. I was surprised I didn't get knocked out. Later, I found out that that Kinney got knocked unconscious when he landed. Before I landed, I saw another chute in the distance and learned many years later it was Denny's."

Bill landed about a mile north of the village of Vaggio near another small village called Montanino. "When I landed, a farmer and two kids came running toward me. The kids were yelling 'Americano, Americano!' and grabbing me. We could hear the distinctive sound of the German vehicles getting closer. Fortunately, I spoke Italian and understood the farmer when he pointed to a wooded hill and told me to run and hide."

Bill didn't waste any time. "As I was hurrying out of my chute, I noticed that the lenses were missing from my goggles. They must have popped out. I couldn't believe it. Then, I took off. I ran as fast as I could up the hill. It was more like a mountain. I ran and ran, all the way to the crest, which ended on a steep cliff. I was totally exhausted, but put my years of infantry training to good use. I found low ground and covered my body with leaves. I was about fifteen feet from the crest of the hill. The woods were thick and there were a lot of leaves on the ground."

Danger soon approached: "Two German soldiers went right by me to the top of the hill. I could hear them and was surprised that they sounded so young. I could also see them. They were yelling something and shooting in the air. I was twenty-seven at the time, so maybe that's why they seemed so young to me. Eventually, they left. That was a close shave. I ended up sleeping in the leaves that night. I was so tired. I slept very well."

Some German soldiers were kids. Nine days later on June 4, when the U.S. Fifth Army liberated Rome after the Germans had evacuated the city, snipers fired at some of the American soldiers in the outskirts of the city. The shots came from three German soldiers, ages twelve to fourteen years. They had camouflage uniforms and high-powered rifles with scopes.[1] Most likely, they were products of Hitler Youth, a paramilitary organization in Germany since 1922. By 1943, Nazi leaders began viewing these youngsters as a military reserve to replenish the manpower being lost in battle. Every available male from sixteen to sixty was conscripted into service.[2]

By the end of the war, some German soldiers were even younger. For example, on April 29, 1945, when American forces liberated Stalag VII-A, a prison camp in Moosburg, Germany, they took as prisoners about 6,000 Germans. Among them were fully-uniformed and armed nine-year-old boys.[3]

Bill awoke to his first day in Nazi-occupied central Italy. He was still wearing his parachute harness and his yellow Mae West life jacket. "I noticed that a piece of leather was torn off the sole of my shoe, and figured it was the result of slamming against the bottom of the plane when I bailed out. As I was sitting there contemplating my next move, a young kid caught my eye. He was about twelve or thirteen years old and walked with a limp. He had an iron leg-brace like my brother's and was wearing a black shirt. It looked like he was just taking a walk through the woods. He saw me and stopped in his tracks. As he was staring at me, saying nothing, I walked over to him and explained to him in Italian that I had been shot down. I also asked him not to tell anyone that he saw me. He listened and nodded, not saying a word, then continued on his way. Because he was wearing a black shirt, I didn't trust him, so I changed my position. I knew that Fascists wore black shirts."

Bill's concern was well founded because young men being indoctrinated in Fascist ideology did indeed wear black shirts. While American boys are encouraged to join the Cub Scouts and later the Boy Scouts, Italian boys were pressured to join a Fascist youth organization called the *Balilla* at ages eight (sometimes earlier) to fourteen, and later the *Avanguardisti* at ages fourteen to eighteen. In both organizations, they were required to wear, among other things, black shirts, and were trained in a regimented manner to become *Fasci di Combattimento*—Fighting Young Fascists.[4]

The Boy Scout promise differs greatly from the *Balilla* promise. The Boy Scout promise is: *On my honor I will do my best to do my duty to God and my country and to obey the Scout Law; to help others at all times; to keep myself physically strong, mentally awake, and morally straight.*[5] The *Balilla* promise was: *I swear to execute without discussion the orders of the Duce and to serve with all my strength and if necessary with my blood the cause of the fascist revolution.*[6]

The closest thing to the *Avanguardisti* program in the United States was probably the Boston School Cadet program of which Bill and every male student over thirteen years of age in Boston were a part. The program's foremost champion and defender, Captain Hobart Moore, later General Moore, said that military training "helps training boys to the habits of obedience, obedience which is prompt, which is unquestioned, and which boys feel to be manly. It develops a more manly spirit in the boy, invigorates his intellect...makes him more graceful and gentlemanly in his bearing, and fits him to the primary duties of life—those of a good citizen."[7] In sum, the military drills were intended to instill a certain sense of duty and discipline, but the Boston program was a far cry from the *Avanguardisti* program.

The requirement to wear black shirts in these Italian youth organizations stemmed from the Blackshirts, Mussolini's henchmen. Mussolini believed in force to achieve his means and from the start of Fascism in 1922, he had squads to carry out this doctrine that were known as Blackshirts, or the Black Militia. By the end of the war, even the Germans thought the Italians hated the Blackshirts more than they hated the Germans.[8] Many people, Bill among them, considered those who wore black shirts to be supporters of Fascism.

"Later that morning, about ten o'clock, I walked down to the farm. I saw the farmer's sons working the field and asked them to get their father. The farmer came back with a bottle of wine and some cheese, and told me to go back in the woods and hide again. He told me he was going to contact somebody to help me."

Partisans to the Rescue

If Bill had been shot down over Italy early in the war, the farmer probably wouldn't have known where to go for help. The Italian Resistance was then in its formative stages. It took a while for the underground network to develop so that farmers and residents of small villages knew who to contact for help.[9] By 1944, the underground resistance was pretty well established, and the farmer knew who could help Bill.

"In the afternoon, about four o'clock, I was hiding in the woods and feeling pretty good because the wine was strong and the cheese was delicious. The farmer knew my approximate location, and directed the partisan to me. He was carrying a bag of civilian clothes.

Goffredo Sarri
Courtesy of the Sarri Family

I changed from my military clothes to my new white shirt and an oxford gray suit. I gave him my clothes, but kept my shoes."

Bill was now engaged in a high-risk venture. While in uniform, if captured, he would become a prisoner of war. As such, he would be subject to humane treatment under the Geneva Convention, even though under wartime conditions existing in Italy at that time this wasn't always the case. Out of uniform, however, even though he wasn't a spy, he might be viewed a spy, and thus be subject to far different treatment, maybe even death.

Bill recalls that the partisan put his clothes in the bag, noting: "The partisan's last name was Sarri. That's all I ever called him." Goffredo Sarri had lived and worked in Figline Valdarno. He owned a shoe factory in that town with fifteen employees until it was destroyed by Allied bombs. In December 1943, the threat of his home being bombed prompted him to move his family to a farm in Vaggio that was owned by a friend who also owned the agricultural company that sold the farm's produce. The farm was operated by a sharecropper who lived on and operated the farm, but shared the produce with the landowner.

Riccardo Becattini's father, Gosto (Costantino) was the sharecropper, and Riccardo and his brother Gigi (Luigi) worked the farm, along with many others. Riccardo, the son of a sharecropper, would risk his life for the two Americans more than once. Interestingly, the most decorated hero of World War II, Audie Murphy, was also the son of a sharecropper.

"After sundown, Sarri instructed me to follow him to his house. So, in my new civilian clothes, I followed him down a dirt road. He was walking about seventy yards ahead of me. While we were walking, two German trucks loaded with soldiers hurried past us. The road led into a village." This was the village of Vaggio.

Over sixty years later, Sarri's son Amerigo would remember that before the Americans parachuted into the area, there were no Germans garrisoned in the village. They had occupied his hometown, Figline Valdarno, a couple of miles down the road west of Vaggio. Now, they were in the village that Bill was walking through, and they were looking for the Americans. Two months later, Bill and Todd would find themselves walking down another road, following Riccardo this time. The trip would also be tense as German soldiers would be lining the road, battle-ready and watching a couple of American airmen disguised as Italian refugees walk past them.

Riccardo Becattini
Courtesy of the Becattini Family

Bill continues: "So, here I was, about 200 miles behind enemy lines, walking through a village occupied by Germans, some fraternizing outside a pub. Sarri was taking me to a farm at the southern edge of the village. At that time, the Germans weren't harassing the Italians, as they were later when more of them were being driven north through the area by the Allies. It is mind-boggling to me that I was able to walk past German soldiers who were looking for me. You can imagine how nervous I was. I put my trust in Sarri and he never let me down. Basically, we always trusted each other. He was a real gentleman and a savior for Todd and me."

The partisans had also helped Todd to evade the enemy. Riccardo followed his chute down to a point just east of the farm, and rushed to get to him before the Fascists or the Germans. Todd landed in a tree in an orchard near the woods. He had to abandon his chute and wrenched his ankle when he dropped from the tree. He heard Jerry fire and limped into the woods. Jerry is a slang term for Germans used by the Allies.[10] Riccardo and other partisans caught up to him, and convinced him that they were friends.

According to Riccardo, he brought Todd to hide in a forest south of the farm and told him to stay hidden until he returned. Later, Riccardo returned with civilian clothing, then brought him to his house, where his family gave him food and bandaged his ankle.[11] He got rid of Todd's military clothes because it was too dangerous to keep them. He also said that a farmer named Begnamino kept Todd's parachute. Later, Riccardo tried to retrieve it, but the farmer only gave him enough fabric to make a shirt that he has since lost.

Bill and Todd were very fortunate to have friends behind enemy lines. Bill notes, "I remember Colonel Smith telling us to be careful never to drop our bombs on farms because the farmers are our friends. He was so right!" They also knew that the Fascists were their enemies. Bill thought that Fascists were for the most part "educated Italians who lived in the cities." He wasn't far from wrong because the civil servants who ran the cities were typically Fascists.

Prisoners of War

Denny landed very close to Todd, just east of him on a farm, but he wasn't as lucky as Bill and Todd. According to Riccardo, "The soldier (Denny) landed in the neighborhood of Tamuresco, close to a small farm managed by a farmer enrolled in the Fascist party who turned him over to the Germans." Whether or not a downed airman became a prisoner of war depended to a large extent on whether or not the Fascists or Germans got to him before the partisans.

Partisans that saw Denny captured told Bill that he was in great pain, and Bill always thought Denny was the person saying "I'm hit!" when their plane was pounded by flak. This was not the case. In 2009, Denny's son Steve said his father had a dislocated shoulder. He had dislocated his shoulder during his training and was unable to lift his arm above his shoulder. When he bailed out and had to hang on to the shroud lines, he dislocated his shoulder again and was in great pain when he landed.

Steve said that his father continued to be in great pain and thought he wasn't going to make it when something happened that changed his attitude toward the enemy. Steve could not recall every detail, but his father told him he was in terrible pain marching in a column with other prisoners when a German soldier ordered him behind a tree and told the others not to look. His father thought he was going to be shot, as did the other prisoners. However, the German pointed to the ground for him to lie down, laid down his rifle, grabbed Denny's bad arm, put his foot on his chest and snapped his shoulder back into the socket. Denny told his son that the pain was excruciating but the soldier knew what he was doing. The soldier smiled at him and ordered him back in line. He felt like the guy saved his life. After that, he realized that this man was just like him, fighting in a war in which he had to kill the guy on the other side.

Denny became a prisoner of war. As was the routine for downed airmen, he was sent to Dulag Luft (*Durchgangslager der Luftwaffe*— the transit prison camp of the Luftwaffe) in Oberursel, Germany, about eight miles northwest of Frankfurt.[12] Nearly all captured Allied airmen were sent to Dulag Luft for interrogation and assignment to a permanent prison camp.[13] Denny was assigned to Stalag VII-A in Moosburg, Germany, about 200 air miles southeast of Oberursel. At the time, Stalag VII-A was a prison camp for enlisted men and non-commissioned officers.[14] He remained imprisoned there until April 29, 1945, just before the war in Europe officially ended on May 8, 1945, V-E (Victory in Europe) Day.[15] Interestingly, Denny had enlisted in the service at Camp Forest in Tullahoma, Tennessee, not only one of the largest World War II training facilities, but also a prison camp for about 24,000 German prisoners of war.[16]

Reynolds didn't have luck on his side either, and would also fall into the hands of Fascists. As he was quietly descending in his chute, he was thinking of Lieutenant George Walsh, a pilot he respected who, along with his crew, was killed in a landing accident eleven days earlier. He was also thinking that this was his thirty-ninth mission and that thirty-nine is three times unlucky number thirteen.

Unlike the other crew members, he had a soft landing: "I landed standing up in a plowed field. I was about 200 yards from a road. They [four men] stopped their jeep and hurried over to me. They were dressed in uniforms similar to the workers in our kitchen at the base. They took my revolver and we walked to the jeep. I thought they might be friendly Italians."

The four Italians brought him to Incisa, the town whose bridge they had just tried to destroy. "In Incisa, they searched me. They motioned for me to face a shed. I didn't. I wanted to see what was happening. One man took my escape package and asked if it was smokes. I indicated yes. He put the escape package back in my pocket."

He got back in the jeep and they took him to Florence, about twelve miles northwest of Incisa. "The streets were narrow and the jeep went fast. They finally stopped at a large castle." This could have been one of a number of large castles in Florence taken over by the Germans. After Florence was liberated, they were turned back over to the city.[17]

He went on: "For supper they gave me a large hunk of rye bread and a large bowl of vegetable soup. The table was ten feet wide and fifty feet long. There were several large chandeliers hanging from the ceiling. The jail was in one corner on the bottom floor. The room was ten feet long, six feet wide and ten feet high, and one small window too high to see out. The door was a large metal door with a peep hole. There was a small barrel for toilet use. The bed had a mattress on chains."

That evening, while Reynolds was pondering his fate, Lieutenant Frederick C. Ritger, the pilot he trained with in the States, was worried about him and expressed his concern in a letter to his folks:[18]

One of my best pals went down today and it hit me as hard as a thing like that could. Lt. Laverne Reynolds the best damn bombardier in the world was knocked down while on a mission over Italy. I have become pretty used to such things but he was such a swell fellow it is mighty hard to see him go. Enough for that now cause I can't express what I feel.

About six months later, Ritger would also be shot down over Italy and would, like Bill and Todd, evade the enemy with the help of a farmer.[19] Three members of his crew would, like Denny and Reynolds, become prisoners of war; and two others would, like Major Hunter, make the ultimate sacrifice, one of whom had been Bill's tent mate in Paestum—Staff Sergeant Stuart L. Huntoon.[20] Danger was ever present on bombing missions, and the air war took its toll.

In the morning, Reynolds was taken to a small building with showers. After he got cleaned up, he was brought to a German who spoke good English. "I was taken to interrogation, and they were able to tell me about my plane and who was on it. I was then put on a train to Venice. That night, I slept on a wooden bed, with no mattress. The rooms were separated with wooden walls. In a room next to mine a woman cried and hollered all night. I didn't sleep much."

The next day, Reynolds was transported by train to Dulag Luft for assignment to a permanent prison camp. He was assigned to Stalag Luft III near Sagan, Germany [now Zagan, Poland], about one-hundred miles south of Berlin. This was the same prison camp known for the unsuccessful "Great Escape" that took place on March 24, 1944.[21] It was a prison camp for airmen who were officers.

Reynolds would eventually be moved to another prison camp, Stalag XIII-D, in Nuremberg, Germany.[22] From there, he would be moved again, this time to the same prison camp as Denny, Stalag VII-A, where conditions would be intolerable and where, like Denny, he also remained a prisoner of war until April 29, 1945.

More Partisans to the Rescue

After the aircraft cleared the Pratomagno Mountains, Kinney bailed out over the Upper Arno River Valley through which the Arno River flowed south from its source at 5,426-foot Monte Falterona. The 150-mile river flowed on a horseshoe course, first south, then west past Arezzo, then northwest past Incisa before it turned again and headed west past Florence to the Ligurian Sea. As Kinney descended into the Upper Arno River Valley, he saw Brickner jump before the aircraft disappeared over the next mountain ridge, the Catenaia Alps.

Kinney had a rough landing on the west wall of the valley. "I hit the ground with some violence and was knocked unconscious."[23] He landed just north of Subbiano, a small town on the Arno River.[24] The Arno River's initial and highest basin extends twenty-one miles from Monte Falterona to Subbiano, which is six miles north of Arezzo. The valley is surrounded by some of the largest forests in Italy, providing good places to hide for partisans and airmen like Kinney.

Kinney awoke to the dangers surrounding him. "When I came to, a deathly quiet was broken by a number of pistol shots in the valley below." Brickner was in the middle of that action. Brickner landed about two miles southeast of Kinney on the east bank of the Arno River, but they never saw each other again. Like Todd, Brickner landed in a tree. By the time he freed himself, he was met by a Fascist and two Germans with their weapons drawn. He was taken prisoner and led to a hut to be interrogated by a German who spoke English fairly well. Just as the interrogator requested his dog tags, partisans attacked the hut and, amidst a hail of bullets, Brickner's captors fled.[25]

The partisans wanted Brickner to join their band, but he expressed a desire to return to Allied territory. They brought him to a place in the forest where escaped Allied prisoners of war were hiding, and he remained in hiding until he was liberated by British troops in Volterrano, a small village about six miles southeast of Arezzo, on July 12, 1944.[26]

When Brickner returned to Allied lines, he reported that a woman who was helping to hide him was approached by a German patrol consisting of a captain, a lieutenant and about a hundred soldiers. During their brief conversation, they told the woman that London radio had announced the Normandy landing and the swift Russian advances. He said the captain told the woman that he believed this theater would fold within two months.[27] Due to the delay tactics of the Germans and a mountainous terrain that favored such tactics, the theater would not fold for at least another ten months.

Kinney was also able to evade capture. He linked up with reliable Yugoslavian partisans operating in Italy who helped him remain hidden until he was liberated by the 56th Reconnaissance Regiment, 78th Infantry ("Battleaxe") Division, British Eighth Army on July 3, 1944. Unlike Bill and Todd, Kinney and Brickner were able to pick up their escape purses and food kits before they bailed out, and put them to good use on the ground.[28]

The Ultimate Sacrifice

When Kinney last saw his aircraft, it disappeared over the Catenaia Alps with Hunter still struggling to control it. On the other side of these mountains was the Upper Tiber Valley through which the Tiber River, the largest river in Italy, flowed south from its source at 4,616-foot Monte Fumaiolo all the way past Rome and into the Tyrrhenian Sea, a distance of about 252 miles. On the far side of the valley loomed the Luna Alps, another ominous hurdle for Hunter to clear.

There is no way of knowing what was going through Hunter's mind as the reality set in that he wouldn't be able to clear the next hurdle and that he didn't have time to save himself. He may have been thinking of his many loved ones—his wife Jean, his son Bill, his mother Shirley, his father Herbert, his grandmother Dora, and/or his brothers Park and Robert. Nobody will ever know, but he was never far from their thoughts then and for years to come.

As to the fate of Major Hunter, Kinney spoke with Italian partisans who witnessed the crash and burial. They told him that the aircraft crashed about six miles northwest of Sansepolcro, and that a man with a shoulder holster and .45- and .38-caliber pistols had been found in it. They said Fascists had stripped the airplane and taken the pilot's personal effects, which consisted of a pocket watch and gold leaves in addition to his two revolvers. This fit the description of Major Hunter. They also told him that Italian natives removed his body from the plane and buried him in a cemetery in Anghiari, about five miles west of Sansepolcro.[29]

It was also reported later that his personal effects consisting of a wallet and money, which were found on his body, were destroyed when the Germans burned the Carabinieri (Police) Headquarters where they were brought after the crash. There was no mention in this report of Hunter's guns, pocket watch and gold leaves that partisans told Kinney had been taken from his body. Identification of the aircraft was made by the number on the tail fins (327650) and the serial number on one of the machine guns (685378).[30] Hunter's family would not learn of his death until August 3, over two months later.

The Caterpillar Club

Bill and the other members of the crew that bailed out were lucky they weren't born too soon. If this were World War I, the entire crew would have perished because parachutes weren't around then. When an aircraft was shot down in that war, those in the aircraft were doomed. Many skillful and courageous pilots went down with their planes during that war. After the war, the pilots who pulled through were pushing for an inventor who could give them a chance for survival when their plane was shot down. That man turned out to be Leslie Irvin.

Irvin had been building model parachutes as a kid in Los Angeles, using odd bits of silk his mother gave him. About the time World War I broke out, he was testing his parachutes on the family cat. Before Irvin's invention, the early parachute case was attached to the plane because it was felt that a person free falling would be too disoriented to open a chute himself. An independent thinker who thought otherwise, Irvin remained obsessed with the idea of a "free fall" parachute while wandering around the country and taking odd jobs. The oddest job he took, as a carnival high diver, helped him pick up a lot of experience in "free falling." Every day, he jumped into water from a seventy-foot platform.[31]

So when the U.S. Army Air Service was searching for someone who could design a parachute, Irvin was ready to meet the call. After World War I, the Army Air Service formed a parachute research team headed by Major E. J. Hoffman, an engineer who was tasked with finding a workable type of free parachute. His team listed a set of conditions and sought a designer. Irvin's design was the only one that satisfied most of the conditions. At last, Irvin had the resources to develop and test the invention that he had been working on since he was a kid.[32]

On April 28, 1919 in historic Dayton, Ohio, where the Wright Brothers began experimenting in flight in 1896 and the site of today's National Museum of the United States Air Force, he got the opportunity to demonstrate his invention and did so in daring style. At that time, most experts felt any man jumping from an aircraft

148

would pass out after falling a short distance, so instead of opening his chute soon after he jumped, he "free fell" for about 600 feet before opening his chute to show them that this wasn't a problem. With that jump, he became the first man in history to make a "delayed release" jump, the first to prove that a free fall of hundreds of feet does not make a man lose consciousness, and of course the first man to jump in a "free-type" parachute.[33]

Irvin jumped from a height of 2,000 feet. Today, people do this for fun. For example, Dana Cochran of West Chester, Ohio, gave her father, Page Eskridge of Anaheim Hills, California, a special gift for his sixtieth birthday—the opportunity to jump with her out of a plane at 2,000 feet, free fall for 1,000 feet, and then open their chutes. Page jumped at the opportunity, and they both enjoyed the experience.

Bill had a far different experience. He jumped at 7,000 feet, slammed against the bottom of the aircraft, felt as though a thousand horses were pulling on his shoulders when his open chute caught the wind, was wondering how he would get out of this mess on the way down, and then hit the ground with a bang. It was anything but enjoyable. It is safe to say that none of the crew on Hunter's aircraft experienced the joy that Dana and her father experienced on that special day.

After his historic jump, Irvin's chute was adopted by the American Air Force, the British Royal Air Force and other air forces around the world.[34] In 1922, the Irvin Air Chute Company started awarding a tiny gold Caterpillar Pin to anyone whose life was saved by parachuting from a disabled aircraft, a testimony to the life-saving ability of its parachutes. In those days, the canopy and shroud lines of parachutes were made from silk spun from the cocoons of silk worms, also called caterpillars. The name also fit because the silk worm lets itself descend gently to earth from heights by spinning a silky thread to hang from, creating an image similar to that of a parachutist descending to earth.[35]

During World War II, nylon replaced silk in parachutes, and it is interesting how this came about. During the 1930's, a research team at DuPont led by Wallace Hume Carothers was trying to develop a synthetic fiber as a substitute for silk because of deteriorating trade relations with Japan, the main source of silk for the United States. This led to the invention of nylon in 1935.[36] In 1939, Nylon was tested on the canopies and suspension lines of parachutes and proved to be stronger. The first nylon parachutes were produced in 1941.[37]

SHOT DOWN OVER ITALY

In December 1943, his nylon parachute saved the life of Joe Bruckler, a gunner on a B-24 that was attacked by enemy fighters in northern Italy. The attack resulted in the deaths of five members of the crew of ten. After Bruckler bailed out, his chute was pierced by shrapnel, resulting in a fast descent and a rough landing in which he sustained shoulder and back injuries. He was told that if his chute had been made of silk, the wind would have ripped the torn canopy to pieces.[38]

Thanks to Irvin, who put the family cat at risk and later himself, and Carothers and his team, who enhanced the fabric used in parachutes, many airmen who were shot down during World War II and survived the experience became members of the Caterpillar Club. It's one of the most exclusive clubs in the world, yet nobody is anxious to join. Despite having made 300 jumps in his lifetime, Irvin himself never qualified for membership because he never jumped from a disabled aircraft.[39] Bill, Todd, Denny, Reynolds, Kinney and Brickner all qualified for membership on May 26, 1944. If it weren't for Major Hunter's skill and courage in controlling his disabled aircraft, some of them might not have had the opportunity to join this exclusive club.

Chapter 7

EVADING THE ENEMY

When Bill Lanza arrived at Sarri's house on the farm during the evening of May 27, 1944, he was greeted warmly by the two families who shared the house, a gathering of about fifteen men, women and children. "Some of the men were sitting around the table, curiously staring at me. Considering that I was seen being shot out of the sky the day before, I guess this was to be expected. Sarri told me they picked up Todd and that he had some cigarettes with him. I was happy to hear that he was safe. I was also happy to hear he had cigarettes because I was a smoker. I had a good night's sleep.

"The next day, I was united with Alfred Todd at Sarri's house. He was limping and his ankle was bandaged. I still couldn't believe that he bailed out with six packs of cigarettes. It was like discovering gold for me. I think he was happy to see me too because I spoke Italian. Sarri's dialect was different and unfamiliar to me, but we understood each other."

The Farm

Sarri's house was on a farm, but his family and the other family who shared the house were not farmers. They were displaced families driven from their homes by the Allied bombing. The Sarri family moved only a couple of miles from their condominium in nearby Figline Valdarno, while the other family moved over four hundred miles from their home in Sicily. The other three families on the farm lived in another housing complex. They were sharecroppers, or tenant farmers, who worked the farm and shared their crops with the landowner. This arrangement had been a way of life in Tuscany since the thirteenth century.[1]

The landowner-sharecropper arrangement is explained in *War in Val d'Orcia: An Italian War Diary 1943-1944* by Iris Origo, who with her husband owned fifty-seven farms on seven thousand acres in Val d'Orcia (Orcia Valley), about forty miles south of Vaggio. She explained the arrangement as the *mezzadria* system, a profit-sharing compact between the landowner and the sharecropper. In Italian, *mezzadro* means sharecropper. It was derived from the word *mezzo*, which means half. The *mezzadria* system called for the landowner to provide and maintain the houses, buy half of what's needed to cultivate and improve the land, and pay for half the stock of animals.[2] In return, the sharecropper lived on the farm, cultivated the land, and shared half his products and profits with the landowner. The landowner was referred to in Italian as the *padrone*.[3]

Iris Origo kept a diary that captured the chaos in Italy during the war. More importantly, it also captured the humanity of the farmers in helping so many people in distress during the war. Of the *mezzadria* system, Origo wrote: "It is not quite that of the landlord and tenant, nor certainly that of the employer and employee—it is more intimate than the former, more friendly than the latter. It is a partnership."[4]

A book written by Pietro Pinti provides a different view of the *mezzadria* system. Pinti was a peasant farmer in Tuscany who was the son of a sharecropper and later became a sharecropper himself. He viewed the relationship between the landowner and sharecropper not as a partnership, but as a master-slave relationship. In his opinion, the landowner was the boss and the peasant had to submit to his will.[5]

When Pinti was young, the landowner told his father that he had to move to another one of his farms. His family didn't want to move, and neither did his father because the land was more difficult to cultivate due to the condition of the soil. Nevertheless, the family had no choice but to move. The landowner didn't own many farms so he had the time to watch closely over them and to make decisions that Pinti's father would have preferred to make.[6] Landowners with many farms such as the Origos, who housed six-hundred people, had a middle man, called a *fattoria*, to watch over their farms.

Pinti, like many farmers, was an anti-Fascist and felt that all the landowners were pro-Fascist and approved of the Fascist policy of keeping both peasant farmers and factory workers in a state of submission. After thirty years of farming under these circumstances, Pinti left farming in his forties for a job as a builder's mate in Florence. This was hard work too, but a big advantage of the new job was that he could rest on weekends and felt free. As a sharecropper, he never felt free.

Fascism did indeed view the *mezzadria* arrangement positively. One of its main principles was to discourage the flight from the countryside into towns.[7] The Fascist government had a special interest in assisting the agricultural regions of Italy to improve the land and make it productive. Consequently, landowners like the Origos were encouraged to develop the land to make Italy more self-sufficient while at the same time preventing clutter in the cities. Landowners were encouraged to introduce modern farming techniques and to plan and implement effective programs to cultivate the land. As a result, many farms had become productive. During the war, the Germans took advantage of this bounty by forcing the farmers to feed them as they retreated through Tuscany.

The farm that Bill and Todd were on was owned by a *padrone* who owned only that one farm as well as an agricultural company whose produce came from that farm. Riccardo's father, Gosto, was the sharecropper who ran the farm and assigned the tasks to the farm workers.

The farm was located in the village of Vaggio, a *frazione*, or fraction (subdivision), of the *comune*, or municipality, of Reggello. A *comune* is similar to a city or town in the United States. It has a mayor and an administration that the city or town and its fractions depend on for basic civil services such as registering the births, weddings, deeds and deaths, and maintaining the local roads and public works. Vaggio is one of thirteen fractions in Reggello, and Reggello is one of forty-four municipalities in the province of Florence. A province is similar to a county in the United States, and Florence is one of ten provinces in the region of Tuscany. A region is similar to a state in the United States, and Tuscany is one of twenty regions in Italy. Two of the regions—Sicily and Sardinia—are islands, and the other eighteen regions form the Italian mainland.[8]

Vaggio is located about two and a half miles east of Figline Valdarno, a town on the Arno River about fifteen miles southeast of

Florence. Figline is in the Arno River Valley (Valdarno in Italian). Today, the international rock star, Sting, finds peace in this valley and considers Figline his "true home."[9] The town just north of Figline on the Arno River is Incisa in Val d'Arno, the site of the bridge Major Hunter's plane was trying to bomb when his plane was shot down.

The farm is located just beyond the southeast end of Vaggio. It overlooks the village and is nestled between the village and thickly wooded hills on its southern perimeter. To reach Figline from the farm, one has to walk north through the village, cross a bridge over the Resco River to the main road, take a left and follow the road which parallels the river for a couple of miles into Matassino, a fraction of both Reggello and Figline Valdarno. In Matassino, the road bends left over another bridge across the Resco River, then bends right toward a third bridge over the Arno River into Figline.

In a couple of months, Riccardo would lead Bill and Todd down this road. The trip would seem like an eternity for the two Americans because German soldiers would be dug in under trees that lined the road, staring at them disguised as Italian refugees.

From Vaggio, the road taken in the other direction forks into two roads—one leading northeast to Reggello three miles away, and the other leading east to Pian di Scò two miles away. While Vaggio is a fraction of Reggello, it is also closely affiliated with Figline Valdarno and Pian di Scò. Montanino, a mile north of Vaggio, where Bill landed, is also a fraction of Reggello. Sixty-three years later, when the author visited Vaggio, he was greeted by the mayors of Figline Valdarno, Pian di Scò and Reggello.

From the farm, if you look east you see picturesque rolling hills interspersed with towns and villages against the background of the Pratomagno Mountains. If you look west, you see out over the Arno River Valley to the Chianti Hills which rise out of the valley. If you look north, you see the rooftops of the village, wooded hills and mountains beyond. If you look south, you see wooded hills beyond which, in about a month and a half, Bill and Todd would see the battlefront approaching Vaggio.

The housing complexes on the farm, like most of those in Tuscany, are rustic and built to last. While farmhouses in America are built primarily of wood, farmhouses in Italy are built primarily of stone or masonry. They have sturdy, thick walls, some from twelve to thirty inches thick, and were in effect natural fortresses that afforded protection against small arms fire and shell fragments from mortar or artillery. Consequently, many were used as command posts during the war by both the German and the Allied armies. One imagines that they looked the same then as they do today.[10]

When Bill and Todd arrived in Vaggio, Riccardo recalls that five families totaling thirty-seven people lived on the farm. The families lived in close quarters in two housing complexes. By the time the front reached the area, Riccardo said that about seventy people were on the farm. Most of them, like Bill and Todd, were being helped by the Becattini and Sarri families.[11]

It was not unusual for families to take in displaced persons whose homes were either destroyed or in harm's way. During the weeks that the Germans were retreating through Montevarchi, about eight miles south of Vaggio, Pietro Pinti and his family were sheltering about sixty people. They slept wherever they could find a spot in his home, including in the stable and cellar, using straw for mattresses.[12]

Both housing complexes on the farm were south of the village. The Sarri family lived in the one closest to the farming fields and the woods beyond. It was a large two-story structure occupied by both the Sarri family and a Sicilian family, whose last name Riccardo cannot recall. Today, the house is a rustic, muted-yellow limestone home with an orange roof of terracotta tiles. It stands behind a large gate entrance that separates it from the second complex just north of it that borders on the village. In 1944, the house was divided into two sections to accommodate the two families.

One section of the house was occupied by the Sarri family, consisting of Goffredo, his wife Grazietta, and their six children: Anna (18), Amerigo (16), Bruno (14), Aldo (9), Grazia (5), and Alfredo (less than a year). Their seventh child, Paolo, came after the war. Goffredo moved his family to the farm from Figline Valdarno after his home was bombed in December 1943. His business had been bombed in June 1943. Goffredo had a shoe business with fifteen employees. He was also a partisan leader fighting for the liberation of his hometown from Fascist rule and Nazi occupation.

According to Bill, "Sarri was a gentleman who always remained calm and did the right thing. We were lucky to have him looking out for us. His wife, Grazietta, was a gracious lady, always with a smile on

155

Farm Complex: Three families totaling 22 people, including the Becattini family, resided in the left complex. Two families totaling 15 people, including the Sarri family, resided in the house on the right.

her face, and her daughter Anna was a mainstay in bringing us food. Rigo [Amerigo] visited us a lot, sometimes with his brother Bruno, and of his visits I have such fond memories."

The other section of the house was occupied by a Sicilian family who sought shelter in Tuscany after the Allied invasion of Sicily drove them from their home. The family consisted of a father, a mother and five children. Riccardo can only recall the names of four of their five children. The three daughters were "La Lilla", Maria, and Angiolina; and one son was Tonino. He cannot recall the name of the other son. Bill remembers that the father was always worried about his family, especially when the battlefront was approaching. Of his daughter Maria, Bill notes: "She was friends with Anna and both of them brought food to the cave regularly. In good weather and bad, they were always there on time, and we were always glad to see them."

The other housing complex consisted of four connected buildings—three houses around a courtyard and a chapel connected to the easternmost house. The complex looked like a small fortress and was occupied by three farming families—the Papi, Becattini and Garuglieri families. The complex was located between the Sarri house and the village. Today, as you walk up to the complex from the village, the first house you see above and to your left behind some trees is the Papi family house, a weathered, rustic, gray-stone house with orange brick patches in rubble-style with a weathered orange roof of terracotta tiles.

In 1944, this house was occupied by the Papi family consisting of Antonio, his wife Ida called "Cencina," and five children. They had three sons, Gianni, Ezio and Angiolino, and two daughters, Gina called "Marisa," and Angiolina. Ezio was not present when Bill and Todd were in Vaggio. He was in a work camp in Germany, but fortunately returned home alive after the war. Said Bill: "I was pleased to hear that after the war Riccardo married Marisa. I knew that they were fond of each other."

When you walk past the Papi house and turn left, you walk into the courtyard. If you turn left again and face north toward the village, you will see that the housing complex is shaped like a horseshoe with the Papi house on the left, the Becattini house in the middle and the Garuglieri house on the right. Today, the gray-orange Papi house melds nicely with the honey-yellow limestone of the Becattini and Garuglieri houses. The orange terracotta-tile roofs adorn the entire complex, which has the seasoned look so characteristic of the stone houses in Tuscany.

The Becattini family consisted of Constantino called "Gosto," his wife Natalina and their six children, one of whom had a family of his own. There were three girls, Giuseppe called "Beppa," Nunzia, and Clementina, and three boys, Riccardo, Roberto and Luigi called "Gigi". Gigi was married to Crelia and they had three children, Margherita (5), Davide (1) and Lido (6 months).

Gosto was the sharecropper responsible for operating the farm. He assigned the tasks to the farm workers. Says Bill, "I never met Gosto, but the farm workers I met were all hard workers and nice people, so I respected the man. Riccardo in particular really knew his way around the farm. You should have seen him handle the oxen. He also knew his way around the woods. I wouldn't want to do battle with him in the woods. Gigi was very strong and an efficient worker who also knew what he was doing, and Beppa worked the fields like a man. However, she was very much a woman with a strong, attractive figure. The family knew its business and was so good to us."

The Garuglieri family consisted of the father, Gino, the mother, Isola, and two sons, Angiolino and Mario. Attached to the Garuglieri house was a chiesetta, a small chapel sometimes found on farms in the rural areas of Italy. Amerigo pointed out that it was deconsecrated and therefore no longer had a religious function. At one time, it may have functioned as a church. Some landowners with many farms had not only a church but a school as well. The Origos had a school for the children on their farms.

The farm had at least ten acres of mostly vineyards, but also grew wheat, corn, potatoes, tomatoes and other fruits and vegetables. Oxen were used to pull the plows, and chickens were raised on the farm. Wheat was an important product for producing bread, pasta and other foods; and corn was important for feeding the animals. Since the wheat and corn were harvested in July when the front was moving into the area, the 1944 harvest would be a challenge. Wine was also an important product, but the grapes were picked and the wine made in the fall.

The Cave

Soon after the arrival of the two Americans, plans were made for their new home. "When Todd and I were brought together, Sarri arranged for Gigi, Riccardo's brother, to dig a cave for us on a steep hill next to the farm. It took about a week to dig the cave in hard clay. He did a great job. Much later, when a bomb landed near our cave, it withstood the concussion."

"While the cave was being dug, we kept out of sight and slept outside. I was used to sleeping outside on the ground because I did enough of it in the Infantry, but Todd hadn't been in the Infantry. He also had a terrible case of dysentery. Sometimes, when the coast was clear, we ate outside on the farm with the Sarri family."

When the cave was ready, Bill and Todd moved into their new home. Bill estimates that the cave was about fifteen feet long by ten feet wide and six feet high. It was about ten to eleven feet from the crest of the hill, and there was a ledge in front of the entrance. Caves were nothing new in Italy. Many people were hiding in caves in the hills and forests of Italy during the war.

The two Americans, who landed in enemy territory without escape kits and in no position to strike out on their own, were fortunate on a number of fronts. First, Bill grew up in a family of Italian immigrants, and spoke the language. Second, Todd grew up on a farm. Third, they had Sarri to look out for them. Bill got along with, respected, and trusted Sarri, and Sarri never let him down.

With the help of the Becattini and Sarri families, Bill and Todd adjusted to being cave dwellers in enemy territory. "We slept on straw mattresses in our cave, but we sometimes washed ourselves and our clothes at a rain basin on the farm. They fed us, usually with soup, bread and wine, and also washed our clothes from time to time."

While they were settling into their new home, the Allies were on the move. The ultimate objective of Operation Strangle, which began on March 19, the day of Bill's first mission, was to wage a sustained and systematic interdiction campaign to cut off troop reinforcements, ammunition, motor fuel, and other supplies by attacking rail, road and sea supply routes to the German front lines.[13] The purpose of air interdiction is to "delay, disrupt, divert or destroy an enemy's military potential before it can be brought to bear against friendly forces."[14] The ultimate objective of Strangle was to make it impossible for the enemy to maintain armies south of Rome, by cutting off its supply lines.[15]

When the spring offensive to break through the Gustav Line and out of the Anzio beachhead was mounted, it was evident that Strangle had accomplished its purpose. In his report to the Combined Joint Chiefs of Staff on the Italian Campaign, General Maitland Wilson, Supreme Allied Commander of the Mediterranean Theater, stated that Operation Strangle, which was carried out from March 19 to May 11, "achieved notable tactical results and contributed heavily to the success of the Allied drive to and beyond Rome."[16]

The success of Operation Strangle led to a more intensive air interdiction campaign in Operation Diadem that began on May 12, coinciding with the spring ground offensive at the Gustav Line and Anzio beachhead. Similar to Strangle, Diadem was to be carried out by medium bombers such as the B-25s and fighter bombers such as the P-47s. Both of these warbirds had something in common—they could take a lot of punishment and keep on flying.

Since the Italian rail network was estimated to account for 80,000 tons of supplies daily to the German front lines, compared to only 700 tons by sea and 800 tons by road, the Allies planned to "strangle" the rail and road networks by establishing an interdiction belt across the width of Italy. Picture the belt as two almost-parallel lines drawn across the waist of Italy north and south of Florence, the top of the belt stretching from La Spezia on the west coast to Rimini on the east coast, and the bottom from Cecina on the west coast to Ancona on the east coast.[17]

Bill and Todd were part of both interdiction campaigns until they were shot down. Now they were in the middle of the interdiction belt and eyewitnesses to the bombing.[18] Their bomb group, the 321st, having flown fifty missions in the hectic month of May, would ramp that up to fifty-three missions in June.[19] This interdiction campaign would cut the German supply lines and enable the Allied ground forces to continue to push the German ground forces up the Italian peninsula.

When Bill and Todd were in Vaggio, the P-47 Thunderbolts of the 57th Fighter Group were operating in the area for the purpose of destroying railroad bridges, marshalling yards, and trains. In addition, they were flying armed reconnaissance, which amounted to attacking anything the pilots felt were targets of opportunity.[20]

The Thunderbolt was a powerful aircraft with exceptional diving capabilities.[21] With an arsenal of 4.5-inch rockets, 500-pound bombs, and 50-caliber machine guns, it weighed over eight tons. It was called the "Jug" as in "Juggernaut." It could fly low through

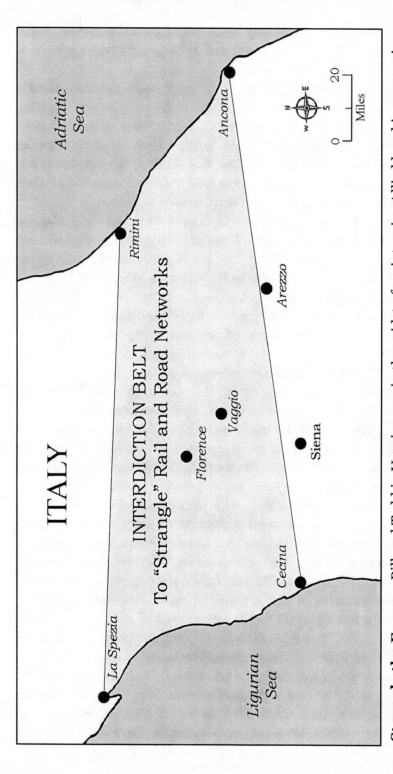

Strangle the Enemy: Bill and Todd in Vaggio were in the midst of an intensive Allied bombing campaign to "strangle" the enemy by cutting off German supplies, equipment and manpower to the Front.

twisting valleys, and not only could it inflict a lot of damage, but it could take a lot of punishment and keep flying.[22] Appropriately, it was also called a "flying tank."[23]

Each of the three squadrons of the 57th had a nickname suitable for an attack aircraft—the 64th "Black Scorpions," the 65th "Fighting Cocks" and the 66th "Exterminators." The 57th flew several missions a day and the strafing of trains was an everyday occurrence, as documented in their history.[24] Two months later, the two Americans would be very thankful for these armed reconnaissance flights when a couple of sweeps by a P-47 may have saved their lives.

Just before Bill's 321st Bomb Group moved to Solenzara, Corsica, to be nearer their targets, the 57th Fighter Group had moved to Corsica for the same reason. The 57th flew out of Alto Landing Field, about forty miles north of Solenzara on the east coast of the French island.[25]

On the morning of June 1, 1944, Lieutenant H. L. Williams led a mission of twelve P-47s from the 64th "Black Scorpions" to bomb a bridge on the Arno River. His mission group assembled into a formation of three flights of four aircraft each, then flew at an altitude of 10,000 feet the sixty miles across the Ligurian Sea to the Italian mainland, and another eighty miles to the target area. When they sighted the target bridge at 10:15 a.m., they dove to 2,000 feet to drop their bombs, cutting the tracks in three places, twice on the north approach and once on the south approach. After effectively knocking out the bridge with their bombs, each flight went searching for targets of opportunity to strafe with their rockets and machine guns.[26]

One flight strafed a train with five flat cars and five box cars, and the result was one smoker. Another strafed another train with ten cars, including six gondola cars (open cars with low sides) loaded with large wooden crates, without result. The third flight had a far different experience. As Bill and Todd watched, their attack yielded significant results. In fact, it would be one of the two most-effective attacks by that squadron for the entire month of June.[27]

Bill recalls: "From the hill, we had a pretty good view over the valley [Arno River Valley], but were always careful not to be seen. We knew that the Germans had good glass [binoculars]. Soon after we moved in, we witnessed P-47 dive bombers attacking a train. We couldn't see the train, but we could hear its whistle in the valley and we could see the P-47s on the attack. We could see them strafing the train, then pulling

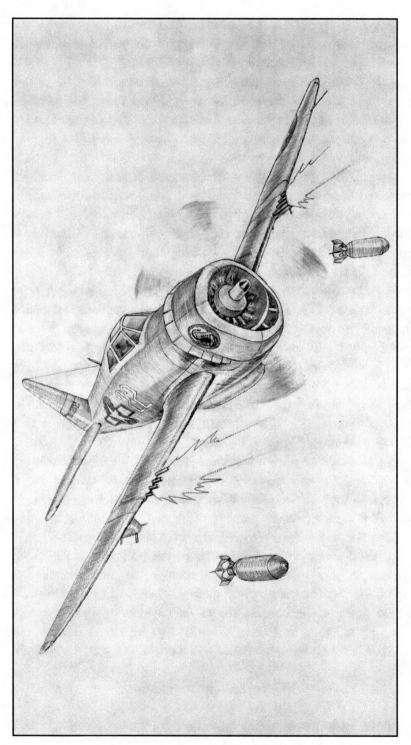

P-47 Thunderbolt on the Attack!

up to avoid the explosion of a direct hit. The first two missed, but the third one was on target. Oh my God! What an explosion! It was so powerful that we could actually feel the concussion!"

According to 64th Fighter Squadron intelligence, the attack occurred in the Arno River Valley near Montevarchi, just south of Bill and Todd. The flight attacked a train with twenty-five cars loaded with gasoline that were "set afire" and "burned furiously," sending black smoke to 8,000 feet.[28]

After the P-47s quickly left the scene, Bill and Todd watched, heard and felt the explosions for most of the day. According to Bill, "The train kept blowing up for hours! What fireworks!" Bill always thought that the train had ammunition as well because of the way it exploded throughout the day. Many years later, Amerigo said he also thought the train was loaded with ammunition.

Bill remembers another instance he thought was related to the train attack: "The next day, one of the natives brought me some tobacco. I wrapped it in some of the propaganda paper being constantly dropped from the sky. I tried to smoke it, but it was too strong. It was like smoking a stogie, only stronger. I liked to smoke, but not tobacco like that." For most of his life, Bill thought the tobacco was blown from that train. Many years later, he learned that it was simply stolen from the Germans.

According to Bill, "The German troops and their vehicles kept off the roads during the day because if a P-47 saw them they didn't stand a chance. One time, a P-47 strafed near us. We could hear it but couldn't see it from our position on the hill. Later, we learned that it clobbered a German vehicle. The troops moved at night to avoid being attacked during the day."

The German infantry feared the P-47 as much as the Allies feared the Stuka dive bomber earlier in the war.[29] Runo Palmquist experienced what Stukas could do when they were dive-bombing his ship on his way from a port in Naples to a beach in Anzio. He could feel the power of the concussions as their bombs hit the water and could only imagine the disaster if one had hit his ship. Likewise, Bill and Todd saw first hand the damage that could be inflicted by a P-47.

Life in Enemy Territory

While their bomb group was receiving kudos for a job well

done in late May and early June, Bill and Todd were being hunted by Germans behind enemy lines.[30] When the two Americans landed in the countryside near Vaggio, the Germans were drawn to Vaggio. Amerigo recalls: "Before William and Alfred arrived in Vaggio, there were no German patrols in the village. After they parachuted into the area, the patrols were looking for them. Whenever we would have a little respite from the German presence, William and Alfred would eat with the family."

Bill recalls: "I spoke Italian and got along well with Sarri, Riccardo and Gigi, so Todd just listened to me. He was a quiet man, a decent man who was easy to get along with. I always thought he would be a good family man. He was very methodical and always organized. For example, he said he had been saving and had money in the bank. I never had any money in the bank. He was a planner, I wasn't. I never got over the fact that he had the presence of mind to bring cigarettes with him when he bailed out. He was always thinking ahead. All I could think of when I bailed out was survival. I imagine he appreciated my being able to communicate so well with the Italians because he never pulled rank on me. One thing we both had in common was that we both had fathers who were very strict. We weren't allowed to step out of line.

"When we first landed in the outskirts of Vaggio, the front lines were about 200 miles away and not too many Germans were in the area. When the coast was clear, we were able to help on the farm but not much because the Germans were looking for us. During the wheat harvest, we helped in threshing the wheat. We also helped in fumigating the grape vines."

The threshing process followed the harvesting process. After the wheat was harvested by cutting the golden fields of wheat stalks with scythes and tying them into bundles to dry, the dry stalks were brought to the cement threshing floor where the two Americans helped to separate the grain seeds from the hay by beating the stalks. The grain seeds were subsequently ground to produce the flour used for making bread, pasta and other foods. The hay, or straw, was also used for animal feed, bedding, compost and other things.

The fumigation process consisted of spraying sulfur on the grapes. The fumes from the sulfur disinfected the vines and protected them from pests. Bill was familiar with fumigation because as a kid he delivered sulfur candles made by his family to stores in the North End of Boston that sold them to Italian immigrants to fumigate their wine barrels, essentially cleaning the barrels to protect them from fungi or bacteria.

Said Bill: "We wanted to help more, but couldn't because of our situation. Still, we were glad to chip in. Later, when the area became infested with Germans, we had to remain out of sight in the woods."

Amerigo was a frequent visitor to the cave. "We liked Rigo and I think he liked us. He used to come up to the cave to keep us company, often sleeping over. We used to play games. One game was someone slapped your hand in the dark and you had to guess who slapped it. Sounds silly, but we tried to make the best of our circumstances, and had a good time playing games."

Many years later, Amerigo characterized the two Americans as follows: "Alfred was blond, tall and rather shy, the classic American. William seemed more Italian than American, was very smart and spoke Italian with a Sicilian dialect."

Bill adds: "Sometimes, Rigo's younger brother, Bruno, would come to the cave with him, but we were concerned about him after hearing that after being scolded by his father once, he threatened to tell the Germans about us. He was a youngster and we figured he might not know the consequences of doing something like that. Fortunately, he never carried out his threat. That always had us on edge.

"Sarri used to visit us regularly. When he did, he would stand on the hill and look out over the valley, careful not to be seen. Once, he asked us if we knew Clark Gable. The Italians liked the American films, especially the Westerns. He knew that Gable had joined the Army Air Forces, and wondered if we might have run across him. We also knew that he signed up, but we never ran across him. A lot of movie stars signed up, hoping that others would follow their lead because people looked up to them."

When Pearl Harbor was attacked, Gable's wife, actress Carole Lombard, a strong patriot, encouraged him to enlist, and then did her part by going on a tour to sell war bonds. Her tour ended in her home state of Indiana on January 15, 1942. Anxious to return to Gable in California, she wired ahead, "You better get into this man's army."[31]

The next day, her plane crashed into a mountain and she was killed. Gable was crushed, but took her advice and enlisted in the Army

Air Forces. He trained as an aerial gunner and received his wings in January, 1943. Even though he was then the "King of the Movies" and a hero to many, he told reporters that his fellow airmen were the real heroes, not him.[32]

Bill continued, "Rigo visited us more often than his father, and was good company. He helped to keep us informed. He listened to the radio and told us what was going on in the war. He also brought his books to the cave and I was surprised to see that he learned in school how to take apart and reassemble a machine gun." Bill had mock rifles in his high school military training that were used mainly for marching drills. While the students of Boston did not handle real guns like the youth of Italy and Germany, the youngsters from rural America grew up with them.

"Riccardo and Gigi were also good company, as were Rigo's older sister Anna and her friend Maria, who brought us food every day. Except for our concern over the threat from Bruno, we were very fortunate to be treated this well behind enemy lines.

"I think we were viewed as a novelty of sorts. We were the center of attraction when we bailed out. Everyone in the village knew what happened. At times, people would be brought to the cave to meet us. Once, Riccardo brought a friend of his, Domenic Messina. He was a young man who was put to work by the Germans as slave labor under the Todt Organization. He gave me his work certificate [printed in German] in case I was ever stopped by a German asking for my identification. I never used it, but I appreciated having it. I still have it." Bill may have been shot if the Germans found it on him and discovered that he wasn't Domenic Messina.

The work certificate was a personal document identifying Messina, age 21, as an Italian citizen born in Giaia Tauro, a seaport on the toe of Italy, who was employed by Romanelli & Co. in Florence and working on behalf of the Todt Organization in the community camp in Vaggio. It allowed the holder to use public roads and places going to and from work during the night curfew. Bill notes: "The Germans would pick you up and put you to work swinging a pick or unloading a truck. You would have to do whatever their engineers wanted to you to do. When you were put to work, they would give you this certificate."

The Todt Organization, named for Fritz Todt, Hitler's chief architect and engineer, was a Third Reich military engineering group that oversaw the construction of roads and military installations in Nazi-occupied countries. The organization forced young men from occupied countries to in effect become slaves to the German Army.[33] Many young Italians headed for the hills to avoid such bondage, often joining partisan bands. Those who didn't flee did the dirty work.

The work could be very dirty. For example, on March 23, 1944, a team of fifteen underground operatives from the U.S. Office of Strategic Services (OSS) were captured while on a mission to destroy a railroad tunnel in Stazione Framura, about eighty-eight miles northwest of Florence. Italian employees from the Todt Organization were ordered to dig a hole for what they were told was a gun emplacement. On March 26, the fifteen operatives were shot and buried in this common grave.[34] As evidenced by this tragedy, the OSS performed high-risk operations. Many clandestine operations took place behind enemy lines during the war.

It is noteworthy that, after the war, the German general who ordered this execution was charged with violating the laws of war under the Geneva Prisoners of War Convention of 1929 by shooting unarmed prisoners of war without a proper trial or hearing. He was found guilty and was subjected to the same fate as his victims—he was shot to death by a firing squad.[35]

The Todt Organization was an important part of the German strategy to build fortifications such as the Gustav Line. While Bill and Todd were living in their cave during the summer of 1944, Todt laborers were being used to build the next imposing German defensive stronghold north of Florence—the Gothic Line. After the Gustav Line fell, the German strategy was to delay the Allied advance until the Gothic Line was completed and ready to become the next major obstacle for the Allied ground forces in Italy.

With the Gustav Line, the Germans already demonstrated their ability to build a formidable obstacle that kept the Allies at bay for five months. However, the Gothic Line was not yet ready, so the Germans had to continue their delaying tactics to bide time before the Allied advance reached this next major obstacle. During the month of June, life behind enemy lines wasn't too bad for Bill and Todd, thanks to the Sarri and Becattini families. However, this situation would change dramatically during the month of July as the battlefront approached Vaggio.

Chapter 8

THE APPROACHING FRONT

After the Allies liberated Rome in early June 1944, they continued to push the front northward up the Italian peninsula, but the pace was slow. There were a number of reasons for this. One, the Germans continued to take advantage of Italy's mountainous terrain, occupying high positions from which to direct accurate artillery barrages against the Allies in pursuit. The Allies were fighting an uphill battle. According to one soldier, "The Germans looked down, we looked up."[1] Two, the terrain itself was a natural obstacle for the effective use of tanks and heavy artillery. Three, the Germans were skillful at creating obstacles to slow the Allied pursuit by blowing up bridges, mining roads, and leaving rear guards and snipers behind when they evacuated a town.

Michael Reynolds, a British Broadcasting Corporation (BBC) correspondent, wrote of the difficult terrain in Italy. After having spent three days with the British 6th Armoured Division at the front when it was just north of Arezzo near the Arno River in mid-July 1944, he reported that Italy was too mountainous and cultivated to allow tanks to manueuver effectively.[2]

In Italy, Allied tanks often had to move in columns down narrow roads surrounded by hills from which the enemy could mount an effective attack. In North Africa, Allied tanks were able to spread out, thereby enhancing their effectiveness in pursuing the enemy. In late July, Bill Lanza and Alfred Todd would see first hand how the German rear guard could be effective in slowing down an Allied tank column traveling on such a road.

To further complicate matters for the Allies, the Germans were adding eight divisions in Italy while the Allies were losing seven divisions in preparation for Operation Dragoon, the invasion of southern France that would occur in mid-August.[3] Bill and Todd would later be in Naples to see a harbor full of ships preparing for that invasion.

Partisans and Reprisals

Despite all the negatives facing the Allies, there was one strong positive. The partisans were becoming a more aggressive force for the Germans to contend with. Kesselring himself, the commander of the German forces in Italy, said in his memoirs that the fall of Rome was the beginning of an all-out guerilla war by the partisans. From then on, he said the partisan war was a menace to his military operations.[4] However, from the vantage point of Bill and Todd (and Brickner and Kinney as well), the partisans were a godsend.

The partisans, whose leaders were typically connected with the Committee of National Liberation, which formed the Resistance in Italy, assisted the Allies in a number of ways. They conducted partisan raids against the Germans. They also acted as scouts and guides for Allied troops and infiltrated towns before Allied infantry troops liberated them, in a sense paving the way for the liberation.[5] The objective of most local partisan leaders was to free their community from Fascist rule and the occupation of the Germans.[6] Consequently, local representatives of the Committee of National Liberation worked closely with Allied leaders to purge a liberated town of its Fascist leadership and to establish law and order under a more democratic form of government.[7]

Goffredo Sarri was one of the partisan leaders in the fight to liberate his hometown of Figline Valdarno. After the war, he would be honored as a "freedom fighter."

German reprisals against partisan activity could be extreme and had been taking place for months. On March 23, 1944, the same day that the fifteen OSS operatives were executed in Stazione Framura, thirty-three German soldiers in Rome were killed by a partisan bomb. In retaliation, the Germans decided to kill ten Italians for every German killed. Consequently, they rounded up 258 political prisoners and 77 Jews who had been taken in raids. They transported the 335 victims to man-made caves in Ardea, a town located between Rome and Anzio in central Italy, and brutally killed them all. This came to be known as the Ardeatine Caves Massacre.[8]

Worse reprisals were yet to come as the Germans retreated up the peninsula. Two of the worst occurred in northern Italy after the front passed through Vaggio. On August 12, 1944, 560 villagers and refugees in Saint Anna di Stazzema, over sixty miles northwest of Vaggio, were rounded up and massacred.[9] Between September 29 and October 1, 1944, 1,830 men, women and children were rounded up in Marzabotto, about fifty miles north of Vaggio, and brutally killed for supporting the partisans.[10]

Between the March massacre in Rome and the September/October massacre in Marzabotto, there were many other instances in which civilians were rounded up and killed in retaliation for partisan activity against the Germans. The Marzabotto massacre was Italy's worst wartime atrocity and was not soon forgotten. In 1998, the German President Johannes Rau made a formal apology to Italy, at which time he expressed his "profound sorrow and shame" to the families of the victims.[11]

When the Italian government surrendered to the Allies in September 1943, many of the prisoners of war from a camp in Laterina, about fourteen miles south of Vaggio, escaped to the Monte Scalari area in Figline Valdarno, where mountainous terrain and thick forests made it a good place to hide. The area also attracted young men from nearby Florence and other towns and villages seeking to avoid the slave labor of the Todt Organization or the draft for the reincarnated Fascist Army of the Salò Republic.[12] Many of them became partisans.

Since the surrender of Italy, the citizens of Figline Valdarno had been helping the escaped Allied prisoners, partisans and others who were hiding in the area.[13] This expression of humanity occurred despite a law passed in October 1943 that made harboring a prisoner of war a crime.[14] The Germans had been circulating messages in occupied countries since 1941 that males who aided the crews of enemy aircraft would be shot on the spot, and women who rendered the same help would be sent to concentration camps in Germany.[15] Helping airmen was a high-risk venture, yet the partisans and the farmers that supported them took this risk. When Riccardo rushed to the aid of Todd after he landed, his life was at risk, and when the farmer in the field and later Goffredo came to the aid of Bill after he landed, their lives were at risk.

At night, the partisans would come down from the hills to conduct guerilla raids against the Fascists and Nazis. As the German soldiers retreated through the area, they would be subject to around-the-clock bombing, daytime strafing by fighter bombers, and nighttime partisan raids. Bill notes: "German troops traveled at night because they would be strafed during the day. As they traveled at night, they would randomly fire into the woods with their machine guns or throw grenades to discourage partisans from sneaking up on them. As a result, it was noisy all night long."

On June 15, Bill's mother Mary received a letter from the War Department that her son was reported missing in action in Italy since May 26, 1944. Among other things, it stated:

> The term "missing in action" is used only to indicate that the whereabouts or status of an individual is not immediately known. It is not intended to convey the impression that the case is closed. I wish to emphasize that every effort is exerted continuously to clear up the status of our personnel. Under war conditions, it is a difficult task as you must readily realize. Experience has shown that many persons reported missing in action are subsequently reported as prisoners of war, but as this information is furnished by countries with which we are at war, the War Department is helpless to expedite such reports.[16]

At the time, Mary Lanza had four sons in the service and three were overseas with a fourth to soon follow. Bill was the son that slipped her money from time to time, so she had a special bond with him. Many miles away, Bill often thought about his mother and how worried she must be. He wouldn't learn how heavy this burden was on her until he returned to the States.

On June 17, Kesselring issued an order that the fight against the partisans "is to be prosecuted with the greatest severity" and that he would "support any commander who in his choice and severity of means goes beyond our customary measures of restraint."[17] This directive led to more massacres of civilians in reprisals for partisan raids.

The next day in Civitella, about twenty miles south of Vaggio, two

German soldiers were killed and the third was wounded by partisans, causing the entire village to evacuate their homes for fear of a reprisal. When the villagers returned to their homes eleven days later on June 29, the Hermann Goering Division killed 212 men, women and children (mostly men) ages one to eighty-four, and burned about a hundred homes, some with the people in them.[18] After the war, Goering was convicted for war crimes and sentenced to death. He committed suicide before his execution.[19]

Soon after Kesselring's order, another tragic reprisal occurred about six miles west of Bill and Todd in Pian d'Albero, an isolated farm surrounded by a forest in the *comune* of Figline Valdarno, the hometown of the Sarri family. This farm, operated by the Cavicchi family, a sharecropping family like Riccardo's, was deep in the forest on hilly terrain near Monte Scalari. It had become a collection center for young men who wanted to become partisans.[20] It had also become a safe haven for wounded partisans.[21] The farmhouse was similar in style to the Papi family's stone-brick house on the Vaggio farm, only much larger. Even today, it looks like a fortress. Somehow, in the roundups taking place in the area, the Germans got wind of the house being a meeting place for partisans.

On the night of Friday, June 19, German soldiers mounted a surprise attack against the Cavicchi farm in what has come to be known as the Battle of Pian d'Albero. Two partisans were killed in the battle and eighteen partisans were captured.[22] One of the partisans killed in the battle was the grandfather of the Cavicchi family, and his son and grandson were among those captured.

Because there were German casualties, a reprisal was in order. On the morning of June 20, about twenty local residents were rounded up and placed under German guard in a local stable. At five o'clock in the afternoon, a German official arrived and the twenty residents were brought to a large space where a table was set up at which the eighteen partisans were ordered to be hanged. They were marched about two-hundred yards past the local church, Saint Andrea of Campaglia, to a grove of mulberry trees where they were hanged in front of the twenty residents.[23]

The eighteen partisans were left hanging there until the afternoon of the next day when the twenty residents were forced to dig a big hole for a mass grave. The parish priest pleaded with the German commander for a proper burial with coffins in a nearby cemetery. His plea was finally heard, but the victims remained buried over the weekend until Monday when their corpses were transferred to coffins and buried in the church cemetery.[24]

The twenty witnesses to the slaughter were worried that they would be next, but the parish priest and the head of the local farm where they were being held prisoner pleaded with the German commander, and he spared their lives. The parish priest also had the task of identifying the eighteen victims, who came from different parts of Italy. Two were the father and son from the Cavicchi family, seven were from Florence, and three just outside of Florence. One was from Bologna to the north and all but one of the others were from southern Italy—two from Rome, one from Naples and one from Taranto on the heel of Italy. The priest was unable to identify the home of one of them.[25]

Vincent Tani, one of the witnesses to the hangings, who knew the Cavicchi family, said that fourteen-year old Aaron was "a very pleasant boy, very nice, who liked to talk a lot." He also said that he didn't cry or moan at the hanging and "died as a hero." Today, the Cavicchi farmhouse stands as a monument to the sacrifice of the three generations of that family who died for "freedom, justice, and peace."[26] They were heroes fighting to be free of Fascism and the Nazis occupying their country.

After the hanging, Tani said the Germans locked them in a stall. For three or four days, they were forced to help the Germans gather animals from surrounding farms to feed the German soldiers. This gave them an opportunity to beg the farmers to tell their families that they were still alive. Fortunately, the Germans had to evacuate the area and left them locked in the stall instead of killing them.[27]

While Bill and Todd did not know of these hangings, they were very much aware of the constant threat of reprisals. Said Bill: "The villagers were always worried about the 'roundups' of innocent people in retaliation for partisan attacks. I remember once when a man in the village was picked up by the Germans. We could hear his wife screaming hysterically when her husband was taken away."

During the middle of June, the front reached Tuscany with Clark's Fifth Army on the west flank and Leese's Eighth Army on the east flank. As the front moved through the southern part of Tuscany, Iris

Origo captured in her diary the death and destruction left in its path as it raged through her farms and the surrounding communities. In her June 22 entry into her diary, she lamented the wastefulness of war and the suffering of civilians in its path.[28]

On June 22, the same day that Origo was reflecting on the devastation of war, Major Hunter's family back in the States was feeling the pain. The family had been informed by telegram on June 11 that Hunter was missing in action, and they wanted to know more.[29] Hunter's grandmother sent a letter to Eisenhower seeking more information. At that point, the Army did not have sufficient evidence to inform the family that he had been killed in action. The family would not learn of his death until August 3.[30] War wears heavily on family members, sometimes too heavily, as it did on Bill's mother.

On June 24, General Leese regrouped for the drive to Arezzo, and the subsequent drive to Florence through the Arno River Valley where Bill and Todd were located. To beef up the British XIII Corps to liberate Arezzo, which was twenty-eight miles ahead of his troops at the time, Leese transferred the British 6th Armoured Division from the British X Corps.[31] With General Clark's U.S. Fifth Army on the west side of Tuscany and his British Eighth Army on the east side, the Allies were ready to drive the German Army northward through Tuscany and beyond.

While the Allies were gearing up for this offensive, the landowners and sharecroppers in their path were fearful not only for their lives and homes, but for their livelihood as well, namely their crops. July was harvest time, and a good harvest was necessary to sustain them. The Origos figured that if the front had passed their farms by the end of June, which it did, they would need every able-bodied man reaping the harvest before they even dug out their hidden possessions.[32] For the farmers in Vaggio, such as Riccardo's family, it would be more challenging because the front would be raging through the farm during harvest time.

On July 1, two weeks after the hanging of the Cavicchi boy and seventeen others, General Alexander, the Allied commander in Italy, appealed to the partisans to intensify their warfare against the Germans. Kesselring, the Axis commander in Italy, countered with orders to arrest a percentage of men in areas of partisan activity and shoot them if acts of violence occur. If any of his men were shot, then reprisals were necessary, such as burning the village and publicly hanging the culprits and ringleaders. To be just, he ordered his men to convene a court-marshal before executing anyone.[33] As seen in the Cavicchi hearing, this was a mere formality preceding the execution. The result of Kesselring's orders was more reprisals and more civilian deaths as the front raged through Tuscany.

In Anghiari, about thirty miles east of Vaggio where Major Hunter was buried by local Italians, the Germans issued a proclamation: "Criminal elements in civilian clothing have repeatedly shot at German soldiers in ambushes. To atone for these crimes, several villages have been burnt to the ground and a portion of the male inhabitants have been shot." The proclamation went on to state: "Municipalities in which attacks on German soldiers or sabotage acts take place will be burnt down and a number of its male inhabitants will be shot."[34]

After the war, Kesselring was tried by a British military court in Venice for the Ardeatine Caves Massacre, as well as for ordering other reprisals against partisan attacks that resulted in the execution of thousands of Italian civilians. He was convicted on both charges and sentenced to death in May 1947.[35] However, the sentence was later commuted to life imprisonment on the notion that this was not a conventional war.[36] What's more, he was pardoned and freed in 1952. A book published in 2009, *Kesselring's Last Battle: War Crimes and Cold War Politics, 1945-1960*, discusses the international politics that led to his being set free.[37]

On July 11 at Arezzo, about twenty-one miles southeast of Vaggio, the 6th Armoured Division was subjected to devastating artillery fire from the Germans. Their Medical Officer, Captain Ian Brown, had to deal with gunshot wounds to all parts of the bodies of men. He attended to face and neck injuries, fractured arms and legs, burns and shrapnel wounds. The same 88-mm cannons that aimed flak to explode near planes were also being used to aim flak to explode over troop concentrations, sending bursts of shrapnel in all directions.[38]

The powerful flak that Major Hunter's plane experienced in the air was directed to burst over Allied troops as well. A BBC correspondent who spent time with the British 6th Armoured Division (of the British XIII Corps) near Arezzo experienced the anxiety of being near flak bursts. He wrote: "...he [the enemy] gave us a tremendous pasting with his self-propelled 88-mm guns. A very uncomfortable afternoon we had lying flat on our faces in a trench, listening to the shells whining overhead and bursting with a crash horribly close to us."[39]

The Germans were defending a front across Italy from Leghorn on the west coast to Ancona on the east coast.[40] The fighting was intense along this front with four Allied corps fighting side-by-side like a belt across Italy. The U.S. IV Corps (Fifth Army) attacked Leghorn, the French Expeditionary Corps (Fifth Army) attacked Poggibonsi, the British XIII Corps (Eighth Army) attacked Arezzo, and the Polish II Corps (Eighth Army) attacked Ancona.

After several days of fighting along the front that spanned the width of Italy, the Allies captured all four strongholds at Leghorn, Poggibonsi, Arezzo and Ancona. The tight belt that the Germans once had across Italy at the formidable Gustav Line was loosened again by Allied troops and pushed further up the Italy peninsula.

You had a chess game of sorts being played up the Italian peninsula. The Allied strategy was for the interdiction campaign to cut the German supply lines to weaken the German front, while the German strategy was to delay the Allied advance with a strong rear guard until its front could be tightened again with another formidable defensive stronghold at the Gothic Line. The Gustav Line was designed to take advantage of mountainous terrain, and the Gothic Line was designed to do the same. To penetrate the Gustav Line, Allied air power was needed, and down the road it would be needed again to penetrate the Gothic Line. On the ground, the battles would continue to be fierce and the casualties high.

There were casualties on the home front as well. On July 13 in Revere, Massachusetts, the burden of having four sons in the service, with one missing in action, was too much to bear for Mary Lanza. Bill's mother died on that day. According to Bill's brother Jim, her health declined after she was notified that Bill was missing in action. Bill would not learn of his mother's death until he got home, but he thought of her all the time. "During my whole tour of duty my mother was my main concern. I knew how worried she must be, and it bothered the hell out of me."

Bill's brother Dan was flown home from New Guinea and his brother Rudy left his ship the USS *Canberra* to return home as well. They didn't get home in time for the funeral, but their brother Tavio made it, coming from Washington, D.C. After a short leave at home,

Dan was reassigned to the Aleutian Islands, going from a warm rainy climate in the South Pacific to a cold rainy climate in the North Pacific. Rudy was reassigned to Okinawa, and after he completed his training Tavio also ended up in Okinawa. Bill was on everyone's mind at the funeral because he was very close to his mother, having worked with her in the store for years. A mother tends to develop a soft spot in her heart for the son who slips her money from time to time.

Danger was always present near the front. Just after Arezzo was captured by the Allies on July 16, the commander of the 6th Armoured Division, General Gerald Templar, became the victim of a mine while traveling in his jeep toward Arezzo on a road that had already been cleared for mines. He was in severe pain when medic Ian Brown arrived to administer morphine for what turned out to be spinal fractures.[41] After treating many casualties resulting from mines, Brown cemented the floor of his jeep to protect himself from land mines.[42] Brown handled severe cases under extreme conditions, earned the respect of the troops, and became a major at age twenty-five, probably the youngest in the Royal Army Medical Corps.[43]

No Peace in the Valley

Even though Arezzo had been badly damaged by German demolitions and Allied bombing, it became an administrative base for the British XIII Corps. It was centrally located in that three main roads that ran from south to north passed through the town. Highway 73 ran from Siena through Arezzo toward Sansepolcro in the Upper Tiber River Valley. Highway 71 ran from Orvieto through Arezzo toward Subbiano and Bibbiena in the Upper Arno River Valley. Highway 69 ran through Arezzo up Arno River Valley, known as Valdarno, past Figline Valdarno, where Bill and Todd would be liberated before the end of the month, and then past Incisa in Val d'Arno, where Hunter's plane was hit by flak.

Above Arezzo, the objective of the British XIII Corps was to advance through the Arno River Valley west of the Pratomagno Mountains toward Florence, about fifteen miles northwest of Vaggio, while the British X Corps advanced east of the Pratomagno Mountains toward Bibbiena, about fifteen miles northeast of Vaggio.[44] More specifically, the 6th Armoured Division and the 4th Infantry Division of the British XIII Corps would be advancing up the Arno River Valley with the 6th Armoured Division on the east flank and the 4th Infantry Division on the west flank. The battles at the front that Bill and Todd were watching were being waged by the 6th Armoured Division heading in their direction.

On July 17, the British 6th Armoured Division reached a deserted town just north of Arezzo but below the Arno River where it flowed west. After setting up their command post on a local farm, people came out of hiding and began retrieving their belongings, which were hidden in the ground and in various places around the farmhouses. Scenes like this were taking place throughout central Italy as towns and villages were liberated by Allied troops.[45]

The 6th Armoured Division next crossed the Arno over Ponte Buriano, one of only three bridges over the Arno River that were not destroyed during the war.[46] It is famous today for being considered the bridge Leonardo da Vinci had in mind when he painted the small bridge over the left shoulder of *Mona Lisa*.[47]

Many bridges in Italy were blown up by both armies, and not just once. Likewise, the bombed-out bridges were rebuilt quickly by the engineers of both armies. The Allies would bomb bridges behind enemy lines to cut off supplies to the front, and the Germans would bomb them at the front to slow down the Allied advance. This kept the engineers on both sides very busy and often in harm's way.

Bill said the British had a terrific bunch of engineers, called "sappers." They were operating in the area where they were hiding. They would clear mines, fill bomb craters, and build bridges so that troops and their artillery could advance. They kept busy. For example, in a single month the sappers of the 6th South African Division built fifty bridges, constructed forty bypasses, and filled in over a hundred craters.[48] The Americans called their engineers "combat engineers," and they were operating west of their hiding place. Mel Brooks, the comedian, was Mel Kaminsky, the combat engineer, during the war. He was responsible for deactivating land mines, and once quipped: "War is loud. Much too noisy."[49] Indeed it is, and it is noisiest at the front.

On July 19, the front was just south of Vaggio. It spanned from Arezzo westward to Montevarchi—near where Bill and Todd saw P-47s strafe a train a month and a half earlier—and further west to Radda in the Chianti Hills. With British troops in the Arno River Valley

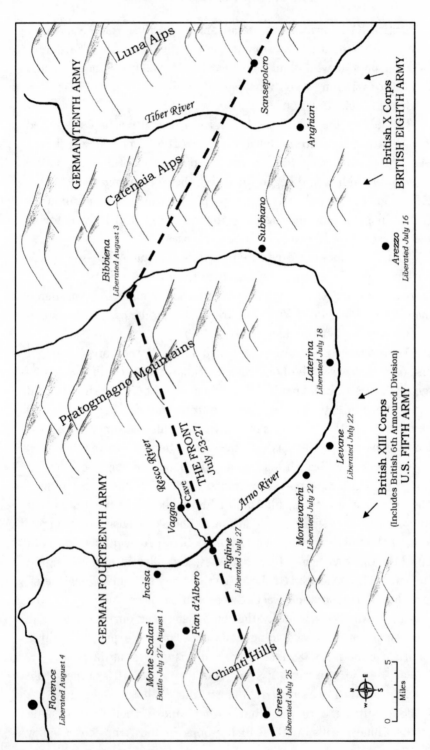

The Front Reaches Vaggio in Late July 1944

pushing the front northward toward Vaggio, the Sarri and Becattini families were trying to figure out what to do as the front drew closer to the farm. At the same time, an anti-Nazi coup d'etat was about to take place to assassinate Hitler at Wolf's Lair, the dictator's military headquarters in the forests of East Prussia. One of the coup's leaders, Colonel Claus von Stauffenberg, had arranged to attend one of Hitler's daily situation briefings. He even arranged to sit near Hitler due to a hearing problem received in combat. The plan was for him to set down his briefcase near Hitler, with a bomb timed to go off after he left the meeting to make a phone call.[50]

On July 20, he placed his briefcase on the side of a massive oak table leg near Hitler. After he left the room, another participant, General Brandt, noticed the briefcase and moved it to the opposite side of the table leg, away from Hitler. When it exploded, the oak table leg saved Hitler's life, but four of the remaining twenty-four people in the room were killed and five were seriously injured. Colonel von Stauffenberg and three of the other leaders of the coup d'etat were soon rounded up and killed. Overall, about five thousand people would be killed for their association with this assassination attempt.[51]

Origo in her diary noted that the German officers she came in contact with were all tired of the war. They had been away from home for five years, were appalled by the bombing now taking place in their homeland, and were depressed by the events taking place in France following the Normandy invasion. Still, she noted, they believed they could not be beaten.[52]

When Kesselring heard of the coup to assassinate Hitler, he didn't think the soldiers under his command would slack off on their military obligations. He thought that the war was too hectic for his men to sit back and contemplate the politics of the war. One point he made was that the youngsters from Hitler's Youth, who were being assimilated into the ranks, were genuinely attached to Hitler and were ready to lay down their lives for him.[53] They worshipped the Fuehrer, the result of years of brainwashing from an early age.

While there was dissention in the ranks of the German high command, Kesselring had more immediate concerns to deal with in Italy. The animosity of the Italian population toward the Germans had greatly increased as a result of the reprisals. The Italians were giving support to the Allies by guiding patrols and giving away German positions. Moreover, partisan raids had become a daily occurrence.[54]

On July 22, the British 6th Armoured Division passed through Levane to Montevarchi where it set up a command post. On July 23, it sustained heavy shelling as the Germans covered their withdrawal with heavy fire, as was their custom.[55] From their hilltop location, Bill and Todd were now at the front and exposed to the shelling. The front extended from Greve in the Chianti Hills eastward through Figline, past Vaggio and over the Pratomagno Mountains to Bibbiena, then over the Catenaia Alps to Sansepolcro, near where Major Hunter was killed in action.[56]

While the 6th Armoured Division tanks, together with artillery observers to direct their fire, pursued the enemy on July 24, some of the troops from the 6th Armoured Division participated in a parade in Arezzo for King George VI who, along with General Alexander, was inspecting the troops after the capture of Arezzo. General Alexander took the opportunity to tell the troops that victory was ahead but that it wouldn't be an easy one.[57]

Also ahead in their path were Bill and Todd. They were at the front in harm's way. The horror of war is most evident at the front and in this war of attrition the casualties were high among civilians as well as soldiers. As the front raged through Italy, many civilians lost their lives, their homes and their possessions. Many towns and villages saw their public utilities destroyed as well as their roads and bridges. Bill and Todd would soon travel over three bridges just before they were blown up by the Germans in retreat.

During the war, the quiet dignity of the Arno River Valley was displaced by the deafening sounds of battle. From their hilltop perch, Bill and Todd saw and heard combat in action. Bombs were dropping, fighter bombers were attacking targets of opportunity, cannons were firing, and shells were exploding. They also grew accustomed to seeing smaller planes called Cubs. When they saw one, they knew that a bombardment was not far behind. There was no peace in the valley.

According to Bill, "It was now dangerous to be on the hill day or night, or anywhere else near the front. During the day, we would see the Cubs and knew that they were sighting targets for the artillery barrages that would follow. During the night, we'd hear a Cub and a flare [on a parachute] would follow that would light up the sky as if it were daytime. Then, the bombs would drop. The Germans' anti-aircraft cannons would kick in, and soon the bombardment looked and sounded like the fourth of July. Since the British bombed at night and the German troops moved at night, this routine went on every night. We used to just sit outside our cave and watch the fireworks, wondering what would happen when the front reached us. We could see it coming."

Bill and others called these light, unarmed, liaison airplanes "Cubs." They all looked like Piper Cubs. Originally, they were designated with an O for observation aircraft and after Pearl Harbor were designated with an L for liaison aircraft. The Cubs were originally simply observer planes used by infantry and artillery divisions for spotting targets and directing artillery fire toward those targets. As their usefulness expanded with other functions, they became known as liaison planes. They are referred to as "L-Birds," in much the same way as the venerable old war planes are referred to as "Warbirds."

The seed for the development of the two-seat army observation and liaison aircraft was planted in 1938 when Hap Arnold, the Chief of the Army Air Corps, was intrigued with the German-built Fiesler-Storch spotter plane, the small plane that flew Mussolini off Gran Sasso. As a result, the Army invited manufacturers in the United States to develop a similar aircraft. Eddie Stinson submitted the winning bid with his Stinson O-49 that later became the Stinson L-1. C. Gilbert Taylor, who developed the "Taylor Cub," followed with the Taylorcraft O-57 that later became the L-2. Next, Jean Roche and an assistant, John O. Dorse, developed the O-58 that later became the L-3. Taylor sold his share of Taylorcraft to William Piper whereupon the "Taylor Cub" became the "Piper Cub" and the Piper Aircraft Corporation produced the L-4. Not to be outdone, Stinson followed with the O-62 that became the L-5.[58]

The competition to develop effective liaison aircraft is a good example of the entrepreneurship that enhanced the ability of the Allies to wage a successful air war. The air war was won not only in the skies but in the research laboratories that designed the aircraft and the factories that built them, and competition was at the core of each. Entrepreneurs such as Stinson, Taylor, Roche and Dorse and Piper were key players in the development of the L-Birds.[59]

In 1941, the L-Birds were all given the nickname "Grasshoppers" by a general who remarked that, as they landed and took off during maneuvers, they looked like grasshoppers in a cornfield.[60] Still, most soldiers simply called them "Cubs." By 1944, the Piper L-4 and the Stinson L-5 were the liaison aircraft of choice.

Terry M. Love, author of *L-Birds*, describes and explains the importance of these liaison aircraft. The high-echelon ground commanders used them to familiarize themselves with their sectors. In fact, General Mark Clark had his own personal Stinson L-5 named the *Rome Express*.[61] Lower-echelon company, regiment and battalion commanders used them to observe the positions of their forward troops as well as the positions of the enemy troops, and to locate and zero in on targets for artillery barrages.[62] They were also used for liaison missions, photographic and visual reconnaissance, supply drops behind enemy lines, and emergency missions. Emergency missions might include evacuating critically-wounded soldiers from remote locations, obtaining critical supplies, or delivering critical information.[63]

They were light, easy to maintain, efficient and effective. The L-4 weighed only 1,200 pounds. It had a sixty-five horsepower engine that could run on gasoline, and its twelve-gallon tank was good for three hours of flight time. If need be, it could land in a field, drain gas from a jeep, truck or tank, and continue on its mission. The L-5 weighed more at 2,200 pounds, was faster than the L-4 at 130 mph vs. 87 mph, and could take more punishment. Still, it could also land and take off in a cow pasture or a wheat field, and was called a "flying jeep" because of its versatility. Despite their size, these planes could, according to Love, "bring greater destructive power to bear on a selected target than any other aircraft in World War II."[64]

There were the obvious concerns that the Cubs might be too vulnerable to enemy fire, but combat experience proved otherwise. They were difficult to shoot down, and even if hit they could glide in for a landing. They could evade speedy fighters by simply landing and hiding. Also, the enemy knew if they shot at one, their position would be exposed and could result in an artillery barrage.[65]

Bill saw plenty of Cubs but he never saw one get shot down. "It was the strangest thing. The Germans would shoot at them, but it must have been hard to hit them, maybe because they were so maneuverable." They were also effective, so much so that enemy soldiers in the Italian Campaign were given a fifteen-day pass for every one they shot down.[66]

The possibility of retribution for going after a Cub was real, so artillery batteries were no doubt hesitant to seek the fifteen-day pass. Pietro Pinti, the Tuscan farmer, called the Cub a *cicogna*, which means stork. He was told it was forbidden to fire at one. He even thought the Germans and Allies had made an agreement about it. In the one instance he saw a German anti-aircraft battery firing at a Cub, Allied bombers appeared five minutes later and "bombed the battery to pieces."[67]

The L-5 went into service with the Royal Air Force as an air observation plane for artillery batteries in Italy, so there is a possibility that the Cubs Bill saw were L-5s. The RAF received them from the United States in silver and painted them dark green and brown with blue sky undersides to camouflage them.[68]

On the other hand, he may have seen Auster IIIs, the most popular British liaison aircraft in World War II.[69] The Auster series of liaison aircraft came about after British industrialist A. Lance Wykes became impressed with the Taylorcraft L-2.[70] He was granted a license by Taylorcraft to become a foreign manufacturer of the American-designed Taylorcraft L-2, and formed Taylorcraft Aeroplanes in the United Kingdom. A British engine was used to avoid the risk of importing American engines during the war, and the British manufacturer produced the Auster IIIs.[71]

Bill remembers one harrowing night drop from a Cub. "The Cubs dropped supplies for the partisans at night. A partisan would signal the location by lighting matches. On that night, Riccardo was in a field near our hill signaling for a drop. The Germans saw the light and unleashed an artillery barrage with shells landing all around us. In a situation like that, you just pray that a shell doesn't land on you."

There was another Cub incident that he never forgot: "One night, the goddam flare went off right over our heads. It lit up the whole area and we were praying nobody saw us on the hill. After the flare went out, we heard a whistling noise. We both knew what that meant. Quickly, I made a beeline for the cave and Todd dove in on top of me. He crushed me and my nose smashed against the floor of the cave. Then, we both felt the concussion. It was so powerful that it lifted us off the ground. We were just lucky that our name wasn't on that bomb. The next day, we heard that the bombing that night killed a civilian in the village."

Bill Mauldin, the Pulitzer prize-winning cartoonist of World War

185

II, who landed with the troops at Anzio, once said: "Bombs sort of lift things up in the air and drop them in a heap."[72] In this case, the things were two Americans thankful for the shelter of a cave built to last, like most everything else in Tuscany. As Bill said of Riccardo's brother, Gigi, who dug the cave: "He knew what he was doing."

As the British drew closer, Bill and Todd had another worry. Sarri had told them to be aware of the Gurhka Indians, known for going behind enemy lines at night and slitting the throats of unsuspecting soldiers.[73] The Gurhka Indians were operating just east of them and stories of their deadly strikes would keep the Germans on edge as well as anyone else hiding in the woods.

"To be honest, we were more scared of the Gurkha Indians that fought for the British than we were of the Germans. Since we were behind enemy lines, we were always worried about them finding our cave at night. When the British were near us, the Germans would machine gun the woods throughout the night because they were also worried about the Gurkhas as well as the partisans."

Their worries were well founded. The book, *Monte Cassino: The Hardest-Fought Battle of World War II*, relates a story about a British major who came across some Gurkha soldiers laughing. When asked what the joke was, he learned that they had come across three German soldiers sleeping in a trench and cut off the heads of two of them. They were laughing about the shock of the third when he awoke to find the other two beheaded.[74]

The Gurkha Indians had been an elite fighting force on the British front lines for a long time. They were fierce fighters and relied on their trusty 'Khukuri' knives to silently kill enemy soldiers. After fearing them in the Anglo-Nepalese War in the 1800s, the British recruited them to fight for them in World War I as well as in World War II.[75] Bill notes: "Since we were in enemy territory, we also felt like potential targets of friendly as well as enemy threats." Interestingly, Bill and Todd would later run across a truckload of Gurkhas on their way back to Rome. They appeared to them as a group of good-looking, friendly young men.

Early in the war, the Germans were the aggressors, but the tide had turned and the Allies were now in pursuit and the Germans were being hammered from all angles. In addition to traditional ground fighting, they were subjected to round-the-clock bombing—the

Americans by day and the British by night. They were also subjected to partisan raids and the threat of having their throats slit by the Gurkhas. Their desperate circumstances led to more atrocities as they retreated in a losing battle.

During the war, Bill saw that, in place of law and order, there was chaos: "In wartime, you had to worry about everything. Not only did the farmers have to worry about the Germans taking what they wanted, but they had to worry about civilians in dire need stealing from them. Once, someone cut and stole wheat from the farm. Another time, someone stole chickens. People were also worried about losing their precious possessions and hid them everywhere. Sarri hid family linens under a haystack. When his wife later sought shelter in the cave, she brought a typewriter which was probably one of her prized possessions.

"We once helped Riccardo hide oxen in a little corral in the woods, but people stopped hiding livestock after the Germans let it be known that they would shoot anyone caught doing this. The oxen were essential for farming the land. Riccardo was worried that the Germans wanted them for food.

"While the partisans were helping us and others, they were also going out on raids at night. I remember once when a Polish guy, who the Germans were using as slave labor through the Todt Organization, defected to join the partisans. He was going on a raid, and I asked Sarri if he could trust this guy, thinking he could be a spy leading them into an ambush. He said we'll find out tonight. That night, the guy was killed."

With death and destruction all around them, the Sarri and Becattini families had to be careful. Said Bill: "They were very courageous because if they were found harboring an American, they would have been shot. Riccardo told me once that the Germans had posted a notice in the village that those who helped Americans would be shot."

Riccardo and Gigi faced another problem when more Germans occupied the area. Their father, Gosto, who operated the farm, was taken away and held as a hostage so that his sons and other farm workers would provide food from the farm for the Germans at the front.

Just after his father was taken hostage, Riccardo visited the cave. Bill remembers: "He was so despondent. He was sitting there with his head in his hands. Since he was sticking his neck out for us, I offered to help him spring his father, but he declined the offer. He was worried that the Germans would retaliate and harm his family.

"As the Allied forces drew nearer, causing the retreating Germans to flood the area, we had to be more careful not to be seen. The Germans were swarming around us like insects. Shells from mortars and heavy artillery were dropping all around us. They knocked the hell out of the trees. We drew fire because three German anti-aircraft flak guns surrounded our hill."

One might wonder how under these conditions the two young ladies were able to bring food to the cave. Many years later, Amerigo explained that his sister Anna and her friend Maria knew different paths through the woods and were able bring food to the two Americans despite the hill being surrounded by Germans.

"Some mornings, the Germans were bivouacking [activity at their temporary encampment] and you could hear them singing. We even saw them practicing with their grenades, and thought they might blow up the haystack that Sarri hid the family linens under. Because the Germans feared the partisan bands so much, they would arbitrarily throw grenades into the brush as they traveled along the roads, so grenades were flying all over." Years later, Amerigo said that everything they had hidden was plundered by the Germans.

"One afternoon, Anna and Maria rushed up to the cave to warn us that Germans were coming. We all took off across the ridge, running deeper into the woods. We ran and ran and ran. Then, whoa! We stopped suddenly in our tracks. Just beyond a big rock was a field filled with Germans bivouacking. We doubled back and hid in the woods for the rest of the afternoon, then returned to our cave. Fortunately, we dodged another bullet." Sixty-three years later, Amerigo explained that the two Germans the girls saw on the farm were deserters who were referred to his father for help, as had been so many other fugitives. Amerigo couldn't recall what became of them.

According to *War of Extermination: The German Military in World War II*, by June 1944 "war weariness among the Germans and the Italians alike was also the emotional horizon that exacerbated atrocity and terror. A tiny minority of German soldiers placed their trust in the Italian strangers and deserted." The two Germans that the girls saw were among them.[76]

"Another time, Riccardo came rushing up to the cave to get us out of the area because the Germans were in the woods looking for partisans. We ended up running deeper into the woods than we ran with the girls and at a much faster pace. When we reached a small clearing, we met up with seven or eight partisans, and stopped to rest. I was a smoker, so I was beat. We stayed in that area for a while and then returned to our cave. I suppose the partisans returned to their hiding places as well. Riccardo stuck his neck out for us more than once."

Amerigo recalls an earlier incident in which he and the two Americans were stopped by an armed patrol in the woods that fortunately turned out to be partisans. The two Americans had to be careful hiding in the woods. They usually stayed in their cave or just outside of it on the ledge, where they could see down the steep, thickly-wooded hill leading up to it.

"I thought we had a pretty good hiding place. I had experience in camouflage from my infantry days, and due to our current circumstances, I was now camouflage happy. We always kept fresh branches hiding the entrance to the cave. Not only that, but we had an alternate hiding place about thirty feet from the cave in a briar bush with just enough space for the two of us. In case of an emergency, our plan was to scurry into the bush and tie the branches together to cover the opening. You would never know we were in there. These were thick woods.

"One day, we were sitting in the cave and, all of a sudden, we froze. We heard German voices, and they sounded nearby. We were panic-stricken because one of our coats was hanging on a tree by the entrance. It was a nice day and we had been sitting outside the cave. We didn't know where the voices were coming from, but they sounded awfully close. Carefully, I crawled out of the cave, retrieved the coat, and crawled back into the cave. We remained quiet and crossed our fingers. We were lucky. They went away. You have no idea what it was like being hunted all the time, knowing that if you were caught you could be killed or sent to a prison camp.

"When the Germans were being driven through our area and shells were falling all around us, Todd was uneasy. He thought we would get caught. I was uneasy too, but I always felt it was my duty to evade capture and had a lot of faith in Sarri and Riccardo to help us. I really trusted those guys."

When the area was being pounded by artillery, Sarri's wife and the children took refuge in the cave. It was safer than being on the farm. Amerigo recalls: "The Germans took possession of the house to provide food for the soldiers at the front. Then the agricultural company became occupied by a commander of the *guastatori*, at which time our family had to seek shelter in the cave."

The *guastatori* were there to prepare the farm for battle as the front approached. They were engineers that created the obstacles to delay the Allied advance, such as laying mines, preparing bridges to be blown up, and making booby traps. Kesselring was buying time until the Gothic Line was done. The Germans were hoping it would become a formidable defensive front like the Gustav Line. Of his delaying tactics, he wrote in his memoirs that he "believed he had fought a most successful rearguard action."[77]

With Germans all around them, Bill remembers what he thought was a strange close call. "I thought we were done. Sarri's wife and her children were in the cave. Riccardo was there too with another partisan, his friend from the farm [Giani, brother of his future wife], who always carried a Spanish revolver. When I came out of the cave, I said to myself, 'Oh, Jesus!' There were two Germans walking up to the cave and they saw me. They didn't look as though they were on duty, but they were Germans. As they approached the entrance, I just nodded my head, ready for anything.

"Just as they looked in the cave, Sarri's wife [Grazietta] rushed out and started talking with them, I thought explaining that we were seeking shelter from the bombing. These soldiers looked like strays, not there on official business. When they saw Todd and the other two men in the cave plus me, I think they decided they didn't want any trouble and left. They may have chickened out. I don't know. They probably thought we were just farmers hiding in a cave. Who knows what they thought? I was worried...but they listened to Sarri's wife and walked away. I'm not kidding."

Over six decades later, Amerigo explained: "The two Germans that William remembers were cooks of a field kitchen. Grazietta knew them because she had been ordered to help with the kitchen." Fortunately, they assumed that those in the cave were simply Italians from the farm seeking refuge from the shelling taking place around the farm. The two Americans had dodged another bullet.

Although it wasn't the case here, there was some evidence to support the thought that some German soldiers avoided trouble. In a story in *Aircraft Down!: Evading Capture in WWII Europe*, a book describing the experiences of several airmen shot down in enemy territory during World War II, an American airman evading the enemy took a number of chances that enemy soldiers didn't want any trouble on their watch if they could help it, and he did well playing these odds. For most of his life, Bill thought the reason the two Germans at the cave didn't start shooting was that they weren't on duty and weren't looking for trouble. This is the human side of war that is seldom depicted.[78] At this point of the war, soldiers on both sides were exhausted and hoping the war would end soon.

"As the British troops neared Vaggio, the artillery barrages got worse and worse, and we were in the middle of the fighting. Once, Rigo was in the cave with us and darted out after a shelling to collect some fragments of a 4.2 mortar shell that had exploded around us. When you see mortar shells and hear machine guns, you know the front is near."

Bill knew all about mortar shells. In the infantry, he had been in charge of a squadron with three mortar launchers. He explains: "A mortar launcher is utilized when you are near the enemy. You launch a mortar shell high into the air over a target. When it gets as high as it can go, it begins a free fall. The shell has a button on the nose that detonates as soon as it hits something. Like a flak burst, it can be deadly for anyone in the area. We were in the woods where mortar shells burst as soon as they hit trees, so we tried to stay under cover in the cave when the shells were falling in the area.

"One of the partisans, who sometimes brought me cigarettes, wanted to prove to me that the British were just over the hill by getting me some of their cigarettes. Sure enough, he came back with the cigarettes, but was shot in the knee. He was limping and his knee was bandaged and bloody.

"This guy had the looks of a tough guy in a Hollywood movie. He was a sidekick of a man they called Nano, who many people in the village were hoping would be put in the can because he pretty much terrorized the village, taking advantage of the turmoil and stealing from both the local citizens and the Germans." According to Amerigo, he was a member of a partisan brigade that operated in a nearby mountain zone, noting that the partisans who operated in his area were from the Pratomagno Mountains.

Pinti, the farmer who was sheltering many displaced people on his farm about eight miles south of Vaggio, suspected that some Italians were posing as Germans to steal someone's possessions. At that time, radio broadcasts instructed people to bury things they wanted to hide, and his family buried a chest of clothes, linen and flasks of oil. A man with a fur factory in nearby Montevarchi brought a couple of suitcases to Pinti's house and hid them in a cupboard. One day, two men dressed as Germans, who Pinti thought were Italians, showed up and found the two suitcases. Pinti felt as though somebody let the cat out of the bag. After relating the above experience, Pinti wrote: "There were many rascals around at that time who took advantage of the general confusion and stole what they could."[79]

With the front approaching, Bill and Todd were bracing for the worst. Fortunately, their savior, Goffredo Sarri, never lost sight of their dire circumstances even amidst the dire circumstances of his family. As Bill said many times, "I put my trust in Sarri and he never let me down. Whenever we would get worried, he would say, 'Be calm.' I don't know how he could always remain calm, but he did, and it really helped us to calm down. When I look back, I think he purposely didn't tell us some of the bad things that were going on around us. I think he was waiting for the right opportunity to get us back to Allied territory."

Chapter 9

LIBERATION

Goffredo Sarri had been in touch with the British and knew that they were near Figline Valdarno and would soon liberate that town. Consequently, he decided to take his family back to the town from which they were driven by Allied bombs eight months earlier. He had moved his family to the farm because he knew the Allies didn't bomb farms. Now that the Germans occupied the farm, it was in harm's way, and he thought his family would be safer in Figline. He also decided that it would be best to move the two Americans to Figline as well.

The Front Arrives

Sarri made arrangements for his family and the Americans to stay at the Don Bosco Salesian Oratory in Figline, not far from his bombed-out home. According to Riccardo, "The day on which we received news that the Allies had arrived near Figline Valdarno, we decided that on the following morning we would leave and face the trip to Figline."

Riccardo continued: "The day before this departure, I went to the commander of the German troops and, with the excuse of having to go to work in the mines of Gaville [a fraction of Figline] with two other workers [Bill Lanza and Alfred Todd], succeeded in getting permission for three persons which would allow us to cross the three bridges on the way."

The plan was for Sarri to bring his family first, with Riccardo to follow with the two Americans. According to Amerigo, "Our travel group was composed of my parents Goffredo and Grazietta, and my brothers and sisters—Anna, Bruno, Aldo, Grazia, the baby Alfredo and me. We were to meet Riccardo, William and Alfred at the Salesian Oratory."

Early in the morning on July 26, 1944 the Sarri family set out for Figline. According to Amerigo, "We had to cross three bridges and we were fortunate because, when we were stopped and searched by the commander of a patrol at the second bridge, he spoke Italian well and helped us get across the bridges. The trip was five kilometers [about three miles] through German emplacements along the side of the road and a continuous cannonade."

After the Sarri family left for Figline, Riccardo went to the cave to get the two Americans. According to Bill, "They didn't always tell us everything that was going on, and we didn't know we would be leaving Vaggio until that morning. Riccardo told us that it was an emergency and we had to get out of there quickly because the place was swarming with Germans."

According to Riccardo, "I tried to disguise William and Alfred with old clothes and told Alfred, who did not speak Italian, to pretend to be a deaf mute and absolutely not to speak for any reason." Riccardo also gave them each a raw egg and some wine to give them a little courage. Bill recalls that he also gave them each a blanket and shoes. Bill remembers the shoes all too well: "They were hard and lumpy the way shoes get after they've been soaked and dried, and they were way too small for me."

Riccardo brought two flasks of wine with him to offer drinks to German soldiers along the way, and it didn't take long to find a candidate for a wine offer. Bill notes: "As soon as we came out of the woods, we saw a German soldier laying wire on the farm and Riccardo offered him some wine. He wasn't interested in the wine, but he let us pass. It looked like he was laying communication wire for the German phones."

They walked north across the farm down into the village of Vaggio where they crossed the bridge over the Resco River. Bill, who had taken a course in demolitions, noticed that the bridge was wired to be blown up. "All you needed to do was connect two wires to complete the circuit. We were careful crossing the bridge." Once over the bridge, they went left and headed west along the road running adjacent to the Resco River toward Figline.

Bill recalls: "The Germans lined the edges of the road to Figline with machine guns covering the road. They were on our right under trees. Some were so close they could touch us with their rifles. They gave us 'lazy looks' as we passed. Some were hanging their clothes to dry and others were dug in with their guns ready for action. They weren't bothering the civilians who were walking on the road. They stayed off the roads under cover. They didn't want to be strafed by an Allied fighter.

"We were following Riccardo, and, boy, were we tense. The trip seemed like an eternity." Before they reached the Arno River, they had to pass through the village of Matassino. In the middle of the village, the road turned left and led to another bridge back over the Resco River. This was the bridge where the Sarri family encountered the German patrol commander who spoke Italian and helped them along.

Riccardo said they made it past the second bridge with a simple offering of wine at the control post, but Bill doesn't recall any German soldiers posted at that bridge. He does, however, recall that they had to walk cautiously over the bridge: "As we crossed the bridge, we had to be careful not to trip the wires. It looked like the Germans were planning to blow up that bridge too." According to Amerigo, the bridge was blown up that afternoon.

Ever since they were driven from Naples at the end of September 1943, blowing up bridges behind them had become routine for the Germans. Before they left that city, Kesselring ordered that anything of use to the Allies had to be destroyed. As a result, ships were sunk in the harbor; port facilities were blown up; and sewers, water and electrical systems were wrecked. The wreckage included even typewriters and accounting machines. The city itself had already been ravaged with bombs and artillery shells.[1] They continued this path of destruction up the peninsula of Italy, doing whatever it took to slow down the Allied advance.

After crossing the bridge in Matassino, they turned right toward the bridge over the Arno River into Figline. They were about a third of a mile from from the bridge when they sensed trouble ahead. According to Bill, "Riccardo was walking in front of us as we approached the bridge over the Arno River. Riccardo was already over the bridge and out of sight. As we neared the bridge, maybe fifty yards away, we saw two German soldiers walking toward us. At that point, I was thinking that maybe it was not such a good idea to cross the bridge during the day, and that our luck had finally run out.

"All of a sudden, by the grace of God, the two soldiers backed off and ran under the cement abutment of the bridge. A P-47 made a sweep and we just kept on walking. When we were crossing the bridge, the plane made another sweep. The soldiers were ducking for their lives."

In wartime, luck is your best friend and the two Americans had it in spades because P-47s were still flying armed reconnaissance in the area looking for targets of opportunity. Fortunately Bill and Todd, disguised as refugees, were not targets of opportunity. On the other hand, German soldiers were prime targets. Bill didn't recall any wires on that bridge, but later thought that it could have been wired underneath because it was a larger bridge that may have handled more traffic.

"After we crossed the bridge, we saw a half-track under a tree and the two German soldiers manning it were staring at us. Maybe they didn't want to expose themselves. Maybe they thought the soldiers on the other side of the bridge challenged us. Who knows? Oh Jesus me... the luck we had...we were so lucky!"

A half-track is an open-topped armored vehicle with light artillery that has wheels in the front and tank-like tracks in the back for better traction over rugged terrain.[2] They were used in the infantry. As an old infantryman, Bill was very familiar with them. They weren't as fast as all-wheel vehicles, but in a country such as Italy with its hills and valleys they were durable and dependable vehicles used by armies on both sides of the war.

Riccardo's recollection of crossing over the Arno River into Figline is different from Bill's. According to Riccardo, they were able to get across the first two bridges with a simple offering of wine. This was not the case at the third bridge. "At the last traffic control post, in the neighborhood of the Arno River, one of the soldiers was a little hesitant regarding Alfred, reading and re-reading the permission signed by the commander. I tried to explain to him that Alfred was a deaf mute and could not hear him. The soldier was at first convinced and let us pass. We succeeded in crossing the river, but as soon as we arrived on the opposite bank, the soldiers started to shoot at us, having uncovered something strange. Fortunately, they did not hit us and by now we were already in the free zone."[3]

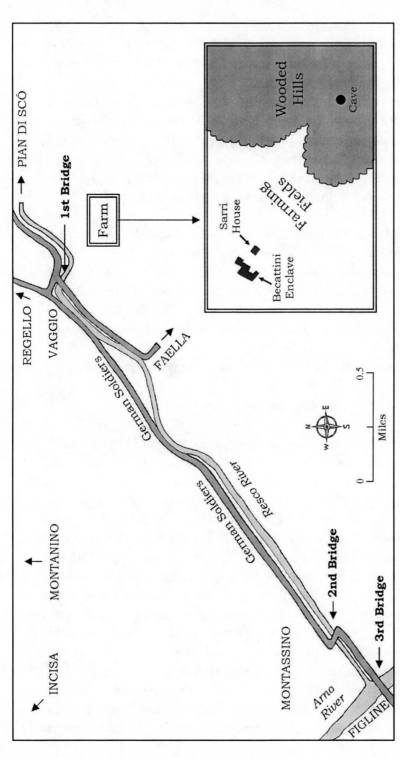

Road to Liberation: Disguised as refugees, Bill and Todd followed Riccardo from the farm, traveling along a road lined with German soldiers, to Figline Valdarno where they were liberated by Allied troops.

Bill said that Riccardo had a tendency to exaggerate when he knew him, so he wasn't at all surprised that his story was more dramatic than his story. What there was no doubt about was that Riccardo was risking his life to help them.

According to Amerigo, the three bridges were all blown up. The bridge over the Resco River in Matassino was blown up that afternoon and the bridge over the Arno River into Figline was blown up that night. Two or three days later, the bridge over the Resco River in Vaggio was blown up. Sarri and Riccardo had once again proven to be saviors to the two Americans, getting them off the farm in the nick of time.

Bill and Todd soon linked up with Riccardo again: "Riccardo was waiting for us after we crossed the bridge. The town was like a ghost town. There wasn't a soul on the streets. Everyone was hiding." Riccardo brought them to the Don Bosco Salesian Oratory in a small square where they met up with the Sarri family. The Oratory was already harboring many displaced people [refugees], all anxiously waiting to be liberated by the Allies. Said Riccardo: "I remember there were warm greetings and strong emotions from having escaped."[4]

Figline Valdarno Liberated

After the emotional meeting, Anna brought the two Americans to see her bombed-out home a short distance away. Meanwhile, her father Goffredo and Riccardo had other business to attend to. Riccardo recalls: "The Allied commander had not yet arrived in Figline. He was in Pavelli, a village five kilometers [about three miles] southwest of the center of Figline. Goffredo and I left in order to inform the Allied commander of the safe arrival to Figline of William and Alfred. We arrived in Pavelli and met the commander, whose name I cannot remember. He welcomed us and told us they would arrive in Figline that evening. [They didn't arrive until the next day.] In the meantime, we told him of the presence of German troops in the village of Vaggio and, looking through binoculars, I indicated the precise area, but told him to aim to the right to avoid a massacre of my family."[5] Had Bill and Todd been still in the cave, they would have been in harm's way.

According to Riccardo, "The commander gave the order immediately to begin the bombardment. At that point, I thought my family

Liberation

remained in the house under the bombardment. I was not able to remain a minute more and ran towards my house immediately. The trip back was particularly difficult because I found myself traveling over a road between the shooting taking place between the Allies and the Nazis."[6]

Riccardo was on a road between Faella, the village just south of Vaggio, and Vaggio. "Shells were falling all around me and one exploded near me. I fell to the ground and found myself buried without a scratch. I was buried alive. I succeeded in opening a passage from my 'tomb' to see light again. I jumped a barbed wire. In a flash, I reached the house where my family members were. Fortunately, I found them all alive."[7]

Faella did not fare very well in the ensuing days. The village was completely destroyed and left in a heap of ruins. The Germans blew up the roads and bridges in order to slow down the Allied advance. They also destroyed an important part of the village's heritage when they blew up two palaces that were a source of pride for the villagers. Despite this destruction, the villagers didn't lose their spirit. After the war, they reconstructed much of what had been lost. Today, Faella is an important fraction of Pian di Scò.[8]

When Bill and Todd returned to the Oratory from Sarri's condo, they were met by a priest. Bill recalls: "He gave me his slippers because my feet were bleeding from walking in shoes that didn't fit. Oh, what a relief that was! Then he took us to a sub-basement to hide." According to Amerigo, the priest was Don Andrea, the Assistant Manager of the Oratory.

The Salesians of Don Bosco are a Roman Catholic religious order founded in the nineteenth century by Saint John Bosco, known as Don Bosco because priests in Italy are addressed with the title of "Don" rather than "Father." Don Bosco was ordained to the priesthood in 1841 and began a youth ministry in Turin, Italy that was focused on bringing education, morality and religion to poor and neglected boys. He found places for them to gather and called these gathering places "The Oratory."[9]

Eventually, his ministry gained support, and acquired property and a permanent building known as the Oratory of St. Francis de Sales. It was named for St. Francis de Sales, a bishop who was known for his kind and gentle manner, and who greatly influenced Don Bosco.[10] Don Bosco had nearly fifty years of youth ministry, and his order has grown over the years.[11] Today, the order has over 40,000 Salesian priests, brothers, sisters and lay people in 120 countries carrying on his youth ministry.[12]

Don Bosco considered an Oratory to be a home where young people were welcome, a school to teach them life skills, a church for prayer and spiritual development, and a playground where fun and joy celebrate life. According to Amerigo, "In Figline, there are the church, the school, the athletic field and other recreational facilities." During the war, it became more than a home to young people. It became a safe haven for refugees.

The two Americans and another family were hidden more securely than others in the Oratory. The other family was a Jewish family for whom being caught meant certain death. Bill recalls: "I can't recall exactly how many people were in the family. There were several, and they kept to themselves. There were cots for all of us to sleep on. We all spent the night sweating it out. Even though shelling was taking place outside, we were so far down that we couldn't hear much." Amerigo said that there were many displaced persons hiding in the large building that night.

To be Jewish in Nazi-occupied territory was a harrowing experience. Of over forty thousand Jews in Italy, nearly eight thousand did not survive the war. Many who did were helped by people of the cloth. In Rome, for example, over five thousand Jews hid in convents and monasteries, as well as in the Vatican.[13]

Many Jews lived in nearby Florence. Of them, Origo noted in her diary on November 24, 1943, "the Germans are continuing the rounding-up of all the Jews. All who can have escaped to the country, or are hiding in friends' houses—but many have been discovered."[14] After many months of this reign of terror, the family sharing the sub-basement with Bill and Todd was now anxiously waiting to be liberated by the Allies.

After the war, a Jewish-Italian sculptor, Arrigo Minerbi, constructed a thirty-five-foot statue of the Madonna (Mary, the mother of Jesus) standing on a globe of the earth, to show his gratitude to the Catholic Church for having shielded him and his family from the Nazis during World War II. The original is a gold statue that sits on a pedestal at the Don Orione Center in the Montemarino district of Rome. In 1954, a full-size bronze replica of the statue was given as a gift to the U.S. national headquarters of the Don Orione order in Orient Heights, a hill section of East Boston.[15] A pedestal was constructed upon which to place the statue. Because placing it atop the pedestal would have created a hazard for the air traffic at Logan Airport, the statue was artfully placed in front of the pedestal to constitute a Madonna Shrine.

The Madonna Shrine is one of the most recognizable icons of East Boston. It overlooks Logan Airport less than a mile away to the south and, coincidently, Bill's old neighborhood a couple of miles to the southwest. Across the street from the shrine on its north side is the Don Orione Home for the Elderly founded by the Don Orione priests. The Shrine and Home were introduced to the public in a 1954 ceremony that featured Jimmy Durante, at that time one of America's most popular entertainers. The author attended that ceremony.

Interestingly, Don Orione was a pupil of Don Bosco and opened his own oratory at the age of twenty, eventually founding schools, boarding houses, agricultural schools, and charitable and welfare organizations. After World War I, his work expanded to other countries in Europe and the Americas.[16] It is indeed an interesting coincidence how threads of the two Don's touched Bill's life.

After a quiet night in the sub-basement of the Oratory, another priest greeted Bill and Todd. Amerigo later identified the priest as Don Biscio, the Director of the Oratory. "He brought us upstairs to a balcony overlooking a small square. He had been a priest in Chicago and spoke English. We spoke to him for about an hour. He was telling us that the Germans were respectful when they first occupied the town, but that things changed as more Germans retreated through the town, causing residents to fear for their lives and their possessions."

Thomas R. Brooks, in his book *The War North of Rome,* wrote: "No question but that the war that involved the Fascists and the Germans, on one side, and the partisans and much of the populace on the other became nastier and nastier as the Allies pressed hard on the heels of the retreating enemy."[17] The nastiness escalated to atrocities committed against civilians. Many were committed in Figline and its fractions as the Germans retreated through the area. Bill and Todd entered Figline after most of the damage was done.

By morning, the remaining Germans had evacuated Figline. The British XIII Corps of the British Eighth Army had broken through the

German resistance. By noon, its troops entered Figline, and people started to come out of hiding.[18] As Bill was talking to the priest, two reconnaissance vehicles drove into the square. "Todd and I were so happy. We went immediately into the square and spoke with a soldier, who brought us to his lieutenant. We explained to the lieutenant that we were Americans who had been missing in action for a couple of months. We were treated almost like prisoners until our identification could be later verified. We were ordered to a truck to bring us to brigade headquarters for interrogation.

"The truck had a driver, two German prisoners, and a guard for the prisoners. There was room for other passengers but we were the only cargo. One of the German prisoners was a staff sergeant and he told us in gestures and some Italian that they were sick of the war. They both showed us their wounds. They were chopped up pretty bad. The eye of one of them looked as though it had been badly damaged.

"Before we left town, we asked the driver to bring us to the Oratory to say goodbye to our friends. When we got there, a crowd started milling around the vehicle because of the two German prisoners. I heard someone say that the German staff sergeant ripped people off, stole some stuff. You could see the crowd getting riled up. The guard drew his pistol and told the driver to get going. I could see Riccardo in the crowd and waved to him. I could also see the guy who got shot in the knee getting cigarettes for me. That was the last I saw of my Italian friends." Amerigo said the two Americans were taken away before the majority of the British troops entered Figline.

Death and Destruction at the Front

The day before, when Bill and Todd were walking to Figline, they could see for themselves how strongly the Arno River Valley was defended by the Germans. Major General S. C. Kirkman, the commander of the British XIII Corps, was well aware that the German Army's main strength lay across the Arno River Valley southeast of Florence. As a result, he decided to mount a major assault toward Florence to the west of the valley through the Chianti Hills to take advantage of the lighter resistance.[19]

The South African 6th Armoured Division, with the help of the New Zealand Division, was charged with mounting a major assault on the western side of the Chianti Hills. Meanwhile, the 4th Infantry Division was battling on the eastern side of the Chianti Hills.[20] On the day that Bill and Todd left Figline, a great six-day battle began on Monte Scalari, a part of the *comune* of Figline, between the 4th Infantry Division's 12th Infantry Brigade and the German rear guards. The Black Watch (the 6th Battalion of the 12th Brigade) led the charge at the crest of the mountain. The taking of Monte Scalari after this bloody battle cleared the way for the beginning of the liberation of Florence.[21]

Hundreds of young Scottish, English, Italian and German soldiers were lost in this battle. In 1995, a War Memorial was erected by the Italian and British people in Figline Valdarno to honor those who died on the mountain in the cause of freedom.[22]

On July 27, the day on which Bill and Todd connected with a British reconnaissance unit in Figline, an artillery regiment of the British 6th Armored Division made their command post in a small farmhouse south of Figline. When they arrived, the farmer took a picture of Mussolini and tore it to pieces. He had just learned that his son had been killed in the hills by a German mortar shell.[23] While Mussolini was once revered by many in Italy, he was now hated by many for bringing this bloody war to Italy.

The partisans' war had become the people's war, and this hatred would climax nine months later on April 28, 1945. On that day, Mussolini, along with his mistress and other loyal Fascists, would be executed by partisans near Lake Como. On April 29, their bodies would be transported to a public square in Milan where they would be kicked and beaten by the crowd, then hung by the feet from the girders of a gas station.[24]

When the battlefront roared through Figline, the civilians in its path suffered greatly. After it passed, the priests of the parishes throughout Figline and its fractions compiled a list of the atrocities committed in their respective parishes. The atrocities were many and can be found in a book entitled *Figline Durante Il Fascismo (Figline During Fascism),* which was written only in Italian by Stefano Loparco. It was given to the author by Amerigo's son, Maurizio.

The parish priest of Saint Martino Altoreggi, Don Luigi Donati, reported on the German vandalism as well as the destruction of a church, an elementary school, a rectory, two civilian houses and a cemetery by Allied strafing. Don Eusebio Giunti of Saint Andrea of

Campiglia reported on the Battle of Pian d'Albero in which two older men were killed in the battle, eighteen others were captured and hanged, and twenty others were rounded up to witness the hanging and bury the victims. He also reported on the plundering of residences, the destruction of bridges, the damage or destruction of ten homes by German mines, and the theft of cattle, wild boar and sheep.[25]

Don Tullio Micheline of Celle reported that the Germans stole personal belongings and food, that five victims of the war had been buried in their cemetery, and that a ten-year old boy was killed by a hand grenade that he found in the woods which burst in his hand. Don Palmiro Matteini of Saint Peiro of Terreno reported that a store clerk was shot by soldiers stealing from him. Don Eugenio Fabbri of Saint Maria of Tartigiliese reported thefts of cattle and agricultural tools, the rounding up of men to dig holes for mines, artillery and ammunition, and the use of women for kitchen service. He also reported that two houses were burned down on July 27.[26]

Don Corrado Bianchi of Saint Michele of Pavelli provided a long list of atrocities in which German soldiers pillaged homes, terrorized the residents, and violated women. He noted that on July 25, the Germans arrested him and fifteen others. They thought they were going to be executed, but instead were put in a wine cellar until the arrival of the Allies. He noted that a local woodcarver, along with two German soldiers and two British soldiers, were killed by bombs and buried in their cemetery. In addition, he told of the death of nine others from the military operations.[27]

Don Angiolo Francioni of Saint Donato in Avane reported of Germans taking cattle, wild boar and smaller livestock as well as commodities like wine and oil; and of families hiding in the forest in fear while German invaders pillaged their homes. Don Pavanello of the Collegiate Institute of the Assumption reported on the plundering of stores and private homes, the damage to homes by mines, the damage to the nitrogen gas plant and the grain silos, the machine-gunning of six men, the shooting of a woman by a German soldier trying to rape her, and the death of nine civilians by shrapnel from cannon fire, two more from mines and even two more from the explosion of a train.[28]

The reports of these parish priests reflect the inhumanity of war. Contrasted with the inhumanity of these atrocities is the humanity of people like the Sarri and Becattini families who helped others at the risk of their own lives. The decency and courage of those families stood out amidst this chaos.

Hope and Recovery After the Front

After the front passed through her farms, Iris Origo wrote: "Destruction and death have visited us, but now—there is hope in the air."[29] The process for Figline and its fractions to recover began with help from the Allied Military Government of Occupied Territory (AMGOT), which appointed a Civil Affairs Officer (CAO) to oversee a temporary military government until the town could get back on its feet. The CAO met with partisan leaders who were fighting for the liberation of their town as well as local representatives of the Committee on National Liberation (CNL). One aim of partisans and CNL was to prevent the likelihood of prominent Fascists remaining in office.[30]

In the case of Figline, the partisan leaders and the CNL acted quickly to appoint as *Sindaco* (mayor) an anti-Fascist, Paschal Poggesi. It was the policy of AMGOT to govern through the *Sindaco*. While the CAO reserved the right to appoint or dismiss the *Sindaco* or other officials, in most cases the choice of the partisans and CNL was respected. The Figline residents referred to the CAO as the Governor, and the Governor set up a Communal Committee for the Administration of the Municipality.

During August, while Bill and Todd were on their way back to the States, the Communal Committee ensured that those most in need of shelter and food were helped. The Committee also took stock of the damage to public facilities and services. All the key roads and bridges were damaged or destroyed, as were public works and buildings. This included the electrical power plant, the silos that stored the community's grain, the railway station and other structures. The temporary military government was an expedient until law and order was established and civil services were once again provided to the community.[31]

On September 6, when Bill and Todd were back in the States, Mayor Poggesi, accompanied by partisan leaders who assisted the Allies in liberating Figline, presented an Administrative Report to the Tuscany Committee of National Liberation. Since the majority of industrial plants that employed laborers had been seriously damaged, one expedient was to utilize unemployed laborers to help rebuild the infrastructure. Appropriately, it was the policy of AMGOT to avoid methods which resembled those of the Todt Organization. Still, reconstruction would be a period of great sacrifice for the residents of Figline.[32]

The partisans were not forgotten by AMGOT. For every tale of German atrocity, there was a tale of partisan bravery. Rest and rehabilitation centers were set up to help demobilized partisans find food and lodging while looking for work. After the war, diplomas for valor, signed by the Commanding General of the Mediterranean Theater of Operations, were presented to partisans who distinguished themselves.[33] Goffredo Sarri would be among those honored.

Goffredo's contribution to the Allied cause didn't end with the liberation of Figline Valdarno. After Figline was liberated, he volunteered for the Italian Army of Liberation in northern Italy and served until June 1945. After that, he resumed his job in Figline. He would in time be honored not only by the Commanding General of the Mediterranean Theater, but by his hometown and his country.

In Harm's Way Again

As soon as Bill and Todd left Figline with two British soldiers and two German prisoners, they found themselves in harm's way again. "We almost got killed! We were traveling along a dirt road next to some hills and a shell landed behind us and exploded. One of the British soldiers said: 'I don't like this. They can see us but we can't see them.' The German rear guard was up in the hills. We kept going and another shell exploded about fifty or sixty yards in front of us, at which point the driver stopped the vehicle, and jumped out quickly. We all followed him. We figured the next shell was destined for us."

The Germans were bracketing them, which is what an artillery battery does to zero in on a target. It involves firing two preliminary shells to gauge the location of the target, setting up the third shell to hit the target.[34] "We ran down an embankment, across a bridge over a small creek and into a barn. A tank commander was outside the barn behind his vehicle. He was on his phone. When we entered the barn, we saw other people hiding, and we took cover behind some farm equipment. Todd and I were staring at each other as if to say 'What's next?' We could hear the commander barking orders. He was guiding his tank column from around the bend, heading in the opposite direction from us.

"The tank commander was small in size but not in stature. He stood tall in the midst of fire, as a shell popped here and there. He was giving orders to his tank column. It seemed to me that the German guns were going off in sequence and that he was timing them so he could advance the tanks in between the barrages. It took a while but he guided his column of tanks past the artillery.

"After things quieted down, the driver of our vehicle left and came back later with a vehicle. It may have been the same vehicle we abandoned, but I didn't ask him. We were just glad he was back, and thankful we were all still in one piece. The six of us then proceeded to brigade headquarters." The two Americans had dodged another bullet. Luck was still with them.

Chapter 10

HOME AT LAST

Bill Lanza and Alfred Todd were interrogated at the Brigade Headquarters of the 6th Armored Division. Bill recalls: "I don't know where we were, but it didn't take that long to get there. It was a bivouac area in a large field with tents pitched, machine guns in place, and a lot of activity. Prisoners were waiting to be processed, and so were we. A British intelligence officer interrogated us, and we gave him all the information he needed to verify our identities. When we were in his tent, two German soldiers were also being interrogated, but in a far different manner. The interrogator was screaming at one of them and took him outside. Then we heard a shot. They made it look like they killed him. The other soldier started talking." Most likely, they were in Pavelli, where on the previous day Goffredo and Riccardo had met with the British commander.

After being missing in action for sixty-five days, the two Americans regained their freedom. "When our identities were verified, everything changed for us and we were treated very well. They fed us and supplied us with British uniforms that included beautiful black leather boots. I felt like a million bucks in those boots. When we got weighed, I weighed the same as I did before we were shot down, but Todd had lost twenty pounds. I couldn't believe I didn't lose any weight, and neither could he.

"We received orders to report to the Headquarters of the Twelfth Air Force in Foggia. We were to get a ride to Rome and then fly to Foggia." Rome is about 135 miles south of Figline, and Foggia is about 160 miles southeast of Rome. "Soon Todd and I boarded an open truck full of soldiers. Many of them were escaped British prisoners of war who headed for the hills when Italy surrendered and the Italian guards let them go. There was also a huge Sengalese Indian on the truck. He was friendly but difficult to understand. However, we understood him when he told us he liked Americans because they were generous and were patriots.

"We spent most of the time talking with two British soldiers who had been hiding in the woods. One of them told us he was captured in North Africa and was one of those who escaped from prison when Italy surrendered. He had been roving around the hills, staying away from big towns. We were all standing up in the back of the truck, and trying to hold on. The driver was a wild man who answered to nobody. He drove like a bat out of hell!

"We passed Infantry troops, tanks and other vehicles headed north. We saw scattered engineers who cleared mines and built bridges. We could see that the front had come through. There were craters from bombs, bombed-out houses, and other signs of destruction. After a while, we stopped in a small village.

"Todd and I walked around the town with the two British soldiers. There was a nice fountain in the middle of the village, and near it was a bar room with a bunch of soldiers standing outside drinking. As we got closer, we saw two guys arguing. One was an Indian and the other a South African. The Indian had a stick with an ivory handle and was waving it around. A British guy, who had escaped from one of the prisoner of war camps in Italy, held the stick while the two of them went at it. The South African flattened the Indian. Oh did he pound him! I felt sorry for the guy."

One might think that soldiers taking a break from the action would be less inclined to spend it fighting. However, the Allies consisted of different nationalities with different cultures, languages and points of view. Away from the discipline of a unit, and with a few drinks in them, soldiers sometimes resorted to fisticuffs to settle differences. Today, differences often escalate to more violence than a fist fight. Again, it was a different time.

The Tuscan village being occupied by Allied troops was most likely a quiet place before the war, but it was now a bevy of activity. "There was a temporary stockade in the town with German prisoners in it. They were like cattle in a circle. The South Africans were throwing them cigarettes. The Germans had stolen things from the Italians, and were searched when they became prisoners. They had watch pockets that were checked for watches.

"We also saw a truckload of Gurhka Indians. They had their battle gear on and were heading toward the front. They were young, good-looking kids. We were surprised because they didn't look like men who would instill fear in you." Audie Murphy was also a young, good-looking kid who didn't look fearful. Yet, he was the most decorated American soldier of World War II. Looks can be deceiving. War is not a fist fight.

"After we had a bite to eat, we got back on the truck and headed for Rome. It was a wild ride again with our reckless driver. We were so glad to get off that truck when we finally reached Rome. We didn't stay in Rome long, catching a flight to Foggia in a B-26." Many airmen like Bill didn't think much of the B-26. He said they called it a "flying coffin."

The Martin B-26 Marauder was a controversial two-engine medium bomber that was more expensive to manufacture than a B-25 Mitchell and more difficult to fly, and it had a higher accident rate.[1] It had a relatively short wing which wasn't conducive to easy handling on landings and takeoffs without a lot of experience. It was also called a "widowmaker." Despite having had its merits during the war, these and other names were hard to live down.[2]

In Foggia, they bumped into men from their bomb squadron: "That evening, we were walking around Foggia and ran across Lieutenant [Keith R.] Matzinger and his crew on the street. They were on leave. It was so good to see familiar faces, but they brought us sad news. That's when we learned that Major Hunter was killed in the plane crash. They told us that he crashed into a mountain."

The Silent Evaders

On August 4, 1944, Bill and Todd were debriefed at the Headquarters of the Twelfth Air Force in Foggia. It was customary for airmen who had escaped from and evaded the enemy to be interrogated for useful information. The result of the debriefing was an Escape and Evasion Report. The report indicated that they were missing in action from May 26, 1944 until they returned to duty on July 29, 1944.[3] While both Amerigo and Riccardo said that the two Americans were liberated in Figline on July 27, Bill said you had to go with the date on the official report.

The report indicated that they received clandestine aid in escaping from and evading the enemy, noting that Bill landed one mile north of the village of Vaggio and Todd just east of the village. The report also explained why Bill and Todd didn't receive their escape purses and food kits before they bailed out. The purses and kits were in the front of the aircraft.[4] Ordinarily, they were left for them in the back of the aircraft, but that was no ordinary day. It was two weeks before D-Day and bombing operations in Italy were hectic as they ramped up bombing activity to divert attention from the impending Normandy Invasion on June 6.[5]

The report also explained why they didn't receive flak suits when they came on board. Due to a shortage of them, the crew of another ship making an earlier mission borrowed them, and didn't return them before their flight. So, for the first time, they flew without the benefit of flak suits. The confusion of war had been the culprit.[6]

During their debriefing, they were also informed that (1) Major Hunter and Reynolds were believed to have been killed in action, (2) Brickner and Kinney had found their way back to Allied lines, and (3) Denny had been captured by Fascists and became a prisoner of war. Bill and Todd already knew that Major Hunter was killed, but they didn't know about the others.[7] Later, they heard that Reynolds had not been killed, but had been captured and sent to a prison camp.

Bill also received a pleasant surprise. He was awarded the Air Medal on June 22 for his actions in the Viterbo mission on April 14 in which his aircraft was pummeled by flak and forced to land in Naples for repair before returning the next day to his home base in Corsica.

During July, unbeknownst to Bill, who was hiding a cave, all of his tent mates were also honored for their service in combat. Mygrant received the Distinguished Flying Cross, and Bufkin, Kane, Harrison and Leonard each received the Air Medal.[8] It may be that they celebrated the occasions with their saved-up whiskey, and perhaps even hoisted one for their missing tent mate.

Near the end of the debriefing session, Bill and Todd were introduced to a certification form that had to be signed by evaders of capture in enemy-occupied territory. The purpose of the form was to prevent an evader from furnishing useful information to the enemy that might jeopardize future evasions.[9] They had to sign the form to certify that "all information concerning their escape, evasion from capture, activities and equipment in connection therewith...is SECRET and must not be disclosed to anyone except the military officials specifically designated." To do so would make them "liable to disciplinary action for failing to safeguard MILITARY INFORMATION."[10] They each duly signed the form.

After the debriefing, they received orders relieving them from assignment to the 321st Bomb Group and instructing them to take a military aircraft for a visit with their friends before shipping out to the States. "We looked forward to visiting our friends in Corsica. That day, there wasn't enough room on the C-47 for both of us, so I volunteered to wait for the next one, and arrived in Corsica a day later."

The Douglas C-47 Skytrain was the standard transport aircraft of the Army Air Corps. It was a two-engine plane that looked like the popular Douglas DC-3 that was used to transport supplies, equipment and troops. About 10,000 were built for the war and General Eisenhower termed it one of the most vital pieces of military equipment used in winning the war. They remained in service long after the war and even saw action in the Korean and Vietnam wars.[11]

According to Kane, he and his tent mates heard that Bill was okay one night in the tent at about 10:00 p.m.: "We went nuts! We were so upset when he didn't return from that mission, and kept hoping and praying that he would be okay." When Bill arrived the next day, he went straight to his tent to see his buddies.

Bill recalls: "It was good to see Mygrant. He was a balanced guy who would land on his feet no matter how you tossed him. He told me that he had taken a trip to Pianosa Island to check on Griffin, who was killed when his plane crash-landed there. He learned from the natives that the Germans gave him an official burial under the Geneva Convention. One of the natives even gave him a photo showing the German soldiers saluting at the burial. He gave me the photo, but I don't know where it is now. I wish I still had it." The humane treatment Griffin received from the Germans on that island was a far cry from the inhumane treatment civilians received in the reprisals that took place on mainland Italy.

Bill also spent time with his other tent mates—Kane, Harrison, Leonard and Bufkin. "Leonard had my [.45-caliber] pistol which I forgot on my last mission. He also had my [.32 caliber] berretta which I bought from an Italian native for twenty bucks. I was happy to hear that Mygrant received the Distinguished Flying Cross for the mission in which he was shot down off the coast of Elba." Many years later, Bill was also pleased to hear that each of his tent mates had received an Air Medal while he was missing in action. Since he was also the proud recipient of that award, it was gratifying that the entire tent was honored in one way or another for their actions in combat.

Aside from his pistols, his other personal effects had been sent to Bastia, the capital of Corsica, about sixty miles north of Solenzara. Bill hitched a ride there and found a pile of letters waiting for him, none of which mentioned the death of his mother.

Back in Corsica, he spent a day at the new club for the enlisted personnel: "Before I was shot down, some of the men built a club that was pretty shabby. When I was away, Colonel Smith knocked it down. He said the men deserved better, and a new club was built that had the atmosphere of a real gin mill. It was great place to meet old friends."

He saw his old friend Dunn who gave him more information about Hunter: "Dunn said that Brickner told him that when he left Major Hunter to bail out, Hunter had his leg on the instrument panel trying to control the aircraft. As I've said so many times over the years, he was one of the true heroes of the war."

Major Hunter surely did a phenomenal job because three eyewitnesses, who were watching his plane after it was hit, said it looked as though it was under control, albeit losing altitude. After he bailed out, Reynolds felt the same way. Meanwhile, inside the aircraft, Hunter was struggling to keep it under control. His quick and deliberate actions enabled everyone to bail out before the plane crashed, sadly with him in it. Bill felt as though he was "all balls," and it looked as though he was "all heart" too.

It was a time of goodbyes. "The last time I saw Todd was in Corsica. I can't remember the exact moment, but he was visiting with his friends while I was visiting with mine, and we ran across each other." Todd had orders to report to Fort Dix, New Jersey, near his home in upstate New York. Brickner had the same orders as Todd, and traveled on the same ship with him from Italy to New York Harbor. Since Brickner was also an evader, he too had to certify in writing that he wouldn't talk about his evasion experiences. Whether or not they discussed them among themselves on the way home is something we'll never know.

Home At Last

After a couple of days in Corsica, Bill caught a plane to Naples, a city where airmen, soldiers and sailors came on their military leaves to rest, relax and spend their money. Bill indulged: "I did pretty well in a crap game. I won big and sent $300 to my mother." Actually, his winnings were in Italian lire of "invasion currency," of which he converted 30,000 lire to the 300 U.S. dollars he sent to his mother in a money order. The son who used to slip his mother money from time to time before the war was still at it, and looking forward to seeing his mother again soon.

Before the Allies invaded Sicily and the Italian mainland, the Americans and British were concerned that if they used their dollars or pounds the Germans might undermine their currencies, either by confiscating them and using them elsewhere in the world or by introducing counterfeits in Italy. They were also concerned that the Germans might impede the ability of the Italians to produce enough lire to enable them to pay their troops and purchase supplies and services from the Italians.[12]

In response to these concerns, the Allied Military Government authorized the production of an "Allied Military Currency," referred to as "invasion currency." The plan was to use the invasion currency until such time as Italy could recover and establish a permanent currency again.[13] An Allied Military Financial Agency was established to work closely with Banca d'Italia, the Italian central bank, in implementing the plan. The invasion currency was authorized by the Allied Military Command to be legal tender in Italy, and on September 24, 1943, the plan was approved by the King of Italy.[14]

While the United States did not authorize the printing of this special currency, it did the printing. Most of the Allied Military currency was printed by the Forbes Lithograph Manufacturing Company plant in Chelsea, Massachusetts, located less than a mile from Bill's home in Revere.[15] Because the U.S. Bureau of Engraving and Printing (responsible for printing the nation's currency) had insufficient equipment to meet the demand, it outsourced the printing to Forbes. For security reasons, representatives of the Bureau and the U.S. Secret Service (responsible for protecting the nation's currency) were sent to the Forbes plant to oversee the top secret operation.

The first printing run produced two types of notes—some half the size of the U.S. dollar to be used for smaller denominations (1, 5, 10 and 50) and some the same size of the U.S. dollar to be used for larger denominations (100, 500 and 1000).[16] The first-run notes did not have the name of the country or its currency because the country to be invaded was highly confidential at the time. They did, however, have printed on both sides "Allied Military Currency," and on the back side the four freedoms specified by President Roosevelt in his January 6, 1942 speech to Congress following the bombing of Pearl Harbor—freedom of speech, freedom of religion, freedom from want and freedom from fear. The four freedoms are now inscribed on Roosevelt's Memorial on the National Mall.[17]

Soon after the Allies invaded Sicily on July 9, 1943, the front side of the notes was overprinted with the country (Italy) and currency (lire) designations. By July 19, two planes carrying seven tons (30,000,000 lire to a ton[18]) of the Italian invasion currency took off for Italy.[19] The temporary currency was pegged to the dollar (100 lire = 1 dollar) and to the British pound (400 lire = 1 pound).[20] However, it could only be used in Italy, and servicemen like Bill had to identify themselves in order to convert it to U.S. dollars, as did Bill before he sent his mother the $300.[21]

After the invasion of southern France on August 15, Naples quieted down and Bill shipped out to the States on August 21. While he was on the high seas, he was thinking about his mother and what a boost to her morale his return would be. He was also very sick: "Oh, did I get seasick. I never got airsick. You could fly me upside down and I was okay in the air, but it was different on the high seas."

While Bill was having a miserable voyage home, his old neighbor Jerry Gray was involved in a project to boost the morale of the war-weary troops. He was meeting with Bing Crosby and Glenn Miller for an upcoming live performance by the two icons to be broadcast to the troops over the BBC network. That was probably where the photograph was taken of Crosby, Gray and Miller that appears in the Glenn Miller display at the United States Air Force Museum near Dayton, Ohio.

At the time, Bing Crosby and Glenn Miller were among the most popular entertainers in show business. Crosby won an Oscar that year for best actor as Father O'Malley in *Going My Way*, which also won the Oscar for the best picture of 1944. On August 31, when Bill was almost home, Crosby and Miller teamed up for a live half-hour recording session at the Paris Cinema in London before three hundred servicemen and women that was simultaneously broadcast by radio to the troops throughout Europe. Pretty soon, Bill would need a morale-booster of his own because sad news awaited him at home.[22] Sad news was also ahead for the Miller family because three months later the patriotic band leader would disappear over the English Channel.

Bittersweet Homecoming

Bill arrived in Newport News, Virginia, on September 1, 1944, which was exactly five years after Germany invaded Poland to start World War II. "As soon as I got back to the States, I called home. My sister Anna answered the phone. When I asked about my mother, she got all choked up and the next thing I knew I was talking to my sister-in-law Dottie. She was happy to hear from me, but was noncommittal on my mother. I knew something was very wrong.

"I had orders to report to Fort Devens in Massachusetts, about an hour from my home in Revere. As soon as I got there, my brother Dan came to see me. When I saw him, I said: 'You don't have to tell me. I know.' I knew my mother had died. I was devastated!

"My mother was very worried about us, and I knew all along that my being missing would weigh heavily on her. I just never expected that she would die. She was only fifty-three years old. I felt terrible that she died never knowing whether I was dead or alive. She was such a great mother and a wonderful person to everyone. This was a sad homecoming. It just changed everything for me. I was so down for a long time. If it wasn't for the girl who later became my wife, I might still be lying on the barroom floor."

After spending a few days home, Bill was ordered to LaGuardia Field in New York. There, on September 7, he had to sign the exact same form he signed in Foggia, certifying once again that he wouldn't disclose any information about his escape and evasion.[23] "I also learned that because Todd and I were behind enemy lines for over two months, we were classified as spies and could have been shot if we had been captured." This also became a possibility months earlier when they turned in their military uniforms for civilian clothes.

Recovery from Combat

After his debriefing at LaGuardia, Bill went through the Army Air Forces Redistribution Program. The Army Air Forces established the

Personnel Distribution Command to pay attention to the problems that war-weary airmen may have when they return to the United States. There were Redistribution Stations No. 1 in Atlantic City and No. 2 in Miami Beach, and rest camps at Lake Lure, North Carolina; Castle Hot Springs, Arizona; and Camp Mystic, Texas. Originally called the Redistribution Center, it became the Personnel Distribution Command on June 1, 1944 and opened additional redistribution stations at Santa Monica and Santa Ana, California; at Camp Davis and Greensboro, North Carolina; and at San Antonio, Texas. The Personnel Distribution Command also acquired more than a dozen convalescent hospitals.[24]

The Personnel Distribution Command routine for airmen consisted of rest and relaxation, evaluation of their physical and mental well-being, and preparation for either reassignment in the military or separation from it. General Hap Arnold set the tone for the program when he summed up the impact of the war on an airman and the responsibility of the Army Air Forces to cushion this impact: "We took him out of civilian life when his future was brightest...when he returns, we want his outlook and his chances for success just as brilliant." Under the program, an airman returning from combat was to be given some choice in the selection of his new assignment. The program was concerned with getting the right people into the right jobs.[25]

Arnold was one of the true champions of air power during the war. He was a protégé of Billy Mitchell, and as the head of the Army Air Corps since 1935 he was its driving force. His name Hap was short for Happy, but he was a difficult taskmaster with a legendary temper. He was an effective leader of the Army Air Corps, but the war took its toll on him, as evidenced by the several heart attacks he suffered during the war.[26] While Arnold could be hard on the men, he cared for them and their families. While he didn't get much rest himself, he knew as well as anyone the importance of rest and relaxation.

Bill's first stop in the program was the Ambassador Hotel in Atlantic City for rest, relaxation and reassignment. Since July 1942, the U.S. Army had leased all the beachfront and side hotels in Atlantic City for use as housing facilities and hospitals.[27] From the Ambassador, Bill was sent to Fort Logan in Denver, Colorado for more rest, relaxation and evaluation.[28] "At Fort Logan, we shared stories. One guy told us that when he bailed out, his chute got caught and he was hanging from the plane, being buffeted by the wind until someone freed him. I could relate to this predicament because the prop wash slammed me against the bottom of plane when I bailed out. Another guy told us that he received help from a German sergeant on the ground. I heard many stories, and I had a few of my own.

"Since I hadn't made any plans for after the war, I was encouraged to return to duty and decided to remain in the service. I was then assigned to Lowry Field, also in Denver, for training in electronics to be a turret maintenance specialist. I studied the operation, installation, maintenance and repair of 30- and 50-caliber machine guns and power turret operations.

"After I completed my training, I was given my choice of airfields. I chose Logan Airport in Boston, close to home, but since there was no military operation there, I ended up at Fort Dix in Trenton, New Jersey. I was assigned to an experimental squadron. We did experimental work on airplanes, made improvements, and had test pilots to check out the improvements. When I was there, they were working on improving the ability to land planes by instruments."

Bill remained in that position until the end of the war. On his free time, he headed for the Big Apple. "New York City was an exciting place, and we took advantage of it. You never knew what you would find there. Once, we saw Gene Kelly in a bar on 42nd Street. He ordered scotch and soda. He was an ensign and had just seen a musical."

During November 1944, while Bill was back in the States, his friend Frank Alvino was a platoon sergeant fighting with Patton's Third Army in Lorraine, a province between France and Germany over which the two countries had been battling for centuries. It had changed hands four times since 1766, most recently in 1940 when Hitler reclaimed it. It was the most direct route from France to Germany. It was also a nasty place to do battle, and Patton was well aware of this.

It was not Patton's choice to do battle in Lorraine. It was Eisenhower's, who wanted to remove as many German forces as possible west of the Rhine River.[29] His plan was to defeat the enemy west of the Rhine, gain a foothold on its east bank, and then march through Germany. Hitler was just as determined to prevent this from happening. No invading army had crossed the Rhine since Napolean in 1805, and Hitler let it be known that any commander surrendering or retreating would be shot.[30]

SHOT DOWN OVER ITALY

Lorraine now stood between Patton's Third Army and the Rhine River, and would soon become the scene of the Third Army's bloodiest campaign.[31] As was the situation in Anzio and Monte Cassino, the terrain and the weather in Lorraine favored the Germans. There were numerous rivers and streams, and it rained for twenty days during the month, causing the worst floods in thirty-five years. The Third Army engineers would build over thirty bridges in Lorraine during November.[32] In addition, there were rolling hills and dense forests that provided cover for snipers, and there were towns and villages with pockets of German resistance. If that wasn't enough, the ground rose from the west to the east, so the Allies were literally fighting another uphill battle.[33]

Lorraine had two principal cities—Metz and Nancy—and Patton issued orders to his men to capture both.[34] Alvino's Yankee Division was fighting with the XII Corps of Patton's Army that attacked Nancy on November 8. Since the Germans held dominant positions and were dug in, they fended off the Allies. It took five days for XII Corps to regroup before it attacked again, and Nancy fell on November 15.

Meanwhile, the forward troops were advancing further east with an objective of capturing the high ground on Hill 310 in Moyenvic, a comune in Lorraine about twenty miles east of Nancy. From Hill 310, the Germans could observe the surrounding area and direct accurate artillery barrages at the attacking troops. Alvino's "I" Company was fighting on the west side of the hill.[35] On November 17, 1944, Alvino found himself in harm's way and was killed in action.

His family was told that he was killed by a sniper when he came to the aid of one of his men. He was among 661 soldiers of the Yankee Division who were killed that month in Lorraine, while another 2000 were wounded.[36] The Lorraine Campaign was a drawn-out, bloody affair that lasted over three months. It resulted in 50,000 casualties to the Third Army, which claimed to have inflicted over 180,000 casualties to the enemy.[37]

Bill learned of Alvino's death in a letter sent from George Tirro, another hometown friend from the Yankee Division. He was greatly saddened by the death of his buddy: "We used to do a lot of things together—play cards, go to town, and we'd even come home together on furloughs. He was a good soldier, and a good friend. I still miss him."

On his next trip home, Bill visited Frank's parents, Anthony and

Carmella. He saw the heavy toll the war took on his own mother, and paid his respects to Frank's mother. Frank also came from a large family—five brothers and four sisters—and all five brothers were serving their country. Ernie and Eddie were in the Army like Frank, and Bob and Charlie were in the Navy.

Alvino was buried in a temporary United States Military Cemetery in Limey, France, about thirty miles west of Moyenvic. His family wanted to bring him home, but it took a while. In 1948, his body was brought by military escort to his hometown in Revere, Massachusetts, where his family and friends paid their final respects before he was laid to rest in Holy Cross Cemetery in nearby Malden, Massachusetts.[38]

Today, a large stone with a commemorative star in Moyenvic honors the soldiers of the 26th Infantry Division—men like Frank—who fought and died in the fight for freedom. Closer to home, a signpost with a commemorative star stands in front of Frank's home in Revere as a lasting tribute to him.

Eight months after Frank's death, Bill was still at Fort Dix when a tragic event occurred in the New York City that involved a B-25. On Saturday July 28, 1945 at 9:49 a.m., an Army Air Forces ten-ton B-25 aircraft crashed into the 79th floor of the Empire State Building. The pilot, Lieutenant Colonel William Smith, was a decorated veteran of a hundred combat missions who went home to Massachusetts for the weekend from his base in South Dakota. He was flying from his home in Bedford, Massachusetts to pick up his commanding officer at Newark Airport before returning to their home base.

Due to a dense fog over New York City, Smith showed up over LaGuardia airport and the tower directed him to land there due to poor visibility over Manhattan. However, he requested and received permission from the military to continue on to Newark. As he flew over Manhattan, he came upon the Chrysler building, at that time the second tallest building in the world. He banked left to avoid it and flew into the world's tallest building.[39]

As with the larger planes that hit the World Trade Towers on 9/11, the high-octane fuel exploded and flames engulfed four floors, from the 78th floor down to 75th floor. All told, fourteen people were killed in the accident, including three members of the crew and eleven office workers. If the accident had occurred during the week, many more would have perished.[40]

Unlike the World Trade Center twin towers, the structural integrity of the building held, and it would be repaired at a cost of a million dollars.[41] The next day, Sunday, Bill took a train from Trenton into the City to see the damage. As he stared up at the aircraft embedded in the building, his thought was simply: "Somebody goofed." On September 11, 2001, when his nephew (the author) was in a tall building in Brooklyn looking at the smoke stemming from an aircraft that hit the north tower of the World Trade Center, he was thinking the same thing, until he saw the second plane hit the south tower.

The 1945 accident made the designers of the twin towers mindful that they were vulnerable to being hit by a large aircraft. As a result, the twin towers became the first structures outside of the military and nuclear industries to be designed to consider the impact of a jet airliner, in this case a Boeing 707. Unfortunately, the two Boeing 767 commercial airplanes that hit the towers on 9/11 were considerably larger and faster than a Boeing 707, and the buildings were not designed to sustain blows from such aircraft.[42]

After witnessing the results of the 1945 weekend tragedy, Bill was almost part of a weekend tragedy. "I hitched a ride to Boston with one of the pilots at the base who borrowed an AT-11 bomber trainer for a weekend visit home." The AT-11 was used to train bombardiers, gunners and navigators. Typically, the crew consisted of a pilot, an instructor and two students. For the weekend trip, there was a crew of three. Notes Bill: "A corporal named Murphy from Cambridge also hitched a ride. The plane was scheduled to land at Bedford Army Air Field, but it was foggy in Bedford. The pilot didn't have the card that qualified him for an instrument landing in bad weather, so we were sent to Logan Airport. Fortunately, it wasn't foggy at Logan and we landed okay, but blew the back tire as we landed. The tire needed to be fixed before we could take off again."

Logan was not a military airport so the tire wasn't fixed in the routine manner of military airports. "We planned to fly home on Sunday when it was still light, but it took a long time to get the tire fixed. We ended up taking off for Fort Dix at around midnight. Murphy was in the co-pilot seat and I was behind the flight deck. As we were flying over New York City, we lost the lights inside the plane and the pilot told us to put on our parachutes. I said to myself, 'Oh no, here we go again.' I groped around in the dark for my parachute, and put it on. It was pretty tense. Boy, was I relieved when the lights came back on in about five minutes."

More trouble lay ahead. "When we came in for a landing, I was standing behind and between the pilot and Murphy with my arms on their seats bracing myself for the touch down. Unbeknownst to us, the wheels weren't down. What a jolt we got when we hit the runway! Suddenly, I was jerked forward and my torso was almost separated from my arms. The next day, my arms were so sore I couldn't lift them. We skidded along the runway in a hail of sparks and were lucky our plane didn't blow up.

"It seemed like fifteen minutes before an emergency crew reached us with their asbestos suits and foam. Fortunately, we didn't need their help. We were already out of the aircraft and sitting on the ground. The next day, Murphy and I were put in separate rooms and questioned about the horn that is supposed to sound when a plane goes into a stall position before the landing and the wheels aren't down and locked in place. It may have sounded, but we didn't hear it."

The experience had a lifelong impact on Bill: "Before that weekend, I had no problem with flying, but afterward I felt as though someone was trying to tell me something. I made a vow to myself never to fly again, and I never did. I was so thankful that we didn't have to bail out again, and that our plane didn't blow up when we were skidding along the runway." Yes, indeed, Bill still had his rabbit's foot that day. Far away, Denny and Reynolds could have used one.

Prisoners of War Left Behind

While Bill, Todd, Brickner and Kinney were all back in the States by the end of the summer of 1944, Denny and Reynolds were not so fortunate. They were still prisoners of war in eastern Germany. Reynolds was in Stalag Luft III in Sagan, Germany (now Zagan, Poland), about one-hundred air miles southeast of Berlin. Denny was in Stalag VII-A in Moosburg, Germany, about 290 air miles southwest of Berlin.

Stalag means permanent camp into which a prisoner of war was placed after a screening process at a Dulag (*Durchgangslager*), or transit camp. The Stalag prison camps were typically for enlisted men and non-commissioned officers. They were run by the Wehrmacht, the German armed forces, which included the army (Heer), navy

(Kriegsmarine) and air force (Luftwaffe). Stalag Luft prison camps were for officers of Allied air crews and were run by the Luftwaffe.[43] If Brickner and Kinney had been captured, they most likely would have gone to Stalag Luft III with Reynolds. If Bill and Todd had been captured, they most likely would have gone to Stalag VII-A with Denny.

By the end of the war, Reynolds and Denny would be among 130,000 prisoners crammed into Stalag VII-A, which was originally built to house only 14,000 prisoners. Without the help of partisans, Bill, Todd, Brickner and Kinney may have been suffering with them.[44]

Prisoners of war were paying a very stiff price in the fight for our freedom. They were cooped up behind barbed wire fences with armed guards and dogs positioned to prevent their escape. Meanwhile, their families and friends back home were worrying about whether or not they would return from the war.

According to a War Department study of American prisoners of war in Germany, conditions in prison camps holding Americans varied greatly. For example, the prisoners of Stalag Luft III were treated better than those of Stalag VII-A. This is because Hermann Goering, a World War I flying ace and now commander of the Luftwaffe, wanted preferential treatment for captured Allied airmen in order to obtain preferential treatment for captured Luftwaffe airmen.[45] By the end of the war, both Reynolds and Denny would both be in Stalag VII-A, subjected to intolerable living conditions, and hoping to be liberated from that overcrowded, awful prison camp.[46]

As bad as the prison camps were, they were a far cry from the concentration camps. There was some humanity in the prison camps. There was no humanity in the concentration camps. The concentration camps were run by the SS. The term SS stems from German word *Schutzstaffel*, which means "protective squadron." It was originally formed to protect Hitler as he rose to power. Once in power, Hitler directed Heinrich Himmler to build it into an elite organization of the most physical, dependable, and faithful men in the Nazi movement.[47] It became the small army that ran the concentration camps and murdered Jews, gypsies, communists and partisans. After the war, the SS was declared a criminal organization at the Nuremberg War Trials, and a large number of its leaders were executed.[48]

There were camps within the prison camps, called compounds, and these also varied greatly. In the officers' camps such as Stalag Luft III, each compound was headed by a Senior Allied Officer (SAO if American and SBO if British, but both called SAO herein). In the enlisted men's camps, such as Stalag VII-A, each compound was headed by a Man of Confidence (MOC), who was usually elected by his fellow prisoners of war, but was sometimes appointed by the Germans.[49]

The SAOs and MOCs represented the prisoners in dealing with the camp commandant concerning grievances such as violations of the Geneva Convention of 1929. The commandant expected them to ensure that the prisoners abided by the strict camp rules. For example, the rules posted in the Center Compound of Stalag Luft III stated that (1) the identity disc received by each prisoner in camp had to be worn permanently and that loss would be punishable; (2) notices would be posted at a defined location for prisoners to read and abide by; (3) military discipline had to be strictly maintained; (4) the use or threat of force by a prisoner against a guard could be punishable by death; (5) possession of arms or lethal weapons was forbidden and the death penalty could be invoked for a violation; (6) prisoners must hand over any pamphlets, arms, ammunition or prohibited articles found after enemy air raids or obtained in any other way; and (6) a prisoner who escapes from the camp may be considered as a saboteur or vagrant and may be treated as such.[50]

Stalag Luft III had six compounds established one after another beginning in March, 1942. One compound housed the German military personnel who ran the prison. The other five compounds housed a total of about 10,000 prisoners.[51] British officers of the different nationalities in the British Commonwealth occupied the East and North Compounds (East merged into North in 1943), and American officers occupied the South, Center and West Compounds.[52]

Each compound had fifteen one-story, wooden barracks which were also referred to as blocks, similar to the cell blocks in most prisons. Each barrack had fifteen rooms ranging in size from twenty-four feet by fifteen feet to fourteen feet by six feet. A barrack could house eighty-two men comfortably, but with the growth of the prison population, rooms for eight men began holding ten, then twelve, and eventually new prisoners had to be consigned to tents outside the barrack. One room in each barrack served as a kitchen, a second as a washroom, and a third as a latrine.[53]

According to Reynolds, who was in the West Compound. "It was surrounded by a large fence and watch towers every so often, and a small wire fence around the inside. I was assigned a room in a barrack. Each room held eight officers, but eventually we had more. Each room had several stacks of bunk beds. I took a top bunk. There was also a table, chairs, a cabinet and a heater."

Of the eating arrangements, Reynolds noted: "There was one room with cooking facilities for each barrack. Each room took turns cooking. There wasn't much to cook, except blood sausage. The Red Cross furnished boxes of food—one box per two persons for one week. The box contained coffee, sugar, powdered milk in a can similar to a coffee can, a chocolate bar, a package of cigarettes, a can of Spam and a can of corned beef. The Germans furnished bread, blood sausage and soup. Some barley soup had little white worms like maggots. The Red Cross saved several lives."

Reynolds wasn't the only one who recognized the humanitarian work of the Red Cross during the war. The International Committee of the Red Cross was the recipient of the 1944 Nobel Peace Prize. It had been six years since the last Nobel Peace Prize had been awarded because war, not peace, had dominated the world during that period. It wasn't until the war ended in 1945 that this honor was bestowed upon the Red Cross for its work during wartime in helping to ensure that the provisions of the Geneva Convention were observed and for lessening the suffering of prisoners of war.[54] As Reynolds noted, it saved lives.

Prisoners of war owe a debt of gratitude to the Red Cross for its continual supply of food and clothing that greatly contributed to their physical health. Likewise, they also owe a debt of gratitude to the Young Men's Christian Association (YMCA) for its continual supply of educational, recreational and religious materials that greatly contributed to their mental health. The generous work of these world-wide humanitarian organizations was a godsend to many prisoners of war.[55]

The YMCA provided the support necessary for holding religious services and Reynolds took advantage of them: "There was one large building where churches of various religions held services every Sunday. I attended almost every Sunday. The only entertainment was walking around the compound. The only other thing we did was dig up tree roots with tin cans and use the wood for our heaters. The Germans lined us up and counted everybody at least once a day. They inspected the barracks several times to make sure nobody escaped.

"One day when we were going back to the barracks in a group, somebody stuck his tongue out at a guard in one of the towers. The guard pointed his rifle in my direction and stopped everybody, and warned us not to do it again.

"When I arrived at the compound, I honestly expected to go home soon. The big D-Day invasion by U.S. troops took place June 6, 1944. I heard about it because someone in another room had a radio." This hope soon waned in the drudgery of prison life: "After being in the compound for one month, it was hard to believe that there was even a place like the U.S. I had almost forgotten what 'life' was like before."

Six months later, things went from bad to worse. The Russians were approaching Sagan from the east, and Hitler was worried they might liberate the 10,000 Allied airmen in Stalag Luft III. Since the Allies already had a powerful air presence, the last thing Hitler wanted was for these experienced airmen to return to the skies. He also wanted to keep them as hostages. When it became evident that they would be liberated unless he acted quickly, he gave the order to immediately evacuate all the prisoners in Stalag Luft III to prisons in southern Germany.[56]

Hitler gave the order at 4:30 p.m. on January 27, 1944, and the various compounds were informed later in the evening.[57] The evacuation order didn't come as a surprise to many of the prisoners because they had been preparing to evacuate for a couple of weeks as a result of the advancing Russian Army. Nevertheless, it was dreadful news because the weather was bitterly cold, the ground was covered with six inches of snow, they didn't know their destination, and they didn't know who would be leading them, some thinking it might be SS troops. The SAOs of the respective compounds told their men to be ready to march, prompting the prisoners to act quickly and pack a minimum of clothes and food in bags, knotted trousers, and make-shift sleds.[58]

According to Reynolds, "The Germans told us we were going to move because the Russians were coming." When asked if he was in disbelief when he learned that they would be marching from the prison on that cold night, he said he wasn't: "When they tell you to march, you march." He simply prepared for the cold: "I had a warm coat. I took the lining and with some straw made a hat. It didn't look like much, but it kept my ears warm."

The exodus would take place in stages, and it was the responsibility of the SAO in each compound to ensure that military discipline was strictly maintained during the evacuation process and the march to the next destination. In addition to the SAO in each compound, there was in the Center Compound the highest-ranking American prisoner of war captured by the Germans—Brigadier General Arthur W. Vanaman.[59]

Vanaman had been the assistant military attaché for air in the U.S. Embassy in Berlin from 1937 to 1941.[60] In May 1944, he became the assistant chief for intelligence for the Eighth Air Force, and a month later was shot down over German territory. Since he spoke German and had lived in Germany, he was an effective representative for the prisoners in the Center Compound. Even in prison, rank has its privileges, and his men would be among the last to march.

Rank is also an earned privilege, the reward for being a good leader, and General Vanaman was that. He ordered his men to arrange themselves by blocks of 150 men in columns of threes with a block commander and a German-speaking officer at the head of each block. Since his compound would be among the last to evacuate at about 3:00 a.m., some of his men had time to make sleds for their belongings. He also ensured that his prisoners would march at a reasonable pace, something the SAOs in the other prison camps were unable to do. According to the SAO of the Center Compound, Vanaman controlled the rate of the march, periods of rest, and the number of marching hours.[61]

Preparing for the march was a harrowing experience for everyone, including the guards who didn't want to march in the cold any more than the prisoners. Some of the men, who feared that the SS troops might be leading the evacuation, were greatly relieved when they learned that the prison guards were leading them because they felt they were in better shape than many of the guards.[62]

The march was most harrowing for the 2,000 prisoners of the South Compound because they were told to march first, had the least time to prepare, and were pushed harder than the other compounds during their march. Their SAO, Colonel Charles G. Goodrich, was informed at 8:00 p.m. to be ready to march in half an hour. It took longer, but they were out of the prison by 11:00 p.m. for an unknown destination that turned out to be a train station in Spremberg, Germany, over fifty miles west of Sagan.[63]

The German officer-in-charge made the march unnecessarily difficult by forcing them to march thirty-five miles in twenty-seven hours from Sagan to Muskau (now Bad Muskau), Germany. They were allowed only one four-hour stop for sleep in weather conditions that amounted to almost a blizzard. Unlike other Compounds which followed them, they were not allowed to stop to rest at some of the small towns along the way.[64]

By the time they reached Muskau at about 2:30 a.m. on January 29, about 15 percent of the men needed assistance to march, and a larger number were on the verge of physical and nervous exhaustion. Colonel Goodrich informed the German officer-in-charge that further marching without a rest would be flatly refused, and the prisoners were given thirty hours to recuperate. Even then, about sixty men were unable to march on to Spremberg. The rest of the prisoners marched the remaining fifteen miles to Spremberg with an overnight rest in the village of Graustein.[65] The others were later picked up by other Compounds as they marched through Muskau on their way to Spremberg.

The West Compound was next to be evacuated. According to Reynolds, "Sometime after midnight, we were marched out of Stalag Luft III. It was cold and some snow was falling part of the time. The next night we stopped at the small town of Muskau. I slept on a pile of potatoes in a barn. The pigs were fed boiled potatoes in troughs. Several of us prisoners had boiled potatoes for breakfast."

All four compounds marched to the Spremberg train station, with thousands of men stretching for miles along the road, enduring sub-zero weather. The Americans in the South and West Compounds arrived on January 31, a trip of three and a half days. The Americans in the Center Compound arrived last on February 4, a seven-day trip. In between, the airmen of the British Commonwealth in the North Compound arrived at the train station on February 2.

From Spremberg, the prisoners were transported by train to two prisons in southern Germany. On January 31, the South Compound, along with 200 men from the West Compound, were jammed into freight cars, fifty men to a car, for a miserable train ride of about 250 miles to Stalag VII-A in Moosburg, Germany. They arrived in Moosburg on February 3.[66] On February 4, prisoners from the Central Compound were also jammed into freight cars for the train ride to Moosburg, arriving on February 7.

The conditions at Stalag VII-A were a far cry from those at Stalag Luft III. The prison camp was extremely overcrowded, it was impossible to get clean, and the food supply was inadequate. If this wasn't bad enough, there was no fuel in February and March to heat the barracks, and this was one of the coldest winters in years.[67]

Denny had been in Stalag VII-A for eight months when the prisoners from Stalag Luft III arrived. He never spoke with his son about his prison experiences until his son became an adult. Some of the things he told him then no child could ever understand. It is even difficult for an adult to understand the inhumanity experienced by prisoners of war in that prison. He told his son that it was so cold that when prisoners died from the intolerable conditions, their bodies would remain in the barracks and were piled up to keep out the wind. These inhumane conditions posed a constant threat to both the physical and mental well-being of the prisoners.

After the South and Center Compounds, along with 200 men from the West Compound, departed from Spremberg on trains to Stalag VII-A, the men in the North Compound and the rest of the men in the West Compound were crammed into trains headed for Stalag XIII-D in Nuremberg, Germany, about 200 miles to the south.[68] According to Reynolds, "We traveled by crowded train box cars to Stalag XIII-D in Nuremberg, Germany and stayed in large barracks."

The conditions at Stalag XIII-D were also deplorable. According to a report by the War Department: "There was no room to exercise, no supplies, nothing to eat out of and practically nothing to eat inasmuch as no Red Cross food parcels were available upon the Americans' arrival. The German ration consisted of 300 grams of bread, 250 grams of potatoes, some dehydrated vegetables and a little margarine."[69] Conditions weren't much better at Stalag VII-A, where there was no fuel to heat the barracks and half the men had either diarrhea or a cold.[70]

It was three weeks before Red Cross food parcels arrived, but the food situation wasn't the only problem. The report states: "Sanitation was lamentable. The camp was infested with lice, fleas and bedbugs." Thousands of men had to sleep on bare floors, the latrine at night was a can in each sleeping room, and the barracks were not heated. Morale was so low in the West Compound that it was difficult for Colonel Darr H. Alkire to maintain the discipline of his men.[71] He had been the SAO for the West Compound at Stalag Luft III and was now the MOC for his men at this prison. In this prison, the Senior Allied Officers were for the most part known as Men of Confidence.

Maintaining discipline had never been a problem for Colonel Alkire. He was a stern and severe disciplinarian. In his book, *50 Mission Crush*, Lieutenant Colonel Donald R. Currier said Alkire was the toughest guy he had yet to meet. In her book, *Those Who Flew*, Virginia Priefert said "he took command of everything." She wrote that it was even said that "he told the Germans they didn't know how to run a POW camp and proceeded to run a disciplined camp for them." The word was that he gave his men assignments and "required them to maintain cleanliness as best they could," noting that "even his captors were afraid of him." He represented his men well and prison life for them was better than most, but even he had a problem operating among the worst of conditions. His leadership was eventually rewarded with a promotion to Brigadier General.[72]

Reynolds recalls one incident in February that provided a ray of hope: "On February 22, 1945, I saw big fireworks, the most I saw in the war. The Allies were bombing Nuremberg and the Germans were trying to shoot them down. Planes were fighting in the sky and the air battle lasted about an hour." Help was indeed on the way, but it would take a couple of months to reach Reynolds.

On April 3, 1945 the prisoners received notice that they had to evacuate Stalag XIII-D, and march to Stalag VII-A. The Men of Confidence decided to make a pitch for the welfare of the men during the march by working out a deal with the German commandant of the camp. They said they would take over full control of the column and preserve order in return for marching no more than twenty kilometers (about twelve miles) a day. The German commandant accepted the deal. On April 4, each prisoner was given a Red Cross food parcel, and the march began.

Reynolds remembers: "We started walking to Stalag Luft VII-A in Moosburg, Germany, which was about 100 [air] miles. About 10,000 prisoners were marching and were stretched for miles. Occasionally, there were young boys [twelve years old or so] with guns helping to watch the prisoners. The country was beautiful. At one point, I took a bath in a small river." Another prisoner of war on that march wrote in his diary that some of the guards were in their sixties and seventies.[73] At this point in the war, all able-bodied men were off fighting somewhere, leaving the Germans with no choice other than to call upon kids and senior citizens to chip in.

At one point in the march, the column found itself in harm's way when passing by a freight marshalling yard that was being dive-bombed by Allied P-47s. Two Americans and one Brit were killed by the friendly fire, and three more men were seriously injured. To prevent further collateral damage, some of the men laid out a large replica of a United States Army Air Corps insignia on the road with an arrow pointing in the direction of their march. Fortunately, they did not encounter another similar incident during their march.[74]

On a positive note, food parcels from the Red Cross for the prisoners were delivered to two towns along the way. On a negative note, when they reached the Danube River on April 9, they had already reached the agreed-upon daily marching limit of about twelve miles, but the Germans insisted they keep going and cross the river. Colonel Alkire refused to cross. With his refusal, the Germans lost control of the march, and prisoners began dropping out of the column. The guards, worried about the rapid advance of the American troops into Germany, made no serious attempt to stop them. The main body of the column, however, stayed together and reached Stalag VII-A on April 20, 1945.[75]

The Danube River was about the half-way point of the march from Nuremberg to Moosburg, and it took five days to cover this leg of the trip. After this confrontation, the pace slackened and it took eleven days to travel the last leg of the trip. As one might logically conclude, the loss of control of the column by the Germans, coupled with tired guards and prisoners, resulted in a much slower pace. Also, many prisoners decided to take their chances by escaping rather than go to another prison camp.[76]

Reynolds remembers one day in particular during the march: "On April 13, we had breakfast on the side of a mountain. There were announcements that President Franklin D. Roosevelt had died." Roosevelt died in Warm Springs, Georgia, of a massive cerebral hemorrhage at 3:35 p.m. on April 12, 1945.[77] The nation was in shock, as were Reynolds and his comrades on the side of the mountain. However, while the world paused to mourn the loss of a great leader, Reynolds and his comrades had to keep marching until they arrived at Stalag VII-A.

Prisoners from other prison camps were also flooding into Stalag VII-A, driven from their prisons by the advancing Allied troops. As a result, there were about 130,000 prisoners crowded into that prison camp.[78] The prisoners represented Allied military personnel from different nationalities (American, British, Russian, French, Polish and others) that had one thing in common. They were all miserable, but hope was in the air.[79]

Every day now, prisoners saw American fighters strafing targets in and around Moosburg. Occasionally, a pilot would fly by the prison and wag his wings. They also saw American bombers flying toward their targets. On the ground, Patton's Third Army, thanks to brave soldiers like Bill's friend, Frank Alvino, had crossed the Rhine River despite Hitler's resolve to stop them. The Third Army was advancing rapidly toward Moosburg, and it was just a matter of time before the prisoners would hear the welcome roar of thunder from distant artillery, drawing closer and closer. It would be a sweet sound indeed for these war-weary prisoners of war.[80]

As the end of April approached, it was evident that the Americans would soon be liberating the prisoners of Stalag VII-A. On April 27, two Swiss representatives of the International Committee of the Red Cross arrived to facilitate the transfer of the prison camp from German to American authorities.[81] This humanitarian institution had the unique role, based on the international humanitarian law of the Geneva Convention, to protect the victims of international or internal armed conflicts, including prisoners of war on both sides of the war.[82]

The German camp commandant asked the two Swiss representatives to act as intermediaries between himself and the representatives of the prisoners, the Men of Confidence. The Americans were advancing so fast that the local commandant of the German Army Corps was brought into the conference, out of which came a proposal that called for a few kilometers around Moosburg to be declared a neutral zone.[83]

At dawn on Sunday, April 29, the proposal was presented to Brigadier General B. H. Karlstad of the 14th Armored Division of Patton's Army, who declared it unacceptable. He gave the German emissary until 9:00 a.m. that morning to return to his headquarters and secure an offer of unconditional surrender or expect an American attack. The German commander rejected the demand, and prepared for the American onslaught.[84]

According to a report by military intelligence, the battle began at 10:00 a.m. and lasted for about two and a half hours. The bullets and shells were flying and the noise was deafening. One shell hit a barrack, injuring twelve guards and killing one. After a lull, General Karlsad's men entered the camp and the guards laid down their arms. The supervision of the prison camp automatically fell to the Men of Confidence.[85]

By order of General Karlstad, some of the German administrative personnel remained at their posts while the remainder, including the guards, became prisoners of war. The Swiss representatives reported that treatment of the German camp authorities by the American troops was correct according to the Geneva Convention.[86]

According to one of the prisoners, Stalag VII-A was the "hellhole of all hellholes." Thus, when the American flag was hoisted to the top of a church steeple in the town of Moosburg, it stirred the emotions of the Americans. At that defining moment, the Americans came to attention and, as liberated men, saluted their flag.[87] At long last, they were free from that hellhole.

On April 29, Hitler knew that there was no hope for him. He received news that Mussolini had been caught by Italian partisans, executed, hung upside down in a public square, and then thrown in the gutter.[88] Fascism had fallen in Italy as violently as it had risen. The next day, Hitler committed suicide, effectively ending the Nazi menace. The following Monday, Germany surrendered unconditionally to the Allied forces. The storm that had torn Europe apart was finally over, and the long process of picking up the pieces and moving forward was just beginning.[89]

According to Steve Denny, as soon as Stalag VII-A was liberated, his father took off running through the woods with a bunch of other prisoners. They had been cooped up in this awful prison for eleven months, and were now free and running through the beautiful Bavarian countryside. Denny told his son that it was a while before they were all together again. His father also told him that the Australians were furious and went after the guards as soon as the prison was liberated, and one can only imagine the result of that pursuit.

Reynolds remained in the prison during the celebration. He remembers that the guards laid down their guns and that when he returned to his tent, he found two bullet holes through it. The next day, American support troops arrived with food for the Allied prisoners of war of all nationalities. The following day, General Patton rolled into Stalag VII-A to visit with the liberated prisoners, now designated as

Home At Last

Recovered Allied Military Personnel (RAMP).[90]

RAMP Reception Centers were established in overseas locations to help freed Allied prisoners of war on their road to recovery. The War Department told them that they and the people at home owed them plenty, and supplied them with new clothes, new shoes, medical care, back pay, and access to a message center for communicating with their families back home. They were put on special strengthening diets and advised what not to eat in order to get fit sooner. They were told that they may not realize how unwell they may be and how important it was to follow their advice. Like those who evaded capture, they were instructed not to reveal any intelligence concerning prison camps and told that some activities within German prison camps must remain secret not only during the duration of the war but in peacetime as well. Reynolds, Denny and other liberated prisoners would pass through these Centers on their way home.[91]

As things settled down after the liberation of Stalag VII-A, volunteers were sought for guard duty in the town of Moosburg, and Reynolds volunteered: "I didn't know who I was supposed to be guarding but it was nice to be out of the prison. I wasn't there very long when a soldier came up to me and said: 'I have been looking for you.' It was Bob Lutz from my hometown, Plankinton, South Dakota. He said he knew I was in Europe and had been looking for me. He went to school with my older brother. We had a short visit and the next day I was lucky and flew to the staging area [a RAMP Reception Center in France] to start home. I got back to the States in June."

When Denny returned from his jaunt through the woods, he too went to a RAMP Reception Center in France. While there, he wrote to his folks back home in Neptune, Tennessee to let them know that he was in good health and coming home. The local paper ran his photo with the byline, "Cheatham County Man Out of Nazi Prison."[92] When he arrived home in June, he received a nice letter from his Congressman:[93]

My dear Sergeant:

I was happy to know that you were found safe when your camp was liberated. I trust that you will have arrived home by the time this letter reaches there.

*We are proud of your military record, for we realize the
sacrifices you have made and the hardships you have undergone.
The Country owes you a debt of gratitude for the service you
have rendered.*

With best wishes,

Sincerely,

Wirt Courtney

Last Man Home

Major Hunter made the ultimate sacrifice in his country's fight
for freedom. He was among more than 300,000 Americans who died
overseas during World War II.[94] Many of them, like him, were first
declared missing in action until sufficient evidence was gathered to
declare them killed in action. The news that a loved one was missing
in action was devastating for a family, and the news that a loved
one was killed in action was way beyond that. In both instances,
the grieving family sought more information. Unfortunately, under
wartime conditions, the process of responding to such inquiries was
painfully slow because of the need to exercise diligent care in order to
avoid mistakes in providing such critical information to the family of
a loved one lost at war.

On June 11, 1944, Jean Hunter was informed by telegram that
her husband had been missing in action since May 26, 1944. At the
time, she was living with her mother and young son Bill in Texas. The
telegram came from the Adjutant General on behalf of the Secretary of
War.[95] Hunter's parents in Indiana, Herbert and Shirley Hunter, were
also notified. This news touched off a long string of correspondence
between concerned family members, who sought more information,
and the War Department, which had to be very careful in providing
such sensitive information.

The War Department depended on two of its offices to handle
such inquiries—The Adjutant General's Office and The Quartermaster
General's Office. The Adjutant General's Corps, referred to as the "AG

Corps," provided personnel and administrative support for the combat commanders. Its tasks included tracking awards and promotions, maintaining personnel records, and handling mail inquiries.[96] The Quartermaster Corps, through its Graves Registration Service, was responsible for the care of deceased military personnel. Its functions included (1) selecting a site for temporary cemeteries; (2) maintaining these cemeteries; (3) identifying and ensuring proper burial of the war dead at these temporary cemeteries pending final disposition as determined by next of kin; (4) receiving, collecting, and safeguarding their personal effects for disposition to next of kin; (5) registering all graves for future identification; and (6) ensuring that the war dead were handled with dignity at all times, and that they were laid to rest with honor in their final burial locations.[97]

The interment of war dead and the operation and maintenance of national cemeteries had been the responsibility of the Quartermaster Corps since 1867, just after the Civil War.[98] As one might guess, since the Corps is responsible for handling such sensitive information, its record-keeping must be meticulous. According to one source, "More repercussions of a military, political, or morale nature can arise from poor regulation of Graves Registration Service than from any other section under the Quartermaster."[99]

Hunter's grandmother, Dora Clark, began the correspondence chain by going straight to the top. On June 22, she sent a letter to General Eisenhower, requesting information about her grandson. She had nice things to say about the General: "I have read of your fine work over there. You are a great general with a kind heart." That said, she asked for the name of her son's squadron commander or of any of the men in his squadron so that she could write to them. Of the war, she wrote: "This war is cruel. It is Hell on Earth. When will it cease? Our fine young men dying on foreign soil for a war they did not make."[100]

Before Dora received a response, the Adjutant General notified the family by telegram on August 3 that Hunter had been killed in action. It wasn't until then that the Secretary of War received evidence that was considered significant enough to establish the fact that he had been killed in action.[101]

The sensitivity of handling family inquiries about the war dead made it necessary for the War Department to proceed with caution. The Report of Death for Hunter wasn't issued by the Adjutant

General's Office until September 23. It listed Hunter's wife as next of kin. It also listed as his beneficiaries his wife and son, as well as his mother and father.[102]

As soon as Dora Clark heard that her grandson had been killed in action, she wanted to be sure. She dispatched a letter on August 4 to the Adjutant General asking if it was true that he was killed in action. She also requested the full story of the crash as it was told by the survivors of his plane. She said she would appreciate and keep the information to herself, noting: "I can rest easy if I know the truth, as it is there is no rest for me."[103]

The following week, on August 10, Shirley Hunter also wrote to the Adjutant General. She requested details of her son's death: "How was his death determined? Was his body found and, if so, where is he buried?" She mentioned their desire to visit his grave sometime if they could learn the location. Further, she requested the names and next of kin of the survivors, stating that they may be able to meet them after the war ends and learn something more about their son. She also asked if there was any way to get information concerning their son's service record, including any citations.[104]

Ten days later, on August 20, Dora dispatched two more letters. One was sent to the Adjutant General's Office. The other was sent directly to General Hap Arnold, the Commanding General of the Army Air Forces. In the letter to the Adjutant General, she sought details: "Did his ship burn when it crashed? Was his body destroyed? Do they bury the dead in a cemetery and mark the grave?" She also asked for the addresses and serial numbers of members of the surviving members of his crew. She wrote: "I wish the details, no matter how sad or severe. I am over seventy and can take it. My only son was in World War I. I will keep confidential anything you tell me. I have a medal for Red Cross work in World War I."[105]

In her letter to General Arnold, she wrote: "I'm sorry to bother you, but you are the only one with authority to tell me the truth. I wish to know the details of my grandson's death no matter how sad it may be." She also asked for the names and addresses of the members of his crew that parachuted to safety.[106]

In response to her June 11 letter to General Eisenhower, Dora received two responses, neither from the general himself. One came from the Adjutant General and the other from the Quartermaster

General. On August 24, the Adjutant General expressed his regrets for her grandson's death and explained that no details were sent with the notice of his death. He also said that, due to combat conditions and the extraordinary volume of correspondence, communications are typically reduced to facts, without detailed descriptions.[107]

On September 9, the Quartermaster General informed her that no information had been received concerning the recovery and burial of her grandson, noting that she would be advised as soon as they receive a report. He added: "Please accept my heartfelt sympathy and condolence in the loss of one so dear. I hope you will receive some consolation in the fact that he will always be among those honored ones who gave their lives that the ideals of a great nation might live."[108]

General Arnold answered Dora's August 20 letter personally on September 8, 1944. He was a busy man, but not too busy to answer a letter from a concerned grandmother of a deceased airman. In a two-page letter, he provided the details of the mission from the Missing Air Crew Report. This included an explanation of the mission and how her grandson's plane was shot down. He also explained that it was customary to accord reverent burial to our dead, even under battle conditions. He explained that the graves are properly marked and recorded to preserve the identity of the dead, and that everything possible is done by military authorities to care for these graves. Further, he pointed out that this procedure is also followed by the governments with which we are at war, through the International Red Cross.[109]

Dora had been part of the Red Cross during World War I, so she already knew of its good work. Arnold also enclosed a list of the names and addresses of the next of kin of the crew members who flew with her son on that fateful day. In closing, he wrote: "I extend my deepest sympathy to you and other members of Hunter's family, and with it the hope that the memory of his faithful service to his Country will comfort you in your sorrow."[110] The Adjutant General responded to her August 20 letter in October 1944, but by that time Dora and Shirley already had the information they sought, thanks to General Arnold.[111]

Shirley received two letters in response to her August 10 letter. On September 2, the Adjutant General regretted having no additional information to provide, but said he referred her letter to the Quartermaster General and the Commanding General of the Army Air Forces. However, he was also the bearer of some good news.

He informed her that her son was presented with the Air Medal on April 27, 1944, and enclosed the citation.[112] On September 18, the Quartermaster General assured her that every effort was being made to obtain a report covering the disposition of her son's body.[113]

Later, Shirley would learn that her son was also awarded the Distinguished Flying Cross for his heroic actions on May 26, 1944. The Distinguished Flying Cross is awarded to a person who "distinguishes himself by heroism or extraordinary achievement while participating in aerial flight. The performance of the act of heroism must be evidenced by voluntary action above and beyond the call of duty."[114]

The information that led the Quartermaster Corps to Hunter's body was probably provided by his navigator, John Kinney. On July 8, 1944, after he made it back to Allied lines, Kinney reported that partisans informed him that Hunter was buried by Italian natives in a civil cemetery in Anghiari, Italy.[115] This information most likely led military personnel trained in identification work to Hunter's gravesite. Because no identification was found on his body, Hunter's dental records were used to identify him.[116] Following identification, his body was moved to a temporary U.S. Military Cemetery pending final disposition of his remains in accordance with the wishes of his next of kin.[117]

A Report of Reburial dated January 24, 1945 indicated that his cause of death was a plane crash, and that he was reburied in the U.S. Military Cemetery in Vada, Italy on January 21, 1945 at 1000 hours (10:00 a.m.). A wooden cross served as his grave marker and for identification purposes, a Form GRS #1 was sealed in a GRS bottle buried with the body and another Form GRS #1 was buried one foot below the grave marker. GRS stands for Graves Registration Service. The airmen buried to his left and right were also indicated. Buried on his right side was Second Lieutenant Vasil V. Vantz of the 85th Bomb Squadron of the 47th Bomb Group and on his left side was Second Lieutenant Vernon B. Williams of the 523rd Fighter Squadron of the 27th Fighter Group.[118]

With end of the war in sight, the War Department was striving to carry out an efficient and reverent operation in identifying the war dead and placing them in temporary military cemeteries. It expected those carrying out this work to act with the dignity befitting the nation's valiant dead. It was a time-consuming, exacting process of great importance.[119]

The Quartermaster Corps had also been busy collecting Hunter's personal effects for the purpose of giving them to his next of kin, his wife Jean. This was another operation that needed to be carried out with care, and it was. The job of collecting, storing, safeguarding and shipping thousands of packages of personal effects, in many cases irreplaceable personal property, was a prodigious one. It involved careful attention to detail because mistakes would have a negative effect on the men who were casualties of war as well as on their families.[120]

When an airman, soldier or sailor in Europe became a casualty (either deceased, hospitalized, captured, interned, or missing) during the war, his unit commander collected all his personal property, inventoried it, removed government property, and forwarded it to a designated overseas Effects Quartermaster, marked with the owner's identification and status.[121]

If the owner was deceased, the property was documented and forwarded to the Army Effects Bureau in Kansas City for transmission to the next of kin through the Kansas City Quartermaster Depot. If the owner was hospitalized, the property was placed in storage indefinitely, subject to disposition instructions from the owner. If the owner was missing in action, as were Bill, Todd, Brickner and Kinney, the property was stored so that each could claim it upon his return to duty, as did Bill when he went to Bastia in Corsica to claim his personal effects. If the owner was captured and interned, as were Denny and Reynolds, the property was also stored so that each could claim it upon his return to duty. If the owner was not returned to duty within a few months, the property was forwarded to the Army Effects Bureau where it could eventually be claimed by the owner or next of kin.[122]

Major Hunter's personal effects at his base of operations in Solenzara, Corsica, were collected on June 14, 1944, carefully safeguarded, and sent to the Kansas City Quartermaster Depot on November 23, 1944 for further disposition to his wife.[123] None of his personnel effects on him when he crashed ever reached his family. Partisans told Kinney that those effects—pocket watch, gold leaves, and two pistols—had been removed by Fascists.[124] According to another report sent to his grandmother by Hap Arnold, his "personal effects consisting of a wallet and money which had either been found on the body or in the plane were destroyed when the Germans burned the Carabineri Headquarters."[125]

The funds of the war dead were handled separately from other personal effects. On January 8, 1945, the Kansas City Quartermaster Depot sent Jean the funds belonging to her husband at the time of his death, a total of $212.60.[126] On May 14, 1945, the Depot sent his other personal effects to her in three packages weighing a total of 160 pounds.[127]

Hunter's personal effects sent to Jean included, among other things, miscellaneous insignias, ribbons, decorations, and wings. While his camera was also sent to Jean, the film was removed as it was deemed to be government property.[128] When Reynolds received his personal effects after he returned from being a prisoner of war, he also received his camera but without the film.

In 1946, the Quartermaster Corps produced a pamphlet for the next of kin of deceased service personnel from World War II. It was entitled *Tell Me About My Boy.* Its purpose was to inform the next of kin that Congress had passed a bill, signed into law by President Truman, which authorized the War Department "to take steps to provide a reverent final burial for those who gave their last full measure of devotion." It explained the program and stated that the Quartermaster Corps would direct it.[129]

In accordance with this program, Hunter's wife Jean was contacted on November 24, 1947 and given four options to have the final burial in (1) a private cemetery in the United States, (2) a private cemetery in another country, (3) a permanent United States military cemetery overseas, or (4) a national cemetery in the United States.[130] Since Hunter's parents desired him to be buried in a private cemetery near his hometown of Williamsport, Indiana, Jean transferred her next of kin designation to them.

The process of arranging to move Hunter's body from Italy to Indiana took time. In 1949, Hunter's parents made final arrangements to have their son shipped home. In keeping with the dignity and reverence of the repatriation program, military escorts accompanied his body at all times. His body arrived home in a casket with a flag of the United States to be used for proper draping of the casket during the funeral service, and to be presented to the next of kin as a keepsake in memory of their son.[131]

Hunter arrived home on June 22, 1949, over nine years after he enlisted on May 12, 1940. The funeral home that received him was owned by a man whose daughter had married Hunter's brother Park. Two guards stood watch over Hunter's body day and night until he was laid to rest. At one point, Shirley wanted to open the casket to obtain closure on her son, but the family talked her out of it.

John Hunter, Park's son, was a young boy and remembers playing outside the funeral home with little Bill, only seven years old at the time. Had Major Hunter survived the war, he would have been thirty years old and in the prime of his life.[132] Sadly, he was among many fathers who gave their lives in the service of their country, and who would never again experience the joys of fatherhood.

Major Hunter left a strong legacy with his family, who always called him by his middle name, Clark. According to Candace Hunter, the daughter-in-law of Clark's brother Park, Clark's wife Jean remarried Herman Glaze, who adopted Bill and was a good father to him. Even though they remained in Texas where Jean had roots, Bill and his family remained close to his Hunter grandparents and the families of Clark's two brothers in Indiana.[133]

Clark's mother Shirley kept his clothes in a free-standing cedar closet for the rest of her life, a long one. She lived to be 104 years old. Near the end when she was knocking on heaven's door, Bill, who looked like Clark and had his mannerisms, paid her a visit and Bill's wife Frances said Shirley thought for a moment he was Clark. When Shirley died, the cedar closet was shipped to Bill in Texas. Included among Hunter's personal belongings were his big-brimmed hat and tall boots.[134] Again, one can see why Bill Lanza thought Major Hunter was a Texan.

When Bill died in 1999, his wife Frances passed his personal effects down to their daughter, Alyson McDonald, who treasures the remembrances of her grandfather. In time, she will no doubt pass them down to her son Ian. The old adage "a man is not dead until he is forgotten" keeps Major Hunter alive in the hearts of his family members, who remain proud of their fallen son for the manner in which he conducted his life and the way he served his country during World War II.

Chapter 11

AFTER THE STORM

The Germans were finally driven from Italy on April 25, 1945, the day celebrated as Liberation Day in Italy. It is the day on which Italy was liberated from the Fascism of Mussolini and the Nazi occupation. It is a national holiday in Italy that honors partisans of the Italian Resistance who fought against Fascism and the Nazi menace. Sixty-three years later, Riccardo Becattini and Amerigo Sarri would be honored on this holiday in memory of Goffredo Sarri.

End of the War

Germany surrendered to the Allies on May 7, 1945 at General Eisenhower's headquarters in Reims, France. The next day, President Truman declared May 8 as V-E (Victory in Europe) Day. The war in the Pacific continued until Japan surrendered on August 14, 1945. However, the United States did not officially declare V-J (Victory in Japan) day until almost three weeks later on September 2, 1945, when Japan signed the terms of surrender aboard the battleship USS *Missouri* in Tokyo Bay.[1]

At long last, the storm that swept across Europe and throughout the Pacific had run its course. Many lives were shattered in its wake, and those who survived the turmoil were left to pick up the pieces and move on. Most of the survivors were ordinary men and women who had extraordinary experiences that they just didn't want to talk about for most of their lives. However, as time marched on, they have come to be appreciated as more than ordinary men and women. Tom Brokaw recognized their unprecedented sacrifices when he characterized them as the "greatest generation."

Reflection

The Italian Campaign involved some of the fiercest fighting in World War II. The Campaign was a war of attrition with both sides sustaining heavy casualties. The "bloody boot" is what historian Donald L. Miller called the Italian peninsula during this Campaign.[2] Since the fighting kept German manpower from being deployed to shore up its defenses in France before D-Day, it played an important role in helping to pave the way for an Allied victory in Europe.[3]

Because Allied ground forces in Italy lost troops to the buildup for D-Day, they were not at full strength during the Italian Campaign. Nevertheless, with the help of the Allied air forces, they were able to effectively cut enemy supply lines and continue to push the Germans up the peninsula of Italy, and ultimately out of Italy.

The Allies forged such an aggressive bombing campaign in Italy that many airmen such as Bill Lanza and Alfred Todd were shot down with interesting stories to tell. However, as evaders they were forbidden to tell their stories. Very little was known about them until the "Missing Air Crew Reports" and "Escape and Evasion Reports" were declassified in 1995. At that time, the accumulation of 1.6 billion pages of classified records between 1940 and 1970 prompted the government to develop a policy of declassifying classified records. The result was a policy to declassify permanent, historical records of twenty-five years old or older that no longer posed a national security threat.[4] Unfortunately, when this occurred, most of the evaders were still unaware that they had the green light to tell their stories.

Bill was one of those who had a chance to tell his story. He reflects on those days: "I can't believe I made it home alive. I am so thankful that the partisans were there to help the airmen shot down during the war. When I think of flying mission after mission with enemy firepower directed at our plane, and of living in a cave with bombs and shells exploding all around us, I find it hard to believe that I came home alive. And when I think of what the troops of Anzio had to go through, I still shudder. I am greatly humbled and so grateful to have made it safely home."

Bob Feller, the first major league baseball player to volunteer to serve his country after Pearl Harbor, once said: "Heroes don't return from war. It's a roll of the dice. If a bullet has your name on it, you're a hero. If you hear a bullet go by, you're a survivor."[5] Those who returned were all lucky, they were all grateful, and they all came away with a deep appreciation of what it took to remain a free nation.

In 1948, Audie Murphy, an American hero of World War II, returned to France at the invitation of the French Government. One morning, he was taken to a small French school, and the students sang to him in French. The experience brought home to him the importance of freedom. He said:[6]

> *"The spirit of freedom was hovering over that play yard as it did all over France at that time. A country was free again. A people had recovered their independence and their children were grateful. They were singing in French, but the melody was freedom and any American could understand that. America, at that moment, never meant more to me. The true meaning of America, you ask? It's in a Texas rodeo, in a political rally, in a newspaper. In all these things, and many more, you'll find America. In all these things, you'll find freedom. And freedom is what America means to the world. And to me."*

After the war, Bill, the members of his crew who were shot down over Italy, and his friends in Italy, went on with their lives. Unfortunately, Major Hunter was unable to go on with his life, but he left a legacy that still makes his family proud and his crew grateful.

The following are (1) a brief account of each crew member after the war, in the order in which they made it home; (2) a brief account of Goffredo Sarri and Riccardo Becattini and their families after the war; and (3) concluding comments on Major Hunter.

Second Lieutenant John H. Kinney

Of all the crew members, John Kinney provided the most information describing the events of May 26, 1944. When he was interrogated by military intelligence after he was liberated, he provided the details about what took place in the aircraft after it was clobbered by flak, and also pieced together what happened to Major Hunter. It was his attention to detail that enabled General Hap Arnold to inform Hunter's grandmother, Dora Clark, of what had happened to her grandson in Italy.

When Kinney married his wife Gwen in 1942, it was the beginning of what his daughter, Judy, said were over "fifty glorious and happy years." The war years, however, weren't that glorious. Not more than a year after they married, Gwen received a dreaded telegram informing her that the love of her life was missing in action.

While her husband was missing, she was saying her prayers and working in the California State Capitol. She was also doing her part to help the war effort, and she had a great comfort system to help her deal with her personal circumstances. The Governor of California, Earl Warren (later to be the Chief Justice of the U.S. Supreme Court), had set up a booth for her in the rotunda of the California State Capitol building where she sold thousands of dollars of war bonds. Daily, the Governor and others would check with her to see if there was any news on her husband.[7]

Fortunately, the story had a happy ending, thanks to the partisans who helped Kinney evade the enemy for thirty-eight days, and to the "Battleaxe" Division of the British Eighth Army that liberated him on July 3, 1944.[8] As soon as he was a free man, he was anxious to call his wife. Late one evening, Gwen picked up the phone and all she heard was: "Don't let that moon get away!" After that phone call, Gwen never went back to work at the State Capitol. Also, for the rest of their lives, whenever Kinney was in a difficult circumstance, he would utter those words to Gwen. It was their own little secret code that would give them the resolve it took to deal with life's many challenges.

Kinney was a group and later a wing navigator. He flew a total of 585 hours in over seven years of service, including seventy-five combat hours flown in a seven-month tour of duty in the Mediterranean Theater. Although he was rated as a bombardier, he did only navigation and no bombing.

When he returned to the States, Kinney was received and processed at the Redistribution Station in Santa Monica, California, and then given a twenty-one day furlough. After that welcome break, he reported back to Santa Monica for reassignment while he and Gwen enjoyed rest and relaxation with various types of entertainment and recreation available to them. They enjoyed the special treatment accorded to former escapees and evaders.

Kinney opted to remain in the Army Air Forces as an instructor and, according to his daughter Judy, served in various locations in Washington, Texas and California. As he moved from one location to another, Gwen made sure that the moon didn't get away. She moved with him. In 1949, Kinney received his honorable discharge.

In civilian life, Kinney, a native of the Golden State, resided in Sacramento, Fresno and Riverbank, California. He worked for the State of California Department of Veterans Affairs for almost thirty-eight years, and touched the lives of many veterans in a positive way. He and Gwen also touched the lives of their two daughters, Diane and Judy, in a positive way. Judy sums it up: "My father was an example of true masculine gentleness, a caring, wonderful and loving husband, father and family provider."

Judy adds: "Ever since I can remember, my father had vegetable gardens, very elaborate gardens. When we built our family home in Riverbank, where he lived for fifty years, it was on an acre of almond trees, and we three girls would assist Dad working those trees each year. He planted every kind of berry imaginable, peppers, carrots (for my horse), sunflowers, lettuces, onions, zucchini and many more wonderful garden delights."

Kinney was also active in a couple of fraternal organizations, one of which is the oldest fraternity in the world. He was a Mason, whose members once included George Washington, Benjamin Franklin and John Hancock.[9] Among other things, Masons are taught that they have a responsibility to make things better in the world, and these founding fathers certainly did that, and so did Kinney. As the Modesto District Manager of Cal Vet Loans, he had the opportunity to make things better for veterans by helping them with their home financing needs.

The other organization Kinney belonged to was "E Clampus Vitus," which is, among other things, dedicated to the study and preservation of lesser known nuggets of history of Western Heritage. There are forty active chapters and thousands of members in California, Nevada and other Western states, but most are in California. The society is known for researching sites of historical interest, although not those of interest to mainstream historians, and erecting plaques to preserve their historical value. One of its members was another man who loved California and its western heritage—Ronald Reagan.[10]

Most importantly, Kinney enjoyed his family and was good to them. According to Judy, "About thirty years ago, he bought some land in Bear Valley and we built a family cabin that took us two years to complete. I truly mean we built it! Now his grandchildren own it." Bear Valley is in northern California and is considered a recreational paradise with many family activities such as biking, fishing, hiking and camping.[11]

She continued: "Dad was a fabulous gardener and cook after retiring. He also loved fishing at Lake Alpine, and especially loved campfires at night with the family around." Lake Alpine is a small, scenic reservoir located near Bear Valley at an elevation of 7,350 feet, and it has five campgrounds with 112 campsites.[12] Thanks to Kinney, his three grandchildren and six great grandchildren will enjoy Lake Alpine and Bear Valley for years to come.

With regard to his wartime experiences, Kinney kept them to himself. His wife, Gwen, said she could never get him to talk about them. Judy added: "My father did not share his war stories. In my adult years, I requested several times that he share some information. However, he continued to be silent. I believe war visions were too troubling for him to repeat."

The author explained why he was silent, and provided the family with a copy of a document he signed on July 8, 1944, certifying that he wouldn't talk about his wartime experiences. It stated:[13]

I understand that any information concerning my Escape or Evasion from capture is SECRET and must not be disclosed to anyone other than an Allied Military Attaché to whom I first report, or to an officer designated by the Commanding General of the Theater of Operations. I understand that disclosure to anyone else will make me liable to disciplinary action.

Now they better understood why he was one of the silent evaders of the greatest generation.

Second Lieutenant Walter H. Brickner

When the war ended, Walt Brickner was back in uniform, only this time it was a baseball uniform. In 1945, he played part of a season for the Albany Senators in Albany, New York, which was a Class A affiliate of the Pittsburgh Pirates, batting only .238. While he played professional baseball until 1951, this was the last time he would play for a major league affiliate.

In 1946, he began the season playing for the Greenville Lions in the Class D Alabama State League, batting .342 in nineteen games, then moved up to the Idaho Falls Russets in the Class C Pioneer League, where he batted .253 in 101 games.[14] One of his teammates on the Russets was a kid who would go on to become a baseball legend.

The kid had just graduated from high school and was playing for a team called the Junior Oaks, which was sponsored by the Oakland Oaks in the Triple-A Pacific Coast League. The Junior Oaks played in exhibitions before the regular Oaks games. The manager of the regular Oaks liked the spirit of this kid—said he reminded him of himself—and recommended him to the Russets, where he signed his first professional contract. The manager was Casey Stengel, and the kid was Billy Martin. To say that Stengel liked Martin is an understatement. He would in time become like a father to him.[15] They would both become New York Yankee legends.

Brickner, on the other hand, had no such luck. Before the war, he had two fine baseball seasons in a row, batting over .300 both years. However, despite some moments in the sun, he struggled after the war. After hitting .342 for the Greenville Lions, he wouldn't hit over .300 again until his last season in 1951 when he hit .319 for the Roswell Rockets of the Eastern League. He even pitched three games for Roswell that year, winning one and losing two.[16]

The 1947 Russets game program stated that Bricker had "an accurate arm, a good batting eye and a great love for baseball," noting that he spent the previous winter in his hometown Philadelphia. It also mentioned that he was forced to bail out of an American plane in enemy territory, but "has never given up faith, and his love for the game has caused him to make a mighty effort to get back to his prewar peak."[17]

Brickner spent nine years playing professional baseball, but never got back to his prewar peak. His batting average over this period was .291 and his slugging average was .380. At the end of the 1951 season, at the age of thirty-one, he left baseball.[18] He moved to California, went to work for the Post Office, purchased a home in Apple Valley, took up golf, and joined the Spring Valley Country Club in nearby Victorville, one of the towns Kinney received training in before he went overseas for combat duty.

Brickner worked for the Post Office for about twenty years, and during those years became a good golfer with a two handicap. He was often paired with Jim Wood, another lefty golfer with a three handicap who belonged to his country club.[19]

According to Wood, "Walt was a quiet and reserved man, one who was hard to get to know. He married late in life to a lady who died after they had been together for about five years. She had a son with two daughters, and he was very fond of one of the daughters. However, after her mother died, the young lady moved to Utah. After that, Walt appeared to be a very lonely man. He liked to play cards at the club, but only with certain people."

Wood continued: "He had diabetes, and after he retired it got so bad that he had to have his leg amputated. I visited him in his home after the operation. He was sitting there with his leg over a chair, with blood dripping on the floor. I took him to the hospital to stop the bleeding. I had a gut feeling that if I didn't pay him a visit, he might have bled to death. He never adjusted to having one leg, and eventually had to move to a rest home. I helped him move, and visited him until he passed away. His stepson and his wife, along with the daughter he was fond of, attended the service. He left each of his stepson's daughters a little something, and they appreciated his thoughtfulness."

Wood remembers him most for his prowess on the links: "In team play, because we were both lefties and had similar handicaps, I would always be paired with him. They figured we would help each other in reading greens, but this wasn't the case because he was a cut putter. He hit the outside of the ball causing it to spin from right to left in a way nobody could believe, especially because he was good at it. Consequently, his read of the greens was very different from my read. He was different, but he was a good golfer and I enjoyed playing with him."

In all the years that Wood golfed with him, Brickner never said much about his baseball or wartime experiences. It's too bad because he had a lot to be proud of. One can only assume that, if more people had been aware of Brickner's baseball and wartime experiences, he might not have died such a lonely man.

After the Storm

Technical Sergeant Alfred J. Todd

Todd's ship arrived in New York Harbor on September 1, 1944, the same day that Bill's ship arrived in Newport News, Virginia. Brickner returned on the same ship, and both of them went from the ship to Reception Station #2 at Fort Dix, New Jersey, where each was granted a furlough of three weeks.[20] The two evaders then headed for home, Todd to Oriskany Falls in New York, and Brickner to Philadelphia.

Three weeks later, Todd went through the Redistribution Center process along with others returning from combat overseas. After that, he was assigned to the Training Department Headquarters at Yuma Army Air Field in Yuma, Arizona, where, like Bill, he did clerical work.[21] When the war ended, he received his honorable discharge, went home, and got a job driving a tractor trailer for the Dairymen's League Cooperative Association. The Cooperative introduced the name "Dairylea" for its many dairy products, which were marketed throughout the Northeast. Today, more than 2,300 member farm families belong to the cooperative, making it the largest supplier of dairy products in the Northeast.[22]

When Todd went to work for Dairylea, Blanche Clark's father was the dispatcher, and he knew a good man when he saw one. Todd's parents sold vegetables and Blanche's parents were among their many satisfied customers. Blanche had trained to be a concert pianist for years, but her career was put on hold when she met Todd. They married on August 16, 1947, and soon started a family that produced four children—Linda, Robert, Mary and Norma. As the kids grew, Blanche put her musical talents to good use by playing the organ in many churches.[23]

In time, the rigors of the road got to Todd. Since he and Blanche worked well as a team, they decided to open a restaurant in nearby State Bridge, and the kids became part of the team. Todd's Inn was opened in 1966, and the family lived upstairs in a very nice, spacious apartment. Todd ran the bar, at which no foul language was allowed; Blanche did the cooking, and the children waited tables.

According to Blanche, Todd always made time to be part of his son's life. Once, he even rented a bus and took Robert's entire Boy Scout troop to Cooperstown to visit the Baseball Hall of Fame. Robert was a good wrestler in high school, and Todd was always there to

253

support his passion. They shared a special bond.

In 1970, tragedy struck the family. Robert, age 19, was killed in an automobile accident. Blanche still has a tough time talking about it. Robert had signed up for the Navy in underwater demolition, and was living and working in Syracuse while waiting to be called up. One weekend, he came home to say goodbye to a friend who was leaving for the Navy. After visiting his friend, he fell asleep at the wheel and hit the cement abutment of a bridge about mile and a half from his parents' house.

The family struggled to deal with the tragedy. It was an especially hard pill for Todd to swallow, and he dealt with it in his own way. One day, he told Blanche to watch over the bar while he attended to some business in Vernon. When he came back, he walked into the packed bar and announced: "The road took my son's life, but I'm going to prove that it won't take mine." He went back to the rigors of the road, working again for Dairylea. Even after he retired from Dairylea, he spent several years transporting standardbred race horses for his son-in-law.

On Christmas Eve following Robert's death, six of his friends, who had been pallbearers at his funeral, spent the evening with the Todd family. The family never forgot that special evening with their son's special friends. One of the six eventually ended up as a son-in-law.

Since Robert loved wrestling so much, the family established the Robert Todd Memorial Wrestling Award in his memory. Every year since, a deserving student-athlete at what is now Vernon-Verona-Sherrill Senior High School in Verona, New York is presented with a scholarship to a summer wrestling camp. The year 2010 will mark the fortieth anniversary of the award. Blanche had an opportunity to meet the 2008 recipient at Appalachian State College in North Carolina, where he was attending a summer wrestling camp on her son's scholarship. She was thinking of her son and her husband when she greeted the young man.

After their parents passed, Todd and Blanche decided in 1988 to retire and move to Pinehurst, North Carolina, near where their youngest daughter, Norma, resided with her family. Her husband trained horses for sulky racing. Since the restaurant business was still in their blood, they purchased the Restaurant at the Pinehurst Training Track and ran it until they retired again. In his final retirement, Todd enjoyed spending time at the track, helping his son-in-law around the stables and transporting his horses on occasion. Their other two daughters, Linda and Mary, now reside in Texas and Virgina, respectively, but keep in close touch with their mother.

According to Blanche, "I had the best husband. Toddy was a family man and a wonderful father. The girls idolized him. Toddy loved to grow vegetables, and Norma built a large, raised vegetable garden that he spent a lot of time in during his retirement." It is interesting that several members of the crew that was shot down over Italy enjoyed gardening during their retirement years.

After they sold the restaurant, Blanche became an assistant teacher at a school for young children with special needs. When Todd's health declined, she stopped teaching to look after her husband. Norma, who lived nearby, used to drop by to put her father to bed every night. Sadly, Alfred Todd died on September 7, 2002. He was laid to rest near his home in rural upstate New York, and a special service was also held in his memory in Pinehurst.

Like Bill, Todd belonged to local veterans' organizations, first in New York and then in North Carolina. In New York, he was a life member of the American Legion Post 404 in Vernon, NY and the Durhamville Veterans Club in Durhamville, NY. He was also a member of VFW Post 7318 of Southern Pines. In addition, he was a fifty-five year member of the Sconondoa Sherill/Vernon Lodge 814 AF & AM in Vernon. Like Kinney, he was also a Mason.[24]

Many times, Blanche tried to get her husband to talk about his wartime experiences, but he never wanted to talk about them. She said he was a very reserved guy when it came to the war. She even doubted that he discussed his experiences with his friends at his veterans' clubs. Once in North Carolina, his post had a dinner honoring those missing in action, and she mentioned to someone that Todd had been one of them. Everyone was surprised. Nobody knew.

When the author first contacted Blanche in 2007, she was very apologetic that she didn't know anything about her husband's wartime experiences. The author helped her understand why by sending her a copy of the document he signed that bound him to secrecy. He pointed out that the purpose of this certification was to protect those who provided clandestine help to the evaders, namely the Sarri and Becattini families. She was surprised to hear about her beloved Toddy's wartime experiences.

SHOT DOWN OVER ITALY

Blanche returned to the classroom after Todd died, and taught youngsters with special needs. After seventeen years in the classroom, she retired from her hands-on work with young children, but still works at the school on a part-time basis. While she was always called Blanche up North, she is known as Miss Blanche down South, and every day Miss Blanche is greeted with a smile by the kids at school. Her daughters and their families still bring great joy to her life, and Toddy and Robert are never far from her thoughts.

Sergeant William A. Lanza

When Bill came home in September 1944 and learned that his mother had died while he was missing in action, he was devastated. He knew she was probably a wreck from news that he was missing in action. He just never thought she would die. It was one of the most difficult times of his life.

He knew a lot of people from working in the store for so many years and, because his mother worked along side of him, many people associated the two very closely. As a result, he received many tearful greetings when he came home. "I'd be walking down the street, see a lady who knew my mother, and she would break out in tears. It wasn't a festive return, but it was nice to be home."

At that difficult time in his life, Yola DiGiulio was there for him. He had met her at a wedding when he was best man and she was the maid of honor. At the time, he was not only attracted to her but was very impressed by how well she treated her sister and mother. When he was assigned to Fort Dix, he kept in touch with her and went on a few dates on weekend trips home, including the weekend of his last plane ride.

By the time he received his honorable discharge on October 14, 1945, he had decided to marry Yola, and she chose November 11, 1945 as the wedding date. At that time, November 11 was Armistice Day, which primarily honored the veterans of World War I. In 1954, it was renamed Veterans Day to honor the veterans of all wars. They had a big wedding in East Boston and a reception at the American Legion Hall in Revere, where his brother Jimmy donated the band that played many of the Glenn Miller tunes arranged by his friend, Jerry Gray.

When Bill left home in March 1941, he figured he would be back in a year to help his friend Muzzy embark on a professional boxing career. After Pearl Harbor stretched his service to almost five years, Muzzy's inside right punch wasn't what it used to be. Fortunately, Muzzy had since hung up his gloves and was driving a checkered cab and starting out in the florist business.

Bill had also changed. His oldest daughter Patty said her mother told her that the war changed her father. Before he went overseas, he liked to be around the boys and to have a good time, but after the war he settled down. Among other things, Bill took advantage of the GI Bill to train as a tailor for men's suits while driving a checkered cab in Boston on a part-time basis.

After deciding that being a tailor wasn't for him, he took a job in a machine shop, continued to drive a cab, and helped Muzzy with his florist shop by making deliveries for him. He started working part-time for the Post Office, and eventually went to work full time. By that time, Muzzy was on his feet in the florist business.

Bill went to work for the Post Office in 1951, and retired in 1980 after twenty-nine years of service. During that time, he and Yola raised three girls—Patty, Suzanne and Anne Marie—and all three settled down with their families in eastern Massachusetts. Patty lived nearby and Bill spent a lot of time with her two sons, Patrick and Brian, until they went off to college. The boys still remain very close to their grandfather. You would be hard-pressed to find a grandfather more proud of his grandsons.

For years after the war, Bill's family lived in a family enclave in Revere with living arrangements not unlike those still found in Italy, whereby relatives live close to each other. In Bill's case, it was as close as you can get. Bill lived in a three-story house with his family on one floor and the families of his brothers, Jimmy and Rudy, on the other two floors. Behind and connected to this house by an annex was a two-story house with living arrangements for his father, his brothers Dan and Tavio, and his sisters Anna and Rita. Dan's best friend, Jack Dodge, also lived there. Interestingly, Jack was a pilot who flew the advertising banners over Revere Beach for years, and who married a girl named Hank. In the backyard, the old man had grape vines from which he continued to make wine, and a large garden with flowers, fruit and vegetables.

Bill and his four brothers were always pretty close. They even played softball together on the same team in Revere. Bill (Air Corps) pitched, Rudy (Navy) played third, Dan (Navy) left field, Tavio (Navy) center field, and Jimmy (Navy Yard) right field. They shared many good times together. Eventually, everyone in the enclave moved to their own homes. Bill's family moved to a single-family home in another part of Revere where he and his wife still live, and where they celebrated their sixty-fourth wedding anniversary on Veterans Day, November 11, 2009.

Patty Fitzgerald says of her father: "He is a kind, gentle man and a wonderful father and grandfather. My kids love him. He always liked the simple things in life. Family and friends are what were always important to him. Material things meant nothing to him. He is a simple man with simple tastes, but with a memory not to be believed."

Her sons Brian and Patrick can vouch for his incredible memory, and for the positive way in which their grandparents have touched their lives. Notes Brian, "One only needs to meet Grandpa twice to appreciate his exceptional memory and ability to tell a story. We've always known Grandpa to be a truly exceptional person, and have sincerely appreciated his and Grandma's participation in our lives and unwavering support for us and our families. Though he appears to have lived modestly, we know he has lived a rich life. In between his stories and discussions about such things as the overabundance of pears growing in his garden or how the Red Sox are doing, he always has a battery of inquiries about our hobbies, jobs and lives."

Like Kinney, Denny and Todd, Bill always had a garden, and it would be a family affair during planting season. He grew tomatoes for his wife's homemade sauce, along with cucumbers and peppers. He had a pear tree and two apple trees that provided bags of fruit for his neighbors and relatives. He has scaled back his garden and now grows only tomatoes and cucumbers. For years after he retired, he participated in a senior citizen summer program in which he worked with and supervised youngsters working to keep community property looking good by cutting the grass, pruning the trees and cleaning the monuments dedicated to people like the veterans in this story.

As close as he was to his family, Bill seldom talked about his wartime experiences with his brothers, his wife or his three daughters. But when he did, people listened. His daughter Patty remembers one time when she had some friends over the house who asked him about the war. He had a few drinks and was feeling pretty good. "My father likes to talk, and started telling us stories. As we sat there mesmerized, I noticed that the hairs on his arm were standing on end."

Bill recalls the time his nephew, a career military man (now Lieutenant Colonel Anthony Sciaraffa), arranged for him to be interviewed by somebody at Camp Edwards, where he received his basic training. Earlier, when Sciaraffa was a student at Boston College, he arranged for a friend to interview his uncle for a term paper, for which he received an "A." In both cases, Bill spoke about being shot down, but didn't provide details of his evasion experiences.

Since four of the surviving crew members certified that they wouldn't talk about their experiences and two others, both prisoners of war, had experiences they preferred not to talk about, it is no wonder that Bill never connected with any crew members after the war, nor had any of them stayed in touch with each other. He did, however, keep in touch with many friends from Massachusetts who served in the Infantry with him, some of whom also served in the Army Air Corps. From 1946 on, Bill religiously attended the annual reunions of Company I, 101st Infantry, 26th Infantry (Yankee) Division.

On May 21, 1996, Bill attended its fiftieth reunion and his local paper, the *Revere Journal*, ran a story about him and two friends from Revere who also served in that company—Ernest Littlehale and George Tirro. Littlehale fought with the Third Army under General George Patton, and Tirro landed on Omaha Beach on June 13 (D-Day plus seven) and fought in Normandy and Northern France with the First Army under General Omar Bradley. These old soldiers kept their friendship going all these years.[25]

Others who attended those reunions were Leo Flanagan from Lawrence, who was shot down in a B-25 on his first mission in the Pacific Theater; Billy Burke from Lowell, who flew sixty-three missions for the 447th Bomb Squadron of the 321st Bomb Group; and Freddie Kidd from Andover, who was shot down over Russia and returned there for a visit after the war. Like Bill, they all started with the Yankee Division, but ended up flying bombing missions with the Army Air Corps.

Bill explains: "The Air Corps for me wasn't like the Infantry. There wasn't a lot of camaraderie. I arrived in Europe as a replacement crew member and never flew with the same crew long enough to develop a camaraderie. I was friends with my tent mates, and some of us flew together at times, but it wasn't like the Infantry where you were with the same men all the time from morning to night. Also, the men I trained with in the Infantry were from the Boston area like me."

He continued: "In the Air Corps, you looked at the board every morning. If you were assigned to a mission, you showed up and flew the mission. If not, your time was your own unless you went on a training exercise. So my loyalty over the years has been with the friends I served with in my Infantry days, some of whom went into the Air Corps like me. Every year, I saw the same eight to ten vets who had similar experiences to mine. We swapped stories and had a nice camaraderie among ourselves. There aren't many of us left."

Unfortunately, one of Bill's closest friends in the Infantry, Frank Alvino, never had an opportunity to enjoy these veteran reunions. However, he was never forgotten by Bill and the other veterans at these reunions, and the signpost honoring him in front of his home in Revere shows that he hasn't been forgotten by his hometown. The author drove by the signpost in July 2009, and it was adorned by two flags and a patriotic red and white flower wreath, inside of which was another flag, his name and the words "American Hero." Bill, who lives less than a mile away, notes: "Every time I drive by, I think of Frank."

Second Lieutenant Laverne E. Reynolds

After he was shot down and sent to a prison camp in Germany, the next eleven months were hell for Reynolds, his wife Aline, and his parents. Aline divided her time between her parents' Louisiana home and his parents' South Dakota home. After Reynolds became a freed prisoner of war, he was sent to a staging area in France, where he boarded a ship headed for the States. When his ship entered New York Harbor, he and his fellow prisoners were greeted by the welcome sight of the Statue of Liberty.

From New York, he traveled by train to Minnesota, and then to his home in Plankinton, South Dakota to spend his three-week furlough. Aline, who had been in Louisiana when he arrived in the States, came quickly to South Dakota to join him.[26]

At the end of three weeks, Reynolds reported to the same Redistribution Station in Santa Monica, California that helped

After the Storm

Kinney adjust to life after war. Also, as was the case with Kinney, his wife joined him. While he and Aline lived in comparative leisure and comfort, Reynolds received a thorough medical examination, discussed his prisoner of war experiences with men who had similar experiences, and received counseling relating to his future.

Reynolds decided to remain in the Army Air Force Reserves and to return to college under the GI Bill. He graduated from South Dakota State College with an electrical engineering degree, and then went to work for the U.S. Army Corps of Engineers where he did electrical engineering for the design and construction of powerhouses. Soon, he and Aline started a family. Roderick was born in South Dakota in 1947, after which they decided to seek a warmer climate.

In 1950, Reynolds transferred to Dallas, Texas, the headquarters for the Southwest Division of the Corps of Engineers. The same year, June Ann was born, and three years later Vange (Evangeline) rounded out the family. In 1958, they moved into the house that he lives in today.

Vange recalls her formative years fondly: "Dad always helped us with our homework and, of course, we thought he was the smartest man in the world. He also took a lot of pictures of us and other family members. My aunts said if it weren't for him, they wouldn't have so many pictures of their kids growing up. And he didn't just take still pictures—when the camcorders came out, he bought one and took family movies."[27]

She continues: "My father is a wonderful, caring person and a true blessing to many people. He has helped people financially, not asking to be repaid. He doesn't gossip or say bad things about people. Everyone gets upset sometimes, but with Dad it was seldom."

She has a special memory of the summer following her college graduation: "When I graduated from college, I was going to get a job. Dad told me to enjoy my summer. He said: 'You will never get another opportunity to have a free and fun summer.' I did not know how true that was. I really appreciate him allowing me that fun summer."

In 1980, Reynolds retired from both the U.S. Army Corps of Engineers and the Air Force Reserves. He started out in the Reserves as a Second Lieutenant, and retired as a Lieutenant Colonel. John Kennedy once said: "And so, my fellow Americans: ask not what your country can do for you—ask what you can do for your country."[28] Laverne Reynolds did a lot for his country by any measure. He also loved his country, saw a lot of it, and appreciated its beauty.

When the kids were growing up, they went on family trips. When he retired, he and Aline bought a customized van and traveled the States. When Aline's mother broke her hip and had to use a cane, they took her on a trip up the West Coast, across the Northern States and back down to Texas. She loved it, and became a frequent traveler with them. When Aline's sister's husband died, they drove to Louisiana and took her on a trip. Over the years, Aline's other two sisters and the husband of one of them took trips with them as well.

Reynolds' grandkids got in on the fun as well. Vange notes: "My parents took me, my sister and her children on vacations with them in the summer." She also points out that her parents went through four vans traveling around the country.

Aline always kept close ties with her family in Louisiana. In August 1999, on a trip to Louisiana to see her sister, her time had come. She had a heart attack and didn't pull through. It was a rough time for Reynolds, and his youngest daughter, Vange, moved in with him. His son, Roderick, and his other daughter, June Ann Boone, both live close by and he sees their families regularly. He has two grandsons, two granddaughters, three great-grandsons and, according to Reynolds, a "great" great-granddaughter. He is proud of all of them.

Roderick went through a rough patch a while back when he lost his wife after thirty-eight years of marriage. He has since remarried and spends quality time with his father on a regular basis: "I try to come over at least once a week to help do things around the house that need to be done. He supervises while I do the work. After working in the yard or the house, we go out to lunch. If there isn't any work that needs to be done, we go out to lunch and sometime do a little shopping. Dad and I also have a tradition of going to the State Fair of Texas in Dallas in October."

Even though Reynolds left Plankinton, South Dakota, in 1950, when the author contacted the *South Dakota Mail* in search of him, Gayle Van Genderen, its owner and publisher, remembered him fondly, stating: "Laverne is one of our favorite Plankinton sons." Her mother was in his high school class.[29]

Reynolds has kept in touch with his family and friends in Plankinton, and during the summer of 2009 he went to his high school reunion. On the way, he took a vacation with his two daughters and great-grandson Tyler to Yellowstone National Park in Wyoming and the Black Hills of South Dakota. He never tired of seeing the beauty of those national treasures. While he was in Plankinton, he visited with Gayle, whose mother died about three years ago. She was happy to see him again, and vice versa. Vange mentioned that Gayle's uncle, Gary Owens, was another Plankinton favorite son. He was the announcer of Rowan & Martin's Laugh In, the popular TV show of the late sixties and early seventies.

In 2009, Reynolds also attended a family reunion of Aline's family as well as the annual Purple Heart POW/MIA Luncheon at Barksdale Air Force Base in Shreveport, Louisiana. According to Vange, he has been attending these reunions for the past fifteen years. He qualifies on all three counts—he received a Purple Heart, was a POW, and was MIA. Vange notes: "They are very moving. They honor these patriots with a ceremony that makes you cry." It must be especially emotional for Reynolds because this is where he met and married his wife Aline.

Sergeant John W. Denny, Jr.

After the war, Denny went to work for the United Methodist Publishing House, which had an interesting history and wasn't always united. In 1844, divisions over slavery split the church, and the South faction selected Nashville as its religious publishing house, making the operation the first major publishing house in the South. During the Civil War, the North seized the Nashville facility and used it for government printing. After the war, Congress reimbursed the facility for wartime damages. It took a while, but in 1939 the northern and southern factions of the church reunited and chose Nashville as the site for the consolidated publishing facility.[30] After the war, Denny ran the presses.

In those days, couples sometimes met at events that you don't see much of anymore. Hunter met his wife at a tea dance, and Denny met his wife, Mildred Wilkerson, on a cake walk. Again, this was a different time. Denny and Mildred married on February 15, 1946, and started a family. Wanda arrived first, and five years later Steve came along.[31]

Denny didn't smoke, drink or cuss, and was active in the church, and so was Mildred. In fact, she and her two sisters, Edna and Jean, were once known as the Wilkerson Trio and sang gospel songs. Jean even found a soul mate who also liked gospel music, Gordon Stoker,

263

who became a legend in the music industry.

During the war, Mildred's mother, Gertie, was one of many women who went to work in a war factory performing tasks previously performed by men. She became a riveter, just like "Rosie the Riveter," the fictional icon representing American women who went to work in the war factories to do their part in the war effort.[32] Gertie worked in a factory in Nashville that made aviation parts such as wings and tail sections for a variety of prime aircraft contractors. Her factory was a division of the Aviation Company, the nation's third-largest producer of war materials during the war.[33]

Denny spent twenty-two years at the publishing house and, according to Steve, was the first one in Nashville to use a five-color press. After that, he took a sales position with MC Sales & Services, and became friends with its owner, Mickey Culler. Culler helped people with good ideas. He helped Denny start his own business, in which he developed, bottled and boxed a chemical agent that was used to clean floors in large supermarkets, such as the Kroger and Winn Dixie chains. Another good idea Culler helped become a reality was that conceived by an engineer from North Carolina to put baby seats on supermarket carts.

Away from work, Denny enjoyed boating and camping with his family. Steve notes: "My father had an old mahogany boat, and he liked to boat on Center Hill Lake and Old Hickory Lake. I was waterskiing by the age of seven. He also liked to pitch a tent and camp out by Center Hill Lake, and we would go on family camping trips. Another thing he liked was gardening, and so do I."

As a note of interest, Center Hill Lake and Old Hickory Lake are among the many lakes managed by the U.S. Army Corps of Engineers, for which Reynolds, his fellow prisoner of war, worked after the war. The lakes are a good example of how the Corps of Engineers enhance the use of the nation's resources by providing social, economic and environmental benefits enjoyed by many Americans such as Denny and his family.[34]

Proudly, Steve notes: "My father was a great guy. He was loved by everyone he came in contact with, and he was color blind. A couple of years after his funeral, I was walking down the street one day and met Theodore Robbins, who used to work for my father when he was in high school. He was in a military uniform, and pointed to the medals and ribbons on his chest and told me my father was the reason he had them."

Steve explained: "When my father started his business, he used to eat at a nearby diner called 'Sweats.' It served country cooking like collard greens that my father liked, and the owner, Morris Sweat, was a friend. Once, my father asked him if he knew a dependable young man who might like a job after school, and he suggested Theodore. My father grew to like Theodore, who was a good football player. He knew that a college education wasn't an option for him, so he encouraged him to pursue a career in the Air Force where he would have opportunities for advancement. Theodore took his advice, and did as well as my father thought he would."

Steve is also proud of his uncle Gordon Stoker, who sang first tenor with the legendary gospel group, the Jordanaires. In 1955, a young man from Memphis, who was a fan of theirs, sought them out after a concert and said if he ever received a major record contract, he wanted them to work with him. In 1956, RCA signed the young man to such a contract, and he was true to his word. The Jordanaires backed him on his first hit, "Heartbreak Hotel."[35]

The young man was Elvis Presley, and for the next fifteen years the Jordanaires backed him in the studio, on the road, and in twenty-nine film soundtracks. When Elvis became a mainstay in Las Vegas, the Jordanaires decided to return to their roots in Nashville. They backed other famous artists over the years, such as Eddie Arnold, Patsy Cline, Loretta Lynn, Ricky Nelson, Kenny Rogers, Conway Twitty, Tammy Wynette and many more.[36]

Their influence was widely felt, even outside country music. For example, Paul McCartney said the Beatles learned to sing harmony by listening to their four-part harmony behind Elvis.[37] The Jordanaires became the most successful studio vocal group in music history. In over fifty years of recording, it was estimated that they have appeared in records that sold more than eight billion copies. Along the way, Uncle Gordon was inducted into eight music halls of fame.[38]

When it came to Denny's wartime experiences, Steve said his father never spoke of them when he was growing up. His Uncle Buddy—Hubert H. Cowell, the husband of Denny's older sister, Edna—was also a prisoner of war.[39] Believe or not, they were in the same prison camp (Stalag VII-A), yet never knew it at the time. Uncle

Buddy was likewise reticent on the subject. When Steve became an adult, his father told him a few things about the prison camp, which helped him to understand why he never wanted to talk to him about it when he was a kid.

In 1988, Denny sent for his POW Medal. Steve said that the day he received it was the proudest of his life. One can see why. He did more than his share in the fight for freedom, and that makes a man proud. Uncle Buddy no doubt felt the same way.

In 1993, Denny took his last breath. He had a large funeral attended by his many friends, both black and white. He had six pallbearers and over twenty honorary pallbearers. One of the pallbearers was Uncle Gordon's son, Alan Stoker, who is a chip off the old block. He is the Sound and Moving Image Curator for the Country Music Hall of Fame and Museum, and won a Grammy in 2004.[40] Alan says of Denny: "My uncle had a great sense of humor. He liked to laugh, and he had a great laugh."

Denny's friends from Mickey's company were also well represented. Mickey is no longer with us, but his nephew, Steve Culler, who now runs the company, remembers Denny fondly: "We all knew that John had been a prisoner of war, but he never talked about it. He was a man who lived his life to the fullest. He was a good-hearted guy who used to give us backstage passes to the Grand Ole Opry. We all love country music down here, and really appreciated those passes."

Denny's wife, Mildred, is along in years and Wanda looks after her. Gospel music is still close to her heart, as are memories of her beloved husband.

Goffredo Sarri and Family

Before the war, Goffredo Sarri was a family man with a business in Figline Valdarno. He and his wife, Grazietta, had three boys and two girls, and he owned a shoe factory with fifteen employees. His family was close, his business was doing well, and he still found time to be an amateur bicyclist. All that changed in 1943 when Italy became a battleground.[41]

Sarri recognized that his wife and children were in danger and moved them to a nearby farm out of harm's way. He acted wisely because both his home and business were bombed during the war.

Sarri Family: Gathered for a wedding in 1968. Amerigo is kneeling. In back of him, from left to right, are Aldo, Grazia, Goffredo, Alfredo's bride Grazia, Alfredo, Grazietta, Paolo, Bruno and Anna. *Courtesy of the Sarri Family*

According to Bill, Sarri was a thoughtful and intelligent man: "He was very careful and didn't make mistakes. He also remained calm under pressure. We trusted him with our lives."

During the war, Sarri and his wife Grazietta gave birth to a sixth child and after the war added a seventh. Despite a large family that depended on him, after Figline was liberated, Sarri volunteered to continue to fight in the War of Liberation, and served his country until the end of the war.

After the war, he resumed his shoe business in Figline, and focused on raising his large family. His contribution to the war effort was soon recognized by the United States when he received from General Joseph J. McNarney, the United States Army Commanding General of the Mediteranean Theater of Operations, a certificate of appreciation for his contribution to the war effort from 1942 to 1945. It stated:

> *This certificate is awarded to Sarri Goffredo* [last names come first in Italy] *as a token of gratitude for and in appreciation of the help given to the Soldiers and Sailors of the United States, which enabled them to escape from, or evade capture by the enemy.*

Two years later, Todd's mother, Corinne, sent a letter to Sarri and his family, thanking them for being so kind to her son and making it possible for them to see him again. The letter meant a lot to the family, and Amerigo has kept it as a family keepsake.[42]

A family photograph was taken in 1968 at the marriage of Alfredo, who was born during the war. The photo shows Anna, who used to bring food to the two Americans, and Amerigo, who used to keep them company in the cave. It is noteworthy that Amerigo, who is kneeling, looks like his father in the photograph that appears earlier in this book.

Four years after this photograph was taken, on February 26, 1972, Goffredo passed on, and left a lifetime of memories for his loving wife and seven children. His family would remain proud of him, as would his hometown and his country. Honors would follow for his valor during the war.

On April 25, 1975, the thirtieth anniversary of Liberation Day, the mayor of Sarri's hometown, Figline Valdarno, presented a posthumous medal and certificate to Sarri for his participation as a freedom-fighter in the War of Liberation. Ten years later, on June 30, 1985, he received another posthumous award, a diploma of honor as a fighter for the freedom of Italy that was signed by the Minister of Defense and the President of the Republic of Italy.

In September 2007, when the author visited Figline, Sarri was among a number of Figline's favorite sons being honored in an exhibit at Chiesa di San Francesco (St. Francis Church), which was built in its present form in the late thirteenth and early fourteenth centuries and is a popular tourist attraction.

Sarri was clearly everything Bill said he was, and more. In a letter to Amerigo in 2007, Bill wrote: "In all these years, not once did I forget what your family has done for me. I idolized your father. He will always be my hero." He added: "Your mother was a fine woman who raised a beautiful family and was a great help to me." Seventeen years after her husband's death, Grazietta died on May 14, 1989, another sad day for the Sarri family.

Thirty-six years after the passing of Goffredo and nineteen years after the passing of Grazietta, their son Amerigo received a special honor. On Liberation Day, April 25, 2008, sixty-three years after the end of World War II, the Mayor of Pian di Scò presented a gold medal to Amerigo for his courage in helping Bill and Todd during the war. What made the medal extra special was that it was presented in the memory of his father, Goffredo.

Riccardo Becattini and Family

Before the war, Riccardo was a farmer. He lived and worked on a farm operated by his father, a sharecropper who shared his crops with the owner of the farm, a man who lived in nearby Florence. Riccardo loved everything about farming, and so it is not surprising that he farmed for the rest of his life.[43]

During the war, Riccardo put his life on the line for the two Americans on a couple of occasions, the most notable one of which was when he disguised them as refugees and escorted them along the German front to Figline Valdarno where they were liberated. In fact, the last familiar face the two Americans saw as they left Figline in a British vehicle was that of Riccardo, with a big smile on it.

Riccardo left Bill with fond memories: "Riccardo was an enthusiastic guy, ready to plunge into anything. He took chances, and that was to our benefit. Todd and I enjoyed his company, and his friendship and courage meant a lot to us."

After the war, Riccardo married Marisa, who lived in one of the three houses in his enclave on the farm. She too had brought food to the two Americans. Bill knew that Riccardo was very fond of her, and was happy to hear that they married after the war and went on to raise a son, Moreno, and a daughter, Laura. Both still live nearby with their families.

In addition to farming, Riccardo liked to go down to the village square to shoot the breeze with his friends, some of whom had also been partisans. While the crew that was shot down over Italy seldom spoke of their wartime experiences, Riccardo and his friends talked about the war all the time. Bill said Riccardo always had a tendency to exaggerate, and wasn't at all surprised that Riccardo's recollection of events are more dramatic than his. That's usually what happens when men get together to tell war stories.

During the late nineties, Riccardo was the subject of a news article in which he explained how he brought the two Americans from Vaggio to Figline to be liberated.[44] His recollection was perhaps exaggerated, but the bottom line is that Riccardo put his life on the line by helping the two American airmen. The Germans had made it known that males who aided the crews of enemy aircraft would be shot on the spot. Riccardo was well aware of this danger, yet he still risked his life to help Bill and Todd.

When the author visited Riccardo in September 2007, he thanked him for risking his life to help the two American airmen. Riccardo replied: "See what Bush can do for me." Apparently, Riccardo had never been publicly honored for his courage, but this oversight was soon to be corrected by his mayor, the mayor of Pian di Scò, Nazareno Betti, who just happened to be translating the exchange.

In a public ceremony on Liberation Day in 2008, Mayor Betti presented a gold medal to Riccardo for his courage back in war times. The good mayor also honored Amerigo in the same ceremony with the same award which was presented in memory of his father Goffredo. This was a timely honor for Riccardo because the following year would be his last.

Honored for Courage: Riccardo Becattini, above left, is presented with a gold medal on Liberation Day in 2008 by Nazareno Betti, mayor of Pian di Scò, Italy. Below, his family and friends join him in celebration of the honor.   *Courtesy of the Becattini Family*

In 2009, Riccardo's wife, Marisa, was having health problems and this wore heavily on him. On March 29, Riccardo left this world in his sleep. The author was notified in an e-mail from Luisa Fortini, the wife of his grandson, Fabio. She wrote:

> *He was fine and fully himself until the day before last. He had bought baby chicks to grow into adult chickens and had bought tomato plants to plant in the near future, so his mind was always projected toward the future and life. It is correct to say that he lived his life 100% right up to the end. He passed away while sleeping very early in the morning. It was very quick.*[45]

Riccardo Becattini was one of those ordinary people who did extraordinary things during extraordinary times. During the war, when chaos gripped his country, he did his part in the fight against the Fascist rule and the Nazi occupation. In so doing, he helped to prevent two American airmen from becoming prisoners of war, and when the time was right, he helped to deliver them to friendly forces. Bill and Todd have always been very grateful for his friendship and courage.

Major William Clark Hunter

There was no "after the war" for Major Hunter. He gave everything he had to give during the war, and what he gave enabled his crew to have "after the war" experiences. He made the supreme sacrifice, which enabled his crew to find their way home.

Bill remembers: "War is tough. Our pilots were so good, flying in tight formations, keeping us on course despite flak flying all around us, controlling the aircraft when hit, and putting their crews ahead of themselves. On the day our plane went down, Major Hunter's skill kept us from hitting the other planes when we broke formation, and his raw courage kept the plane under control until everyone but him had bailed out. I consider myself very lucky because there were so many courageous men like Major Hunter who weren't so fortunate. They were the real heroes. We were fighting for a good cause, our freedom, but the cost was very, very high. God bless our heroes."

Epilogue

When I dropped by my Uncle Willie's (Bill Lanza's) house for a visit on June 8, 2006, I could never have guessed that I would be spending the next four years of my life writing a story around his experiences during World War II. What began as a simple exercise of taking notes to pass on to my kids ended up consuming my life for the next four years. However, I have to say that I was primed for something like this. I had read and appreciated many of the books written about the valor and fortitude of World War II veterans. What's more, I had just retired and returned from a visit to the beaches of Normandy, a powerful emotional experience that gave me an even deeper appreciation of the scope of the sacrifices that enabled us to remain a free nation.

When I learned that my uncle and another airman lived in a cave in enemy territory for two months, and that a couple of families risked their lives to help them, I wanted to know more. I began reading about the war in Italy, and I set out to find Alfred Todd, the man he shared the cave with during the summer of 1944. Ten months later in April 2007, I learned that he had died, and found his widow, Blanche Todd. She told me that he never wanted to talk about his wartime experiences. From that point on, Mrs. Todd was very supportive of my efforts, as she joined my uncle and me on this trip down memory lane.

Early on, I needed help in researching the 321st Bomb Group that my uncle served with, and received the most help from John Fitzgerald. In memory of his father, with whom my uncle once flew, John had been painstakingly gathering information on the history of the 321st Bomb Group. He has done a remarkable job in honoring his father's memory, and has been a valuable resource for me and many others. The men of the 321st all owe a debt of gratitude to John for his fine work.

John also put me in touch with Michele "Mick" Becchi of the *Istituto Storico della Resistenza (Historical Institute of the Resistance)* in Italy. Mick helped me connect with the mayors of three beautiful Tuscan towns—Figline Valdarno, Pian di Scò and Reggello—that surround the village of Vaggio, where I found the families of Amerigo Sarri and Riccardo Becattini.

Communicating with these officials and their staffs in a language I don't speak became the next challenge. Air Force Major Lia Mastronardi (now a retired Lieutenant Colonel), the daughter of an old friend, connected me with Mauro Zanotti, the general manager of the Hotel Londra, one of the nicest hotels in Venice, who was glad to help me write formal letters to the mayors of these historic towns. Mauro is also a pilot who flies in air shows and has a high regard for the venerable ol' B-25 warbird. With the help of Mick and Mauro, I was able to connect with these mayors, whose staffs worked together to put me in touch with both Amerigo and Riccardo.

My wife Diana, my daughter Kelly and I had planned to visit Italy when I retired, and my retirement coincided nicely with my new project, so we decided to go to Italy in September 2007. Scheduling became a problem, and it wasn't until the week before our trip that I learned that I would be able to meet with Amerigo. I didn't learn that I would be able to meet with Riccardo until after I arrived in Italy. While we were sightseeing in Venice, Rome, Siena, Florence and Milan, I took two side trips to Vaggio, where I had many pleasant surprises in store for me.

The first surprise was the closeness of the families. I felt as though I went back in time because families there still live together and near other family members. When I was growing up, this is how I lived, and it reminded me of that. I felt very much at home in this family atmosphere, and could see why my uncle felt the same way during the summer of 1944.

On the day of my arrival in Tuscany, Amerigo was organizing a bicycle race, which told me that the fruit didn't fall very far from the tree since his father, Goffredo, was a competitive amateur bicyclist. His son, Maurizio, and his wife, Marina, met me at the train station in Florence, and brought me to meet Amerigo in Figline Valdarno, where the two Americans were liberated by the British in July 1944. Not far from the Don Bosco Salesian Oratory, where the two Americans hid the day before they were liberated, Amerigo greeted me with a big hug and tears in his eyes, and I might add in mine as well.

He was anxious for me to see a local exhibit of Figline's native sons who fought in past wars, and brought me to one of those timeless churches you see in Tuscany. Among the photos and documents on display were those of his father, Goffredo Sarri. I could see that his father had been honored by his hometown, his country and our country. I thought to myself that I must have inherited my uncle's rabbit foot because my visit could not have been timed more perfectly. It was great to see that the man who was a savior to my uncle and Todd was not a forgotten man.

My uncle felt that Goffredo Sarri was the salt of the earth, and you could see that Amerigo was very proud of his father, as was Maurizio of his grandfather. One of the priests gave us a tour of the exhibits, with Maurizio translating for me. Later, as we walked around Figline, it was readily apparent that Amerigo and Maurizio were well known and highly regarded in the community. I was so happy that I had embarked on this project.

Later, we drove from Figline to Vaggio, crossing the Arno River and following the same route traveled by Riccardo, my uncle and Todd years before, but in the opposite direction and under far different circumstances. The road was as described to me by my uncle. The Resco River flowed parallel to the road and mountains rose in the distance. As we approached Vaggio, wooded hills on my right rose above the village. One of those hills was once the summer home of the two Americans.

I had a wonderful evening at the Sarri home, where Amerigo and his wife Clementina live with Maurizio and his wife Marina and their son Nicolé. It is a comfortable home on the south bank of the Resco River, not far from the farm and the cave. Marina rolled out the red carpet with a delicious meal, and served it in the charming surroundings of their backyard. Two of Amerigo's brothers—Alfredo and Paolo—and their spouses dropped by, and we talked about the two Americans throughout a memorable evening. Amerigo's recollections of that summer were in sync with those of my uncle.

The following morning, we walked to Riccardo's home, just around the corner and up the street. As we approached his house, we could see above the village rooftops the wooded hill with the cave. We could also see a large gathering ahead of us.

You can imagine my surprise when we were greeted not only by Riccardo and his family, but by the mayors and staff members of the three Tuscan towns that surround Vaggio—Pian di Scò, Reggello and

Figline Valdarno. A newspaperman from a Florence newspaper was there as well.

It was an overwhelming reception, and I could only think of how much my uncle and Todd would have enjoyed it. I learned later that Riccardo's heroism in helping the two Americans had been the subject of a newspaper article about ten years ago, and that Riccardo was trying to find Bill and Todd at that time. This gathering would result in another article about Riccardo, and me, and how he saved my uncle and Todd.

It was a pleasure to meet the town officials who helped me connect with Amerigo and Riccardo. After exchanging warm greetings, we all walked uphill to the nearby farm. To my surprise, what I had envisioned as wood farmhouses that you'd find in New England turned out to be a complex of sturdy Tuscan stone and masonry structures. I was also surprised at the size of the wooded hill. I had envisioned it to be much higher, but when I considered that everything south of Amerigo's house was uphill, I could see that the hill was in fact higher than it seemed when standing next to it. Later, on top of the hill, I could see out over the Valley of the Arno River, or in Italian "Valdarno."

Photos for the local paper in Florence were taken of the group near the hill with the cave. After most of the group departed, Amerigo, Riccardo, Nazareno Betti (the mayor of Pian di Scò), and I were left by the wooded hill. Fortunately, Mayor Betti spoke English. There were tracks all over the field near the hill and I learned they were boar tracks. I was anxious to see the cave but not a boar. I was told that there had been two caves—a small lower cave and a large upper cave. My uncle never mentioned a lower cave; he only spoke of the upper cave.

When we entered the woods, I found them to be much thicker than I had envisioned. Riccardo showed me where the lower cave had been near the bottom of the hill and I could see how difficult it would be to detect in those woods. The hill to the upper cave was much steeper than it seemed from outside the woods. Nobody was up for climbing the hill, and I could understand why.

(I figured I would return to Vaggio later in the week to look for the upper cave, the only one my uncle recalls ever being in. When I did, Riccardo brought me into the woods and along a trail south of

276

the smaller cave, then pointed up a steep incline. I was on my own. On a positive note, I did not encounter a boar. On a negative note, I did not find the cave. Two years later, I read a book about a B-25 co-pilot who was also shot down over Italy and lived in a cave north of Vaggio. His son, even with help of local residents, couldn't find his cave.[1] The thickness of the brush foiled both of us.)

While Riccardo's wife, Marisa, and their daughter, Laura, were preparing a meal, Mayor Betti brought Amerigo, Riccardo and me to his office, located in an architectural gem of a building, then to the Church of St. Maria in Pian di Scò, which he proudly pointed out would be a thousand years old in 2008. The sturdy, dignified Romanesque church, which went through a restoration process during the sixties, has three apses and a bell tower, and looks as though it will last for another thousand years.[2]

When we returned to Riccardo's house, his family was there to greet us with a meal fit for a king. Riccardo had made the wine we drank, the chicken came from his farm, and the ham came from a boar shot and seasoned by his son, Moreno. Riccardo said to be sure to tell my uncle that I had the same wine, chicken and ham that he ate sixty-three years ago. (Later, I made sure I did.) The fruits and vegetables were home grown, and the pasta was home made. As with the Sarri family, I could see that the two Americans were in good hands with the Becattini family.

Marisa told me that she used to bring food to the two Americans, and the whole family knew all about Guglielmo (Bill) and Alfredo (Todd). While the Americans never talked about their wartime experiences, it was evident that Riccardo and his family never stopped talking about them. It was a special time for me. I kept thinking of how much my uncle and Todd would have enjoyed what I was experiencing.

When I mentioned to the Sarri and Becattini families that I was thinking of writing a book and dedicating it to them, they thought this was a great idea. That is when I decided for sure to write a book. Since then, Marina has been my liaison with the Sarri family and Luisa Fortini, the wife of Riccardo's grandson Fabio, has been my liaison with the Becattini family. They have been nothing short of wonderful, and I am so grateful for their help. While I cannot speak or understand spoken Italian, I have learned to write and read letters and e-mails in Italian, thanks to language software and thanks to the patience of my friends in Italy.

It took me a long time and many books to understand the ground war, air war, intelligence war and civil war in Italy. I purchased over seventy books and was on a steep learning curve for a couple of years. At first, I spent most of my time on websites, but soon learned that, in contrast to books, anyone can put anything on a website without substantiating it. Thereafter, I spent most of my time in books but still found many websites to be very helpful, especially those dedicated to World War II veterans and those providing links to military documents and reports.

After I had a pretty good understanding of the war in Italy, the Mitchell B-25 medium bomber, the men who flew it in combat, and the help provided by the Sarri and Becattini families to the two Americans, I set out in March 2008 to learn more about the crew that my uncle and Todd were shot down with, especially the pilot, Major Hunter.

Locating the families of World War II veterans is a slow process that requires patience, persistence and perseverance. My initial focus was on locating the family of Major Hunter, who my uncle thought was from Texas. The trail I was following, however, led to Hunter's Individual Deceased Personnel File from which I learned that he was from Williamsport, Indiana, not Texas. In August 2008, I connected with the families of two sons of Hunter's younger brother Park, who continue to carry on the family farming tradition. I received a warm reception from them, which again strengthened my resolve to do a nice job with this project.

Candace Hunter, the wife of Park's son John, was my first contact with the family. She and her sister-in-law, Linda Hunter, the wife of Park's son Ben, graciously briefed me on the family history. That's when I learned that Hunter had a young son, Bill, who was almost two years old when his father was killed in action. Although Major Hunter's wife, Jean, remarried and remained close to her roots in Texas, she made sure that Bill stayed close to his father's roots in Indiana.

I was saddened to learn that Bill passed in 1999, but it was nice to hear that his wife, Frances, and their daughter, Alyson, and her son, Ian, have remained close to the Hunter family in Indiana. What's more, Bill passed down his father's wartime keepsakes to Alyson, who in time will no doubt pass them down to Ian, whose middle name is Clark, the same as his great grandfather.

Once, in reflecting about her grandfather and others who were killed in action, Frances wrote in an e-mail: "All of this conjures up in my imagination as to what their lives were and what they might have been. These brave men and women truly were the Greatest Generation. I'm so proud to be an American, even with all the turmoil of today. We're so blessed!" When I read this, I felt blessed to be engaged in a project in which I was meeting people like Frances.

Frances told me that Betty Blackburn knew a lot about Clark in the war days because she lived through them with her sister, Jean, Clark's wife. Soon after Jean learned that her husband was killed in action, Betty learned that her husband, also a pilot, had become a prisoner of war. Betty was notified just before she was to have a son. She and Jean suffered together in those days. She even knew that Hunter carried two guns, and told me she and her sister called him "Two-Gun Tex." Once again, I could see why my uncle thought he was from Texas.

As I was learning about Hunter from his family, I was multi-tasking by searching for the rest of the crew. My research on Laverne Reynolds, the bombardier, led me to Plankinton, South Dakota, where I was happy to learn that he was still alive. The editor of the local paper, Gayle Van Genderen, knew him well. She referred my inquiry to his daughter, Vange, who contacted me on December 1, 2008. At that time, I learned that the family moved to Dallas, Texas in 1950.

As I would do with the families of other crew members, I shared information from my research, and sent along some questions. Vange, her sister and her niece got together with Reynolds to review the questions. I was pleasantly surprised when Reynolds sent me a letter that not only addressed my questions, but provided a lot of other information, including his experiences as a prisoner of war. Vange told me that she asked him if it depressed him to think about those experiences, and he said yes.

Since that time, I have spoken with Mr. Reynolds on many occasions. Among other things, we have tried to figure out exactly where he landed after he bailed out. While I am pretty sure I know where all the others landed, he and I are not sure where he landed, but I knew he landed somewhere between where Denny landed in Vaggio and where Kinney landed over the Pratomagno Mountains. It was a pleasure piecing things together with him, and to see that he was part of a tight-knit family. I am still amazed that he was never nervous on bomb runs.

It took me quite a few phone calls before I found someone in Kinney's family. On February 3, 2009, I located his wife, and soon began a correspondence with his daughter Judy, who had loads to share about her "fabulous" father, but nothing about his wartime experiences because he never spoke of them. As I did with Mrs. Todd, I sent her the document her father signed that required him to remain silent on his evasion experiences. Like Mrs. Todd, she was so appreciative of what I was doing, and I was so appreciative of her support.

In researching John Denny, I found an application he completed in 1988 to obtain his Prisoner of War Medal. When I saw that he lived on General George Patton Road in Nashville, Tennessee, I couldn't believe it because Patton liberated him from Stalag VII-A. It was so fitting that he lived on a street honoring his liberator. After a number of phone calls, I found his son, Steve, also of Nashville, on February 17, 2009.

By this time, I was not surprised when he told me his father spoke little of his wartime experiences, especially his prisoner of war experiences. What little his father told to him appears in this book. Of his prisoner of war experiences, his father mentioned something when he was an adult that made Steve understand why he didn't want to talk about them. As with everyone else, I shared the information I had about his father, and have enjoyed our conversations about his father.

Walt Brickner was tough to find. I knew he had been a minor league baseball player, and it was through this association that I tracked him down. After I found his obituary, I obtained his death certificate, on which was the name of someone who turned out to be his good friend, Jim Wood. They belonged to the same country club, and often golfed together. As expected, Walt never spoke with Jim about his wartime experiences, and it's too bad because he had a lot to be proud of. As much as he loved baseball, he put his baseball career on hold to fight for his country, and that is indeed something to be proud of.

Originally, I had planned to dedicate this book to Goffredo Sarri and Riccardo Becattini and their families for their courage and humanity. However, after getting to know more about the crew that was shot down over Italy, especially Major Hunter, I decided

Epilogue

to include them in my dedication. I spent the first two years of this project learning about the war in Italy and how the Sarri and Becattini families helped Bill and Todd evade the enemy. Then, I began to realize that I might be able to make contact with the families of all the crew members. This resulted in an exciting and dramatic enhancement to the book, and elevated my already high regard for these valiant men.

Acknowledgements

When you engage in a four-year project to write a book, especially your first book, you have a lot of people to thank. The book itself is a thank you to the Sarri and Becattini families for their courage and humanity, and to the seven-man crew of that ill-fated plane who served their country well, especially Major Hunter who gave his life to save his crew. Here, I wish to also thank those who provided valuable support to me in researching and writing this book.

Overall Support

- William "Bill" Lanza – My Uncle Willie's amazing memory and story-telling ability made this book possible. It has been great bonding with him, and I am thankful that my Aunt Yola kept him on the ball all these years.
- Diana Lanza – Without my wife Diana's love, understanding and encouragement, along with her proofreading and wise counsel, I would still be writing and my kids would still be asking me why it was taking so long. All kidding aside, I have been blessed with a great support group in John, Jr., Mark, Brett, Jeff and Kelly.
- John Hetland – I always viewed John as a pocket of brilliance, and he shined his light on me as my sounding board throughout the process, and by editing my work. His help is appreciated beyond measure.

Help in Finding the Sarri and Becattini Families

- As noted in the Epilogue, Michele "Mick" Becchi and Mauro Zanotti helped me to connect with the mayors of three Tuscan towns, for which I am grateful.
- I am also grateful to the mayors of those towns and their staffs for bringing me together with the Sarri and Becattini families, and for arranging a warm reception for me in Vaggio. I wish to thank Sergio Benedetti, the mayor of Reggello; Riccardo Nocentini, the mayor of Figline Valdarno; and Nazareno Betti, the mayor of Piani

Pian di Scò; and their staffs. I'll never forget that day.

- I offer special thanks to Maria Pia Babini and Sabrina Fazzini of the Reggello mayor's office, and Sandra Zinanni of the Figline Valdarno mayor's office for contacting Amerigo and Riccardo in advance of my trip to Italy, and setting the stage for our meeting.

Support from the Sarri and Becattini Families

- Amerigo Sarri – He was a teenager who befriended my uncle and Todd during the war, and sixty-three years later he befriended me and was gracious in sharing his memories of the summer of 1944. It was such a pleasure to visit with him.
- Maurizio Sarri – Amerigo's son, Maurizio, was a splendid host and interpreter when I was in Italy, at which time he became my favorite professional soccer coach.
- Marina Pazzaglia – Maurizio's wife, Marina, has been my liaison with the Sarri family for the past few years, and I owe her a debt of gratitude for helping me communicate with her family in a language I don't speak.
- Riccardo Becattini – Riccardo put his life on the line for my uncle and Todd during the war, and it was a pleasure to spend some time with him and get his recollections of the war. I was so happy that he and Amerigo were honored for their courage in 2008, and I was so sad that Riccardo left us in 2009.
- Marisa and Laura Becattini – Marisa and Laura, Riccardo's wife and daughter, were wonderful hosts during my visit, and I will never forget the marathon meal with their family. It was also a pleasure to meet Riccardo's son, Moreno, during my visit.
- Luisa Fortini – Luisa, the wife of Riccardo's grandson, has been my liaison with the Becattini family for the past few years, and I appreciate her generous assistance in helping me to communicate with her family. During our correspondence, she and her husband Fabio had their first child, Raul, Riccardo's great-grandson, who will no doubt grow up to be proud of his special great-grandfather.

Support from the Families and Friends of Hunter's Crew

- William Lanza Family – In addition to my Uncle Willie and Aunt

Acknowledgements

Yola, their daughters (my cousins) Patty, Suzanne and Anne Marie have always been there for their parents. Also, it would be difficult to find two grandsons that are nicer to their grandparents than Patrick and Brian Fitzgerald.

- Alfred Todd Family – One of the pleasures of this project was getting to know Blanche Todd through numerous conversations, and to see how strong her love remains for her husband "Toddy" and her son Robert. Mrs. Todd appreciated learning about her husband's wartime experiences, and kept her three daughters— Linda, Mary and Norma—in the loop during our trip into the past.

- William Clark Hunter Family – I am thankful to Candace and Linda Hunter for sharing the Hunter family history with me. I am also grateful to Frances Glaze, Major Hunter's daughter-in-law, and her daughter, Alyson McDonald, keeper of Hunter's wartime remembrances, for kindly sharing with me memories and photos of Major Hunter, a true hero of the war. I was impressed by the patriotic grace of Frances, and am thankful for the memories that her mother's sister, Betty Blackwell, shared with me. I wish Frances's husband, Bill, could have seen this book that honors his father.

- Laverne Reynolds Family – One of the highlights of this project was to find Laverne Reynolds alive and in good hands. He was glad that I was writing a book about Major Hunter's crew, and he and his family, especially his daughter Vange, went above and beyond to help. After I sent him some questions, he teamed with his two daughters and a granddaughter to provide more information than I ever imagined, and this effort was deeply appreciated. Likewise, I am grateful to his son, Roderick, for sharing his thoughts with me about his father. As with my uncle, I feel as though I am living history when I speak with Mr. Reynolds.

- John Kinney Family – When I first connected with Kinney's daughter, Judy, she thanked me for all my investigative work, and has been cheering me on ever since. She shared with me many nice, moving stories about her parents, which I never expected but greatly appreciated. Her father would be proud to see how much he is loved by his family.

- John Denny Family – It made me feel good when Denny's son, Steve, said his father would have gotten along well with me. Denny is never far from Steve's thoughts, since his father's POW medal hangs in his room and his flag is encased in his office. I enjoyed hearing about his father from Steve, as well as from a former business associate, Steve Culler, and a talented nephew, Alan Stoker. Many thanks to all for sharing these memories with me.

- Walter Brickner's Friend – I would like to thank Walt's friend and golfing buddy, Jim Wood, for sharing his memories of Walt with me. I would also like to thank Clint Chavin and Jack and Faye Bridwell in Moultrie, Georgia; and Judy House and LaDean Harmston at the Museum of Idaho, for helping me to find a photo of Walt for this book.

Creative Support

- Gregory Stone – I have admired the artwork of Gregory Stone (www.gregorystoneartist.com) for a long time, and consider myself very lucky to have had an artist of his caliber do the cover for this book. My good fortune is related to the fact that his brother, Rocky Stone, was my college roommate. The Force was with me on this one.
- Brian Bromborsky – Brian played his senior football season on a bad knee and performed well, which always impressed me. I knew from his father that he loved art, and I followed his career through the Ringling College of Art and Design. When I needed some artwork, I sought him out, and am so pleased with his fine silhouette art and illustrations.
- Giovanni D'Orefice – I met Signor D'Orefice during my visit to the *Museo Historeale di Cassino* in Italy. At that time, he asked if I would provide written comments on my experience at the museum. I gladly obliged, after which he gave me a book of photos and told me I could use any of them in my book. I took him up on his offer, and I wish to thank him for being so kind.
- Todd Slater – I've known Todd for a long time as he is a good friend of one of my sons. I knew he was a talented graphic artist with a good eye for detail. Consequently, I sought his help in laying out the book and its cover, and he did a fine job for which I am thankful.
- Nancy True – Nancy is a professional indexer who is also a friend of one of my sons. I was so happy when she took an interest in the book, and so pleased with the index she created. I think readers will share my appreciation for her work.

Acknowledgements

Aviation Expertise

- Jack Mastronardi – Jack is a retired Air Force and Delta pilot, whom I have known and greatly respected my entire life. His oldest daughter Lia is a retired Air Force Lieutenant Colonel, but before she retired she helped me link up with one of her friends in Italy who also helped me with this project. Jack, whose son Nick is a Captain and a Professor at the Air Force Academy, helped me in trying to understand what happened to Major Hunter's aircraft after it was clobbered by flak. For that and our lifelong friendship, I am thankful.
- Tom Griffin – Tom is one of Doolittle's Raiders, a genuine national hero. He was kind enough to read what I wrote on the Raiders, and gave me information to add. I am also grateful to Bob Anning of Cincinnati, Ohio, for connecting me with Major Griffin and for arranging a tour for me of the Tri-State Warbird Museum in Batavia, Ohio.
- George Bartlett – George is a retired Brigadier General who flew seventy-five missions as a navigator-bombardier in the Pacific during World War II in the Marine version of the B-25J. He is a tough, proud Marine who appears in the James Bradley book, *Why Marines Fight*, and was a wonderful resource for me.
- Larry Kelley – Larry has his own B-25J, which he flies at air shows to raise awareness for Disabled American Veterans. In 2009, he did a flyover at the Indianapolis 500, and in 2010 he organized a flyover of seventeen B-25s at the 68th Reunion of the Doolittle Raiders. Larry also helped me with a couple of questions. I thank him, and I applaud and greatly respect what he does.
- Fred Smith – Fred flew sixty-six missions in a B-25J during the war, and was a valuable resource in helping me out with a few issues, in addition to providing me with a nice story involving a Doolittle Raider, Bill Pound.
- John Dell Isola – John flew a B-25J for eight years after the war, and I appreciate his help in trying to understand how an aircraft handles in a crisis situation. He and his wife Pat and I spent a pleasant afternoon together at an air show in New Hampshire.
- Paul Gale – Paul was a navigator on a B-25 during the war. He helped me understand the navigator position, for which I am thankful.
- Roger Hansen – Roger gave me a tour of the Tri-State Warbird

Museum in Batavia, Ohio, including the inside a B-25J. I wish to thank Roger. I also wish to thank David O'Maley, the museum's founder, for making this museum possible.

Translation Support

- Mauro Zanotti – Mauro is a class act. He runs one of the nicest hotels in Venice, is a pilot who appreciates the warbirds, has good taste in baseball players (his favorite baseball player is my favorite player—Ted Williams), and writes correct, effective Italian. He helped me craft letters to Italian officials, which paved the way for me to meet Amerigo Sarri and Riccardo Becattini.

- Franco DiGangi – Franco is my barber, whose barber shop had its 50th anniversary in 2007. I don't have as much hair to cut anymore, so he throws in a translation. Since he was a teenager in Italy during the war, he also threw in a couple of stories that appear in the book.

- Patrick Fitzgerald – Patrick is my uncle's grandson who, despite being incredibly busy, has from time to time done translations for me, for which I am grateful.

- Phyllis Ignozza – Phyllis is a professional translator who has also done a fine job in translating news articles for me.

- Dr. A. Donald Angeletti – Dr. Angeletti is my doctor. He has also helped me with translations. When he saw one of the letters Mauro Zanotti helped me craft, he said to be sure the recipient knows I didn't write it because it was written in impeccable Italian.

- Dr. Pasquale Collura – Dr. Collura is my next door neighbor, who is fluent in French and Italian. He's a good neighbor from whom I borrowed a translation.

Research Assistance

- John Fitzgerald – John has helped me more than anyone else in my research. His website on the 321st Bombardment Group History (http://57thbombwing.com/321stBombGroupHistory.php), dedicated to his father, has been a valuable resource for me and many others researching the valiant men of the 321st Bombardment Group. My uncle once flew a combat mission with his father.

Acknowledgements

- Victor Hancock – Victor is the editor of *Men of the 57ᵗʰ Bomb Wing,* a quarterly journal of stories about airmen who served their country well during World War II. The journal helped me to appreciate those airmen who served with valor during the war, and for that I am most grateful. I'm also glad that he likes the book.
- Deborah Cooney – Debby is an independent archival researcher at the National Archives. She has found many documents, reports and maps that have helped me immensely in writing this book, and it has been a pleasure to work with her.
- David Charville – David, who has a website that honors his grandfather, shared with me operations orders for my uncle's combat missions, and advised me on how to use my time effectively at the National Archives, where I obtained more detailed information on my uncle's missions.
- Yvonne Kinkaid – Ms. Kincaid at the Air Force Historical Studies Office was extremely helpful in providing information, as well as directing me to others for information.
- Joseph Caver – Mr. Caver at Air Force Historical Research Agency helped me obtain reports of reconnaissance missions, as well other information that was helpful to me. He was a pleasure to deal with.
- Anne O'Connor – Ms. O'Connor, also at the Air Force Historical Research Agency, was very helpful in my research into the prison camps.
- Captain Nicole M. Dubnicay – Captain Dubnicay, another helpful researcher at the Air Force Historical Research Agency, assisted me in locating escape and evasion reports, for which I am grateful.
- Lynne Gamma – Ms. Gamma, also at the Air Force Historical Research Agency, helped me obtain missing air crew reports that were much appreciated.
- Lynne Douglas – Lynne, the Director of Marketing and Community Relations at Columbia Metropolitan, graciously shared with me historical information about Columbia Army Air Base, where many B-25 crews trained during the war.
- Staff at National Personnel Records Center – Many staff members helped me locate information about the crew of Major Hunter's plane, and I appreciate their efforts.
- Steve Cole – I would like to thank Steve for his maps of the Italian Campaign which were a godsend to me on this project. The maps

appear in his website (www.custermen.com) dedicated to the 85th "Custer" Infantry Division with which his father served during World War II.

Other

- Jim McHale – I don't know anyone who reads more history books, and who gets more enjoyment out of them, than Jim. Consequently, I asked him if he would read my book and let me have it from the hip. His comments were helpful and appreciated, and resulted in valuable enhancements to the book.
- Marilyn Jeffers Walton – Marilyn is an author who has written a fine book, *Rhapsody in Junk: A Daughter's Return to Germany to Finish Her Father's Story,* which is a tribute to her father and his crew who were shot down over Germany during the World War II. She encouraged me on this project, and I am very thankful for her "can do" attitude.
- Dimitri Raugei – Dimitri is a lifelong resident of Florence who has appeared in a couple of movies set in Tuscany—*Tea for Mussolini* and *Up at the Villa.* On my second visit to Vaggio, he spent the day with me as my excellent guide and interpreter, and we had a very good day. His grandfather was a partisan, so he was very interested in what I was doing.
- Runo Palmquist – Runo is a friend of my brother, Ron. Runo fought on the beaches of Anzio, and was among the troops that broke out of the Anzio beachhead to capture Rome. He and his wife, Norma, graciously welcomed me into their home, where I felt as though I was living history as this humble, strong and compassionate man discussed his war remembrances with me.
- Harry Desko – I wish to thank Harry Desko who, with his wife, Alice, worked at the North American Aviation plant in Kansas City that built the B-25J's during the war. He proudly shared some of his memories with me.

Special Thanks

- Family – I wish to thank my mother, Dorothy, who looked exactly like Amelia Earhardt and had the same spunk, for instilling in me

Acknowledgements

the importance of being a good person; my father, Jim, for being such a good person; my brothers, Ron and Tom, for a lifetime of wonderful memories; and my pal, Ralph Ferragamo, for being such a great friend through the years.

I think that those who helped me were glad to help because they appreciated and understood the hard times endured by that generation, and how it emerged from the doldrums as a great generation. Many relatives of that generation are, like me, trying to recapture in some way what made them give so much of themselves, yet remain humble and satisfied with life. The Great Depression had depleted their money, and World War II took many of their loved ones, yet they emerged from this turmoil with goodness and grace. My uncle said: "It made life easier for me because the smaller things in life became more important. I've lived a simple life, but I was happy to have what I had."

About the Author

John Lanza (center), the author, is shown with Amerigo Sarri (left) and Riccardo Becattini (right) during a visit to Italy in 2007. He thanked them and their families for risking their lives to help his uncle, William Lanza, and Alfred Todd to evade the enemy during World War II.

John grew up in Revere, Massachusetts. After graduating from Bates College in 1967, he was a banker in New York City for almost forty years, retiring from JPMorgan Chase in 2006. He has an MBA from Baruch College, and has taught undergraduate and graduate courses on payments systems for over twenty-five years.

John has five grown children and four grandchildren, and lives with his wife, Diana, in Caldwell, New Jersey. He is an avid reader and has always been involved with team sports as a player, coach, booster, writer and photographer. He was once a Red Sox prospect and later a Yankee bird dog scout, at which time his father accused him of treason.

John planned to write books when he retired, and logically assumed his first would be his evolving text for his courses on payments systems. However, upon his retirement, while taking care of his 92-year old father, he spent some time with his 90-year old uncle and learned of the story that became this book.

Notes

Preface

[1] Douglas Brinkley, *The Boys of Pointe Du Hoc: Ronald Reagan, D-Day, and the U.S. Army 2nd Ranger Battalion* (New York: Harper Perennial, 2006), 5-6.

[2] Tom Brokaw, *The Greatest Generation* (New York: Random House, 1998), xxx.

[3] Mauer Maurer (ed.), "321st Bombardment Group," *Air Force Combat Units of World War II*, http://libraryautomation.com/nymas/usaaf5.html (accessed March 23, 2007).

[4] "History of Veterans Day," United States Department of Veterans Affairs, http://www1.va.gov/opa/vetsday/vetdayhistory.asp (accessed January 15, 2010).

[5] Michael R. Gary, "Highlights of an Interview with World War II Veteran William Lanza," Boston College Term Paper, April 13, 1984.

[6] C. L. Sulzberger, *The American Heritage Picture History of World WarII* (New York: American Heritage/Bonzanza Books, 1966), 373.

Chapter 1: BEFORE THE STORM

[1] "The War to End All Wars", Special Report, BBC News, Tuesday, November 10, 1998, http://news.bbc.co.uk/1/hi/special_report/1998/10/98/world_war_i/198172.stm (accessed April 18, 2008).

[2] "World War II Casualities," *Spartacus International*, http://www.spartacus.schoolnet.co.uk/FWWdeaths.htm (accessed April 18, 2008).

[3] Margaret E. Wagner, Linda Barrett Osborne, Susan Reyburn and the Staff of the Library of Congress, *The Library of Congress World War II Companion* (New York, London, Toronto, Sydney: Simon & Schuster, 2007), 35.

[4] "Exploring Boston's Neighborhoods—Boston Landmarks Commission," http://www.eastboston.com/eastbost.htm (accessed February 11, 2008).

[5] Columbia Theater, Cinema Treasures, http://cinematreasures.org/theater/12260/ (accessed February 11, 2008).

[6] "March of Dimes Story," http://www.marchofdimes.com/789_821.asp (accessed March 3, 2009).

[7] Ibid.

[8] "Franklin D. Roosevelt: The Man on the Marching Dime,"http://www.pcgs.com/articles/article984.chtml (accessed March 3, 2009).

[9] *Jerry Gray and His Orchestra, Live from the Palladium*, CD Inside Cover produced for Collector's Choice Music by WE Music Inc., P.O. Box 1571, Glendale, CA 91209.

10 Richard Grudens, *Chattanooga Choo Choo: The Life and Times of the World Famous Glenn Miller* (Stonybrook, NY: Celebrity Profiles Publishing Company, 2004), 131-132.

11 "Jerry Gray, 61, Band Leader, Composer and Arranger, Dies," *The New York Times*, August 11, 1976, www.nytimes.com (accessed April 18, 2008).

12 Eric Olsen, "Artie Shaw Remembered," http://blogcritics.orgarchives/2005/01/11/200310.php (accessed April 18, 2008).

13 George T. Simon, *Glenn Miller and His Orchestra* (New York: Da Capo Press, 1980), 189.

14 Ibid, 191.

15 "Pact of Steel (Italy-Germany [1939])," *Encyclopaedia Britannica*, http://www.britannica.com/eb/topic-564710/Pact-of-Steel (accessed April 18, 2008).

16 Richard Grudens, *Chattanooga Choo Choo: The Life and Times of the World Famous Glenn Miller* (Stonybrook, NY: Celebrity Profiles Publishing Company, 2004), 131-132.

17 George T. Simon, *Glenn Miller and His Orchestra* (New York: Da Capo Press, 1980), 191.

18 Kathryn Shenkle, Historian, Arlington National Cemetery, "Historical Information on Glenn Miller," http://www.arlingtoncemetery.org/historical_information/glenn_miller.html (accessed April 16, 2008).

19 George T. Simon, *Glenn Miller & His Orchestra* (New York: Da Capo Press, 1980), 324.

20 "(Alton) Glenn Miller—Life and Career, Military Service, Disappearance, and Personality," *Cambridge Encyclopedia, Vol.1,* http://encyclopedia.stateuniversity.com/pages/19/-Alton-Glenn-Miller.html (accessed October 20, 2008).

21 Kathryn Shenkle, Historian, Arlington National Cemetery, "Historical Information on Glenn Miller," http://www.arlingtoncemetery.org/historical_information/glenn_miller.html (accessed April 16, 2008).

22 George Simon, *Glenn Miller and His Orchestra* (New York: Da Capo Press, 1980), 4-5.

23 "Biography of Glenn Miller," *The Internet Movie Database*, http://www.imdb.com/name/nm0001895/bio (accessed April 16, 2008).

24 Kathryn Shenkle, Historian, Arlington National Cemetery, "Historical Information on Glenn Miller," http://www.arlingtoncemetery.org/historical_information/glenn_miller.html (accessed April 16, 2008).

25 Ibid.

26 *World War Cultural Association*, http://www.worldwar.it/forum/topic.asp?TOPIC_ID=6360 (accessed January 5, 2008).

27 Clayton K. S. Chun, *The Doolittle Raid: America's first strike back at Japan* (Oxford: Osprey Publishing, 2006), 15.

28 "Throngs Greet Col. Lindbergh on Boston Visit," *Christian Science Monitor*, July 22, 1927, 1.

Notes

[29] Ibid.

[30] "Logan International Airport: Then and Now," *Massport*, http://www.massport.com/ LOGAN/about_histo.html (accessed January 5, 2008).

[31] "Throngs Greet Col. Lindbergh on Boston Visit," *Christian Science Monitor*, July 22, 1927, 1.

[32] A. Scott Berg, *Lindbergh* (New York: Berkley Books, 1999), 165.

[33] "A History of the Boston School Boy Cadets," http://bambinomusical.com/David/ Cadets.html (accessed January 5, 2008).

[34] "Boston Schools Put 17,000 Cadets In Annual Parade," *Christian Science Monitor*, June 3, 1932, 1-2.

[35] David Kruh, "A History of the Boston School Boy Cadets," http:www.bambinomusical .com/David/Cadets.html (accessed January 5, 2008).

[36] James Doolittle and Carroll V. Glines, *I Could Never Be So Lucky Again* (New York, Toronto, London, Sydney and Auckland: Bantam 2001), 25-32.

[37] Jennifer Jordan, "Wine During Prohibition," http://ezinearticles.com/ ?Wine-During-Prohibition&id=297426 (accessed January 5, 2008).

[38] H.W. Brands, *A Traitor to His Class: The Privileged Life and Radical Presidency of Franklin Delano Roosevelt* (New York: Doubleday, 2008), 108.

Chapter 2: PREPARING FOR THE STORM

[1] "26th Infantry Division—One Page History," http://www.geocities.com/ armored50th/26th_Infantry_Division.html (accessed 23 March 2007).

[2] Chief Warrant Officer E.J. Kahn and Technical Sergeant Henry McLemore, *Fighting Divisions* (Washington, D.C.: Infantry Journal Press, 1945), 33.

[3] Dennis A. Connole, *The 26th "Yankee Division" on Coast Patrol Duty, 1942-1943*, Table of Contents, http://www.mcfarlandpub.com/book-2.php?id=978-0-7864-3142-7 (accessed July 14, 2009).

[4] Louise Pettus, "Army War Games—The Carolina Maneuvers," http://www.rootsweb .ancestry.com/~sclancas/history/wargames.htm (accessed July 14, 2009).

[5] "WC51 Weapons Carrier," http://www.robertsarmory.com/wc51.htm (accessed July 14, 2009).

[6] "26th Infantry Division—One Page History," http://www.geocities.com/ armored50th/26th_Infantry_Division.html (accessed July 6, 2009).

[7] "Famous Cases: George John Dasch and the Nazi Saboteurs," Federal Bureau of Investigation, http://www.fbi.gov/libref/historic/famcases/nazi/nazi.htm (accessed February 26, 2009).

[8] Craig Nelson, *The First Heroes: The Extraordinary Story of the Doolittle Raid— America's First World War II Victory* (Boston: Penguin Books, 2003), 277.

9 Ibid.

10 Ibid.

11 Chief Warrant Officer E.J. Kahn and Technical Sergeant Henry McLemore, *Fighting Divisions* (Washington, D.C.: Infantry Journal Press, 1945), 33.

12 C. C. Elebash, "Was It the Air Corps or Army Air Forces in WW II?" June 2000, Army Air Forces Historical Association, http://www.aafha.org/aaf_or_aircorps.html (accessed September 16, 2009).

13 "Flexible Gunnery Training in the AFF," Army Air Forces Historical Studies: No. 31, Assistant Chief of Air Staff Intelligence Historical Division, USAF Historical Archives, ASI (ASHAF-A), Maxwell AFB, Alabama, 15-16.

14 Clayton K. S. Chun, *The Doolittle Raid: America's first strike back at Japan* (Oxford: Osprey Publishing, 2006), 14.

15 "A Brief History of the Columbia Army Air Base," acquired from Lynne Douglas, Marketing Director of Columbia Metropolitan Airport, on October 28, 2008.

16 "North American B-25 Mitchell," last revised March 6, 2000, http://www.joebaugher.com/usaf_bombers/b25_2.html (accessed March 20, 2010).

17 "A Brief History of the Columbia Army Air Base," acquired from Lynne Douglas, Marketing Director of Columbia Metropolitan Airport, on October 28, 2008.

18 Clayton K. S. Chun, *The Doolittle Raid: America's first strike back at Japan* (Oxford: Osprey Publishing, 2006), 15 and 35.

19 David Tomlin, "Dangerous Mission: Doolittle Plotted Raid 20 Years Ago This Month," *Associated Press*, published in *The Columbia Record* on Wednesday, March 28, 1982, acquired from Lynne Douglas, Marketing Director of Columbia Metropolitan Airport, on October 28, 2008.

20 Ibid.

21 Doolittle Raid Exhibit at the National Museum of the United States Air Force at Wright-Patterson Air Force Base in Ohio, visited by author on January 23, 2008.

22 Ibid.

23 2nd Lieutenant Alyson Smith,"Doolittle Raider looks back on turning point in U.S. history," 96th Air Base Wing Public Affairs, Courtesy of Air Force Materiel Command News Service, http://www.af.mil/news/story_print.asp?id=123019181 (accessed November 2, 2007).

24 Craig Nelson, *The First Heroess: The Extraordinary Story of the Doolittle Raid—America's First World War II Victory* (Boston: Penguin Books, 2003), 15.

25 "Doolittle Raid," http://www.absoluteastronomy.com/topics/Doolittle_Raid (accessed September 6, 2009).

26 Written comments from Tom Griffin received in package sent by him to author dated February 20, 2009.

Notes

[27] Mitsuo Fuchida and Masatake Okumiya, *Midway: The Battle that Doomed Japan, the Japanese Navy's Story* (Annapolis: Bluejacket Books, 2001), 93, http://books.google .com/books?id=oayw_I6QkfgC&pg=PA93&lpg=PA93&dq=Japanese+picket+boat+No.+ 23+Nitto+Maru&source=bl&ots=vLwSUfY2AV&sig=QkFfWhcHpQTbpnYUJd4rfv3Jbp Q&hl=en&ei=6TaXSra1FY-w8Qa2NCZDA&sa=X&oi=book_result&ct=result&resnum= 1#v=onepage&q=&f=false (accessed August 27, 2009).

[28] Clayton K. S. Chun, *The Doolittle Raid: America's first strike back at Japan* (Oxford: Osprey Publishing, 2006), 49.

[29] Mitsuo Fuchida and Masatake Okumiya, *Midway: The Battle that Doomed Japan, the Japanese Navy's Story* (Annapolis: Bluejacket Books, 2001), 96, http://books.google .com/books?id=oayw_I6QkfgC&pg=PA93&lpg=PA93&dq=Japanese+picket+boat+No.+ 23+Nitto+Maru&source=bl&ots=vLwSUfY2AV&sig=QkFfWhcHpQTbpnYUJd4rfv3Jbp Q&hl=en&ei=6TaXSra1FY-w8Qa2NCZDA&sa=X&oi=book_result&ct=result&resnum= 1#v=onepage&q=&f=false (accessed August 27, 2009).

[30] Ibid, 96.

[31] "80 Brave Men, The Doolittle Tokyo Raiders Roster," http://www.doolittleraider .com/80_brave_men.htm (accessed February 26, 2009).

[32] Clayton K. S. Chun, *The Doolittle Raid: America's first strike back at Japan* (Oxford: Osprey Publishing, 2006), 83-85.

[33] Ibid, 84-85.

[34] Craig Nelson, *The First Heroes: The Extraordinary Story of the Doolittle Raid— America's First World War II Victory* (Boston: Penguin Books, 2003), 275.

[35] Ibid, 277.

[36] "Billy Mitchell the Prophet," Billy Mitchell exhibit at the National Museum of the United States Air Force at Wright-Patterson Air Base in Ohio, visited by author on January 23, 2008.

[37] "Billy Mitchell," http://www.u-s-history.com/pages/h1437.html (accessed September 16, 2009).

[38] Billy Mitchell exhibit at the National Museum of the United States Air Force at Wright-Patterson Air Base in Ohio, visited by author on January 23, 2008.

[39] "Henry H. Arnold," http://www.airpower.maxwell.af.mil/airchronicles/cc/arnold.html (accessed February 26, 2009).

[40] "80 Brave Men, The Doolittle Tokyo Raiders Roster," http://www.doolittleraider .com/80_brave_men.htm (accessed February 26, 2009).

[41] "Combat Crew and Unit Training in the AAF 1939-1945," Air Historical Office, Headquarters, United States Air Force, August 1949, http://afhra.maxwell.af.mil/ numbered_studies/studies2.asp (accessed February 26, 2009).

[42] Army Air Forces Aircraft: A Definitive Moment, Air Force Historical Studies Office, http://www.airforcehistory.hq.af.mil/PopTopics/AAFaircraft.htm (accessed February 23, 2010).

⁴³ Melvin D. Saunders, "Are We Already Learning In A Subliminal Way?" http://www .mind-course.com/subliminal.html (accessed 27 May 2008).

⁴⁴ "Army Air Forces: A Definitive Moment," http://www.airforcehistory.hq.af.mil/ PopTopics/AAFaircraft.htm (accessed May 29, 2008).

⁴⁵ N. Manocchio, "Skeet," http://www.bristolfishgame.com/skeet.htm (accessed May 29, 2008).

⁴⁶ *Merriam-Webster's Collegiate Dictionary*, Tenth Edition (Springfield, Massachusetts: Merriam-Webster, Inc., 2001), 88.

⁴⁷ Thomas J. Stada, David W. Dantzler, Greg K. Yarrow, and J. Benjamin Burroughs, "History of the 'Infamous Buist Tract' and Its Wilderness," *The Independent Republican Quarterly*, A Publication of the Horry County Historical Society,Vol. 40, No. 1-4 (Conway, SC: 2006), 6, http://www.clemson.edu/cafls/departments/forestry/horry _county/documents/buist_tract.pdf (accessed September 16, 2009).

⁴⁸ "Development of AAF Base Facilities in the United States," U.S. Air Force Historical Study No. 69, USAF Historical Division, Air University, 1951, 150-151, http://afhra. maxwell.af.mil/numbered_studies/467658.pdf (accessed November 14, 2007).

⁴⁹ "Recruitment and Training of Medical Personnel," The United States Army Air Forces in World War II, http://www.usaaf.net/ww2/medical/mspg4.htm (accessed October 22, 2009).

⁵⁰ "How S.C. Helped Win World War II," http://www.thestateonline.com/history/files/ 20050814_D4.pdf (accessed March 24, 2007).

⁵¹ "Biography," Mark W. Clark Collection, The Citadel Archives and Museum, http:/www .citadel.edu/museum/Clark_Biography.pdf (accessed March 24, 2007).

⁵² Ed Castens, *The 446ᵗʰ Revisted* (Published under the auspices of the 446ᵗʰ Bombardment Group Association—no publication date), 46.

⁵³ "Atlantic Air Routes of World War II," *Heritage Herald*, Issue Number 34, May 2004, http://www.heritageleague.org/brian/34final.pdf (accessed April 15, 2008).

⁵⁴ "United States of America and Guyana, Treaty Agreement No. 11963," May 26, 1966, http://untreaty.un.org/unts/1_60000/24/14/00046660.pdf (accessed May 29, 2008).

⁵⁵ Ed Castens, *The 446ᵗʰ Revisted* (Published under the auspices of the 446ᵗʰ Bombardment Group Association—no publication date), 46.

⁵⁶ "Slang Used In The 5ᵗʰ AAF In The SWPA During WW2," http://www.kensmen.com/ slang.html (accessed May 29, 2008).

⁵⁷ "Combat MilTerms," http://www.combat.ws/S4/MILTERMS/MT-S.HTM (accessed May 29, 2008).

⁵⁸ "Feature—Famous Short Snorters," *History Detectives*, http://www.pbs.org/ opb/historydetectives/investigations/502_famoussnorters.html (accessed May 29, 2008).

⁵⁹ Kent Hannon, "The Aviator," *Georgia Magazine*, Vol. 87, No. 3, June 2008, http:// www.uga.edu/gm/artman/publish/aviator.html (accessed May 29, 2008).

Notes

⁶⁰ "Fast Facts About Brazil," Consulate General of Brazil in New York, http://en.brazilny
.org/index.php?/consulado/anchor/fast_facts_about_brazil/#five (accessed
February 11, 2008).

⁶¹ Michael Astor, "Brazil to Crack Down on Amazon Cattle Invasion," *Associated Press*,
June 4, 2008, http://www.boston.com/news/world/latinamerica/articles/2008/06/04/
brazil_to_crack_down_on_amazon_cattle_invasion/ (February 29, 2008).

⁶² "World War Aircrew Buried In Arlington National Cemetery," Arlington National
Cemetery Website, February 1998, http://www.arlingtoncemetery.net/
ww2crew.htm (accessed February 29, 2008).

⁶³ "About Ascension Island," Ascension Island Government, http://www.ascensionisland
.gov.ac/aig/ascension-island-about.htm (accessed April 15, 2008).

⁶⁴ Ibid.

⁶⁵ Ibid.

⁶⁶ Jack Valenti, *This Place, This Time: My Life in War, the White House and Hollywood*
(New York, Harmony Books, 2007), 128.

⁶⁷ Ibid, 132.

⁶⁸ Joe Razes, "Pigeons of War," *America in WWII, The Magazine of a People at War,
1941-1945*, http://www.americainwwii.com/stories/pigeons.html (accessed April 15,
2008).

⁶⁹ Ibid.

⁷⁰ Ed Castens. *The 446ᵗʰ Revisted* (Published under the auspices of the 446ᵗʰ
Bombardment Group Association—no publication date), 47.

⁷¹ "Overview of Ella Logan," http://www.geo.ed.ac.uk/scotgaz/people/
famousfirst1477.html (accessed March 30, 2007).

⁷² "Individual Training in Aircraft Armament by the AAF 1939-1945," Air Forces
Historical Studies: No. 60, Air Historical Office, Army Air Forces, July 1947, http://afhra
.maxwell.af.mil/numbered_studies/467649.pdf (accessed March 30, 2007).

⁷³ "Constantine," *Brittanica Precise Encyclopedia, Answers.com*, http://www.answers
.com/topic/constantine-algeria?cat=travel (accessed March 24, 2007).

⁷⁴ Ibid.

⁷⁵ Ibid.

⁷⁶ Winfried Heinemann, "Salerno—A Defender's View," *Army History: The Professional
Bulletin of Army History*, Spring 2008, http://bookstore.gpo.gov/images/
army-history67.pdf (accessed March 25, 2009).

⁷⁷ "12ᵗʰ Air Force Organization, January 1, 1944," The 498ᵗʰ Bombardment Squadron in
Corsica, http://www.warwingsart.com/12thAirForce/airforcetable2.html
(accessed March 24, 2007).

⁷⁸ "The Mount Vesuvius Eruption of March 1944," http://web.archive.org/web/

20010419235636/http://sbl.salk.edu/~dkaiser/Vesuvius.html (accessed August 10, 2007).

[79] "History of the 310th, 321st and 340th Medium Bombardment Groups 1944 to 1945," last updated November 18, 2005, http://members.northrock.bm/~ehetzel/57th.html (accessed March 24, 2007).

[80] "West Pointer Assumes Job," *321 In The News*, March 26, 1944, 14, http://www .warwingsart.com/12thAirForce/spinglerheadlines2.html (accessed March 24, 2007).

[81] "57th Bombardment Wing Now Is Combat Operational Unit," *321 In The News*, March 1, 1944, 15, http://www.warwingsart.com/12thAirForce/spinglerheadlines2.html (accessed March 24, 2007).

[82] Jack Valenti, *This Place, This Time: My Life in War, the White House and Hollywood* (New York, Harmony Books, 2007), 128.

[83] 2nd Lt. Alyson Smith, "Doolittle Raider looks back on turning point in U.S. history," 96th Air Base Wing Public Affairs, Courtesy of Air Force Materiel Command News Service, http://www.af.mil/news/story_print.asp?id=123019181 (accessed November 2, 2007).

[84] Doolittle Raid Exhibit at the National Museum of the United States Air Force at Wright-Patterson Air Force Base in Ohio, visited by author on January 23, 2008.

[85] Craig Nelson, *The First Heroess: The Extraordinary Story of the Doolittle Raid— America's First World War II Victory* (Boston: Penguin Books, 2003), 12.

[86] "Carl Norden, Inventor/Engineer," National Aviation Hall of Fame, Inc., Dayton OH, http://nationalaviation.blade6.donet.com/components/content_manager_v02/view _nahf/htdocs/menu_ps.asp?NodeID=2007013156&group_ID=1134656385& Parent_ID=-1 (accessed January 27, 2009).

[87] "John H. Lienhard, "Norden's Bombsight," http://www.uh.edu/engines/epi1004.htm (accessed March 24, 2007).

[88] Jacklyn Lazar, "Sergeant Joseph A. Lappen," http://nhs.needham.k12.ma.us/ cur/wwii/05/p2-05/brooke-jal-p2-05/WWII_Lappen.html (accessed October 22, 2007).

[89] Steve Pace, *B-25 Mitchell Units of the MTO* (Oxford: Osprey Publishing, 2002), 22-23.

[90] "History of the 310th, 321st and 340th Medium Bombardment Groups 1944 to 1945," http://members.northrock.bm/~ehetzel/57th.html (accessed October 22, 2008).

[91] "Mission and Operations Reports of the 321st BG," (28 Reports from March 19, 1944 to May 26, 1944). Obtained from the National Archives in College Park, MD.

[92] Steve Pace, *B-25 Mitchell Units of the MTO* (Oxford: Osprey Publishing, 2002), 23.

[93] "Mission and Operations Reports of the 321st BG," (28 Reports from March 19, 1944 to May 26, 1944). Obtained from the National Archives in College Park, MD.

[94] "History of the 310th, 321st and 340th Medium Bombardment Groups 1944 to 1945," last updated November 18, 2005, http://members.northrock.bm/~ehetzel/57th.html (accessed March 24, 2007).

[95] *Pilot Training Manual for the Mitchell Bomber B-25*, AAF Manual No. 50-11, Published by Headquarters, AAF, Office of Flying Safety, revised April 1, 1945, 124.

Notes

Obtained from *B-25 Mitchell Briefing Time Multi-Media CD* purchased from MidAtlantic Air Museum, Reading Regional Airport, Reading, PA.

Chapter 3: ITALY IN CHAOS

[1] *Merriam-Webster's Collegiate Dictionary*, Tenth Edition (Springfield, Massachusetts: Merriam-Webster, Inc, 2001), 422.

[2] "Benito Mussolini," http://www.comandosupremo.com/Mussolini.html (accessed September 16, 2009).

[3] "Italy: Harvest and Headaches," *Time*, July 18, 1938, http://www.time.com/time/printout/0,8816,760008,00.html (accessed September 24, 2009).

[4] "Italy: Banzai!" *Time*, May 9, 1938, http://www.time.com/time/printout/0,8816,759599,00.html (accessed September 24, 2009).

[5] Ibid.

[6] "Italy: Aprilia Furrow," *Time*, May 4, 1936, http://www.time.com/time/printout/0,8816,882628,00.html (accessed September 24, 2009).

[7] R.J. B. Bosworth, *Mussolini's Italy: Life Under the Fascist Dictatorship, 1915-1945* (Boston: Penguin Books, 2007), 505.

[8] Paul Halsall, "Modern History Sourcebook: Benito Mussolini: What is Fascism, 1932," *Internet Modern History Sourcebook*, http://www.fordham.edu/halsall/mod/mussolini-fascism.html (accessed March 28, 2008).

[9] Rick Atkinson, *The Day of Battle: The War in Sicily and Italy, 1943–1944* (New York: Henry Holt and Company, 2007), 13.

[10] Ibid, 15.

[11] Ibid, 13.

[12] Philip A. Smith, *Bombing to Surrender: The Contribution of Air Power to the Collapse of Italy, 1943,* (Thesis for The School of Advanced Air Power Studies, Maxwell Air Force Base, Alabama, June 1997, 60-80), http://www.8thafhsoregon.com/8th/analysis/Bombing-Italy-To-Surrender-smith_pa.pdf (accessed March 8, 2008).

[13] William L. Shirer, *The Rise and Fall of the Third Reich, A History of Nazi Germany* (New York: Simon and Schuster, 1960), 997.

[14] Iris Origo, *War in Val d'Orcia: An Italian War Diary, 1943–1944* (Boston: David R. Godine, Publisher, Eighth Printing, 2007), 53.

[15] Ibid, 65.

[16] "Sicily-Rome American Cemetery and Memorial," The American Battle Monuments Commission, Nettuno, Italy, Handout Received During Visit in September, 2007, p. 5.

[17] Rit Nelson, "George S. Patton, Jr., 1885-1945, American General During WWII," http://www.hyperhistory.net/apwh/bios/b4pattong.htm (accessed March 8, 2008).

[18] Matthew Parker, *Monte Cassino: The Hardest Fought Battle of World War II* (New

York: Anchor Books, 2005), 31.

[19] Michael Wright, ed., *The Reader's Digest Illustrated History of World War II* (London: Reader's Digest Association, Ltd., 1989), 279.

[20] Dr. John Pimlott, *The Atlas of World War II* (Philadelphia: Courage Books, 2006), 140.

[21] Brigadier Peter Young, ed., *Atlas of the Second World War* (New York, G.P. Putnam's Sons, 1974), 121.

[22] "Proclamation of Italian Surrender by Marshal Pietro Badoglio, Head of Italian Government," Rome Radio, September 8, 1943, The Italian Surrender Documents of World War II, World Conflicts Documents Projects, http://www.geocities.com/iturks/html/documents_11.html (accessed March 26, 2009).

[23] "This day in the war in Europe 65 years ago: September 3, 1944" and "September 4, 1944," wwIIaircraft.net, http://www.ww2aircraft.net/forum/ww2-general/day-war-europe-65-years-ago-6116-73.html (accessed October 16, 2008).

[24] *Encarta Dictionary: English (North)*, Microsoft Word 2003, s.v. "partisan."

[25] "The Partisan Fight Takes Shape," The Resistance in Italy, Historical Background, http://www.cifr.it/Chapter_02.html (accessed 12 August 2007).

[26] Stefano Loparco, *Figline Durante Il Fascismo* (Signa, FIorence, Italy: Masso delle Fate Edizioni, 2004), 171.

[27] Harry Elmer Barnes, "Winston Spencer Churchill: A Tribute," Institute for Historical Review, *http://www.ihr.org/jhr/v01/v01p163_Barnes.html* (accessed October 17, 2009).

[28] Greg Annussek, *Hitler's Raid To Save Mussolini: The Most Famous Commando Operation of World War II* (New York and Washington D.C.: Da Capo Press, 2005), 9-16

[29] Ibid, 119.

[30] Ibid, 174.

[31] Ibid, 221-225.

[32] "Brief History of the L-5 Design," Sentinel Owners and Pilots Association, http://www.geocities.com/akdhc2pilot/history.html (accessed April 12, 2008).

[33] Greg Annussek, *Hitler's Raid To Save Mussolini: The Most Famous Commando Operation of World War II* (New York and Washington D.C.: Da Capo Press, 2005), 231-232.

[34] Ibid, 241.

[35] Ibid, 121.

[36] Miller, Donald L, *The Story of World War II* (New York: Simon & Schuster Paperbacks, 2006), 221.

[37] "Sicily-Rome American Cemetery and Memorial," The American Battle Monuments Commission, Nettuno, Italy, Handout Received During Visit in September, 2007, 15.

Notes

[38] Greg Annussek, *Hitler's Raid To Save Mussolini: The Most Famous Commando Operation of World War II* (New York and Washington D.C.: Da Capo Press, 2005), 244-245.

[39] Ibid, 242-243.

[40] Ibid, 245.

[41] "The Resistance in Italy 1943-1945: Historical Background," http://www.cifr.it/Chapter_02.html (accessed August 13, 2007).

[42] Matthew Parker, *Monte Cassino: The Hardest Fought Battle of World War II* (Anchor Books, 2005), 31.

[43] Ibid, 32.

[44] Ibid, xv.

[45] Ibid, xv.

[46] Rick Atkinson, *The Day of Battle: The War in Sicily and Italy, 1943–1944* (New York: Henry Holt and Company, New York, 2007), 535.

[47] Matthew Parker, *Monte Cassino: The Hardest Fought Battle of World War II*, (New York: Anchor Books, 2005), xiv.

[48] Ibid, 37.

[49] Colonel J. H. Green, *Cassino 1944 (Before, During and After)* (Cassino, Italy: Lamberti Editore, 1989), 18.

[50] Dr. John Pimlott, *The Atlas of World War II* (Philadelphia: Courage Books, 2006), 142.

[51] Iris Origo, *War in Val d'Orcia: An Italian War Diary, 1943–1944* (Boston: David R. Godine, Publisher, Eighth Printing, 2007), 108-109.

[52] Sister Margherita Marchione, "Pope Pius XII: Rome's 'Righteous Gentile'," *Italian America*, Winter 2007, http://www.osia.org/public/pdf/IA_Winter_07_Pg14-15.pdf (accessed July 29, 2009).

[53] Patrick K. O'Donnell, *Operatives, Spies and Saboteurs: The Unknown Story of WWII's OSS* (New York: Citadel Press Books, 2006), 278-279.

[54] Malcolm Tudor, *At War in Italy 1943: True Adventures in Enemy Territory* (Woodlands, United Kingdom: Emilia Publishing, 2007), 60-62.

[55] Iris Origo, *War in Val d'Orcia: An Italian War Diary, 1943–1944* (Boston: David R. Godine, Publisher, Eighth Printing, 2007), 112.

[56] H. Maitland Wilson, "Report by The Supreme Allied Commander Mediterranean to the Combined Chiefs of Staff on the Italian Campaign 8 January 1944 to 10 May 1944," (Washington, D.C., U.S. Government Printing Office, 1946), 1.

[57] Colonel J. H. Green, *Cassino 1944 (Before, During and After)* (Cassino, Italy: Lamberti Editore, 1989), 15 and 43.

58 "Allied Forces Bomb Monastery at Monte Cassino, February 15, 1944," Chronology of the Second World War, *Spartacus Educational*, http://www.spartacus.schoolnet.co.uk/2WWmonte.htm (accessed September 16, 2009).

59 "Congressional Gold Medal Recipient Ira C. Eaker," *Congressional Gold Medal.com*, http://www.congressionalgoldmedal.com/IraCEaker.htm (accessed March 26, 2008).

60 Craig Nelson, *The First Heroes: The Extraordinary Story of the Doolittle Raiders—America's First World War II Victory* (New York: Penguin Books, 2003), 306-307.

61 Matthew Parker, *Monte Cassino: The Hardest Fought Battle of World War II* (New York: Anchor Books, 2005), 69.

62 Donald L. Miller, *The Story of World War II* (New York: Simon & Schuster Paperbacks, 2006), 229.

63 "Landings Made at Anzio," *321 In The News*, January 22, 1944, 12, http://www.warwingsart.com/Internet.12thAirForce/spinglerheadlines2.html (accessed March 29, 2007).

64 "Product Description of *James Arness: An Autobiography*," http://www.amazon.com/James-Arness-Autobiography/dp/0786412216 (accessed September 16, 2009).

65 Matthew Parker, *Monte Cassino: The Hardest Fought Battle of World War II* (New York: Anchor Books, 2005), 118.

66 Simon Goodenough, *War Maps: World War II, From September 1939 to August 1945, Air, Sea and Land, Battle by Battle* (New York: St. Martin's Press, 1982), 72.

67 Clayton D. Laurie, "Anzio 1944," Brochure of the U.S. Army Center of Military History, http://www.history.army.mil/brochures/anzio/72-19.htm (accessed June 16, 2009).

68 Donald L. Miller, *The Story of World War II* (New York: Simon & Schuster Paperbacks, 2006), 229.

69 "General Lucas and the US 5th Army Land at Anzio, January 22, 1944" Chronology of the Second World War, *Spartacus Educational*,http://www.spartacus.schoolnet.co.uk/2WWlucasJ.htm (accessed March 26, 2007).

70 Matthew Parker, *Monte Cassino: The Hardest Fought Battle of World War II*, (New York: Anchor Books, 2005), 118-119.

71 H. Maitland Wilson, "Report by The Supreme Allied Commander Mediterranean to the Combined Chiefs of Staff on the Italian Campaign 8 January 1944 to 10 May 1944" (Washington, D.C., U.S. Government Printing Office, 1946), 19.

72 Alan Axelrod, *The Real History of World War II, A New Look at the Past* (New York: Sterling, 2008), 209.

73 Colonel J. H. Green, *Cassino 1944 (Before, During and After)* (Cassino, Italy: Lamberti Editore, 1989), 43.

74 Matthew Parker, *Monte Cassino: The Hardest Fought Battle of World War II*, (New York: Anchor Books, 2005), 164.

75 Ibid.

[76] Brother Bernhard Thomas Blankenhom, "St. Thomas Aquinas," http://www.opwest. org/sap/alt/library/st_thomas.htm (accessed March 26, 2008).

[77] H. Maitland Wilson, "Report by The Supreme Allied Commander Mediterranean to the Combined Chiefs of Staff on the Italian Campaign 8 January 1944 to 10 May 1944" (Washington, D.C., U.S. Government Printing Office, 1946), 25.

[78] David Hapgood and David Richardson, *Monte Cassino: The Story of the Most Controversial Battle of World War II* (New York and Washington D.C.: Da Capo Press, 2002), 224.

[79] "Allied Forces Bomb Monastery at Monte Cassino, February 15, 1944," Chronology of the Second World War, *Spartacus Educational*, http://www.spartacus.schoolnet.co.uk/ 2WWmonte.htm (accessed 24 March 2007).

[80] "Frequently Asked Q's and A's About *Historeale*," Handout from the *Museo Historeale di Cassino* in Cassino, Italy. Obtained during visit to *Museo Historeale di Cassino* in September 2007.

Chapter 4: BOMBS AWAY

[1] Colonel J. H. Green, *Cassino 1944 (Before, During and After)* (Cassino, Italy: Lamberti Editore, 1989), 56.

[2] "Allied Forces Bomb Monastery at Monte Cassino, February 15, 1944," Chronology of the Second World War, *Spartacus Educational*, http://www.spartacus.schoolnet.co.uk/ 2WWmonte.htm (accessed March 24, 2007).

[3] Chris Bishop and Chris McNab, *Campaigns of World War II Day by Day* (London: Amber Books, 2006), 131.

[4] Rick Atkinson, *The Day of Battle: The War in Sicily and Italy, 1943–1944* (New York: Henry Holt and Company, 2007), 23.

[5] "New Tactics Are Started," *321 In The News*, March 26, 1944, 14, http:// www.warwingsart.com/12thAirForce/spinglerheadlines2.html (accessed March 24, 2007).

[6] "War Diary for March 1944," Headquarters, 321ˢᵗ Bombardment Group, AAF APO 650, Department of the Air Force, Air Force Historical Studies Office, AF/HOH (Library), Bolling Air Force Base, Washington, D.C.

[7] "Allied Troops Take Monte Cassino, May 18, 1944," Chronology of the Second World War, *Spartacus Educational*, http://www.spartacus.schoolnet.co.uk/2WWmonte.htm (accessed 24 March 2007).

[8] F.M. Sallagar, "Operation 'Strangle' (Italy, Spring 1944): A Case Study of Tactical Air Interdiction," A Report Prepared for United States Air Force Project Rand (Santa Monica, CA: Rand [R-851-PR], February, 1972), 16.

[9] Ibid, 14.

[10] "The Gustav Line," The United States Army Air Forces in World War II, http://www.usaaf.net/ww2/africa/africapg6.html (accessed 29 March 2007).

[11] "New Tactics Are Started," *321 In The News*, March 26, 1944, 14, http://

www.warwingsart.com/12thAirForce/spinglerheadlines2.html (accessed March 29, 2007).

[12] Ibid.

[13] "The '88' Flugabwehr-Kanone 8.8 cm Flak 18, 36 and 37," *44th Infantry Division*, http://efour4ever.com/88.htm (accessed August 13, 2007).

[14] "WWII German Flak," http://yarchive.net/mil/ww2_flak.html (accessed August 13, 2007).

[15] Gordon Rottman, *US Army Air Force (1) (Elite)* (Oxford: Osprey Publishing, 1993), 47-48.

[16] "Outline History for March 1944," Headquarters, 321st Bombardment Group, AAF APO 650. Obtained from the Department of the Air Force, Air Force Historical Studies Office, AF/HOH (Library), Bolling Air Force Base, Washington, D.C.

[17] "489th Yearbook," *B-25J Mitchell Briefing Time Multi-Media CD*, MidAtlantic Air Museum, Reading Regional Airport, Reading, PA.

[18] "Mission Report for March 30, 1944," (Mission No. 246/Operations Order 284), 321st Bombardment Group, AAF, APO 650. Obtained from the National Archives in College Park, MD.

[19] Ibid.

[20] Ibid.

[21] Ibid.

[22] "448th BS War Diary, March 30, 1944," 321st Bombardment Group History, 57th Bomb Wing Association, http://57thbombwing.com/321stHistory/321_BG_1944-03.pdf (accessed March 29, 2009).

[23] "Mission Reports for March and April 1944," 321st Bombardment Group, AAF, APO 650. Obtained from the National Archives in College Park, MD.

[24] "Mission Report for April 14, 1944," (Operations Order No. 299/Mission No. 298), Headquarters, 321st Bombardment Group, AAF, APO 650. Obtained from the National Archives in College Park, MD.

[25] "448th BS War Diary," 321st Bombardment Group History, 57th Bomb Wing Association, http://57thbombwing.com/321stHistory/321_BG_1944-03.pdf (accessed March 29, 2009).

[26] "Missing Air Crew Report 4188," Headquarters, 321st Bombardment Group, AAF, APO 650, April 18, 1944. Obtained from the National Archives in College Park, MD.

[27] Ibid.

[28] The Air Medal Citation for William A. Lanza, June 22,1944. Obtained from William A. Lanza.

[29] Judy Ellen Kinney, e-mail message to author, April 16, 2009.

[30] "Missing Air Crew Report 4193," Headquarters, 321st Bombardment Group, AAF, APO

650, April 30, 1944. Obtained from the National Archives in College Park, MD.

[31] Ibid.

[32] Ibid.

[33] "Tactical Operations (Twelfth Air Force), April 29, 1944," Combat Chronology, U.S. Army Air Forces, Mediterranean—1944, Part 1, http://www.milhist.net/usaaf/mto44a.html#44apr (accessed September 21, 2009).

[34] "Corsica," Your French Connexion, LLC, http://www.yourfrenchconnexion.com/france-info/corse.htm (accessed September 21, 2009).

[35] "Corsica Description and Information," *french-property.com*, http://www.french-property.com/regions/corse/about.htm (accessed September 21, 2009).

[36] Telephone conversation with Ronald J. Kane on September 18, 2009.

[37] John Tagliabue, "Corsicans Remember Americans of World War II," *New York Times* (Europe), June 10, 2008, http://www.iht.com/articles/2008/06/10/europe/journal.php?page=2 (accessed September 20, 2009).

[38] "USAAF Chronology: Combat Chronology of the US Army Air Forces for April 1944," http://paul.rutgers.edu/~mcgrew/wwii/usaf/html/Apr.44.html (accessed 31 March 2007).

[39] F.M. Salagar, "Operation 'Strangle' (Italy, Spring 1944): A Case Study in Tactical Air Interdiction," A Report Prepared for the United States Air Force Rand Project (Rand, Santa Monica, California, February 1972), 23-24. Obtained from the National Archives in College Park, MD.

[40] Matthew Parker, *Monte Cassino: The Hardest Fought Battle of World War II* (New York: Anchor Books, 2005), 326.

[41] Colonel J. H. Green, *Cassino 1944 (Before, During and After)* (Cassino, Italy: Lamberti Editore, 1989), 66-67.

[42] Chris Bishop and Chris McNab, *Campaigns of World War II Day by Day* (London: Amber Books, 2006), 131.

[43] "The Breaking of the Hitler Line," Italy Volume II: From Cassino to Trieste, *New Zealand Electronic Tech Center*, http://www.nzetc.org/tm/scholarly/tei-WH2-2Ita-c1-5.html (accessed September 16, 2009).

[44] "Anzio 1944," http://www.army.mil/cmh-pg/brochures/anzio/72-19.htm (accessed March 31, 2009).

[45] Enzo Agelucci and Paolo Matricardi, *Complete Book of World War II Combat Aircraft* (Vercelli, Italy: VMB Publishers, 2006), 125.

[46] Margaret E. Wagner, Linda Barrett Osborne, Susan Reyburn and the Staff of the Library of Congress, *The Library of Congress World War II Companion* (New York, London, Toronto, Sydney: Simon & Schuster, 2007), 567.

[47] Michael Wright, *The Reader's Digest Illustrated History of World War II* (London: Reader's Digest Ltd., 1989), 285.

[48] "Military, Chapter 4, Defensive Operations," *globalsecurity.org*, http://www.globalsecurity.org/military/library/policy/army/fm/3-50/Ch4.htm (accessed April 12, 2009).

[49] "Addendum to the History for the Month of May," Public Relations Release, June 1, 1944, 57th Bomb Wing. Obtained from 321st Bombardment Group History, 57th Bomb Wing Association, http://57thbombwing.com/321stHistory/321_BG_1944-03.pdf (accessed March 29, 2009).

[50] "May Marked Heaviest Group Losses," *321 In the News*, June 14, 1944, 17, http://www.warwingsart.com/12thAirForce/spinglerheadlines2.html (accessed March 24, 2007).

[51] "Narrative History for May 1944," 446th Bombardment Squadron, 321st Bombardment Group, AAF APO 650. Obtained from 321st Bombardment Group History, 57th Bomb Wing Association, http://57thbombwing.com/321stHistory/321_BG_1944-03.pdf (accessed March 29, 2009).

[52] "Drive on Rome Begins," *321 In The News*, May 12, 1944, 16, http://www.warwingsart.com/12thAirForce/spinglerheadlines2.html (accessed March 24, 2007).

[53] "HQ 321st BG War Diary," 321st Bomb Group History, 57th Bomb Wing Association, http://57thbombwing.com/321stHistory/321_BG_1944-05.pdf (accessed March 29, 2009).

[54] "Drive on Rome Begins: 321 Is Flying Close Attack," *321 In the News*, May 12, 1944, 16, http://www.warwingsart.com/12thAirForce/spinglerheadlines2.html (accessed March 29, 2007).

[55] "13 May 1944, Alesan Field, Corsica," A History of the 57th Bomb Wing, http://budslawncare.com/57/index7.htm (accessed April 23, 2008).

[56] Ibid.

[57] Ibid.

[58] "448th BS War Diary: Additional Narrative for May 1944," 321st Bombardment Group History, 57th Bomb Wing Association, http://57thbombwing.com/321stHistory/321_BG_1944-03.pdf (accessed March 29, 2009).

[59] Edward F. Logan, Jr., *Jump, Damn It, Jump! Memoir of a Downed B-17 Pilot in World War II* (Jefferson, N.C.: Mcfarland & Company, 2006), 99.

[60] Susan Heller Anderson, "Mildred Gillars, 87, of Nazi Radio, Axis Sally to an Allied Audience," *New York Times*, July 2, 1988, http://www.nytimes.com/1988/07/02/obituaries/midred-gillars-87-of-nazi-radio-axis-sally-to-an-allied-audience.html (accessed September 21, 2009).

[61] "Mission Report for May 15, 1944," (Operations Order No. 331/Mission No. 330/Group Mission No. 290), 321st Bombardment Group History, 57th Bomb Wing Association, http://57thbombwing.com/321stHistory/321_BG_1944-03.pdf (accessed March 29, 2009).

[62] Ibid.

[63] "Saw Britons Rescue Yanks," News article provided on March 7, 2007 by John T. Fitzgerald, son of retired Colonel John Fitzgerald of the 446th Bombardment Squadron,

Notes

321st Bombardment Group.

64 "Mae West," *AphaDictionary,com*, http://www.alphadictionary.com/goodword/word/ Mae+West (accessed October 19, 2007).

65 "Missing Air Crew Report 4844," May 25, 1944, 321st Bombardment Group, AAF, APO 650. Obtained from the National Archives in College Park, MD.

66 Ibid.

67 "World War II Prisoners of War Data Files, 12/7/1941-11/19/1946," Access to Archival Databases, http://aad.archives.gov/aad/series-description.jsp?s=644&cat=WR26&bc=,sl (accessed March 31, 2008).

68 Elizabeth Feizkhah, "Traveler's Advisory," http://www.time.com/time/ magazine/1998/int/980615/travelers_advisory.trave5.html (accessed April 12, 2008).

69 "The Devil's Island," *waytuscany.net*, April 2002, http://www.waytuscany.net/ rooten/incontaminati_938.html (accessed April 24, 2008).

70 Thomas R. Brooks, *The War North of Rome, June 1944–May 1944* (New York: Sarpedon, 1996), 94.

71 Iris Origo, *War in Val d'Orcia: An Italian War Diary 1943–1944* (Boston: David R. Godine, Eighth Printing, 2007), 57.

72 "Joseph Heller's Catch 22," The Acquilla Theatre Company, http:// www.statetheatrenj.org/media/pdfs/keynotes_catch22.pdf (accessed April 24, 2008).

73 Ibid.

74 Brad Lockwood, "Joseph Heller," www.brooklyneagle.com/categories/ category.php?category_id=12&id=19034 (accessed April 24, 2008).

75 Harry D. George and Harry D. George, Jr., *Georgio Italiano: An American Pilot's Unlikely Tuscan Adventure* (Victoria, British Columbia, Canada: Trafford Publishing, 2000), 73.

76 R. J. Overy, *The Air War 1939–1945* (New York: Stein and Day, 1981), 146-145.

77 Bert Kinzey, *B-25 Mitchell* (Carrolton, Texas: Squadron/Signal Publications, 1999), 30-31 and 60-62.

78 "NAA-K Bomber Builders Reunion, Wyandotte County Museum," http:// skyways.lib.ks.us/genweb/wyandott/htm (accessed February 18, 2009). In addition, author had telephone conversation with Harry Desko on February 18, 2009.

79 Jack Valenti, *This Place, This Time: My Life in War, the White House, and Hollywood* (New York: Harmony Books, 2007), 124.

80 Ibid, 125.

***Chapter 5*: SHOT DOWN**

1 "Bailey Bridge," Maybey Bridge & Shore, Inc., http://www.mabey.com/About/ BaileyBridge/tabid/140/Default.aspx (accessed September 16, 2009).

[2] R.J. Overy, *The Air War 1939–1945* (New York: Stein and Day, 1981), 121.

[3] "Mission Reports for April and May 1944," Headquarters of the 321st Bomb Group, AAF, APO 650. Provided by David Charville, grandson of First Lieutenant Leighton "Danny" Charville of the 445th Bomb Squadron of the 321st Bomb Group via mail.

[4] "Historic Aerospace Site: Purdue University Airport," *American Institute of Aeronautics and Astronautics*, http://www.aiaa.org/Participate/Uploads/05-0443westlafayette.pdf (accessed November 3, 2009).

[5] "Purdue University Army ROTC History," http://www.purdue.edu/armyrotc/Program_Overview/history.php (accessed November 3, 2009).

[6] "A Brief History of Kelly AFB," Office of History, San Antonio Logistics Center, Kelly Air Base, Texas, http://proft.50megs.com/kelly.html (accessed September 16, 2009).

[7] "A History of Military Aviation in San Antonio," Air Education and Training Command History and Research Office (Private publication by Air Force historians: Revised September 2000 by Thomas A. Manning, Command Historian), http://www.aetc.af.mil/library/history/index.asp (accessed December 16, 2008), 20.

[8] Scott Huddleson, "Air Force Took Flight in San Antonio," *San Antonio Express-News*, posted to website November 1, 2008, http://www.printthis.clickability.com/pt/cpt?action=cpt&title=San+Antonio+News%2C+Weather%2C+Sports+%3A+mySA.com+%7C+ExpressNews&expire=&urlID=33061474&fb=Y&url=http%3A%2F%2Fwww.mysanantonio.com%2FAir_Force_took_flight_in_San_Antonio.html&partnerID=345404 (accessed December 14, 2008).

[9] Ibid.

[10] "Mission Report for May 17, 1944," (Operations Order No. 334/Mission No. 333/Group Mission No. 293), Reports of the 321st Bomb Group, AAF, APO 650. Obtained from the National Archives in College Park Maryland on October 24, 2007.

[11] "Mission Report for May 19, 1944," (Operations Order No. 337/Mission No. 336/Group Mission No. 296), 321st Bombardment Group, AAF, APO 650. Obtained from the National Archives in College Park Maryland on October 24, 2007.

[12] "446th BS Mission Summary, May 25, 1944," USAAF Chronology: MTO Operations (12 AF). Provided by John Fitzgerald, Jr., son of 446th BS pilot, John Fitzgerald.

[13] "Precision Bombing Praised," MAAF Headquarters, *321 In The News*, November 21, 1944, 1. Provided by Bob Ritger, proud nephew of 1st Lt. Frederick C. Ritger (321st, 446th), http://57thbombwing.com/321stHistory/321st_Headlines.pdf (accessed May 21, 2009).

[14] "446th BS Mission Summary, May 25 1944, USAAF Chronology: MTO Operations (12 AF). Provided by John Fitzgerald, Jr., son of 446th BS pilot, John Fitzgerald.

[15] "HQ 321st BG War Diary: Additional Narrative for May 1944," 321st Bombardment Group History, http://57thbombwing.com/321stHistory/321_BG_1944-05.pdf (accessed May 21, 2009).

[16] "World War II Figures," Learning More from History (Page 6.38), *whittsflying.com*, http://www.whittsflying.com/web/page6.38Learning_More_from_History.htm (accessed October 15, 2007).

[17] "Telegram with New Primary Targets from General Knapp," Found with papers of Mission Report for May 26, 1944," (Operations Order No. 347/Mission No. 346/Group Mission Number 306), 321st Bombardment Group, AAF, APO 650. Obtained from the National Archives in College Park, Maryland on October 24, 2007.

[18] Ibid.

[19] Carlton M. Smith, "The S-2 Story," http://www.303rdbg.com/sp-s2personnel.html (accessed January 28, 2009).

[20] "Escape and Evasion Report No. 85," Headquarters Twelfth Air Force, Office of Assistant Chief of Staff, A-2. Provided by Department of the Air Force, Air Force Historical Research Agency, Maxwell Air Force Base, Alabama on October 8, 2008.

[21] "Mission Report for May 26, 1944," (Operations Order 347/Mission No. 346/Group Mission No. 306), 321st Bombardment Group, AAF, APO 650. Obtained from the National Archives in College Park, Maryland on October 24, 2007.

[22] Edward F. Logan, Jr., *Jump, Damn It, Jump! Memoir of a Downed B-17 Pilot in World War II* (Jefferson, N.C.: Mcfarland & Company, 2006), 95.

[23] Ibid, 96.

[24] Alan Batens, "US Army WW2 Dog Tags," available at http://home.att.net/~steinert/us_army_ww2_dog_tags.htm (accessed November 7, 2008).

[25] "Escape and Evasion Report No. 89," Headquarters Twelfth Air Force, Office of Assistant Chief of Staff, A-2. Provided by Department of the Air Force, Air Force Historical Research Agency, Maxwell Air Force Base, Alabama on May 17, 2007.

[26] "War Diary for Month of May, 1944," Headquarters 321st Bombardment Group, AAF APO 650. Obtained from the Department of the Air Force, Air Force Historical Studies Office, AF/HOH (Library), Bolling Air Force Base, Washington, D.C.

[27] "446th BS Mission Summary for May 26, 1944," USAAF Chronology: MTO Operations (12 AF). Provided by John Fitzgerald, Jr., son of 446th BS pilot, John Fitzgerald.

[28] "Mission Report for May 26, 1944," (Operations Order No. 348/Mission No. 347/Group Mission No. 307), 321st Bombardment Group, AAF, APO 650. Obtained from the National Archives in College Park, Maryland on October 24, 2007.

[29] "Walt Brickner Minor League Statistics & History," *baseball-reference.com*, http://www.baseball-reference.com/minors/player.cgi?id=brickn001wal (accessed May 13, 2009).

[30] Ibid.

[31] "Moultrie Packers," *baseball-reference.com*, http://www.baseball-reference.com/bullpen/Moultrie_Packers (accessed May 13, 2009).

[32] "Walter H. Brickner," World War II Army Enlistment Records, Access to Archival Databases (AAD), The National Archives, http://aad.archives.gov/aad/record-detail.jsp?dt=893&mtch=1&cat=all&tf=F&q=walter+h.+Brickner&bc=&rpp=10&pg=1&rid=3633145 (accessed May 13, 2009).

[33] "Escape and Evasion Report No. 85," Headquarters Twelfth Air Force, Office of Assistant Chief of Staff, A-2. Provided by Department of the Air Force, Air Force Historical Research

Agency, Maxwell Air Force Base, Alabama on October 8, 2008.

34 Personal information on Laverne E. Reynolds provided by Laverne E. Reynolds, mostly in e-mail dated January 12, 2009.

35 "Captain Donald Smith," Submitted on April 18, 2001 by the Belle Fourche Chamber of Commerce, http://www.state.sd.us/military/vetaffairs/sdwwiimemorial/SubPages/ stories/story14.htm (accessed May 13, 2009).

36 "Missing Air Crew Report 6613," Obtained from the Department of the Air Force, Air Force Historical Studies Office, AF/HOH (Library), Bolling Air Force Base, Washington, D.C.

37 Personal information on John H. Kinney provided by his daughter, Judy Ellen Kinney.

38 "Some Basics," Basic Navigation–General, http://www.navfltsm.addr.com/ basic-nav-general.htm (accessed May 14, 2009).

39 Pilot Training Manual for the Mitchell Bomber B-25, AAF Manual No. 50-11, Published by Headquarters, AAF, Office of Flying Safety, revised April 1, 1945, 11. Obtained from B-25 Mitchell Briefing Time Multi-Media CD purchased from MidAtlantic Air Museum, Reading Regional Airport, Reading, PA.

40 R.J. Overy, The Air War 1939–1945 (New York: Stein and Day, 1981), 122.

41 Personal information on John Denny provided by his son, Steve Denny.

42 "Laverne E. Reynolds," Information Releasable Under the Freedom of Information Act, Request Number: 1-4848375293, National Personnel Records Center, Military Personnel Records, 9700 Page Avenue, St. Louis, Missouri 63132-5100, September 9, 2009.

43 "Missing Air Crew Report 6613," Obtained from the Department of the Air Force, Air Force Historical Studies Office, AF/HOH (Library), Bolling Air Force Base, Washington, D.C.

44 Pilot Training Manual for the Mitchell Bomber B-25, AAF Manual No. 50-11, Published by Headquarters, AAF, Office of Flying Safety, revised April 1, 1945, 13. Obtained from B-25 Mitchell Briefing Time Multi-Media CD purchased from MidAtlantic Air Museum, Reading Regional Airport, Reading, PA.

45 "Missing Air Crew Report 6613," Obtained from the Department of the Air Force, Air Force Historical Studies Office, AF/HOH (Library), Bolling Air Force Base, Washington, D.C.

46 "North American B-25 Mitchell," http://www.acepilots.com/planes/b25.html (accessed June 19, 2009).

47 "USAAS-USAAC-USAAF-USAF Aircraft Serial Numbers—1908 to Present," http://home. att.net/~jbaugher/usafserials.html (accessed June 19, 2009).

48 Steve Pace, B-25 Mitchell Units in the MTO (Oxford: Osprey Publishing, 2002), 33.

49 "Missing Air Crew Report 6613," Obtained from the Department of the Air Force, Air Force Historical Studies Office, AF/HOH (Library), Bolling Air Force Base, Washington, D.C.

50 Ibid.

Notes

51 "Mission Report for May 26, 1944," (Operations Order No. 348/Mission No. 347/Group Mission No. 307), 321st Bombardment Group, AAF, APO 650. Obtained from the National Archives in College Park, Maryland on October 24, 2007.

52 Ibid.

53 Harry D. George and Harry D. George, Jr., *Georgio Italiano: An American Pilot's Unlikely Tuscan Adventure* (Victoria, British Columbia, Canada: Trafford, 2000), 117.

54 Steve Pace, *B-25 Mitchell Units of the Mediterranean* (Oxford: Osprey Publishing, 2002), 70.

55 "Norden M-9 Bombsight," Fact Sheet from National Museum of the USAF, http://www .nationalmuseum.af.mil/factsheets/factsheet.asp?id=8056 (accessed September 16, 2009).

56 Frank B. Dean, "Flak Guns In The Brenner Pass," http://budslawncare.com/57/brenner .htm (accessed February 8, 2009).

57 Vladimir Ratkin, translated by James F. Gebhardt, "B-25: Familiarization with its construction, mastery [by Soviet pilots], and employment, based on the combat experience of 14th Guards Bomber Air Division and 4th Guards Air Corps," http://lend-lease.airforce .ru/english/articles/ratkin/index.htm (accessed September 16, 2009)

58 "Mission Report for May 26, 1944," (Operations Order No. 348/Mission No. 347/Group Mission No. 307), 321st Bombardment Group, AAF, APO 650. Obtained from the National Archives in College Park, Maryland on October 24, 2007.

59 "Missing Air Crew Report 6613," Obtained from the Department of the Air Force, Air Force Historical Studies Office, AF/HOH (Library), Bolling Air Force Base, Washington, D.C.

60 "Escape and Evasion Report No. 85," Headquarters Twelfth Air Force, Office of Assistant Chief of Staff, A-2. Provided by Department of the Air Force, Air Force Historical Research Agency, Maxwell Air Force Base, Alabama on October 8, 2008.

61 "Escape and Evasion Report No. 80," Headquarters Twelfth Air Force, Office of Assistant Chief of Staff, A-2. Provided by Department of the Air Force, Air Force Historical Research Agency, Maxwell Air Force Base, Alabama on October 8, 2008.

62 Harry D. George and Harry D. George, Jr., *Georgio Italiano: An American Pilot's Unlikely Tuscan Adventure* (Victoria, British Columbia, Canada: Trafford Publishing, 2000), 120.

63 "Escape and Evasion Report No. 85," Headquarters Twelfth Air Force, Office of Assistant Chief of Staff, A-2. Provided by Department of the Air Force, Air Force Historical Research Agency, Maxwell Air Force Base, Alabama on October 8, 2008.

64 "Aircraft Pitch Motion," National Aeronautics and Space Administration, Glenn Research Center, http://www.grc.nasa.gov/WWW/K-12/airplane/pitch.html (accessed July 25, 2009).

65 "Ailerons," National Aeronautics and Space Administration, Glenn Research Center, http://www.grc.nasa.gov/WWW/K-12/airplane/alr.html (accessed July 30, 2009).

66 "Vertical Stabilizer—Rudder," National Aeronautics and Space Administration, Glenn Research Center, http://www.grc.nasa.gov/WWW/K-12/airplane/rud.html (accessed July

30, 2009).

[67] Meryly Getline, "From the Cockpit with Captain Meryly Getline," http://www.fromthecockpit.com/Aircraft_Hydraulic_Leak.html (accessed July 25, 2009).

[68] Harry D. George and Harry D. George, Jr., *Georgio Italiano: An American Pilot's Unlikely Tuscan Adventure* (Victoria, British Columbia, Canada: Trafford Publishing, 2000), 117.

[69] Conversations with former Air Force and Delta pilot, Jack Mastronardi.

[70] "Specifications of the North American B-25J Mitchell," B-25 Mitchell "Heavenly Body" Website, http://www.b25.net/pages/b25spec.html (accessed July 30, 2009).

[71] "Emergency Operation," *Flight Handbook for B-25J Series Airplanes,* AAF AN 01-60GE-1, revised 25 April 1953, 53. Obtained from *B-25 Mitchell Briefing Time Multi-Media CD* purchased from MidAtlantic Air Museum, Reading Regional Airport, Reading, PA.

[72] Telephone conversations with Laverne E. Reynolds on December 22, 2008 and August 27, 2009.

[73] "Mission Report for May 26, 1944," (Operations Order No. 348/Mission No. 347/Group Mission No. 307), 321st Bombardment Group, AAF, APO 650. Obtained from the National Archives in College Park, Maryland on October 24, 2007.

[74] Ibid.

[75] "Mission Summary for May 1944," 446th Bombardment Squadron, 321st Bombardment Group, AAF APO 650. Obtained from the Department of the Air Force, Air Force Historical Studies Office, AF/HOH (Library), Bolling Air Force Base, Washington, D.C.

[76] "Escape and Evasion Report No. 80," Headquarters Twelfth Air Force, Office of Assistant Chief of Staff, A-2. Provided by Department of the Air Force, Air Force Historical Research Agency, Maxwell Air Force Base, Alabama on October 8, 2008.

[77] "Map of Tuscany," Euro Cart, Studio E.M.B. Bologna, Rastingnano di Pianoro, Bologna (Purchased in Italy in 2007).

[78] *Pilot Training Manual for the Mitchell Bomber B-25,* AAF Manual No. 50-11, Published by Headquarters, AAF, Office of Flying Safety, revised April 1, 1945, 140-141. Obtained from *B-25 Mitchell Briefing Time Multi-Media CD* purchased from MidAtlantic Air Museum, Reading Regional Airport, Reading, PA.

[79] "Missing Air Crew Report 6613," Obtained from the Department of the Air Force, Air Force Historical Studies Office, AF/HOH (Library), Bolling Air Force Base, Washington, D.C.

[80] "Missing Air Crew Report 5145," Obtained from the Department of the Air Force, Air Force Historical Studies Office, AF/HOH (Library), Bolling Air Force Base, Washington, D.C.

[81] "Escape and Evasion Report No. 80," Headquarters Twelfth Air Force, Office of Assistant Chief of Staff, A-2. Provided by Department of the Air Force, Air Force Historical Research Agency, Maxwell Air Force Base, Alabama on October 8, 2008.

[82] Ibid.

Notes

[83] "Missing Air Crew Report 6613," Obtained from the Department of the Air Force, Air Force Historical Studies Office, AF/HOH (Library), Bolling Air Force Base, Washington, D.C.

[84] "Trimmed Aircraft," National Aeronautics and Space Administration, Glenn Research Center, http://www.grc.nasa.gov/WWW/K-12/airplane/trim.html (accessed July 10, 2009).

[85] "Escape and Evasion Report No. 80," Headquarters Twelfth Air Force, Office of Assistant Chief of Staff, A-2. Provided by Department of the Air Force, Air Force Historical Research Agency, Maxwell Air Force Base, Alabama on October 8, 2008.

[86] "Missing Air Crew Report 6613," Obtained from the Department of the Air Force, Air Force Historical Studies Office, AF/HOH (Library), Bolling Air Force Base, Washington, D.C.

[87] "Escape and Evasion Report No. 85," Headquarters Twelfth Air Force, Office of Assistant Chief of Staff, A-2. Provided by Department of the Air Force, Air Force Historical Research Agency, Maxwell Air Force Base, Alabama on October 8, 2008.

[88] Ibid.

[89] "Escape and Evasion Report No. 80," Headquarters Twelfth Air Force, Office of Assistant Chief of Staff, A-2. Provided by Department of the Air Force, Air Force Historical Research Agency, Maxwell Air Force Base, Alabama on October 8, 2008.

[90] "Missing Air Crew Report 5145," Obtained from the Department of the Air Force, Air Force Historical Studies Office, AF/HOH (Library), Bolling Air Force Base, Washington, D.C.

[91] Ibid.

[92] "Missing Air Crew Report 6613," Obtained from the Department of the Air Force, Air Force Historical Studies Office, AF/HOH (Library), Bolling Air Force Base, Washington, D.C.

[93] Ibid.

Chapter 6: PARTISAN HELP

[1] "It Was Patton's Idea, The History of An Unusual World War II Unit," Based Upon "General Patton's Secret Weapon" by Werner L. Larson, Lt. Col., USA (Retired), Condensed and Edited by John R. Fisher, Lt. Col. (USAR) (Retired), Published in USA by the 443rd AAA Association, Copyright©1984 1998 443rd AAA Association, 443rd Antiaircraft Artillery Automatic Weapons Battalion, Texas Military Forces Museum, http://www.texasmilitaryforcesmuseum.org/36division/archives/443/44375.htm (accessed April 5, 2007).

[2] "Hitler's Boy Soldiers, 1939-1945," *The History Place*, http://www.historyplace.com/worldwar2/hitleryouth/hj-boy-soldiers.htm (accessed September 16, 2009).

[3] Frank D. Murphy, "The Liberation of Moosburg," *Moosburg Online*, Stalag VII A: Oral History, February 2002, e-mail by Frank D. Murphy, forwarded by Dave Kanzler, to *Moosburg Online*, October 2004, http://www.moosburg.org/info/stalag/murphyeng.html (accessed December 12, 2008).

[4] Munro, Ion Smeaton, *Through fascism to world power: A history of the revolution in*

Italy (Freeport, New York: Books For Libraries Press, reprinted 1971) 397-98.

[5] "Boys Scouts of American, National Council," http://www.scouting.org/Media/FactSheets/02-503a.aspx (accessed December 12, 2008).

[6] "Education in Fascist Times Through Pictures and Reports," http://uk.geocities.com//fkaprotz1/onbt.html (accessed December 12, 2008).

[7] David Kruh, "The Boston School Boy Cadets," http://www.davidkruh.com/the-boston-school-boy-cadets (accessed June 16, 2009).

[8] Thomas R. Brooks, *The War North of Rome, June 1944–May 1945* (New York: Sarpendon, 1996), 131.

[9] Philip D. Caine, *Aircraft Down!: Evading Capture in WWII Europe* (Washington, D.C.: Potomac Books, Inc., 2005), 4.

[10] "Escape and Evasion Report No. 89," Headquarters Twelfth Air Force, Office of Assistant Chief of Staff, A-2. Provided by Department of the Air Force, Air Force Historical Research Agency, Maxwell Air Force Base, Alabama on May 17, 2007.

[11] Ibid.

[12] "Response to Inquiry for Information on John W. Denny, September 19, 2008," National Personnel Records Center (Military Personnel Records, 9700 Page Avenue, St. Louis, Missouri), MO 63132-5100.

[13] "The Luftwaffe Interrogators at Dulag Luft – Oberursel," Stalag Luft I Online, http://www.merkki.com/new_page_2.htm (accessed February 24, 2010).

[14] World War II Prisoner of War Data File for John W. Denny, Jr., The National Archives, Access to Archival Databases, http://aad.archives.gov/aad/record-detail.jsp?dt=466&mtch=1&cat=all&tf=F&q=John+w.+denny&bc=sl,sd&rpp=10&pg=1&rid=58932 (accessed February 9, 2009).

[15] "Cheatham County Man Out of Nazi Prison," Unknown Newspaper, Neptune, TN, May 25, 1045. Obtained from National Personnel Records Center, St. Louis, MO on September 19, 2008.

[16] "A Brief Look at Camp Forrest," Camp Forest, Tullahoma, Tennessee, http://www.campforrest.com/table_of_content.htm (accessed February 9, 2009).

[17] Jessica Gilker, "Shifting Roles for the Palazzi of Florence," *FlorenceNow.net*, a multimedia project of the Department of Communication at Berry College in Mount Berry GA, http://fssweb.berry.edu/~bcarroll/florence/ (accessed February 9, 2009).

[18] "446th Bomb Squadron, War Diary of Frederick Charles Ritger, Letter to Home, Friday, May 26, 1944," 321st Bombardment Group History, http://57thbombwing.com/321stHistory/321_BG_1944-05.pdf (accessed November 18, 2009).

[19] "Message Posted on 57th Bomb Wing Association Message Board on May 22, 2007 by Bob Ritger, nephew of Fred Ritger," http://57thbombwing.com/phpBB57/viewtopic.php?t=94&sid=23fa8f3511d221d86a46d87531329788 (accessed November 18, 2009).

[20] "446th Bomb Squadron Extracts from Missing Air Crew Report # 10385," Extracts included Individual Casualty Questionnaire (completed by Frederick C. Ritger) and

Certification Statement (signed by Ritger) concerning his aircraft that was shot down over Italy on December 10, 1944, 321st Bombardment Group History, http://57thbombwing.com/321stHistory/321_BG_1944-12.pdf (accessed November 18, 2009).

21 "The Greatest Escape of All," October 9, 2004, *The Independent* (Europe), http://www.independent.co.uk/travel/europe/the-greatest-escape-of-all-543053.html (accessed February 9, 2009).

22 World War II Prisoner of War Data File for Laverne E. Reynolds, The National Archives, Access to Archival Databases, http://aad.archives.gov/aad/record-detail.jsp?dt=466&mtch=1&cat=&tf=F&q=Laverne+e.+Reynolds&bc=sl,sd&rpp=10&pg=1&rid=107315 (accessed February 9, 2009).

23 Certified Statement by John H. Kinney, July 8, 1944, Found in Missing Air Crew Report 6613, Obtained from the Department of the Air Force, Air Force Historical Studies Office, AF/HOH (Library), Bolling Air Force Base, Washington, D.C.

24 "Escape and Evasion Report No. 80," Headquarters Twelfth Air Force, Office of Assistant Chief of Staff, A-2. Provided by Department of the Air Force, Air Force Historical Research Agency, Maxwell Air Force Base, Alabama on October 8, 2008.

25 "Escape and Evasion Report No. 85," Headquarters Twelfth Air Force, Office of Assistant Chief of Staff, A-2. Provided by Department of the Air Force, Air Force Historical Research Agency, Maxwell Air Force Base, Alabama on October 8, 2008.

26 "Escape and Evasion Report No. 80," Headquarters Twelfth Air Force, Office of Assistant Chief of Staff, A-2. Provided by Department of the Air Force, Air Force Historical Research Agency, Maxwell Air Force Base, Alabama on October 8, 2008.

27 "Escape and Evasion Report No. 85," Headquarters Twelfth Air Force, Office of Assistant Chief of Staff, A-2. Provided by Department of the Air Force, Air Force Historical Research Agency, Maxwell Air Force Base, Alabama on October 8, 2008.

28 Ibid.

29 "Missing Air Crew Report 5145," Obtained from the Department of the Air Force, Air Force Historical Studies Office, AF/HOH (Library), Bolling Air Force Base, Washington, D.C.

30 Attachment to Letter dated September 7, 1944 to Mrs. Dora E. Clark (grandmother of Major William Clark Hunter) from General Hap Arnold, Commanding General, Army Air Forces. Obtained from the Department of the Army, U.S. Army Human Resources Command, Alexandria, Virginia, August 18, 2008.

31 Gerald Bowman, *Jump For It!* (London: Evan Brothers Limited, 1955), 28.

32 Ibid, 30.

33 Ibid, 31.

34 Ibid, 31.

35 "The Caterpillar Club—Irvin Parachute Co.," http://www.merkki.com/caterpillarclub.htm (accessed May 10, 2008).

36 Mary Bellis, "The History of Nylon and Neoprene," http://inventors.about.com/library/weekly/aa980325.htm (accessed May 10, 2008).

37 Gordon Rottman, *US Army Air Force (1) (Elite)* (Oxford: Osprey Publishing, 1993), 29.

38 Walt Hehnert, "An American Airman Remembers Stalag 17," Buffalo Commons Storytelling Festival, http://www.buffalocommons.org/story.php?id=27 (accessed September 22, 2009).

39 Gerald Bowman, *Jump For It!* (London: Evan Brothers Limited, 1955), 32.

***Chapter 7*: EVADING THE ENEMY**

1 Iris Origo, *War in Val d'Orcia: An Italian Diary 1943–1944* (Boston: David R. Godine, Publisher, Eighth Printing, 2007), 9.

2 Ibid.

3 Pietro Pinti and Jenny Bawtree, *Pietro's Book: The Story of a Tuscan Peasant* (New York: Arcade Publishing, 2004), 181-182.

4 Iris Origo, *War in Val d'Orcia: An Italian Diary 1943–1944* (Boston: David R. Godine, Publisher, Eighth Printing, 2007), 9.

5 Pietro Pinti and Jenny Bawtree, *Pietro's Book: The Story of a Tuscan Peasant* (New York: Arcade Publishing, 2004), 40.

6 Ibid, 59.

7 Iris Origo, *War in Val d'Orcia: An Italian Diary 1943–1944* (Boston: David R. Godine, Publisher, Eighth Printing, 2007), ix.

8 "Understanding Italy's Regions, Provinces & Towns," http://www.angelfire.com/ok3/pearlsofwisdom/saviello4.html#understanding (accessed September 17, 2009).

9 "Iliaria Ciuti, "Toscana My Love," *Firenze Magazine*, 40. Author clipped this article from magazine during visit to Tuscany in September 2007.

10 "Combat in Cities and Towns (Section 6, Chapter 3)," *A Military Encyclopedia Based on the Operations of the Italian Campaigns 1943-1945*, Prepared by G-3 Section, Headquarters 15 Army Group Italy, http://www.milhist.net/docs/milencyc/MilEncyc.03G3.pdf (accessed September 22, 2008).

11 Riccardo Becattini, e-mail to author from Luisa Fortini with information provided by Riccardo Becattini, February 25, 2008.

12 Pietro Pinti and Jenny Bawtree, *Pietro's Book: The Story of a Tuscan Peasant*, (New York: Arcade Publishing, 2004), 93.

13 F.M. Sallagar, "Operation 'Strangle' (Italy, Spring 1944): A Case Study of Tactical Air Interdiction," A Report Prepared for United States Air Force Project Rand (Santa Monica, CA: Rand [R-851-PR], February, 1972), 23.

14 Colonel Clifford R. Krieger (USAF), "Air Interdiction," *Airpower Journal* (Spring 1989), http://www.airpower.au.af.mil/airchronicles/apj/apj89/spr89/krieger.html (accessed August 25, 2009).

15 Ibid, 41.

Notes

[16] H. Maitland Wilson, "Report by The Supreme Allied Commander Mediterranean to the Combined Chiefs of Staff on the Italian Campaign, 8 January 1944 to 10 May 1944" (Washington, D.C.: U.S. Government Printing Office, 1948), 33.

[17] F.M. Sallagar, "Operation 'Strangle' (Italy, Spring 1944): A Case Study of Tactical Air Interdiction," A Report Prepared for United States Air Force Project Rand (Santa Monica, CA: Rand [R-851-PR], February, 1972), 24-25.

[18] Ibid, 24-25.

[19] "321st BG War Diary: Additional Narrative for June 1944," 321st Bomb Group History, 57th Bomb Wing Association, http://57thbombwing.com/321stHistory/321_BG_1944-05.pdf (accessed July 29, 2009).

[20] Yvonne Kincaid, Department of the Air Force, Air Force Historical Studies Office Research, e-mail to author dated April 30, 2008.

[21] "P-47 Thunderbolt," *World-War-2-Planes.com*, http://www.world-war-2-planes.com/p-47.html (accessed September 17, 2009).

[22] Chris Cant, *The Essential Aircraft Identification Guide: Allied Fighters 1939-1945* (Minneapolis, MN: Zenith Press, 2008), 145.

[23] Heather Sheldon, "A Son's Memorial," *Times-Standard.com*, Eureka, CA, May 27, 2001, http://www.awon.org/local/eureka.html (accessed May 1, 2008).

[24] Yvonne Kincaid, Department of the Air Force, Air Force Historical Studies Office Research, e-mail to author dated April 30, 2008.

[25] William W. Hahn, "From Stratofighter to Dive Bomber," *Air Classics*, February 2002, http://findarticles.com/p/articles/mi_qa3901/is_200202/ai_n9083019/ (accessed August 10, 2007).

[26] "Operational & Intelligence Summary No. 373," Operations for June 1, 1944, Headquarters Fifty Seventh Fighter Group (AAF) (RG 18, AAF, WWII, Entry 7, Box 3317). Obtained from the National Archives in College Park, Maryland in August 1944.

[27] Ibid.

[28] Ibid.

[29] William W. Hahn, "From Stratofighter to Dive Bomber," *Air Classics*, February 2002, http://findarticles.com/p/articles/mi_qa3901/is_200202/ai_n9083019/ (accessed August 10, 2007).

[30] "321st BG War Diary: Additional Narrative for May 1944," 321st Bomb Group History, 57th Bomb Wing Association, http://57thbombwing.com/321stHistory/321_BG_1944-05.pdf (accessed March 29, 2009).

[31] "Carole Lombard Biography," http://www.murphsplace.com/lombard/bio.html (accessed July 2, 2009).

[32] "Clark Gable in the Eighth Air Force," http://www.geocities.com/cactus_st/article/article143c.html (accessed July 2, 2009).

[33] Margaret E. Wagner, Linda Barrett Osborne, Susan Reyburn and the Staff of the Library

of Congress, *The Library of Congress World War II Companion* (New York, London, Toronto, Sydney: Simon & Schuster, 2007), 185.

[34] Patrick K. O'Donnell, *Operatives, Spies and Saboteurs: The Unknown Story of WWII's OSS* (New York, Citadel Press, 2004), 59-60.

[35] "The Dostler Case, Trial of General Anton Dostler, Commander of the 75th German Army Corps," United States Military Commission, Rome, October 8-12, 1945, http:// www.ess.uwe.ac.uk/WCC/dostler.htm (accessed April 10, 2009).

Chapter 8: THE APPROACHING FRONT

[1] Thomas R. Brooks, *The War North of Rome, June 1944–May 1945* (New York: Sarpedon, 1996), 46.

[2] Frank Beckett, *Prepare to Move: With the 6th Armoured Division in Africa and Italy* (Grimsby, South Humberside, Great Britain: Frank and Eileen Beckett, 1994), 202.

[3] Thomas R. Brooks, *The War North of Rome, June 1944–May 1945* (New York: Sarpedon, 1996), 36.

[4] Ibid, 122.

[5] "Control of Partisan Activities (Chapter 2, Section 9)," *A Military Encyclopedia Based on Operations in the Italian Campaigns 1943-1945*, Prepared by G-3 Section, Headquarters 15 Army Group Italy, http://www.milhist.net/docs/milencyc/MilEncyc.02G2.pdf (accessed August 15, 2007).

[6] Ibid.

[7] Ibid.

[8] Tom W.Glaser, "The Massacre at the Ardeatine Caves, 24 March 1944," http://www.zchor.org/italy/caves.htm (accessed 15 August 2007).

[9] Elisabeth Zimmermann, "German War Crimes in Italy: Part One," October 7, 2004, http://www.wsws.org/articles/2004/oct2004/germ-007.shtml (accessed 15 August 2007).

[10] Richard Lamb, *War in Italy, 1943-1945: A Brutal Story* (New York and Washington D.C.: Da Capo Press, 1996), 68.

[11] Ibid.

[12] Stefano Loparco, *Figline Durante Il Fascismo* (Signa, Florence, Italy: Masso delle Fate Edizioni, 2004), 171.

[13] Ibid, 171.

[14] Roger Absalom, "A Strange Alliance: Aspects of Escape and Survival in Italy, 1943-1945," *The Journal of Modern History*, Vol. 66, No. 2 (University of Chicago Press, June, 1994), 409-411, http://www.jstor.org/pss/2124309 (accessed August 15, 2007).

[15] Philip D. Caine, *Aircraft Down!: Evading Capture in WWII Europe* (Washington, D.C.: Potomac Books, 2005), 3.

[16] Major General J.A. Ulio, The Adjutant General, Letter to Mrs. Mary Lanza, June 15,

Notes

1944, War Department, Washington, D.C. Obtained from William A. Lanza.

[17] Thomas R. Brooks, *The War North of Rome, June 1944–May 1945* (New York: Scarpedon, 1996), 133.

[18] "The Trial of German Major War Criminals," *The Nizkor Project*, http://www.nizkor.org/hweb/imt/tgmwc/tgmwc-09/tgmwc-09-80-05.shtml (accessed August 15, 2007).

[19] "Biography of Reichsmarschall Herman Goering," The World at War: Hermann Goering, http://www.euronet.nl/users/wilfried/ww2/goering.htm (accessed August 15, 2007).

[20] John Baldini, "The Battle of Pian d'Albero," *ResistenzaToscana* (Resistance of Tuscany), http://www.resistenzatoscana.it/storie/la_battaglia_di_pian_d_albero/ (accessed May 18, 2008).

[21] "Florence Consul Moira Macfarlane Commemorates WWII Partisans (22/06/07)," UK in Italy, Foreign & Commonwealth Office, http://ukinitaly.fco.gov.uk/en/newsroom/?view=News&id=2076104 (accessed September 23, 2008).

[22] Stefano Loparco, *Figline Durante Il Fascismo* (Signa, Florence, Italy: Masso delle Fate Edizioni, 2004), 171.

[23] Ibid, 171-2.

[24] Ibid, 172.

[25] Ibid, 172.

[26] Vincenzo Tani, "Pian d'Albero—June 1944," http://www.eccidi1943-44.toscana.it/testimonianze/20_giugno_44.htm (accessed May 18, 2008).

[27] Ibid

[28] Iris Origo, *War in Val d'Orcia: An Italian Diary 1943–1944* (Boston: David R. Godine, Publisher, Eighth Printing, 2007), 216.

[29] Dora Clark Letter to General Eisenhower, June 22, 1944, Individual Deceased Personnel File of William C. Hunter, Department of the Army, U.S. Army Human Resources Command, 200 Stovall Street, Alexandria, VA 22332-0400, August 18, 2008.

[30] Shirley Hunter letter dated August 10, 1944 to Robert H. Dunlop, Brigadier General, The Acting Adjutant General, (In letter, Mrs. Hunter referenced War Department telegram to her dated August 3, 1944), Individual Deceased Personnel File of William C. Hunter, Department of the Army, U.S. Army Human Resources Command, 200 Stovall Street, Alexandria, VA 22332-0400, August 18, 2008.

[31] Thomas R. Brooks, *The War North of Rome, June 1944–May 1944* (New York: Scarpedon, 1996), 52.

[32] Iris Origo, *War in Val d'Orcia: An Italian War Diary, 1943–1944* (New York: David R. Godine, Eighth Printing, 2007), 226.

[33] Thomas R. Brooks, *The War North of Rome, June 1944–May 1944* (New York: Scarpedon, 1996), 133.

[34] Hannes Heer, Klaus Naumann, and Roy Shelton, *War of Extermination: The German*

Military in World War II, 1941-1944 (New York: Berghahn Books, 2000), 198-199, http://books.google.com/books?id=Sh77amvItIMC&pg=PT1&lpg=PT1&dq=Hannes+Heer,+Klaus+Naumann,+and+Roy+Shelton,+War+of+Extermination:+The+German+Military+in+World+War+II,+1941-1944&source=web&ots=kiiBbM2B67&sig=n-3i4Wk8_ULs_apRoUPDOEPCXs&hl=en&sa=X&oi=book_result&resnum=1&ct=result (accessed August 20, 2008).

[35] "The Trial of Albert Kesselring," British Military Court at Venice, Italy, February 17–May 6, 1947 (Source: Law-Reports of Trials of War Criminals, the United Nations War Crimes Commission, Volume VIII, London, HMSO, 1949), http://www.ess.uwe.ac.uk/WCC/kesselring.htm (accessed July 31, 2009).

[36] Richard Lamb, *War in Italy, 1943-1945: A Brutal Story* (New York and Washington D.C.: Da Capo Press, 1996), 76.

[37] University of Kansas Review of Kerstin von Lingen's *Kesselring's Last Battle: War Crimes Trials and Cold War Politics, 1945-1960* (Lawrence, Kansas: University Press of Kansas, 2009), http://www.kansaspress.ku.edu/vonkes.html (accessed July 31, 2009).

[38] Frank Beckett, *Prepare to Move: With the 6th Armoured Division in Africa and Italy* (Grimsby, South Humberside, Great Britain: Frank and Eileen Beckett, 1994), 189.

[39] Ibid, 203.

[40] Ibid, 189.

[41] Ibid, 191

[42] Ibid, 200.

[43] Ibid, 277.

[44] Thomas R. Brooks, *The War North of Rome, June 1944–May 1944* (New York: Scarpedon, 1996), 78.

[45] Frank Beckett, *Prepare to Move: With the 6th Armoured Division in Africa and Italy* (Grimsby, South Humberside, Great Britain: Frank and Eileen Beckett, 1994), 200.

[46] Ibid, 197.

[47] Anthony Mason, *Leonardo Da Vinci* (Milwaukee, Wisconsin: World Almanac Library, North American Edition, 2004), 33, http://books.google.com/books?id=9kdP3QVoXYC&printsec=copyright&dq=buriano+bridge+and+mona+lisa&source=gbs_toc_s&cad=1#PPA29,M1 (accessed August 20, 2008).

[48] Thomas R. Brooks, *The War North of Rome, June 1944–May 1944* (New York: Scarpedon, 1996), 45.

[49] "Historical Vignette 109 - Mel Brooks Was a Combat Engineer in World War," U.S.Army Corps of Engineers, Headquarters, http://www.usace.army.mil/History/hv/Pages/109-Mel_Brooks.aspx (accessed January 12, 2010).

[50] Margaret E. Wagner, Linda Barrett Osborne, Susan Reyburn and the Staff of the Library of Congress, *The Library of Congress World War II Companion* (New York, London, Toronto, Sydney: Simon & Schuster, 2007), 771.

Notes

[51] "Assassinaton Attempt on Hitler Fails," *Project 60—"The First Fight Against Fascism"— Archives*, July 1944, http://www.bartcop.com/arc4407.htm (accessed October 3, 2008).

[52] Iris Origo, *War in Val d'Orcia: An Italian War Diary, 1943–1944* (New York: David R. Godine, Eighth Printing, 2007), 206.

[53] Thomas R. Brooks, *The War North of Rome, June 1944–May 1944* (New York: Scarpedon, 1996), 101.

[54] Ibid, 122.

[55] Frank Beckett, *Prepare to Move: With the 6th Armoured Division in Africa and Italy* (Grimsby, South Humberside, Great Britain: Frank and Eileen Beckett, 1994), 203-205.

[56] Colonel Conrad H. Lanza, "The War in Italy (19 July to 18 August 1944)," *Field Artillery Journal*, October 1944, 711, http://sill-www-army.mil/FAMAG/1944/OCT_1944/ OCT_1944_PAGES_711_720.pdf accessed October 17, 2008).

[57] Frank Beckett, *Prepare to Move: With the 6th Armoured Division in Africa and Italy* (Grimsby, South Humberside, Great Britain: Frank and Eileen Beckett, 1994), 203-205.

[58] Terry M. Love, *L-Birds: American Combat Liaison Aircraft of World War II* (New Brighton, MN: Flying Books International, 2001), 15, 21 and 28.

[59] R. J. Overy, *The Air War 1939–1945* (New York: Stein and Day, 1981), 2-3.

[60] Terry M. , *L-Birds: American Combat Liaison Aircraft of World War II* (New Brighton, MN: Flying Books International, 2001), 23.

[61] Ibid, 38,

[62] "Command Reconnaissance (Section 6, Chapter 3)," *A Military Encyclopedia: Based on Operations in the Italian Campaigns 1943-1945*, Prepared by G-3 Section, Headquarters 15 Army Group Italy, http://www.milhist.net/docs/milencyc/MilEncyc.03G3.pdf (accessed October 3, 2008).

[63] Terry M. Love, *L-Birds: American Combat Liaison Aircraft of World War II* (New Brighton, MN: Flying Books International, 2001), 6.

[64] Ibid, 29, 32, 33, 42, and 44.

[65] "Evolution of the Liaison-Type Airplane 1917-1944," Army Air Forces Historical Studies: No. 44, Army Air Forces Historical Office, Headquarters, Army Air Forces, USAF Historical Archives, ASI (ASHAF-A), Maxwell Air Force Base, Alabama.

[66] Terry M. Love, *L-Birds: American Combat Liaison Aircraft of World War II* (New Brighton, MN: Flying Books International, 2001), 32-33.

[67] Jenny Bawtree and Pietro Pinti, *Pietro's Book: The Story of a Tuscan Peasant* (New York: Arcade Publishing, 2004), 95.

[68] Ray Merriam, *U.S. Warplanes in World War II* (Bennington, VT: Merriam Press, 2000), 26-27, http://books.google.com/books?id=R7GjzzNMpu4C&pg= PA26&lpg=PA26&dq=%22l+5%22+sentinel+in+world+war+ii+in+italy&source= web&ots=0d8eIPPoj9&sig=KNWYhdSNpPo3BY1MrV8TPh7jJq8&hl=en#PPA26,M1 (accessed August 20, 2008).

[69] Terry M. Love, *L-Birds: American Combat Liaison Aircraft of World War II* (New Brighton, MN: Flying Books International, 2001), 19.

[70] Ibid, 72.

[71] Ibid, 19.

[72] Matthew Parker, *Monte Cassino: The Hardest Fought Battle of World War II* (New York; Anchor Books, 2005), 57.

[73] Ibid, 152.

[74] Ibid, 152.

[75] William J. McCarthy, "Brief History of Nepal," November 2000, *One Planet Education Network*, http://www.oneplaneteducation.com/Past_nepal.asp (accessed March 31, 2007).

[76] Hannes Heer, Klaus Naumann and Heer Naumann, *War of Extermination: The German Military in World War II* (Providence, Oxford: Berghahn Books, 2004), 207, http://books.google.com/books?id=Sh77amvItIMC&pg=PA191&lpg=PA191&dq=pratomagno+mountains&source=web&ots=kijz6K_H9a&sig=WP9ltgdDQOLZQB2C86jieJUB4ik&hl=en&sa=X&oi=book_result&resnum=2&ct=result#PPA192,M1 (accessed March 31, 2007).

[77] Richard Lamb, *War in Italy, 1943-1945: A Brutal Story* (New York and Washington D.C.: Da Capo Press, 1996), 78.

[78] Philip D. Caine, *Aircraft Down!: Evading Capture in WWII Europe* (Washington, D.C.: Potomac Books, Inc., 2005), 15.

[79] Jenny Bawtree and Pietro Pinti. *Pietro's Book: The Story of a Tuscan Peasant* (New York: Arcade Publishing, 2004), 93-94.

Chapter 9: LIBERATION

[1] Matthew Parker, *Monte Cassino: The Hardest Fought Battle of World WarII* (New York: Anchor Books, 2005), 31.

[2] "Half-Track," *Britannica Online Encyclopedia*, http://www.britannica.com/EBchecked/topic/252417/half-track (accessed September 22, 2009).

[3] Information provided by Riccardo Becattini through an e-mail from Luisa Fortini on February 25, 2008.

[4] Ibid.

[5] Giorgio Grassi, "Eroe per caso (Hero by Chance)," Part of an article from a local newspaper in Tuscany given to author by the Becattini family. The newspaper is not indicated on the part of the article given to the author. The author had the article translated into English. Presumably the newspaper was *La Nazione* in Florence since Giorgio Grassi is a writer for that newspaper.

[6] Ibid.

[7] Ibid.

8 "Pian di Scò (Faella is a Fraction of Pian di Scò)," http://www.comune.pian-di-sco.ar.it/storia.asp (accessed September 30, 2008).

9 "Salesian Youth Mininstry," http://www.salesianym.org/ministries/index.htm (accessed September 5, 2008).

10 "Salesians of Don Bosco," www.salesians.org/salesians.html (accessed September 6, 2008).

11 "Salesian Youth Mininstry," http://www.salesianym.org/ministries/index.htm (accessed September 5, 2008).

12 "Salesians of Don Bosco," www.salesians.org/salesians.html (accessed September 6, 2008).

13 Rick Atkinson, *The Day of Battle, The War in Sicily and Italy, 1943–1944* (New York, Henry Holt and Company, 2007), 476.

14 Iris Origo, *War in Val d'Orcia: An Italian War Diary, 1943–1944* (Boston, MA: David R. Godine, Publisher, Eighth Printing, 2007), 112.

15 "Don Orione Madonna Shrine," http://eastboston.povo.com/Don_Orione_Madonna_Shrine (accessed September 21, 2009).

16 "Luigi Orione (1872-1940)," http://www.vatican.va/news_services/liturgy/saints/ns_lit_doc_20040516_orione_en.html (accessed September 21, 2009).

17 Thomas R. Brooks, *The War North of Rome, June 1944–May 1945* (New York: Sarpedon, 1996), 131.

18 Stefano Loparco, *Figline Durante Il Fascism* (Signa, Florence, Italy: Masso delle Fate Edizioni, 2004), 173.

19 "A Change in Plan," Italy Volume II: From Cassino to Trieste, *New Zealand Electronic Text Center*, http://nzetc.org/tm/scholarly/tei-WH2-2Ita-c4-1.html (accessed September 20, 2008).

20 Ibid.

21 Stefano Loparco, *Figline Durante Il Fascism* (Signa, Florence, Italy: Masso delle Fate Edizioni, 2004), 172.

22 "Area Monumentale di Sant'Andrea (Monuments of Saint Andrea)," *Resistenza Toscana.it* (Tuscany Resistance), http://translate.google.com/translate?hl=en&sl=it&u=http://resistenzatoscana.it/&ei=zSfJSYifDNLmnQf77aDKAw&sa=X&oi=translate&resnum=2&ct=result&prev=/search%3Fq%3DResistenza%2BToscana.it%26hl%3Den%26sa%3DG (accessed September 20, 2008).

23 Frank Beckett, *Prepare To Move: With the 6th Armoured Division in Africa and Italy* (Grimsby, South Humberside, Great Britain: Frank and Eileen Beckett, 1994), 205.

24 C.L. Sulzberger, *The American Heritage Picture History of World War II* (New York: American Heritage/Bonanza Books, 1966), 556. Also, "Mussolini Death," *YouTube*, http://www.youtube.com/watch?v=ty4sVI-R8Vo (accessed March 23, 2009).

25 Stefano Loparco, *Figline Durante Il Fascism* (Signa, Florence, Italy: Masso delle Fate

Edizioni, 2004), 174-75.

[26] Ibid, 175-76.

[27] Ibid, 176-78.

[28] Ibid, 178.

[29] Iris Origo, *War in Val d'Orcia: An Italian War Diary, 1943–1944* (Boston, MA: David R. Godine, Publisher, Eighth Printing, 2007), 239.

[30] "Local Government (Section 8, Chapter 14)," *A Military Encyclopedia Based on Operations in the Italian Campaigns, 1943-1945*, http://www.milhist.net/docs/milencyc/MilEncyc.14AMG.pdf (accessed September 30, 2008).

[31] Stefano Loparco, *Figline Durante Il Fascism* (Signa, Florence, Italy: Masso delle Fate Edizioni, 2004), 179.

[32] Ibid, 179-80.

[33] "Partisans (Section 23, Chapter 14)," *A Military Encyclopedia Based on Operations in the Italian Campaigns, 1943-1945*, http://www.milhist.net/docs/milencyc/MilEncyc.14AMG.pdf (accessed September 30, 2008).

[34] Definition of Bracket, *U.S. Military Dictionary, Answers.com*, available from http://www.answers.com/topic/bracket (accessed September 30, 2008).

Chapter 10: HOME AT LAST

[1] "Martin B-26 Marauder," (last revised March 12, 2000), http://home.att.net/~jbaugher2/b26_1.html (accessed March 20, 2009).

[2] "B-26B Marauder: American Bomber in World War II," *HistoryNet.Com*, http://www.historynet.com/b-26b-marauder-american-bomber-in-world-war-ii.htm (accessed March 20, 2009).

[3] "Escape and Evasion Report No. 89," Headquarters Twelfth Air Force, Office of Assistant Chief of Staff, A-2. Provided by Department of the Air Force, Air Force Historical Research Agency, Maxwell Air Force Base, Alabama on May 17, 2007.

[4] "Missing Air Crew Report 6613," Obtained from the Department of the Air Force, Air Force Historical Studies Office, AF/HOH (Library), Bolling Air Force Base, Washington, D.C.

[5] "Escape and Evasion Report No. 89," Headquarters Twelfth Air Force, Office of Assistant Chief of Staff, A-2. Provided by Department of the Air Force, Air Force Historical Research Agency, Maxwell Air Force Base, Alabama on May 17, 2007.

[6] Ibid.

[7] Ibid.

[8] "446th BS War Diary: Additional Narrative for July 1944," 321st Bombardment Group History, http://57thbombwing.com/321stHistory/321_BG_1944-07.pdf (accessed September 21, 2009).

Notes

[9] Ibid.

[10] Ibid.

[11] "C-47 Skytrain Military Transport," Boeing History, http://www.boeing.com/history/mdc/skytrain.htm (accessed July 20, 2009).

[12] "Money: Second Sicilian Invasion," *Time*, August 23, 1943, http://www.time.com/time/magazine/article/0,9171,885066,00.html (accessed September 30, 2009).

[13] Ibid.

[14] Frank A. Southard, *The finances of European liberation with special reference to Italy* (New York: Arno Press, 1979), 22.

[15] Centennial History Staff, Treasury Department, *History of the Bureau of Engraving and Printing: 1862–1962* (Washington, D.C.: U.S. Government Printing Office, 1962), 146.

[16] "Allied Military Currency," http://www.strictly-gi.com/currency.html (accessed September 30, 2009).

[17] "The Four Freedoms," *Our Heritage*, Historic Manhein Preservation Foundation, Inc., July 2009, http://www.manheim1762.org/files/July_2009_Newsletter3.pdf (accessed September 30, 2009).

[18] "Money: Second Sicilian Invasion," *Time*, August 23, 1943, http://www.time.com/time/magazine/article/0,9171,885066,00.html (accessed September 30, 2009).

[19] Centennial History Staff, Treasury Department, *History of the Bureau of Engraving and Printing: 1862–1962* (Washington, D.C.: U.S. Government Printing Office, 1962), 145-146.

[20] Frank A. Southard, *The finances of European liberation with special reference to Italy* (New York: Arno Press, 1979), 22.

[21] Phil M. Goldstein, "Notes on Collecting Allied Military Currency," http://www.antiquetintoy.com/notesmilcurr.htm (accessed September 30, 2009).

[22] Richard Grudens, *Chattanooga Choo Choo: The Life and Times of the World Famous Glenn Miller Orchestra* (Stonybrook, NY: Celebrity Profiles Publishing Company, 2004), 155-158.

[23] "Amended Instructions Concerning Publicity in Connection with Escaped Prisoners of War, to Include Evaders of Capture in Enemy-Occupied Territory and Internees in Neutral Countries (Form AG 383.6)," War Department, The Adjutant General's Office, Washington, D.C. (Signed by William A. Lanza on September 7, 1944).

[24] W.F. Craven and J.L. Cate, editors, *The Army Air Forces in World War II* (Washington, D.C.: Office of Air Force History, 1983), 551. Purchased CD from BACM Research, Iselin, New Jersey.

[25] "Faces Up," *Time*, November 8, 1943, http://www.time.com/time/magazine/article/0,9171,796274-2,00.html (accessed October 25, 2008).

[26] "Henry H. Arnold," http://www.airpower.maxwell.af.mil/airchronicles/cc/arnold.html (accessed January 20, 2009).

[27] "World War II, The Second Era of Expansion," http://www.herelocal54.com/ news.php?s_id=&appid=db15580&action=view&id=18492 (accessed October 16, 2007).

[28] "Fort Logan History," http://www.cdhs.state.co.us/cmhifl/ftlhistory.htm (accessed October 16, 2007) & "A Brief History of Lowry Air Force Base," http:// www.wingsmuseum.org/lowryafb.php (accessed October 16, 2007).

[29] Dr. Christopher R. Gabel, "The Lorraine Campaign: An Overview, September– December, 1944," Command and General Staff College, U.S. Army Combined Arms Center, Combined Arms Research Library, February 1985, http://www-cgsc.army.mil/carl/ resources/csi/gabel3/gabel3.asp (accessed July 14, 2009).

[30] "Crossing the Rhine February–April 1945," *World War II Multimedia Database*, http:// www.worldwar2database.com/html/rhine.htm (accessed August 20, 2009).

[31] Dr. Christopher R. Gabel, "The Lorraine Campaign: An Overview, September– December, 1944," Command and General Staff College, U.S. Army Combined Arms Center, Combined Arms Research Library, February 1985, http://www-cgsc.army.mil/carl/ resources/csi/gabel3/gabel3.asp (accessed July 14, 2009).

[32] Ibid.

[33] Ibid.

[34] Ibid.

[35] "World War II," *26th Infantry Division, The Yankee Division of W.W. II*, http://yd-info.net/page5/page21/index.html (accessed August 20, 2009).

[36] William M. Cosgrove, "The Lorraine Campaign (Chapter 9)," *Time on Target: The 945th Field Artillery Battalion in World War II* (New York: William M. Cosgrove, 1997), http://www.timeontarget.us/book-chapter9.html (accessed July 14, 2009).

[37] Dr. Christopher R. Gabel, "The Lorraine Campaign: An Overview, September– December, 1944," Command and General Staff College, U.S. Army Combined Arms Center, Combined Arms Research Library, February 1985, http://www-cgsc.army.mil/carl/ resources/csi/gabel3/gabel3.asp (accessed July 14, 2009).

[38] "Individual Deceased Personnel File of Frank Alvino," Department of the Army, U.S. Army Human Resources Command, 200 Stovall Street, Alexandria, Virginia, 22332-0400, August 7, 2009.

[39] William Roberts, "July 28, 1945—Plane Hits Building—Woman Survives 75-Story Fall," *Elevator World*, http://www.elevator-world.com/magazine/archive01/9603-002.htm (accessed March 20, 2009).

[40] Jennifer Rosenberg, "The Plane That Crashed Into the Empire State Building," *About.com: 20th Century History*, http://history1900s.about.com/od/1940s/a/ empirecrash.htm (accessed March 20, 2009).

[41] Alan Bellows, "The B-25 That Crashed into the Empire State Building," July 12, 2006, *DamnInteresting.com*, http://www.damninteresting.com/?p=179 (accessed March 20, 2009).

[42] Therese McAllister, Jonathan Barnett, John Gross, Ronald Hamburger, Jon Magnusson, "Introduction (Chapter 1)," *World Trade Center Building Performance*

Notes

Study: Data Collection, Preliminary Observations, and Recommendations, Federal Emergency Management Agency, Federal Insurance and Mitigation Administration, Washington, DC, FEMA Region II, New York, New York, FEMA 403, May 2002, http://www.fema.gov/pdf/library/fema403_ch1.pdf (accessed February 27, 2009).

[43] "Abreviations: POW Camp Listings," The National Ex-Prisoner of War Association, http://www.prisonerofwar.org.uk/camp_list.htm (accessed September 22, 2009).

[44] "Stalag Luft 3 (The March, Evacuation of Moosburg)," *WWW.B24.NET*, Research provided by the United States Air Force Academy and permission to use granted by William Newmiller at http://www.usafa.af.mil, http://www.gps-practice-and-fun.com/stalag-luft-3.html (accessed March 20, 2009).

[45] "American Prisoners of War in Germany," Report Prepared by Military Intelligence Division, War Department, July 15, 1945, Assistant Chief of Air Staff, Intelligence, Microfilm Reel A 1320, Air Force Historical Research Agency, AFHRA/RSA, Maxwell Air Force Base, Alabama.

[46] "American Prisoners of War in Germany," Report Prepared by Military Intelligence Division, War Department, November 1, 1945, Assistant Chief of Air Staff, Intelligence, Microfilm Reel A 1320, Air Force Historical Research Agency, AFHRA/RSA, Maxwell Air Force Base, Alabama.

[47] "Nazi Conspiracy & Aggression, Volume I, Criminality of Groups and Organizations, The Schutzstaffeln (SS) (Part 1 of 16)," *The Nizkor Project*, 173, http://www.nizkor.org/hweb/imt/nca/nca-02/nca-02-15-criminality-05-01.html (accessed March 20, 2009).

[48] "Schutzstaffel (SS)," *Spartacus Educational*, http://www.spartacus.schoolnet.co.uk/GERss.htm (accessed March 20, 2009).

[49] "American Prisoners of War in Germany," Report Prepared b Military Intelligence Division, War Department, November 1, 1945, Assistant Chief of Air Staff, Intelligence, Microfilm Reel A 1320, Air Force Historical Research Agency, AFHRA/RSA, Maxwell Air Force Base, Alabama.

[50] "History of Center Compound, Stalag Luft III, Sagan, Germany (Part II, Camp Standing Orders, Stalag Luft III), August 1, 1943 to April 30, 1945," Assistant Chief of Air Staff, Intelligence, Microfilm Reel A 1320, Air Force Historical Research Agency, AFHRA/RSA, Maxwell, Air Force Base, Alabama.

[51] "Stalag Luft 3 Sagan on the Map," *GPS-Practice-and-fun.com*, http://www.gps-practice-and-fun.com/stalag-luft-3.html (accessed March 20, 2009).

[52] "American Prisoners of War in Germany," Report Prepared by Military Intelligence Division, War Department, November 1, 1945, Assistant Chief of Air Staff, Intelligence, Microfilm Reel A 1320, Air Force Historical Research Agency, AFHRA/RSA, Maxwell Air Force Base, Alabama.

[53] Ibid.

[54] Gunnar Jahn (Chairman of the Nobel Committee), "Presentation Speech to Award the Nobel Peace Prize of 1944 to the International Red Cross," December 10, 1945, http://nobelprize.org/nobel_prizes/peace/laureates/1944/press.html (accessed September 21, 2009).

[55] "History of United States Army Air Forces Prisoners of War of the South Compound,

Stalag Luft III (General Summary), September 1, 1943 to April 30, 1945," Assistant Chief of Air Staff, Intelligence, Microfilm Reel A 1320, Air Force Historical Research Agency, AFHRA/RSA, Maxwell Air Force Base, Alabama.

[56] "Stalag Luft 3 (The March, Evacuation of Moosburg)," *WWW.B24.NET*, Research provided by the United States Air Force Academy and permission to use granted by William Newmiller at http://www.usafa.af.mil, http://www.gps-practice-and-fun.com/stalag-luft-3.html (accessed March 20, 2009).

[57] Ibid.

[58] "American Prisoners of War in Germany (Stalag Luft III, Sagan Evacuation)," Report Prepared by Military Intelligence Division, War Department, November 1, 1945, Assistant Chief of Air Staff, Intelligence, Microfilm Reel A 1320, Air Force Historical Research Agency, AFHRA/RSA, Maxwell Air Force Base, Alabama.

[59] Anthony Read and David Fischer, *The Fall of Berlin* (New York: Da Capo Press, 1995), 146, http://books.google.com/books?id=88g5qBy4_Q4C&printsec=copyright&dq=the+fall+of+berlin+by+anthony+read#PPP9,M1 (accessed March 19, 2009).

[60] Ibid.

[61] "History of Center Compound, Stalag Luft III, Sagan, Germany (Part V), August 1, 1943 to April 30, 1945," Assistant Chief of Air Staff, Intelligence, Microfilm Reel A 1320, Air Force Historical Research Agency, AFHRA/RSA, Maxwell Air Force Base, Alabama.

[62] "History of Center Compound, Stalag Luft III, Sagan, Germany (Part III), Daily Diary of Center Compound, August 1, 1943 to April 30, 1945," Assistant Chief of Air Staff, Intelligence, Microfilm Reel A 1320, Air Force Historical Research Agency, AFHRA/RSA, Maxwell Air Force Base, Alabama.

[63] "American Prisoners of War (The Journey)," Report Prepared by Military Intelligence Division, War Department, November 1, 1945, Assistant Chief of Air Staff, Intelligence, Microfilm Reel A 1320, Air Force Historical Research Agency, AFHRA/RSA, Maxwell Air Force Base, Alabama.

[64] Ibid.

[65] Ibid.

[66] Ibid.

[67] "History of Center Compound, Stalag Luft III, Sagan, Germany (Part IV, Stalag VII-A, Moosburg), August 1, 1943 to April 30, 1945," Assistant Chief of Air Staff, Intelligence, Microfilm Reel A 1320, Air Force Historical Research Agency, AFHRA/RSA, Maxwell Air Force Base, Alabama.

[68] Ibid.

[69] "American Prisoners of War (Stalag 13D Conditions)," Report Prepared by Military Intelligence Division, War Department, November 1, 1945, Assistant Chief of Air Staff, Intelligence, Microfilm Reel A 1320, Air Force Historical Research Agency, AFHRA/RSA, Maxwell Air Force Base, Alabama.

[70] "History of Center Compound, Stalag Luft III, Sagan, Germany (Part IV, Stalag VII-A, Moosburg), August 1, 1943 to April 30, 1945," Assistant Chief of Air Staff, Intelligence,

Microfilm Reel A 1320, Air Force Historical Research Agency, AFHRA/RSA, Maxwell Air Force Base, Alabama.

[71] "American Prisoners of War (Stalag 13D Conditions)," Report Prepared by Military Intelligence Division, War Department, November 1, 1945, Assistant Chief of Air Staff, Intelligence, Microfilm Reel A 1320, Air Force Historical Research Agency, AFHRA/RSA, Maxwell Air Force Base, Alabama.

[72] Virginia Priefert, *Those Who Flew: Aviation History of Thayer County, Nebraska* (Paducah, Kentucky: Turner Publishing Company, 2002), 101-102.

[73] George Rubin, "George Rubin: In the Skies Over Germany, World War II Plants the Seeds of a Personal Philosophy of Quaker Pacifism," *TheWire*, February 9, 2002, http://www.nyc10044.com/wire/2213/rubin.html (accessed July 4, 2009).

[74] "American Prisoners of War (Nuremberg Evacuation)," Report Prepared by Military Intelligence Division, War Department, November 1, 1945, Assistant Chief of Air Staff, Intelligence, Microfilm Reel A 1320, Air Force Historical Research Agency, AFHRA/RSA, Maxwell Air Force Base, Alabama.

[75] Ibid.

[76] Ibid.

[77] H.W. Brands, *A Traitor to His Class: The Privileged Life and Radical Presidency of Franklin Delano Roosevelt* (New York: Doubleday, 2008), 812.

[78] "History of Center Compound, Stalag Luft III, Sagan, Germany (Part IV, Stalag VII-A, Moosburg), August 1, 1943 to April 30, 1945," Assistant Chief of Air Staff, Intelligence, Microfilm Reel A 1320, Air Force Historical Research Agency, AFHRA/RSA, Maxwell Air Force Base, Alabama.

[79] "American Prisoners of War (Stalag 7A)," Report Prepared by Military Intelligence Division, War Department, November 1, 1945, Assistant Chief of Air Staff, Intelligence, Microfilm Reel A 1320, Air Force Historical Research Agency, AFHRA/RSA, Maxwell Air Force Base, Alabama.

[80] Frank D. Murphy, "The Liberation of Moosburg," February 7, 2002, http://www.100thbg.com/mainpages/history/history4/murphy_fd1.htm (accessed March 21, 2009).

[81] "American Prisoners of War (Stalag 7A)," Report Prepared by Military Intelligence Division, War Department, November 1, 1945, Assistant Chief of Air Staff, Intelligence, Microfilm Reel A 1320, Air Force Historical Research Agency, AFHRA/RSA, Maxwell Air Force Base, Alabama.

[82] Gunnar Jahn (Chairman of the Nobel Committee), "Presentation Speech to Award the Nobel Peace Prize of 1944 to the International Red Cross," December 10, 1945, http://nobelprize.org/nobel_prizes/peace/laureates/1944/press.html (accessed September 21, 2009).

[83] "American Prisoners of War (Stalag 7A)," Report Prepared by Military Intelligence Division, War Department, November 1, 1945, Assistant Chief of Air Staff, Intelligence, Microfilm Reel A 1320, Air Force Historical Research Agency, AFHRA/RSA, Maxwell Air Force Base, Alabama.

[84] Ibid.

[85] Ibid.

[86] Ibid.

[87] Frank D. Murphy, "The Liberation of Moosburg," February 7, 2002, http://www.100thbg.com/mainpages/history/history4/murphy_fd1.htm (accessed March 21, 2009).

[88] William J. Shirer, *The Rise and Fall of the Third Reich: A History of Nazi Germany* (New York: Simon and Schuster, 1960), 1131-1133.

[89] Ibid, 1139.

[90] Frank D. Murphy, "The Liberation of Moosburg," February 2002, http://www.moosburg.org/info/stalag/murphyeng.html (accessed March 21, 2009).

[91] "Recovered Allied Military Personnel, Reception Center, Channel Base Section," (Transcribed from an original booklet welcoming soldiers to the Reception Center. The original booklet belonged to Byron Ellis of Battery "B" of the 203rd Anti-Aircraft Artillery Battalion and his son, Mark Ellis, transcribed it.), http://www.7tharmddiv.org/docrep/X-RAMP-Booklet.doc (accessed March 23, 2009).

[92] "Cheatham County Man Out of Nazi Prison," Archival Record Reproduction Services, National Personnel Records Center, Military Personnel Records, 9700 Page Avenue, St. Louis, MO 63132-5100.

[93] "Response to Inquiry for Information on John W. Denny, September 19, 2008," National Personnel Records Center (Military Personnel Records, 9700 Page Avenue, St. Louis, Missouri), MO 63132-5100.

[94] *Tell Me About My Boy*, 1946 Pamphlet Produced by the Quartermaster Corps for Next of Kin of Deceased Service Personnel from World War II, http://qmfound.com/about_my_boy.htm (accessed March 23, 2009).

[95] "War Department Telegram to Jean Hunter, June 13, 1944," Department of the Army, U.S. Army Human Resources Command, 200 Stovall Street, Alexandria, VA 22332-0400, August 18, 2008.

[96] "Adjutant General's Corps," *GlobalSecurity.org*, http://www.globalsecurity.org/military/agency/army/ag.htm (accessed March 20, 2009).

[97] "Graves Registration Service," World War II Medical Research Center, http://med-dept.com/gps.php (accessed March 23, 2009).

[98] Ibid.

[99] "Quartermaster (Chapter 10)," *A Military Encyclopedia Based on Operations in the Italian Campaign, 1943-1945*, http://www.milhist.net/docs/milencyc/MilEncyc.10QM.pdf (accessed March 23, 2009).

[100] "Dora Clark Letter to General Eisenhower, June 22, 1944," Individual Deceased Personnel File of William C. Hunter, Department of the Army, U.S. Army Human Resources Command, 200 Stovall Street, Alexandria, VA 22332-0400, August 18, 2008.

[101] "Shirley Hunter Letter to Robert H. Dunlop, Brigadier General, The Acting Adjutant General, August 10, 1944" (Referenced War Department Telegram to Shirley Hunter, August 3, 1944), Individual Deceased Personnel File of William C. Hunter, Department of the Army, U.S. Army Human Resources Command, 200 Stovall Street, Alexandria, VA 22332-0400, August 18, 2008.

[102] "Report of Death (September 23, 1944)," War Department, The Adjutant General's Office, Washington 25, D.C., Individual Deceased Personnel File of William C. Hunter, Department of the Army, U.S. Army Human Resources Command, 200 Stovall Street, Alexandria, VA 22332-0400, August 18, 2008.

[103] "Dora Clark Letter to A.P.O. 650, c/o Postmaster, New York, New York, August 44, 1944," Individual Deceased Personnel File of William C. Hunter, Department of the Army, U.S. Army Human Resources Command, 200 Stovall Street, Alexandria, VA 22332-0400, August 18, 2008.

[104] "Shirley Hunter Letter to Robert H. Dunlop, Brigadier General, The Acting Adjutant General, August 10, 1944" (Referenced War Department Telegram to Shirley Hunter, August 3, 1944), Individual Deceased Personnel File of William C. Hunter, Department of the Army, U.S. Army Human Resources Command, 200 Stovall Street, Alexandria, VA 22332-0400, August 18, 2008.

[105] "Dora Clark Letter to Officer (Directed to The Adjutant General), August 20, 1944," Individual Deceased Personnel File of William C. Hunter, Department of the Army, U.S. Army Human Resources Command, 200 Stovall Street, Alexandria, VA 22332-0400, August 18, 2008.

[106] Ibid.

[107] "Major General J.A. Ulio, The Adjutant General, Letter to Dora Clark, August 24, 1944," Individual Deceased Personnel File of William C. Hunter, Department of the Army, U.S. Army Human Resources Command, 200 Stovall Street, Alexandria, VA 22332-0400, August 18, 2008.

[108] "Lieutenant Colonel Mayo O. Darling, Q.M.C., Assistant, Letter to Dora Clark, September 9, 1944," Individual Deceased Personnel File of William C. Hunter, Department of the Army, U.S. Army Human Resources Command, 200 Stovall Street, Alexandria, VA 22332-0400, August 18, 2008.

[109] "General Hap Arnold, Commanding General of the Army Air Forces, Letter to Dora Clark, September 8, 1944," Individual Deceased Personnel File of William C. Hunter, Department of the Army, U.S. Army Human Resources Command, 200 Stovall Street, Alexandria, VA 22332-0400, August 18, 2008.

[110] Ibid.

[111] "Major General J.A. Ulio, The Adjutant General, Letter to Dora Clark, October 10, 1944," Individual Deceased Personnel File of William C. Hunter, Department of the Army, U.S. Army Human Resources Command, 200 Stovall Street, Alexandria, VA 22332-0400, August 18, 2008.

[112] Ibid.

[113] Ibid.

[114] "Distinguished Flying Cross," *gruntsmilitary.com*, http://www.gruntsmilitary.com/

dfc.shtml (accessed May 26, 2009).

[115] "Missing Air Crew Report 5145," Obtained from the Department of the Air Force, Air Force Historical Studies Office, AF/HOH (Library), Bolling Air Force Base, Washington, D.C.

[116] "Memo Routing Slip to Director of Memorial Division, Quartermaster Corps, with attachments including the dental and medical records of Major William C. Hunter," Casualty Branch. Investigations and Correspondence Section, Individual Deceased Personnel File of William C. Hunter, Department of the Army, U.S. Army Human Resources Command, 200 Stovall Street, Alexandria, VA 22332-0400, August 18, 2008.

[117] "Report of Reburial, Graves Registration Service, January 24, 1945," Individual Deceased Personnel File of William C. Hunter, Department of the Army, U.S. Army Human Resources Command, 200 Stovall Street, Alexandria, VA 22332-0400, August 18, 2008.

[118] Ibid.

[119] *Tell Me About My Boy*, 1946 Pamphlet Produced by the Quartermaster Corps for Next of Kin of Deceased Service Personnel from World War II, http://qmfound.com/about_my_boy.htm (accessed March 23, 2009).

[120] Colonel A.C. Ramsey, Q.M.C., "Effects Depot," *The Quartermaster Review*, September-October 1945, Army Quartermaster Museum, Fort Lee, Virginia, http://www.qmmuseum.lee.army.mil/WWII/effects_depot.htm (accessed March 23, 2009).

[121] Ibid.

[122] Ibid.

[123] "Inventory of Effects for William C. Hunter, June 14, 1944 and War Department Warehouse Packing List, November 23, 1944," Individual Deceased Personnel File of William C. Hunter, Department of the Army, U.S. Army Human Resources Command, 200 Stovall Street, Alexandria, VA 22332-0400, August 18, 2008.

[124] "Missing Air Crew Report 5145," Obtained from the Department of the Air Force, Air Force Historical Studies Office, AF/HOH (Library), Bolling Air Force Base, Washington, D.C.

[125] "Attachment to Letter dated September 7, 1944 to Mrs. Dora E. Clark (grandmother of Major William Clark Hunter) from General Hap Arnold, Commanding General, Army Air Forces dated September 7, 1944." Obtained from the Department of the Army, U.S. Army Human Resources Command, Alexandria, Virginia, August 18, 2008.

[126] "Letter to Jean Hunter, January 8, 1945," Captain F.A. Eckhardt, Q.M.C. Assistant, Kansas City Quartermaster Depot, Individual Deceased Personnel File of William C. Hunter, Department of the Army, U.S. Army Human Resources Command, 200 Stovall Street, Alexandria, VA 22332-0400, August 18, 2008.

[127] "Letter to Jean Hunter, May 4, 1945 and Jean Hunter Return Receipt to Army Effects Bureau, Kansas City Quartermaster Depot, May 14, 1945," 2nd Lieutenant P. L. Koob, Q.M.C.Assistant, Kansas City Quartermaster Depot, Individual Deceased Personnel File of William C. Hunter, Department of the Army, U.S. Army Human Resources Command, 200 Stovall Street, Alexandria, VA 22332-0400, August 18, 2008.

[128] "Order for Shipment from Army Services Forces, Army Effects Bureau, to Jean

Hunter, May 4, 1945 (Included notation that films were removed. As per Army Effects Bureau Inventory, there were five films.)," Individual Deceased Personnel File of William C. Hunter, Department of the Army, U.S. Army Human Resources Command, 200 Stovall Street, Alexandria, VA 22332-0400, August 18, 2008.

[129] *Tell Me About My Boy*, 1946 Pamphlet Produced by the Quartermaster Corps for Next of Kin of Deceased Service Personnel from World War II, http://qmfound.com/about_my_boy.htm (accessed March 23, 2009).

[130] "Letter to Jean Hunter, November 24, 1947," Major General Thomas B. Larkin, The Quartermaster General, Individual Deceased Personnel File of William C. Hunter, Department of the Army, U.S. Army Human Resources Command, 200 Stovall Street, Alexandria, VA 22332-0400, August 18, 2008.

[131] *Tell Me About My Boy*, 1946 Pamphlet Produced by the Quartermaster Corps for Next of Kin of Deceased Service Personnel from World War II, http://qmfound.com/about_my_boy.htm (accessed March 23, 2009).

[132] "Receipt of Remains of the Late William C. Hunter, Signed by Earl A. Hamilton of Williamsport, Indiana, June 22, 1949." Individual Deceased Personnel File of William C. Hunter, Department of the Army, U.S. Army Human Resources Command, 200 Stovall Street, Alexandria, VA 22332-0400, August 18, 2008.

[133] Letter from Candace and John Hunter to John Lanza dated August 27, 2008. John Hunter's father Park is a brother of Major William Clark Hunter.

[134] Interview with Frances Glaze on November 25, 2008. Mrs. Glaze's father-in-law is Major William Clark Hunter.

Chapter 11: AFTER THE STORM

[1] "What are V-E Day and V-J Day?" *History Fact Finder*, http://www.enotes.com/history-fact-finder/war-conflict-twentieth-century/what-v-e-day-v-j-day (accessed April 7, 2009).

[2] Donald L. Miller, *The Story of World War II* (New York: Simon & Schuster Paperbacks, 2001), 214.

[3] "Introduction to the Italian Campaign," *World War II History Info*, http://www.worldwar2history.info/Italy (accessed April 6, 2009).

[4] "History of Veterans Day," United States Department of Veterans Affairs, http://www1.va.gov/opa/vetsday/vetdayhistory.asp (accessed January 15, 2010).

[5] "Rapid Robert, Still Hero at 88," *USA Today*, Cover Story, Sports, Section C, July 26, 2007.

[6] "Quotes of Audie Murphy," Audie Murphy Memorial Website (Webmaster Richard L. Rogers), http://www.audiemurphy.com/documents/doc31/quotesofaudiemurphy.pdf (accessed January 25, 2010).

[7] Personal information about John H. Kinney provided by his daughter, Judy Ellen Kinney.

[8] "Escape and Evasion Report No. 80," Headquarters Twelfth Air Force, Office of Assistant Chief of Staff, A-2. Provided by Department of the Air Force, Air Force Historical Research Agency, Maxwell Air Force Base, Alabama on October 8, 2008.

9 "What's A Mason?" http://www.trowel.com/flamason/what.htm (accessed May 12, 2009).

10 Jesse McKinley, "Promoting Offbeat History Between the Drinks," *New York Times*, October 13, 2008, http://www.nytimes.com/2008/10/14/us/ 14california.html?pagewanted=1&_r=1&hp (accessed September 22, 2009).

11 "Bear Valley and Lake Alpine," http://www.alpinecounty.com/area/ index.php?area=1 (accessed May 12, 2009).

12 "Lake Alpine," http://www.fs.fed.us/r5/stanislaus/visitor/lakealpine.shtml (accessed May 12, 2009).

13 "Safeguarding Information Concerning Escape, Evader or Released Internee (Form AG 383.6)," Headquarters Twelfth Air Force, APO 650, Signed by John H. Kinney on July 8, 1944. Provided by Department of the Air Force, Air Force Historical Research Agency, Maxwell Air Force Base, Alabama on October 8, 2008.

14 "Walt Brickner Minor League Statistics & History," *Baseball-Reference.com,* http:// www.baseball-reference.com/minors/player.cgi?id=brickn001wal (accessed May 12, 2009).

15 "The Unofficial Billy Martin Homepage," http://www.geocities.com/Colosseum/Loge/ 1695/english.html (accessed July 5, 2009).

16 "Walt Brickner Minor League Statistics & History," *Baseball-Reference.com,* http://www.baseball-reference.com/minors/player.cgi?id=brickn001wal (accessed May 12, 2009).

17 This recap was provided by Judy House and LaDean Harmston of the Museum of Idaho, located in Idaho Falls, Idaho.

18 Ibid.

19 Personal information about Walt Brickner provided by his friend, James A. Wood.

20 "Special Orders for Alfred J. Todd and Others," Army Services Forces, New York Port of Embarkation, Camp Kilmer, New Brunswick, New Jersey, September 2, 1944 & "Orders for Alfred J. Todd and William A. Lanza," Headquarters Twelfth Air Force, APO 550, August 5, 1944. Provided by Blanche Todd, wife of Alfred J. Todd on February 5, 2009.

21 Letter from Alfred J. Todd to the Commanding General, AAF Western Flying Command, 1104 West 8th Street, Santa Ana, California, requesting a transfer from Yuma Army Air Field to one of four fields of his preference. Provided by Blanche Todd, wife of Alfred J. Todd on February 5, 2009.

22 "Dairylea Cooperative, Inc.," http://www.dairylea.com/default.htm (accessed May 13, 2009).

23 Personal information on Alfred J. Todd provided by his wife, Blanche Todd.

24 Obituary of Alfred J. Todd provided by his wife, Blanche Todd.

25 "3 Old Soldiers from Revere Are Far From Fading Away," *The Revere Journal*, 1996 (exact date not known, probably late May or early April). Obtained from William A. Lanza.

26 Personal information about Laverne E. Reynolds provided by Laverne E. Reynolds himself.

Notes

[27] Evangeline (Vange) Reynolds provided quotes and additional information about her father and his family in e-mail to author, August 18, 2009, as well as in other e-mails.

[28] "Ask Not What Your Country Can Do For You Speech," Inaugural Address by John F. Kennedy, January 20th 1961, http://www.inspiring-quotes-and-stories.com/ask-not-what-your-country-can-do-for-you.html (accessed August 19, 2009).

[29] E-mail from Gayle Van Genderen (owner and publisher of the *South Dakota Mail*, Plankinton, SD), November 28, 2008.

[30] "United Methodist Publishing House," *The Tennessee Encyclopedia of History and Culture*, http://tennesseeencyclopedia.net/imagegallery.php?EntryID=U006 (accessed May 13, 2009).

[31] Personal information on John Denny provided by his son, Steve Denny.

[32] "Rockwell's Rosie the Riveter Painting Auctioned," http://www.rosietheriveter.org/painting.htm (accessed September 22, 2009).

[33] "Nashville Site History," Vought Aircraft Industries, Inc., http://www.voughtaircraft.com/newsFactGallery/factsheets/sites/nashville.htm (accessed May 13, 2009).

[34] "Center Hill Lake," Value to the Nation, Fast Facts, US Army Corps of Engineers, http://www.vtn.iwr.usace.army.mil/recreation/reports/lake.asp?ID=75 (accessed May 13, 2009).

[35] Michael McCall, "Nashville Cats: Gordon Stoker and Ray Walker of the Jordanaires," October 25, 2008, http://www.countrymusichalloffame.com/site/experience-events-detail.aspx?cid=3878 (accessed May 13, 2009).

[36] Ibid.

[37] Dave Schieber, "Death Pays a Call to the Pied Piper," *St. Petersburg Times*, August 5, 2002, http://www.kki.pl/elvisal/elvisnews_august04august09.htm (accessed July 5, 2009).

[38] Michael McCall, "Nashville Cats: Gordon Stoker and Ray Walker of the Jordanaires," October 25, 2008, http://www.countrymusichalloffame.com/site/experience-events-detail.aspx?cid=3878 (accessed May 13, 2009).

[39] "World War II Prisoners of War Data File," The U.S. National Archives & Records Administration, http://aad.archives.gov/aad/record-detail.jsp?dt=466&mtch=&tf=F&q=hubert+h.+cowell&bc=sl,sd&rpp=10&pg=1&rid=55640 (accessed May 13, 2009).

[40] Rick Clark, "Nashville Skyline," August 1, 2005, http://mixonline.com/mag/audio_nashville_skyline_78/ (accessed May 13, 2009).

[41] Personal information on Goffredo Sarri and his family provided by Goffredo's son, Amerigo Sarri, either in person or via e-mails from Marina Pazzaglia, the wife of Amerigo's son, Maurizio Sarri.

[42] Letter provided by Amerigo Sarri.

[43] Personal information on Riccardo Becattini and his family provided by Riccardo Becattini himself, either in person or via e-mails from Luisa Fortini, the wife of Riccardo's grandson, Fabio.

[44] Giorgio Grassi, "Eroe per caso (Hero by Chance)," Part of an article from a local newspaper in Tuscany given to author by the Becattini family. The newspaper is not indicated on the part of the article given to the author. The author had the article translated into English. Presumably the newspaper was *La Nazione* in Florence since Giorgio Grassi is a writer for that newspaper.

[45] E-mail from Luisa Fortini dated March 30, 2009.

Epilogue

[1] Harry D. George and Harry D. George, Jr., *Georgio Italiano: An American Pilot's Unlikely Tuscan Adventure* (Victoria, British Columbia, Canada: Trafford Publishing, 2000), 232.

[2] "Pieve di Santa Maria (Church of Saint Mary)," *toscanaviva.com*, http://translate.google.com/translate?hl=en&sl=it&u=http://www.toscanaviva.com/Pian_di_Sco/pieve_di_santamaria.htm&ei=k2xFSsHVDeOwtgevvry5Ag&sa=X&oi=translate&resnum=9&ct=result&prev=/search%3Fq%3Dpieve%2Bdi%2Bsanta%2Bmaria%2Bpian%2Bdi%2Bsco%26hl%3Den%26sa%3DG (accessed July 1, 2009).

Index

Photos, illustrations, and maps are indicated in **bold**.

Index

and actions during final mission, 124, 126, 132

background and training, 108, 110

bailing out, landing, and evasion, 132, 146–147

and life after the war, 214, 250–252

playing baseball and golf, 108, 110, 250–252

as silent evader, 5, 214

bridges, 80–81, 83, 99, 103, 107–108

Resco River bridge wired to blow up, 194, 195

Briles, 2nd Lt. Connally O., 31, 34

British 56th Reconnaissance Regiment, 147

British 6th Armoured Division, 169, 175, 176–177, 182, 203, 209

advancing toward Vaggio, 178–179

British 6th Battalion "Black Watch" of the 12th Brigade, 203

British 78th Infantry "Battleaxe" Division, 147

British Air-Sea Rescue, 93–94

British debriefing, 209

British Eighth Army, 55, 58, 64, 147, 174–175

British Ministry of Defense, 13

British Royal Air Force, 13

British Royal Army Medical Corps, 178

British VIII Corps, 175

British X Corps, 175

British XIII Corps, 177, 201–202

Britton, Sgt. William W. Jr., 84

Brokaw, Tom, 1, 246

Brooks, Mel (Mel Kaminsky), 181

Brooks, Thomas R., 203

Brown, Capt. Ian, 176, 178

Bruckler, Joe, 150

Bufkin, Sgt. Francis P., 86, 212, 213

Burandt, Lt. Charles, 120, 128

Burke, Billy, 259

Burrow, Sgt. Isom, 94

C-47 (transport aircraft), 213

Calabria, Italy, 60

camaraderie in Infantry, 259–260

Camp Claiborne, LA, 111

Camp Davis, NC Redistribution Station, 218

Camp Edwards, MA, 21, 23, 259

Camp Forest, TN, 144

Camp Gordon, GA, 23, 25

Camp Mystic, TX, 218

Cantor, Eddie, 10

Cape Cod, MA, 20, 21, 23

Capodochina Airfield, Italy, 91

Carlsbad Army Airfield, NM, 111

Carolina Maneuvers, 22

Carothers, Wallace Hume, 149, 150

Casablanca, Morocco, 37, 42–43

Cassino. *See* Monte Cassino

Castle Hot Springs, AZ, 218

casualties

of bombing missions, 84, 85, 86

from bombing missions, 93–94

Catch-22, 95–96

Catenaia Alps (*Alpe di Catenaia*), 129, 134, 147

Caterpillar Club, 149–150

Catholic Church, 68–69, 198–202

cave of Lanza and Todd, 157, 158–159, 166, 186, 188–190

author's visit to, 276–277

caves, civilians living in, 186

Cavicchi family, 173–174

Cecina, Italy, 128

Center Hill Lake, TN, 264

Cerisano, Italy, 60

Chelsea, MA, 215

Chianti Hills, Italy, 154, 202–203

Chicago, IL, 31

Chiesa de San Francesco (St. Francis Church), Italy, 269

China, airfields for Doolittle Raiders, 28, 29

Chrysler Building, NY, 221

Church of St. Maria, Pian di Scò, Italy, 277

Churchill, Winston, 39

on Italy, 55, 67, 71, 73, 74

Ciano, Galeazzo, 65

Cicero, 68

Citadel, The, SC, 36

Civil Affairs Officer (CAO), 205

civilians hiding valuables, 179, 187, 188, 192

Civitella, Italy, 172–173

Clark, Dora (Maj. Hunter's grandmother), 147, 236, 238–240, 243

Clark, Gen. Mark W., 36, 58, 184

as controversial leader, 36

and Gustav Line, 75

and liberation of Rome, 88

and Salerno beachhead, 58, 62, 64, 74

and Tuscany, 174–175

Clark Field, Philippines, 30

Clark Todd, Blanche (Sgt. Todd's wife), 3, 253–256, 273

Class C Pioneer League, 251

Class D Alabama State League, 251

Cline, Patsy, 265

Cobb, Alvie, 94

Cochran, Dana, 149

Cohen, Sam, 9

Coleman, S/Sgt. Seaton, 120, 134

Collegiate Institute of the Assumption, 204

Collins Hunter Glaze, Jean (Maj. Hunter's wife), 102, 147, 236, 241–243, 278–279

343

Index

347

Index

background and training, 107, 110–113
  and honors, 127, 263
  and life after the war, 260–263
  as prisoner of war, 132, 144–145, 212, 223, 230–235
  as silent evader, 4
Reynolds, Aline Gates (wife), 111, 260–263
Reynolds, Evangeline "Vange" (daughter), 261–263, 279
Reynolds, Michael (BBC), 169
Reynolds, Roderick (son), 261–262
Reynolds Boone, June Ann (daughter), 261, 262, 279
Rhine River, Germany, 219
Ritger, Lt. Frederick C., 111, 144–145
Robbins, Theodore, 264–265
Robert Todd Memorial Wrestling Award, 254
Roberts Field, Liberia, 42
Roche, Jean, 183
Rogers, Kenny, 265
Rome, Italy, 56, 69, 73, 200, 211
  liberation of, 88, 169
Rome Express (Clark's plane), 184
Roosevelt, Franklin Delano, 10, 39, 232
  and four freedoms, 216
Rosie the Riveter, 264
Roswell Rockets baseball team, 251
Royal Air Force, 13
Royal Army Medical Corps, 178
rural developments in Italy, 54

saboteurs, German on U.S. coast, 23
Sacred Cow (Roosevelt's plane), 39
Sagan, Germany (now Zagan, Poland), 24, 145, 223
Saint Andrea of Campiglia, Italy, 203–204
Saint Anna di Stazzema massacre, 171
Saint Donato in Avane, Italy, 204
Saint Maria of Tartigiliese, Italy, 204
Saint Martino Altoreggi, Italy, 203
Saint Michele of Pavelli, Italy, 204
Saint Peiro of Terreno, Italy, 204
Salerno, Italy, invasion at, 58, 64
Salk, Dr. Jonas, 10
Salò Republic, 65, 70
Samson, Lt. Alan, 128
San Antonio, TX Redistribution Station, 218
San Stefano, Italy, 63
Sansepolcro, Italy, 147
Santa Ana Army Air Base, CA, 111, 113
Santa Ana, CA Redistribution Station, 218
Santa Monica, CA Redistribution Station, 218, 260–261
"sappers" (engineers), 181
Sarri, Aldo (son of Goffredo), 155, 194, **267**
Sarri, Alfredo (son), 155, 194, 268, 275

Sarri, Amerigo "Rigo" (son), 128, 136, 189, 191, **267**
  author's visit with, 274–277
  on churches, 158, 199, 200, 201
  as eyewitness, 128, 136, 164
  on Germans, 140, 165, 188, 190
  and honors, 246, 269, 270
  during journey to Figline Valdarno, 193–195, **197**, 198
  with Sgts. Lanza and Todd, 157, 166, 189, 202, 268–269
Sarri, Anna (daughter), 155, 194, 198, **267**, 268
  bringing food, 157, 167, 188
Sarri, Bruno (son), 155, 157, 166, 167, 194, **267**
Sarri, Clementina (wife of Amerigo), 275
Sarri, Goffredo, 1, 135, **139**, 142
  and family, 155, **267**, 268
  helping Lanza and Todd, 166, 192
  and honors, 206, 268–269, 275
  and life after the war, 266–269
  moving his family, 65, 72, 140, 193
  as partisan leader, 135, 170, 198
Sarri, Grazia (daughter), 155, 194, **267**
Sarri, Grazietta (wife), 155, 190, 266, **267**, 268–269
Sarri, Marina Pazzaglia (wife of Maurizio), 274
Sarri, Maurizio (grandson), 274
Sarri, Nicolé (great-grandson), 275
Sarri, Paolo (son), 155, **267**, 275
saturation bombing, 46–47
Schroeder, Harvey, 111
Sciaraffa, Lt. Col. Anthony, 259
Senior Allied Officer (SAO), 224–225, 227–228
shakes, 95
sharecroppers, 140, 151–153
Shaw, Artie (Artie Arshawsky), 10–11
Shenkle, Kathryn, 13
short snorters, 39–40
Shreveport, LA, 263
Sicily, Italy, 55, 57, 60, 151, 157
Signal Corps, use of pigeons, 41–42
silent evaders and prisoners of war
  Brickner, 2nd Lt. Walter H. (co-pilot), 5, 214
  compared to talkative Italians, 6, 270, 277
  Denny, Sgt. John W., Jr. (engineer/gunner), 230, 235, 266, 280
  Kinney, 2nd Lt. John H. (navigator), 4, 250, 280
  Lanza, Sgt. William A. (tail gunner), 1–2, 3, 65, 212–213, 217, 258–259

351

Index

SHOT DOWN OVER ITALY

LaVergne, TN USA
02 December 2010

207171LV00003B/6/P